Libraries – A Design Manual

A DESIGN MANUAL

Libraries

Nolan Lushington
Wolfgang Rudorf
Liliane Wong

CONTRIBUTIONS BY

Norma Blake

Mohamed Boubekri

Rebecca Chestnutt

Michael Franke-Maier

Ursula Kleefisch-Jobst

Karl-Heinz Schmitz

Frank Seeliger

Aat Vos

Klaus Ulrich Werner

Birkhäuser
Basel

Note to North American readers
The plan terminology in this book follows the European convention throughout. Hence the street and access level of a building is referred to as ground floor. The next level (second floor in North American usage) is called first floor and so on for all following stories. All dimensions are metric except where U.S. standards are made reference to. In those cases the imperial measurements are given in parentheses.

Layout and cover design:
Reinhard Steger, Christian Schärmer, Maria Martí Vigil
PROXI, Barcelona

Graphic concept "Design Manual" series:
Oliver Kleinschmidt, Berlin

Project texts: Wolfgang Rudorf (wr), Liliane Wong (lw)

Translation into English (pp. 22–37, 44–48, 62–67, 106–119): Julian Reisenberger, Weimar

Editor: Ria Stein, Berlin

Production: Katja Jaeger, Berlin

Typeface: Frutiger

Paper: 150 g/m² BVS matt

Lithography: Oriol Rigat, Barcelona

Printing: Medialis, Berlin

Cover: Stadtbibliothek am Mailänder Platz, Stuttgart, Germany

Cover photograph: Stefan Müller, courtesy of Eun Young Yi

This publication is also available as an e-book (ISBN PDF 978-3-03821-630-8; ISBN EPUB 978-3-03821-459-5) and in a German language edition (ISBN 978-3-0346-0570-0).

Library of Congress Cataloging-in-Publication data
A CIP catalog record for this book has been applied for at the Library of Congress.

Bibliographic information published by the German National Library. The German National Library lists this publication in the Deutsche Nationalbibliografie; detailed bibliographic data is available in the Internet at <http://dnb.ddb.de>.

P.O. Box 44, 4009 Basel, Switzerland
Part of Walter de Gruyter GmbH, Berlin/Boston

Printed on acid-free paper produced from chlorine-free pulp. TCF ∞
Printed in Germany
ISBN 978-3-0346-0826-8
9 8 7 6 5 4 3 2 1
www.birkhauser.com

PRINCIPLES OF THE LIBRARY BUILDING

SELECTION OF PROJECTS

University Libraries

Appendix

Wolfgang Rudorf
Liliane Wong

Preface

The library as a building typology has a history spanning millennia in time. The lengthy history chronicling its development was irrevocably altered in the late 1990s with the advent of digital technology. The introduction of digitized material and the birth of a new type of book redefined the field, casting doubts on the future of the book as an object of paper and ink, and with it the relevance of the library as a space of collections and readers.

Digitized material has not replaced the physical collection, rather it has been assimilated into the institution as another salient component of a greater structure. Instead, the typology of the library has been expanded upon to provide new experiences within the library, broadening its provision of knowledge. From retail, entertainment and the arts to healthcare and secondary education, new programs are incorporated into the library to better serve, maintain and attract existing and new patrons. These programs, determined in the most part by geography and the socio-economic needs of the communities, form a unique development in the library typology. A pluralistic type emerges as evidenced by the development in the name "library". Around the world this appellation has been augmented and even replaced by new titles such as learning center, information center, media center, learning commons, mediatheque, culture house, community center and "idea" store. With this flowering of the library as an institution of new and diverse experience the library has retained its relevance in society and secured its own future.

A publication of this type in the second decade of the 21st century on the subject of libraries demonstrates the strength of both the institution and the bond between the book and society. That is not to say that digitized content has not had an enormous impact on society. The gradual disappearance of bookstores is evidence of its far-reaching effect. Rather, it is a testament to a Darwinian will toward survival and adaptation that has enabled the library as an institution to redefine itself in the terms of a digitized world.

This book comprises international case studies from the late 1990s to the present. The selection of these case studies was extremely difficult as well-designed and beautifully executed libraries were in abundance. The range is to demonstrate multi-directional strategies to stave off extinction, maintain and even strengthen this institution.

The conversation regarding these fascinating issues began in 1997 when we worked on the refurbishment and addition of the Hartford Public Library. We became acquainted with Louise Blalock, the Director of the library, and her husband, Nolan Lushington. Both librarians, their knowledge of the workings of the library was vast and forwardthinking. In the design of Hartford we faced many of the same issues confronting libraries in the late 20th century as discussed herein. Our chats were the foundation of our collaboration here. The numerous discussions on what the future might hold have, 18 years later, become reality. It is exciting to have witnessed this moment in the history of the library and to document it in this volume. A single regret is that Nolan, who passed away in 2013, will not be with us to open the book in its completed form. We feel fortunate, however, to have shared in the making of this work with such a knowledgeable, kind and gentle colleague.

We would like to thank, most of all, our editor Ria Stein for her belief in this project and for her infinite patience, wisdom and guidance that made the realization of this book possible. Special thanks to Patricia Lomando, our RISD graduate student assistant, whose enthusiasm and organization were invaluable to the completion of this book. We are also grateful to RISD student assistants Seo Yeon Ji and Chad Echols, who shared in our early vision of this book. Finally, to Franzi, Hanna, and Maria Rudorf and Clara Halston, our enormous appreciation for the contribution of "smaller" hands.

Boston, October 2015

Reading room at CINiBA – Centrum Informacji Naukowej i Biblioteka Akademicka, Uniwersytet Śląski, Katowice, Poland

Liliane Wong
with Nolan Lushington

The Library in its Social Context

The Reading Room of the British Museum, previously the British Library, is exemplary of academic and research libraries founded upon private collections of the 18th century.

The library is a service institution. A collection made accessible to a particular community, the library is defined by its contents and the society it serves. The development of the library is inextricably linked with the evolution of these two elements. As the concepts of the collection and its accessibility shift through time with cycles of seminal discoveries and the changes brought about by such inventions, they redefine the library's role in society.

Cycles of Change

The earliest collections consisted primarily of hand-copied manuscripts. Pre-historic archives in cuneiform were records of dynastic warriors and rulers, great libraries of the ancient world were the property of kings, libraries of the Middle Ages the realm of the church, Renaissance libraries the exclusive collection of wealthy patrons and the great research and reference libraries the domain of private universities. While there is record of public access to scrolls in the Roman Republic of the first centuries A.D., collections after the fall of the Roman Empire remained for many centuries the realm of the literate and, by necessity, the wealthy.

This concept of the library was dramatically altered by the 1439 invention of the moveable printing press. The resulting growth of printed matter led to increased literacy in a society in which the book was no longer the property of a few. Yet these opportunities primarily benefited an enlightened middle class of teachers, scholars, and scientists rather than the general public. The growth of private collections in universities was a direct result. These libraries are still in existence today and include the Bibliothèque nationale de France (previously the Royal Library of Charles V), the Bodleian Library (previously Humphrey's library at Oxford), the British Library (founded as part of the British Museum), the Laurentian Library, the Vatican Library and the German State Library in Berlin. These institutions are the basis of today's academic and university libraries that continue to serve scholars in their research needs.

The emergence of the public library, with accessibility for all, had its origins in the 18th century. Prior to this time, the few public libraries known were but sporadic and unique endeavors. Some well-known examples are the public library associated with London's Guild Hall, dating back to 1425, and the Bibliothèque Mazarin, the private collection of Cardinal Mazarin that opened to the public in 1643. Circulating and lending libraries of the 18th century further extended accessibility to collections.

The development of the library as a public institution, not surprisingly, parallels the progress of individual rights from the period of the Enlightenment. In late 18th century France, the overthrow of the monarchy had direct impact on the formation of their public libraries, many of which "... find their origin in the Revolutionary

The Town Library at Peterborough, New Hampshire, established in 1833, was the first American free library established through the use of local taxes.

Early 20th century libraries such as the New York Public Library from 1911 were constructed as civic monuments in formal architectural language.

The first computers – here the first digital computer at Argonne National Laboratory in Illinois from 1953 – led the way for current technology in which it is posited that a whole library can be stored on a single chip.

decree of November 2, 1789, which declared that all the possessions of the clergy, including their libraries, was national property."[1] In Victorian England, at a time of demands for rights and representation, the Public Libraries Act was enacted as law in 1850 through the advocacy of Ewart, Brotherton and Edwards.[2] In the U.S. of the 19th century, the public library, as a concept, was embraced as part of the democratic ideal. The realization of the public library was often made possible through the support of individual citizens. The Peterborough Town Library of New Hampshire, established in 1833, was the first free library in the U.S. to be established through the use of local taxes. This was the start of a long tradition as community-based funding still accounts for 90 % of American libraries today.[3] By the close of the 19th century, the institution of the library had evolved to an established resource in a society where "books and other library resources should be provided for the interest, information and enlightenment of all people of the community the library serves."[4]

Constructed as civic monuments, the design of public libraries in the early 20th century reflected the esteem placed by that society on knowledge. This esteem was expressed in the building through a monumental scale, references to Classical architecture and an imposing interior. The development of the public library in the next 75 years mirrored the transformation of that society away from such formalism. These changes were visible on the design of the exterior and the interior but also in the programmatic make-up of the library itself. The open-stack library of the 1930s and 1940s with popular materials, browsing collections, and children's and young adults' collections and reading rooms was the precursor to the model of the functional library outlined by the American Library Association in 1948. Espousing accessibility and functionality, one principle was that "the public library building of the future should be planned and equipped as a modern educational center."[5] In the following decades libraries were provided with meeting rooms, audio-visual facilities, projection rooms, listening rooms, children's rooms and collections that included the then new forms of media such as records, tapes, CDs and movies. The inclusion of such amenities and familiar domestic objects together with the later addition of food and drink in the form of cafés demonstrates the changing role of the library in the last quarter of the 20th century. This transformation from the formal library of the 1900s to the familiar "living room" of the city reflects the changes in the society served by the institution of the library.

The Impact of Information Technology

The invention of the printing press wielded an impact on libraries that lasted for a period of almost five centuries. This cycle concluded with the institution fully established in society, upholding a universal mission as information resource for both research and popular culture. Mid- to late 20th century libraries were relatively similar from one to the next until the 1990s when this continuity was broken by the initial integration of information technology into the library. When the term was coined in 1958 by Leavitt and Whisler to define a branch of engineering that "includes techniques for processing large amounts of information rapidly",[6] information technology was no longer new. The 1951 introduction of the first real-time computer at MIT was followed by four decades of developments resulting in the present-day panoply of operating systems, microprocessors, desk top computers, removable disks, differentiated hardware and software, notebook computers, storage devices, digital imaging and image scanning. In the last quarter of the 20th century, libraries adapted to these developments in the form of electronic workstations, electronic reference and online public access computers (OPAC). The emergence of the Internet for public use in the early 1990s marks a turning point. "From the mid-90s to the present, all things related to the Internet can only be described in terms of exponential change, from capabilities of base technologies to the creation and accumulation of digital content to the number of users and possibilities for use."[7] The advent of Internet commerce in which the library's commodity of books and information are exchanged online heralds a new cycle of change in the development of the library in society.

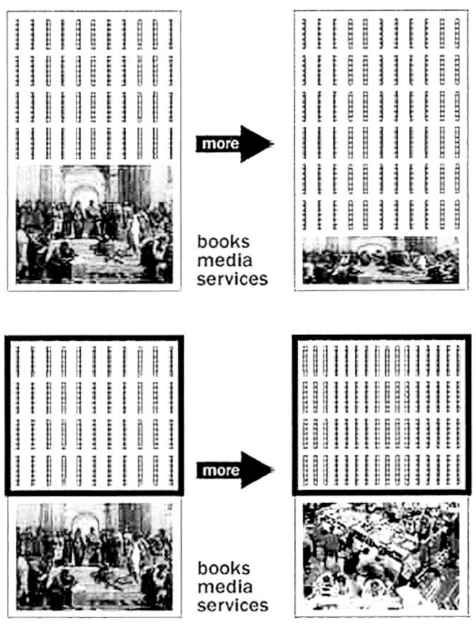

The diagram from the "Concept Book" for the Seattle Central Library illustrates the need for flexibility in the library.

Completed in 2004, the Seattle Central Library's highly sophisticated architecture served as a symbol of change for the library of the 21st century.

Changing Library Concepts

Most libraries today exist as hybrid models, offering both the services of the conventional library and ones enhanced by digital technology. The activities of searching, storing, archiving and, more recently, online searching, using digitized and scanned collections, and digital archiving, all exploit the digital era's "promise of indefinite memory".[8] The success of these new services led to the obsolescence of some library standards such as the card catalogue or microfiche. While this promise of infinite memory has its limitations, its legacy of digital archives, e-books and virtual storage has radically changed the spatial needs of the library and the demands of the patrons. With competition from numerous digital resources such as Internet bookstores, e-books, free digitized collections – all of which are accessible from one's personal computer – the future of the library in the age of the Internet is in question. With the demise of many bookstores around the world, an undercurrent of uncertainty is palpable with regard to the role of libraries in such an era. Advocates on each side extol the virtues and drawbacks of the bookless library, a mirror of a society divided in opinion and in opportunity. The library of the 21st century is an institution grappling with its own significance in a society transformed by the output of digital technology.

Public Libraries

The public library with its mission to serve the broad and varied interests of its community intersects with digital technology on many different planes. With the goal of providing information free of charge to its constituents, the public library is a vital resource especially in a society dominated by the presence of the Internet. For those without digital access, the library serves as an opportunity to increase digital equity. A 2010 survey conducted by the Bill and Melinda Gates Foundation found that "67 % of libraries ... are the only provider of free public access computers and Internet in their communities."[9] The public library remains a source of information and access not only for the underprivileged but also for students, citizens, small businesses, the young and the old. In searching for an identity within a new technological order, the public libraries of this decade are very different from one to the next, demonstrating the pluralism that currently exists in this building typology.

The Seattle Central Library, completed in 2004 (pp. 154–157), marks the beginning of this quest for self-definition. Premised on OMA's prescient 1999 proposal observing that "the contents of a whole library can be stored on a single chip or ... that a single library can now store the digital content of all libraries",[10] the design of Seattle Central recognized the need for a "potential re-thinking"[11] of the library as a type. At Seattle, the library program is reapportioned to accommodate books as well as new forms of media. A new flexibility is demonstrated in which an efficient accommodation of printed matter (the "Book Spiral", designed for a sequential 700,000 volume capacity) permits the "consolidation of the apparently ungovernable proliferation of programs and media."[12] Leading the dialogue on new forms of media and the possibility of a bookless future, Rem Koolhaas' embrace of new media in the Seattle Central is achieved primarily through the use of a highly sophisticated architecture, on both the exterior and the interior, as visual symbols of change. The success of such provocative architecture is due in great part to its acceptance by the highly progressive community that it serves. The library has benefited from the positive notoriety it has achieved from this "starchitecture" status.

Other libraries have followed suit in employing architecture to create identity. The unmistakable marks of renowned architects such as Frank Gehry or Alsop + Störmer – the Lewis Library at Princeton University (2008, pp. 230–231) or the Peckham Library in London (2000, pp. 174–177) – have elevated the status of the institutions themselves.

Architecture is used to create identity as in Frank Gehry's Lewis Library on the Princeton University campus, completed in 2008.

The Idea Store at Whitechapel, Adjaye Associates, 2005, utilizes commercial branding to market a "new" institution of the library in London.

While the byproducts of digital technology such as the e-book or the ability to access books and information from non-specific locations have not led to the demise of the book, there is speculation on the viability of the library as an institution of only books and information. Public libraries today fear the loss of relevance not only from the Internet but also from the changes in the society they serve. Recognizing the lure of commerce, both physical and electronic, in modern life, another approach to public library design acknowledges the multitude of attractions – shopping, eating out, attending the cinema – that compete with excursions to the library. Designs of some libraries posit the institution of the library as one such competitive venue of entertainment. David Adjaye's Idea Store at Whitechapel, London (pp. 184–187), the first of the UK Idea Stores, is overt in its adoption of commercial branding to market a "new" institution of a library that distances itself from the formidable and underused institutions of the previous generation. In cosmopolitan Amsterdam, Jo Coenen's OBA – Openbare Bibliotheek Amsterdam (pp. 158–163) is an urban destination for its citizens of all ages with the inclusion of not only books and electronic media but also an art gallery, a café, a restaurant, a theater and a rooftop bar. In Norwich, England (Millennium Library, Michael Hopkins Architects, 2001, pp. 150–153) the library is incorporated into a shopping mall that is a tourist destination in the historic district. In suburban Cerritos, California, the public library is designed to entertain, emulating its neighboring attraction and competitor for young readers, Disneyland. Inspired by the drive-in commerce of the American West, the Arabian Public Library near Phoenix (Richärd + Bauer, 2007, pp. 190–191), sited in the vast, arid landscape of the Arizona desert, offers a drive-in counter where books ordered online may be picked up by car.

Frequently viewed as a place in which digital equity can be achieved through free access, some public libraries have expanded their role beyond that of a bridge to span the "digital divide". While many mid- to late 20th century public libraries, often termed "living rooms of the city", transformed into places of refuge for the homeless, recently public libraries in underserved neighborhoods have adopted more proactive programs with objectives steeped in economic egalitarianism. The Biblioteca España

The art gallery, restaurant, theater, bar and café at the OBA – Openbare Bibliotheek Amsterdam, Jo Coenen, 2007, demonstrate the concept of the library as urban destination.

Provocative architecture elevates the status of the institution of the library itself as in Alsop + Störmer's Peckham Library, 2000, in London.

Set in an underserved neighborhood of Medellín, Columbia, the Biblioteca España, Giancarlo Mazzanti, 2007, was achieved through the progressive agenda of the city mayor.

Robotic retrieval book storage, here at the University of Utah, is one of many ways in which technology has changed the functioning of the library.

(Giancarlo Mazzanti, 2007, pp. 194–197), sited in an impoverished neighborhood of Medellín, Columbia, includes a community center and a daycare facility for its users – all achieved through the vision of a progressive mayor's agenda of "social urbanism". Its celebrated black monumental forms have rendered it an architectural destination and the establishment of public transportation to and from the city was an unexpected and long overdue benefit to its underserved citizens. At Usera, a high-crime neighborhood of Madrid, the Biblioteca Pública (Ábalos & Herreros, 2004, pp. 178–181) is designed as a protective fortress for its youth with an urban art interior inspired by graffiti, the language of the streets. At the Idea Store at Whitechapel, a learning center of secondary education is integrated into the library for the immigrant community it serves. According to the Director of the Seattle Public Library system, today "libraries are more than functional buildings; they are monuments to the values of education and democracy ... They are a symbol for the community that we're investing in our children and investing in our immigrants and refugees."[13] Interestingly enough, this can be read as continuing the tradition of Andrew Carnegie's concept of the free public library as "a cradle of democracy upon the earth ... where neither rank, office, nor wealth receives the slightest consideration."[14]

Academic Libraries

Less confined by the wide-ranging patron demands of the public library, the academic library's integration of digital technology is directed mainly at a focused mission of research. Significant academic libraries such as the Philological Library at the Freie Universität Berlin (Norman Foster, 2005, pp. 226–229), the Law Library at the Universität Zürich (Santiago Calatrava, 2004, pp. 220–221) or the Jacob-und-Wilhelm-Grimm-Zentrum at the Humboldt Universität in Berlin (Max Dudler, 2009, pp. 232–237) all accommodate a physical collection while incorporating many aspects of digital technology. In contrast, the engineering library of the University of Texas at Austin as well as the Library Learning Terrace of Drexel University in Philadelphia opened without book collections. At Stanford University's engineering library all but 10,000 volumes were culled. While digital collections are suited to some research libraries – such as in the field of engineering – it is by no means a universal direction for the future of academic research. Copyright protection remains a major obstacle in the digitization of many publications. Some subjects of research rely on original texts with their patina of markings and annotations while publications related to obscure subjects of study are not often included in digitization projects. According to Professor Adrian Johns of the University of Chicago, who specializes in the history of the book, the world is "nowhere near the point when people doing serious research, especially on historical topics, can rely solely on digital sources. ... Compared to the variety that exists out in the printed world, Google is just skimming the surface."[15] The Rolex Learning Center in Lausanne (SANAA, 2010, pp. 238–243), a single fluid space without boundaries, combines physical collections, a learning technologies lab and public space for an "avant garde approach that combines computer interfaces with real world instruction."[16] Helmut Jahn's Mansueto Library at the University of Chicago (2011, pp. 244–247) exemplifies the best of both the analog and the digital with a design that emphasizes the physical collection while utilizing the most advanced technology of robotic retrieval for its storage.

Digital Libraries

While the full impact of digital technology for both the public and the academic library remains to be revealed, the adoption of digital technology has taken flight in virtual endeavors called "digital libraries". Digital libraries exist only online and their materials are free of charge and accessible in multi-lingual formats. The term is currently used to refer to "systems that are very different in scope and yield very diverse functionality. These systems range from digital object and metadata repositories, reference-linking systems, archives, and content administration systems, which have been mainly developed by industry, to complex systems that integrate advanced digital library services."[17] Some significant examples are Europeana,

europeana
think culture

Digital libraries include digital access points such as Europeana with its digitized items of books, films, paintings and museum objects.

"a single access point to millions of books, paintings, films, museum objects and archival records that have been digitized throughout Europe",[18] with European cultural and scientific institutions as its sources; the World Digital Library, "significant primary materials from countries and culture around the world",[19] developed by a team that includes the U.S. Library of Congress, partner institutions in many countries, UNESCO and a number of private companies; and the Google Book Project, which in 2012 scanned 20 million books with institutional partners such as Harvard University, Oxford University, Stanford University and the New York Public Library. An online resource, DLD, the Digital Library Directory, is a portal to some of the best digital library resources within the categories of arts and humanities, business and reference, health and medicine, science and technology and social sciences. While these digital libraries do not yet offer services of conventional libraries, they have eliminated boundaries for global access to information. The potential accessibility of such collections from around the world is awe-inspiring even though many issues such as copyright, universal accessibility and relevant formats are yet to be resolved.

The evolution of the role of the library in society over the centuries from private resource to civic monument to functional building to living room of the city is today in flux. Fueled by advancements in information technology the developments of this century are far-reaching ones for the growth of the library as an institution. As a collection made accessible to a particular community, the library has evolved dramatically. The concept of the collection to include virtual objects is one that illustrates the speed of change since the mid-19th century. While the integration of technology and the Internet into everyday life has caused speculations about the existence of the book and hence the library in the foreseeable future, the many solutions that recent libraries have adopted in redefining their role in this society are indicative of a new spirit. From library shopping centers, library restaurants, libraries without collections, virtual libraries, library community centers, library daycare centers, libraries as acts of redemption to libraries as cultural icons, the pluralism of roles confirms the strength of the institution itself. In this multiplicity of roles the library extends itself further in service of a multi-faceted society, challenging conjectures of its impending obsolescence. In this new cycle of library development the breadth and extent of these new opportunities come nearest to fulfilling the ideal expressed by Thomas Jefferson in 1807 that "... knowledge is the common property of mankind."[20]

References

1 James C. McIntosh, "Public Libraries in France", *Occasional Papers*, University of Illinois Library School, no. 41, February 1955.

2 Edwards was a supporter of universal suffrage and eventually served as the Chief Librarian of the Manchester Public Library.

3 Ruth A. Wooden, "The Future of Public Libraries in an Internet Age", *National Civic Review*, Wiley Periodicals, Winter 2006, p. 4.

4 Policy 1 from the "Library Bill of Rights", adopted June 19, 1939, by the American Library Association (ALA) Council.

5 Carleton B. Joeckel, Amy Winslow, *A National Plan for Public Library Service*, Chicago: American Library Association, 1948, p. 126.

6 Harold Leavitt, Thomas Whisler, "Management in the 1980s", *Harvard Business Review*, November 1958.

7 Stephen M. Griffin, "Funding for Digital Libraries Research Past and Present", *D-Lib Magazine*, vol. II, no. 7/8, July/August 2005.

8 "Digital Archiving: History Flushed, the Digital Age Promised Vast Libraries, but They Remain Incomplete", *The Economist*, April 28, 2012.

9 Omar L. Gallaga, "Digital Challenges for U.S. Public Libraries", *All Tech Considered – Technology News and Culture*, June 21, 2010.

10 OMA/LMN Architects, "Concept Book", Seattle Public Library proposal, December 1999, http://www.spl.org/prebuilt/cen_conceptbook, p. 12.

11 Ibid.

12 Ibid. p. 22.

13 Mark Bergin, "Deborah Jacobs is no Ordinary Librarian, and her Seattle Masterpiece is no Ordinary Library", *WORLDmag*, issue "Building a city", March 24, 2007.

14 "Quotes About Librarians, Libraries, Books and Reading", *The International Federation of Library Associations and Institutions*, Iowa Library Services, State Library of Iowa. http://www.statelibraryofiowa.org/ld/t-z/tell-library-story/scpt/quotes-about-libraries

15 Marc Parry, "A High-Tech Library Keeps Books at Faculty Fingertips – With Robot Help", *The Chronicle of Higher Education*, July 24, 2011.

16 EPFL – École Polytechnique Fédérale de Lausanne Rolex Learning Center, press information, June 7, 2010.

17 "Digital Library Manifesto", *The Digital Library Reference Model*, DL.org project, (www.dlorg.eu), 2009.

18 http://pro.europeana.eu

19 World Digital Library, http://www.wdl.org/en/about/

20 Thomas Jefferson, "Letter to Henry Dearborn", 1807.

Norma Blake

The Library User as Customer

In the 21st century, libraries have had to share their role as the primary institution for information provision with several technological rivals. In 2005, a study by the non-profit computer service and research organization OCLC showed that search engines have superseded libraries as a primary source of information.[1] Google, Barnes & Noble and Amazon are strong competitors for libraries; a vast amount of information is available 24/7; it is sometimes well-organized and easily retrieved. What can libraries offer that people do not find on Google? Will libraries still be viable in the future? In order to play an important information retrieval role in the future, libraries must focus their services more strongly on the needs and desires of the libraries' customers. This enhancement is not only necessary in the provision of content, but also in the availability of technical equipment and appropriate physical environments. Library staffs have started to emphasize libraries' role as the information gateway for people seeking authenticated information. Library strategies for retaining and enhancing their customer base include: becoming the community center, becoming a center of excellence, providing technology and expertise, providing innovative service models and capturing funding and recognition through advocacy and marketing.

The Community Center

In his bestselling book *Tribes*, author, blogger and marketing expert Seth Godin argues that the Internet has revived a human social unit from the distant past, the tribe – i.e. a group of people connected to each other and to an idea. The elimination of the barriers of geography, cost, and time fostered new communication channels such as blogs and social networking sites, which help existing tribes to get bigger. At the same time, the author emphasizes that people still crave a place where they belong, where they feel accepted and welcome, a place where they meet people with similar interests. They seek a place where they are noticed and where they are missed if they are absent.[2] The library can provide such a place, being an anchor and a social haven. This is of particular importance in a society where personal contacts grow broader but at the same time shallower. Many people in the Western world live in an isolation that would have been unimaginable to our ancestors, in a state of unprecedented alienation while being highly connected and electronically accessible. "We were promised a global village; instead we inhabit the drab cul-de-sacs and endless freeways of a vast suburb of information," as the Canadian columnist Stephen Marche puts it. The decrease in confidants – that is, in quality social connections – has been dramatic over the past 25 years. In a U.S. survey, the mean size of networks of personal confidants decreased from 2.94 people in 1985 to 2.08 in 2004. By 2004, 25 % of Americans claimed they had nobody to talk to, and 20 % had only one confidant.[3]

At Cerritos Millennium Library in Cerritos, Orange County, California, Charles Walton Associates, 2002, the children's department features a lighthouse, a Tyrannosaurus Rex and a story-telling banyan tree. Furnishings throughout the building vary and use a variety of styles. The Old World Reading Room features wood paneling and is decorated accordingly.

The Umpqua Bank in Portland, Oregon, has reinvented retail banking with a design-conscious environment. This branch is a community gathering spot to enjoy coffee, music, even Wii competitions.

A place like the library offers a sense of "being", something that neither Google nor online book shopping can provide. The library can offer comfortable seating and an environment that fosters tranquility and contemplation as well as inspiration and intellectual stimulation; in other words, a sense of community. For this reason, newer libraries have different spaces with different designs, customized to the needs of various user groups.

Cerritos Millennium Library in Orange County, California, bills itself as the "Wow" library with a "cruise ship mentality" (Charles Walton Associates, 2002). The children's area includes an aquarium, interactive screens, a lighthouse, a large Tyrannosaurus Rex and a banyan tree. Furnishings throughout the building vary from Mission style to Art Deco. Going to the library is experiential. The longer one stays, the more one uses the goods and services. This concept, which takes its cues from nearby Disneyland and regards entertainment as a part of the contemporary library's job, has generated many new library users: In the library's first six weeks of operation in 2002, attendance went from 58,770 to 185,765 compared to the previous year; library cards issued grew from 792 to 5019 and circulation increased from 84,372 to 136,286.[4]

When considering new directions in library concepts, the New Jersey State Library staff studied the Umpqua Bank Innovation Lab model in Portland, Oregon. In this locally founded and community-based bank, ceiling-to-floor windows provide daylighting everywhere and create transparency. There are café tables with wireless computers, touch screens showing customer-generated scenes of the community, merchandise of local vendors on display, a community information chalkboard, a computer bar with a live "bartender" with free advice and coffee plus many, many meetings and programs for residents. All this is offered to start community conversation. Umpqua Bank creates a sense of community that keeps members coming back and investing in the bank.

Libraries have engaged in worthwhile partnerships. The lobby of the Salt Lake City Library in Utah (Moshe Safdie, 2003) has community businesses and non-profit spaces on the right and library spaces on the left. The Amsterdam Public Library OBA (Jo Coenen, 2007, pp. 158–163) offers a full-service restaurant. The library in Gainsville, Florida, offers the "Library Partnership", providing space for a rotating network of about 30 agencies that work on family services. The library in East Brunswick, New Jersey, issues passports, and the Camden County Library, also in New Jersey, opened a branch at the local shopping mall. There are pop-up libraries, libraries in housing projects and mobile technology libraries, such as the Pike County Public Library District's Mobile Center library in Kentucky.

The Urban Room, the breathtaking lobby of the Main Public Library in Salt Lake City, Moshe Safdie, 2003.

Many New Jersey libraries have special areas for targeted guests, usually teen spaces. In Old Bridge, however, a part of the library was restructured to offer attractive spaces for active older adult and senior guests. It includes a conversation circle with rocking chairs and large touch screens easily used by the visually impaired. There are large-print books and digitizing devices for vinyl records. Specific programs for senior citizens such as Scrabble and Bridge are run by senior volunteers in their own program room.

Concierge and reception areas, well-established in the hospitality industry, have been introduced in some libraries. ImaginOn in Charlotte, Charlotte-Mecklenburg County, North Carolina, has a welcoming concierge desk (Holzman Moss Bottino, 2005, pp. 182–183). Many libraries like the East Brunswick Library in New Jersey have small, moveable desks for "hip to hip" information services where staff and guests can view screens together and hold convenient consultations.

"Trading Spaces" was a project that started at the Mount Laurel Public Library in New Jersey. The library received U.S. $ 15,000 each from the regional library cooperative, the State Library, and the local Friends of the Library. With just U.S. $ 45,000 spent on revitalizing the interior of the library with bookstore-style furnishings, borrowing

In Old Bridge, New Jersey, a part of the public library was refurbished to create attractive spaces for senior visitors with comfortable furniture.

more than doubled the first year. This led the New Jersey State Library to start the SWAT team projects in local libraries. Librarians who had done such revitalization in their libraries went on to help other libraries who were also awarded small grants to remake parts of their interiors. The excitement generated by such projects brought local volunteers and local money that could be added to enlarge the projects.

Centers of Excellence

Libraries strive to be centers of excellence in unique ways to become solutions to problems in their communities. Libraries in Massachusetts received Federal Emergency Management Agency certification to formally assist residents after natural disasters. Many New Jersey libraries became essential ports of respite after the hurricanes Sandy and Irene damaged their communities. The libraries provided wireless networks and the opportunity to charge everything from phones to hair curlers. The libraries helped residents file claims and apply for aid. Now many of the libraries also conduct preparedness workshops.

After the U.S. went into recession in 2008, many communities in New Jersey experienced high unemployment. The libraries became the first place many came to for job-seeking assistance. The libraries provided computer training and helped people download employment forms and upload resumes. Libraries sponsored programs on topics of interest to job-seekers.

As early as 2005, a study yielded that – while the ratings for library products were mostly positive – there were many complaints about its service: limited or poor hours of operation, fees and policies associated with using the library, stringent return dates and other limits on circulation, use of the online catalogue and generally poor service.[5] Since then, however, libraries have slowly come to emphasize aspects of hospitality, service and ambience. As part of these efforts and because libraries wanted to be seen in a positive light as most excellent organizations, the New Jersey State Library staff decided to look at customer service experiences in the hospitality industry. New Jersey has a major casino town, Atlantic City, where librarians laud the customer service. A free seminar was conducted for about 100 librarians at the Trump Taj Mahal in Atlantic City; so popular was the program that the registration spots were gone within hours. From the casino marketing experts, librarians learned that on average happy customers talk to three to five friends each to share their experience while dissatisfied visitors relate their experience to ten to 20 other persons. It also became clear that it takes roughly five to six times as much effort to gain a new client as opposed to keeping an existing client. Studies conducted by the casino showed that among non-returning customers, only 3 % did not return because they had moved away and 1 % had died; 14 %, however, were dissatisfied with what was offered and a staggering 82 % had been alienated by the treatment they had received. In this respect, libraries can learn a lot from the casino industry. Both casinos and libraries have stiff internet competition, and they have to provide welcoming and pleasant experiences that make customers choose to return, since they have other options.

Technology and Technology Expertise

Every day more and more people are coming to libraries virtually. Those who choose to come to the library, often come to use the libraries' technology or to learn how to use their own devices. The Philadelphia Library in Pennsylvania trains staff on various e-readers and waits for the onslaught of customers after holiday gift-giving, when visitors rush in to the library to learn how to use their devices and how to download the library's e-content. The New Jersey State Library lends libraries Mobile Device Discovery kits that have e-readers and tablets to use when training staff and customers. More than 100 libraries have signed up to borrow the kits. Many libraries now have technology centers to make state-of-the-art technology available for consumers to generate their own products. New York's Fayetteville Library has a lab that includes a 3D printer. The library in Orlando, Florida, houses labs for visual arts and digital media. Above-mentioned Charlotte-Mecklenburg County Library in North Carolina has GarageBand software for teens to use to produce their own music.

Innovative Services

Libraries have migrated from simply housing and safe-guarding materials to becoming knowledgeable providers of different and rewarding experiences. Every librarian's motto should be: "We want you to come back." Library customers' expectations are much higher than they were 20 years ago. They expect at a minimum comfortable lounge furniture, long opening hours, interesting programs and materials for all ages and interests, cafés, and state-of-the-art technology. At the Princeton Public Library in New Jersey, the "red box" dispensers make audio-visual materials available at all times. In San Francisco, California, the GoLibrary system dispenses library materials to commuters.

A trend that was introduced in Denmark was live books or local experts who could be "checked out" for 30 minutes at a time. They are available to discuss with individuals or groups all aspects of a topic of interest. For instance, at the Bainbridge Island Library in Washington, a paralyzed young man in a wheelchair explained to a group of students how he organizes his life. This and other libraries have a database of valuable social capital, which also emphasizes the role of community members. Often these volunteers are retired individuals who bring their years of knowledge and capabilities to the community. The library can be the place that organizes this trading of skills. How valuable would it be to not only check out a book on caring for roses, but also to check out a professional gardener who can offer practical advice on the subject and answer questions.

Libraries offer consumers all kinds of collections that are unique: tools, seeds and musical instruments are just a few of these collections. The Topeka-Shawnee Library in Kansas offers its health books in a health "neighborhood" next to the blood pressure cuff donated by the local hospital. The travel books are in travel bags by locale, and community members who travel are encouraged to donate their travel books upon return from a trip. Monroe Township Library in New Jersey has a drive-in window for borrowing and returns, very popular with mothers who do not have to unbuckle children from their car seats to carry out a library transaction. Houston Public Library in Texas has "HPL to Go", i.e. curbside delivery so customers can park outside, call the library and have a "car hop" bring the materials to the car.

Marketing and Advocacy

Libraries are making the connection between marketing and advocacy. This is of particular importance in the United States, where 80 % of funding for public library operations comes from local tax receipts while state and federal taxes provide a relatively small portion of operating funds. The OCLC report *From Awareness to Funding* summarizes the findings from a study on how marketing and advocacy techniques could be employed to create awareness and ultimately increase funding for public libraries.[6] Individuals surveyed believe that the library is a noble place, important and relevant to the community. They see the library as a transformational force and a vital community resource like public schools, fire and police departments. To this end, when faced with cuts, the New Jersey State Library started a "Tell Us Your Story" campaign, which resulted in television and radio ads, "skins" on buildings and buses, and roadside billboards and road signs. The campaign illustrated for funders and members of the community how their friends and neighbors successfully used libraries to improve the quality of their lives. Constituents explained in their own words the value of libraries to library funders. In New Jersey, libraries received U.S. $6 million for the Knowledge Initiative when business persons told funders how science and

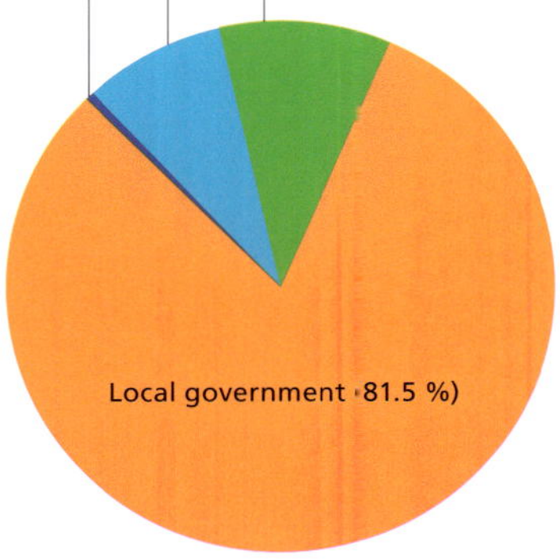

In the United States, public libraries are mostly funded by local tax receipts.

At ImaginOn in Charlotte in North Carolina, Holzman Moss Bottino, 2005, the entrance is given a sculptural presence and a number of spaces address children of various ages. The check-out desk is reminiscent of a hotel reception, thus underlining the impression of hospitality.

health information databases accessed through libraries helped entrepreneurs get established and retain their businesses in the state. This program won a national innovation award.

In a similar vein, New Jersey started a project called "Snapshot: One Day in the Life of NJ Libraries" to show what libraries did for people in just one day. On the first Snapshot Day on February 19, 2009, 161,367 people visited New Jersey libraries or four times the number of people who visited Disneyland in a day. Librarians counted visitors and asked why they came to the library that day. From Snapshot Day, librarians could tell, for example, that about 30,000 people a month likely get employment assistance at New Jersey libraries. Legislators were impressed with the 1,200 pictures taken as well. Snapshot Day was adopted by the American Library Association and was replicated in at least 31 states across the USA.

In Conclusion

The reason that libraries continue to exist is their ability to adapt. Libraries adapt to changing priorities and the changing economic status of their service areas. Libraries are adept at understanding the needs of their communities and making the library part of the solution to community problems. Today with social media, the libraries serve many customers who never even come to the library. Yet libraries must continue to build flexible spaces to accommodate new uses and new technologies. While libraries may need to house fewer physical materials, they need space for their members to generate their own materials and space for the community to come together to share ideas.

References

1 *Perceptions of Libraries and Information Resources*. Dublin, Ohio: OCLC – Online Computer Library Center, 2005. http://www.oclc.org/de-DE/reports/2005perceptions.html, last accessed October 29, 2013, pp. 1–7.

2 Seth Godin, *Tribes: We Need You to Lead Us*. New York: Portfolio Hardcover, 2008.

3 Stephen Marche, "Is Facebook Making Us Lonely?", *Atlantic Monthly*, April 2, 2012. http://www.theatlantic.com/magazine/archive/2012/05/is-facebook-making-us-lonely/308930/, accessed October 29, 2013.

4 Sarah Dalton, "The New Cerritos Library", *Connection*, a Publication of the California State Library, Sacramento, July 2002, No. 25.

5 The study analyzed more than 1,300 comments by users on existing library services in the U.S., Canada, the UK, Australia, India and Singapore. The response to user services was overwhelmingly negative: 1,106 were negative and only 238 positive. See *Perceptions of Libraries and Information Resources*. Dublin, Ohio: OCLC – Online Computer Library Center, 2005. http://www.oclc.org/de-DE/reports/2005perceptions.html, accessed October 29, 2013, pp. 3–20.

6 *From Awareness to Funding: A Study of Library Support in America*. Dublin, Ohio: OCLC – Online Computer Library Center, 2008. http://www.oclc.org/en-CA/reports/funding.html, accessed October 29, 2013.

Ursula Kleefisch-Jobst

On the Typology of the Library

The illustration from the *Codex Amiatinus*, one of the oldest surviving manuscripts of the Bible, shows a scriptor in front of an open armarium.

According to the *Reallexikon zur Deutschen Kunstgeschichte* (Encyclopaedia of German Art History), the term library – over the ages also known as *bibliotheca*, *liberaria*, *libraria* or *liberey* – is used indiscriminately in literature from the Middle Ages and Antiquity to denote either an entire building, a room or simply just a cupboard for storing books, as evidenced by the occasional use of the term *armarium* (a locked closet or chest). In the sixth of Vitruvius Pollio's *Ten Books on Architecture*, which he dedicated to the Emperor Augustus (at around 33 BC), he uses the plural term *bybliothecae*, from which Luciano Canfora infers that the Roman architect and engineer was referring to the cupboards in which the scrolls were kept: "Bedrooms and libraries ought to have an eastern exposure, because their purposes require the morning light," he wrote, noting that when stored in such cupboard-like *bybliothecae* the books "will not decay."[1]

In his treatise "De re aedificatoria", written between 1442 and 1452 and based in part on Vitruvius' writings, Leon Battista Alberti further differentiates between public and private libraries. In a private residence ("works of individuals"), the library should be adjacent to the husband's bedroom. Like Vitruvius, Alberti supports the notion of orienting the library eastwards in "the direction of the sunrise at equinox".[2] In Book Eight on "Ornament to Public Secular Buildings", Alberti has more to say about libraries, remarking on what they contain but revealing nothing about the building or the room itself: "The principal ornament to any library will be a large collection of rare books .... It would also be an ornament to have mathematical instruments ... or the map that Aristarchus is said to have made of the whole world and all its provinces engraved upon a metal plate."[3] Alberti may be referring here to the descriptions of libraries from Antiquity that he makes mention of elsewhere in Book Eight.

It would seem that up until the early modern period, libraries had not yet developed into a separate building with specific typical characteristics. That certainly applies to the Baroque period up until well into the 18th century: libraries were usually housed within a larger building or complex of buildings such as a castle or monastery. It was not until the 19th century that the library as we know it today came about: landmark buildings that are a characteristic element of the townscape.

The typology of the library developed initially from its internal structure outwards. Over centuries, it was defined by the design of its interior: beginning as a simple room for storing written scrolls, it later became a place to study books. This simple space would later turn into a central reading room. The appearance of libraries in the urban realm as buildings in their own right, i.e. no longer as part of another building complex, is closely connected to their being made accessible to the broader public. For centuries, libraries were only accessible to those who could read and write. Today, libraries are open for everyone and their users are not just from the educated classes.

Study Libraries in the Middle Ages

In the Romanesque period, libraries were only to be found in monasteries. As most of the books were liturgical scriptures for services, the books were kept near the altar in the sacristy. The books were therefore part of the church's sacred items and stored securely in cupboards or almeries in the sacristy. In many cases they were stored in rooms directly over the sacristy. As the stock of books gradually expanded to include theological and juridical works for the monks' education, it became less and less necessary to house them in the sacristy, and over time the library moved to a position on the east side of the church but still close to the choir and choir stools. The book presses served solely as a repository for the books, the monks withdrawing to their cells for the purposes of study.

The plan of the Monastery of St. Gall is instructive for the development of the library. Conceived as a kind of ideal plan around the time of the Benedictine reforms shortly before the year 800 AD, the plan shows an almost square two-story building next to the presbytery on the northeast transept. The legend says *"infra sedes scribentiu(m), supra bibliot(h)eca"*; the scriptorium, or writing-room, was on the lower floor illuminated by seven windows in the north and east walls, while the library was on the upper floor and could be reached by a stair from the presbytery: *"introitus in bibliotheca sup(ra) cripta superius."*[4] It is conceivable that there was also a stair directly from the scriptorium.

The plan of the Monastery of St. Gall shows one of the earliest examples of a free-standing building for the scriptorium and library – at least in an ideal plan. We have no knowledge of whether such a building was actually built. When the library was not located above the sacristy, it was instead placed between the choir and the chapter house in the eastern wing of the cloister.

With the founding of the first universities, the purpose of libraries changed from being that of a mere repository to becoming a place of study. Because the libraries were now made available to a broader section of society, the commonly used writings were laid out on raked lectern-like desks and anchored with chains. A rectangular room with windows along the long sides and the raked desks arranged at right angles began to crystallize.

One of the first libraries of this kind was in the Sorbonne in Paris in 1289, of which all that remains is a written account: it was a separate hall-like building that contained a room measuring 40 × 12 paces with 19 windows along each long side and 28 inclined desks. This was the so-called *magna libreria*, while the *parva libreria*, which probably contained the bookcases, was located in an adjoining room.[5] Such library spaces were usually unobstructed by columns, but in some larger library rooms in Germany, there is a row of columns down the center, while in Italy one sometimes sees two parallel rows of columns creating a narrow nave-like space down the center.

Plan of the Monastery of St. Gall from around 800 AD showing one of the earliest examples of a separate library building (gray)

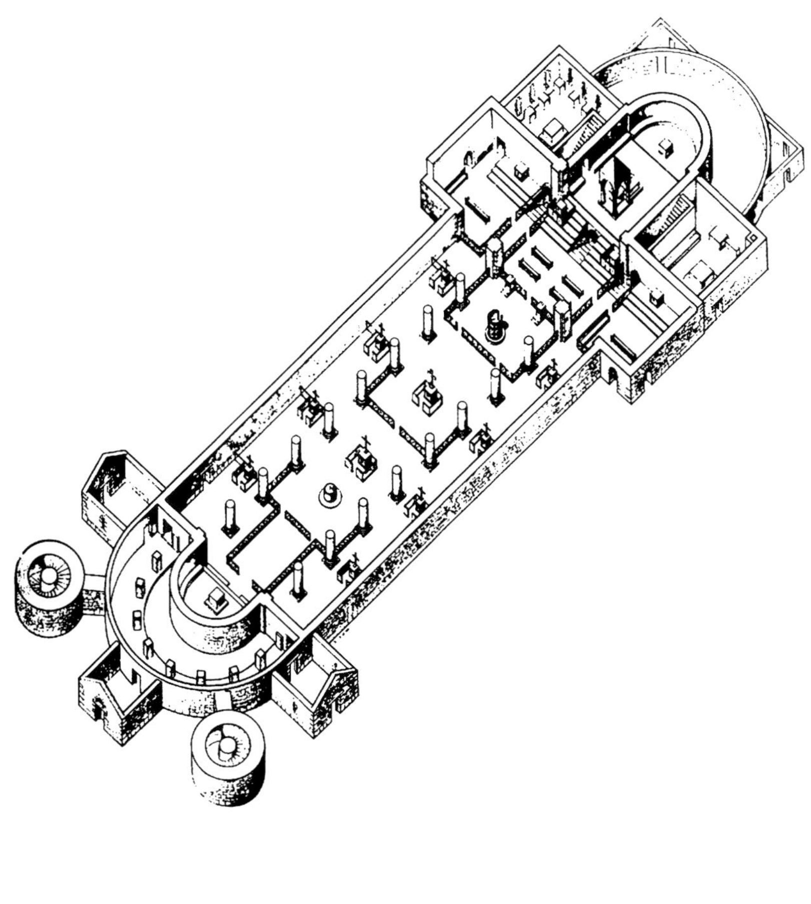

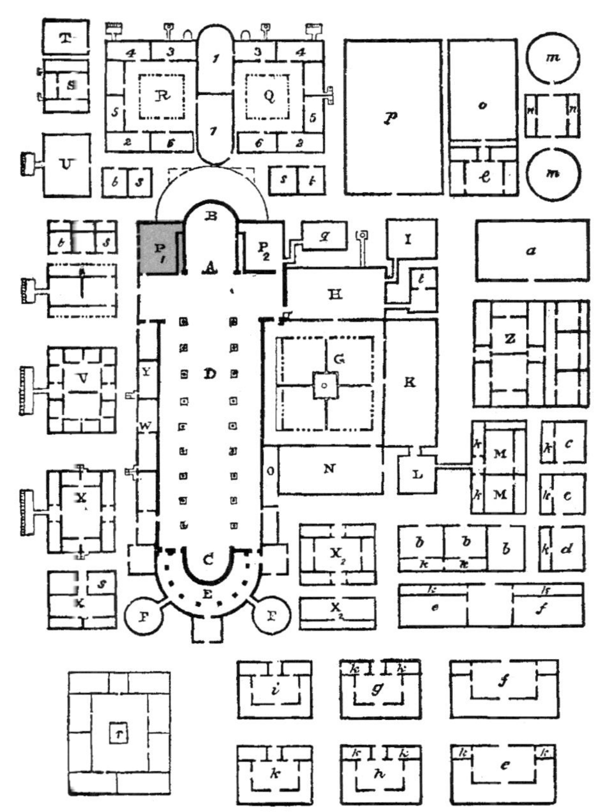

This type of narrow, long room as a space for study quickly became the dominant arrangement in the monasteries of the day, especially among the mendicant orders for whom scholarly study was part of the order's rules. To begin with, the library spaces were still located in the region of the east cloister, near to the chapter house, and often over it. But as the libraries began to attract visitors from outside the order, their position shifted gradually during the 15th century, usually into the upper story of a side wing east of the quadrangle. This enclosed position of the library can be seen in monasteries throughout the 16th century.

The free-standing library building of the Augustinian Friars' monastery in Erfurt, Germany, built at the beginning of the 16th century is an exception. Its plain, unadorned exterior is reminiscent of a free-standing chapel building. And indeed, libraries were also known to have been built above chapels.

Libraries in the Renaissance – First Public Appearances

With the Renaissance in Italy came the creation of a large number of new representative public buildings in the powerful cities and city-states. These new buildings also included isolated instances of library buildings, commissioned without exception by well-educated and influential persons.

In 1524, Pope Clement VII, formerly Cardinal Giulio de Medici, commissioned Michelangelo to construct a library for the valuable manuscripts owned by the Medici family that until then had resided in the family's Palazzo in Florence. The plan to build such a library goes back to the year 1519 in conjunction with plans to build a new sacristy on the transept of San Lorenzo as a tomb for the Medici family. The church and monastery of San Lorenzo are located in the direct vicinity of the Medici Palazzo. Plans for the library were resurrected with Guilio's elevation to the papacy but were again delayed due to lack of money and the library eventually opened in 1571. Following medieval precedence, the library was located adjacent to the cloister of San Lorenzo, but the entrance vestibule, the *ricetto*, with its cascade of steps leading to the library itself, was an entirely new and extraordinary architectural space. The walls of this vestibule are subdivided by a high plinth on which pairs of monumental half-columns rest, each of which frames an aedicula between them, with pilasters continuing the rhythmic articulation on the upper story. The wall treatment echoes that of the exterior of the building, giving the vestibule the character of a representative, public entrance courtyard. By relocating the library from the Medici Palazzo to the complex of the monastery, it relinquished its private character. Michelangelo designed the library interior itself as a large hall devoid of columns with rows of desks arranged in the traditional manner along each of its long sides.

Parallel to Michelangelo's Biblioteca Laurenziana, another library was being built in enice on the Piazzetta opposite the Doge's Palace: the Libreria Vecchia or Biblioteca Marciana. Started in 1537 on the side facing the Campanile, it was built to plans by Jacopo Sansovino and completed after his death by Vincenzo Scamozzi from 1588–1591. It was commissioned by the powerful Procurators of San Marco, who were the custodians of St. Mark's wealth and goods and were the most influential public officials in the Venetian State. The building was originally designed to close the gap between the Zecca (the mint) at the Baccino di San Marco and the Campanile. Only after construction had begun did the Procurators decide to house a valuable collection of Greek and Latin manuscripts in the building. Sansovino developed a plan for a vast reading room on the upper story of the seven bays that adjoined the Campanile, reached by a sumptuous foyer in the central axis of the building.

Biblioteca Marciana, Venice, Jacopo Sansovino and Vincenzo Scamozzi, 1591. The building opposite the Doge's Palace closes the square.

The Laurentian Library, Florence, Michelangelo, 1571, was built to house the manuscripts belonging to the Medici family. The vestibule, with its cascade of steps leading up to the library, forms a prestigious entrance.

Although the building was not originally erected to house a collection of books, it is remarkable that a library was even conceived for such a prominent and representative building in the city's innermost bastion of power. The building's appearance follows typical classical patterns, with stout doric columns on the ground floor and slender, richly decorated ionic columns on the upper story, characterizing the library as a public building. Sansovino followed Alberti's recommendations, orienting the library eastwards. Like in the Laurentian Library, the main room is an elongated hall free of columns. The room is decorated with a series of scholarly iconographic paintings: personifications of music, wisdom and fame on the roof and a cycle of philosophers' portraits around the walls.

In 1603, the learned Cardinal Federico Borromeo of Milan, who was a patron of Jan Brueghel the Elder – the so-called "Flower" Brueghel –, commissioned the building of a library to house his collection of 30,000 books and 15,000 manuscripts from all over the world. The library was named after Ambrose, the patron saint of Milan. The entrance to the Biblioteca Ambrosiana opens onto the Piazza San Sepolcro with a projecting entrance *al antica* that announces its presence to the urban surroundings. The two-story reading room, the Sala Federiciana, is covered by a long barrel-vaulted ceiling with two semi-circular Diocletian windows at the ends for illumination. For Alberti,[6] the barrel vault was itself a mark of distinction as the temples of Antiquity were, according to the Renaissance architect, roofed over by barrel vaults. Federico, well-versed as he was, would have been aware of this.

However, what is most exceptional about this building is its open shelving in which the books and manuscripts are stored. They appear to cover, indeed to constitute, the entire surfaces of the wall. A gallery running around the perimeter provides easier access to the upper bookshelves. The Biblioteca Ambrosiana is probably the first library to be equipped with shelving of this kind. From this point on, all of the fundamental elements that constitute a library had been developed: a long, column-free space, open shelves and galleries. These elements were then further refined over the course of the Baroque era. The galleries in particular developed into elements that defined the space, and shelves transitioned from being items of furniture into an integral part of the walls.

Biblioteca Ambrosiana, Milan, Lelio Buzzi and Francesco Maria Richini, 1618. Cardinal Federico Borromeo commissioned the building of a library to house his extensive collection of books and manuscripts. The projecting entrance building announces the building to its surroundings. On the interior the open shelves act as walls.

The library in El Escorial near Madrid by Juan de Herrera, completed in 1584, is a unique combination of ecclesiastical and royal library.

From the above it is clear that the library interior was subject to a process of continual development, but no such progression can be observed for the library's outward appearance. In this context, it is instructive to take a short look at the library in El Escorial in Madrid. The Bibliotheca Escorialensis is unique in that it is both an ecclesiastical as well as a royal library: the complex of El Escorial is both a monastery as well as a royal palace built by King Philip II of Spain. The church lies in the center of the complex, framed by a courtyard on either side with several courtyards arranged in front as a means of entrance. The library is housed in the wing facing the street over the main entrance portal. It is located on axis with the church, directly on the boundary between the royal and the monastic areas. Colossal doric and ionic columns demarcate the presence of the library on the building's facade. Above the main cornice, the facade is set back slightly, evoking the impression of a church front. The long reading room with a low barrel vault and lunette caps probably derives not from Alberti's understanding of the temples of Antiquity but from its origin in the royal gallery of the castle building. Free-standing cabinets and globes are arranged along the central axis of the room.

The Library as a *Gesamtkunstwerk*

While the Baroque period did not bring forth any further fundamental typological advancements, the libraries developed into sumptuous *Gesamtkunstwerke* – a blend of architecture, painting and stucco that expressed the overall extravagant mentality and splendor of the era. By the second half of the 17th century, libraries in monasteries had advanced to become as important as the refectory or the communion hall. The library was often built over the refectory, the two spaces contained in a single building that extended like a spur off the quadrant of the cloister, its built mass acting as a counterpart to the church. This arrangement can be seen, for example, in the new library at the Benedictine monastery at Neresheim in the German state of Baden-Württemberg, built from 1699 onwards to plans by Michael Wiedemann. The library's prominent status was often reflected in the architectural treatment of its facade as a projecting *risalit* in one of the courtyards in the immediate vicinity of the church. El Escorial is one of the earliest examples of this.

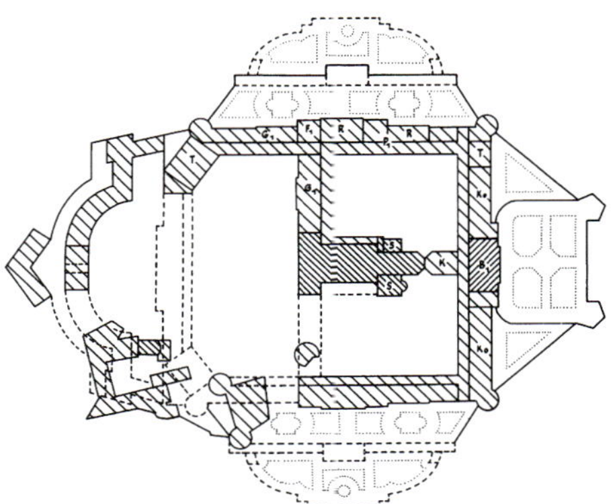

In the Benedictine abbey at Göttweig, the library is housed in the east wing of the cloister. In this case, the central *risalit* is wider than the reading room behind and therefore does not expressly denote the library on the exterior of the building.

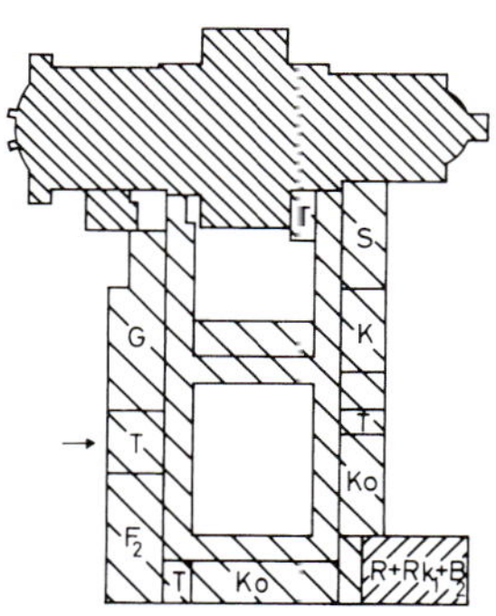

In the Benedictine monastery at Neresheim, built from 1699 by Michael Wiedemann, the library is arranged above the refectory, the two forming a spur that extends out of the plan, its built mass acting as a counterpart to the church.

The lavishly decorated library at Göttweig was established when the abbey was rebuilt from 1718 onwards according to plans by Lucas von Hildebrandt.

Library at the Benedictine abbey of Wiblingen, Christian Wiedemann, 1744. The gallery rests on red and green columns, its curved balconies projecting into the room.

In the Benedictine abbey at Göttweig in Austria the library is located in the east wing of the cloister courtyard and is arranged perfectly on axis with the choir and the adjacent chapter house. Here, however, the central *risalit* that visually structures the long facade of the building overlooking the Danube is much wider than the reading room behind it, and in this case it does not therefore explicitly denote the library on the facade. The library was established as part of plans to rebuild the abbey from 1718 onwards by Lucas von Hildebrandt. The real show of splendor occurred, as in the past, in the design of the interior. Libraries started to be modeled after the representative rooms of the nobility such as ceremonial halls, antiquaria and cabinets of curiosities, and especially churches. Given that science was seen as being one step beneath divine knowledge, it is no surprise that the key aspect of some libraries bore similarities to sacred spaces.

This can be seen in two characteristic examples that illustrate two of the most commonly employed spatial systems of Baroque churches. The library at the Benedictine abbey at Wiblingen near Ulm, Germany, is believed to have been built by Christian Wiedemann in the mid-18th century. Its elegantly winding gallery with curved balconies that project into the room, rests on 32 scagliola columns made to resemble red and green marble. Standing between them on low plinths are wooden statues, rendered entirely in white, that portray allegories of the virtues and the disciplines.

The Abbey Library of St. Gall, Peter Thumb, 1766. The system of wall pilasters used in the church to connect the galleries was also applied to the library where they are lined with bookcases.

In St. Gallen in Switzerland, construction began for the new Abbey of St. Gall around 1760, which included the abbey library completed in 1766 to a design by the architect Peter Thumb from Vorarlberg. For the church interior, the architect developed a system of pilasters that connect the perimeter galleries, a system that he also applied to the library's reading room. Here the pilasters are completely lined with bookcases. The ultimate example of Baroque splendor is the imperial library in the Hofburg palace in Vienna. Soon after his inauguration, Emperor Charles VI embarked on an extensive program of building, which included a library building for the Habsburg dynasty's extensive collections of books, which until then had been stored in the Hofburg. In 1722, the Emperor commissioned Johann Bernhard Fischer von Erlach to construct a new library making use of an existing riding school building from 1681. As such, the wing in which the library was to be housed was predetermined. Fischer von Erlach elected to introduce a new element in the middle of the central axis of the elongated rectangular wing, the top two stories of which house a magnificent oval reading room with a high-domed roof. Fischer therefore gave the building a new definition of its own, decorated on the outside with vast ionic orders, and containing a dramatic interior space, the *Prunksaal* (Splendid Hall), from which the side wings lead off. The transition between the oval dome and the side wings was originally much more fluid, but 40 years after completion it became necessary to strengthen its structural stability.

Imperial library, Hofburg palace, Vienna, Johann Bernhard Fischer von Erlach, from 1722. The Splendid Hall is tripartite with two side wings and an oval dome.

The Pantheon of Knowledge

In the 17th century, the idea of the library as a centrally planned building gained increasing favor. As part of modernization work on the renaissance Blankenburg Castle in the Harz region of Germany in 1705, the court architect of Brunswick, Hermann Korb, installed a library above the castle chapel, a square plan with an octagonal arrangement of free-standing columns within it. This centrally planned arrangement may have been more a matter of chance than anything but it probably influenced Korb's later design for the Court Library in Wolfenbüttel designed a year later and built from 1706 to 1710. The Court Library was a two-story rectangular building containing an oval rotunda with two galleries, one above the other. The building's exterior and interior were comparatively plain and unadorned due to a lack of money, which also resulted in sections of the building being built as a timber frame construction, which in turn ultimately led to the building being demolished in 1887. A lantern with 24 windows ensured the room was well-illuminated. The two galleries provided ample space for books.

Court Library, Wolfenbüttel, Hermann Korb, 1710. Painting by Ludwig Tacke.

However, the idea of housing a library in a centrally planned building had a greater significance. In documents from the 18th century, the library is also referred to as the "Pantheon of Wolfenbüttel". Ever since the Renaissance, centralized building layouts have been regarded as an ideal figure for buildings, and the most famous of these is certainly the Roman Pantheon. In the fourth of Palladio's books on architecture, printed in Venice in 1570, he speaks of centrally planned churches as being a man-made "image of God's world". As such, what better way to house the "knowledge of the world" than also in an ideal building figure? Correspondences of these kinds played an important role in the age of early Classicism because they showed that it was about more than the simple resurrection of models from Antiquity but rather their interpretation through the lens of the Renaissance. The pantheon epitomizes the adoption of ideal forms in architecture. This reference took on particular importance as the library began to liberate itself from the confines of the monastery and palace and became a public educational institution in its own right. And it was here, as before in the Middle Ages, that the universities were to play a key role.

Radcliffe Camera, Oxford, James Gibbs, 1747. A two-story main room is illuminated by a domed roof.

Christopher Wren designed a building of such universal aspirations, modeled on the Pantheon in Rome, in 1676 for Trinity College Library in Cambridge. His initial design shows a square building with an ionic portico arranged in front of a rotunda crowned by a dome and lantern. The interior envisaged the colloquium in the plinth, with a two-story library above it with bookcases extending to the base of the dome, its windows allowing light to stream into the interior. Possibly Hermann Korb was aware of Wren's first unbuilt design and used it as inspiration for his own building.

A pupil of Wren's and a scholar of Palladian architecture, James Gibbs, completed the construction of a library to house the collection of the famous doctor John Radcliffe in 1747. Built in the campus of Oxford University, it was known as the Radcliffe Camera. The main two-story room is set upon a rustic plinth and illuminated by a tholobate and dome. The bookcases are arranged in the galleries that run around the perimeter of the space behind the arcades.

Etienne-Louis Boullée drew up a design for an ideal form for a public library in 1784 that features a monumental domed central space. The bookshelves are arranged beneath the vast semi-circular dome in four staggered tiers beneath one another in the manner of rows of theater seating. Boullée became increasingly influential as a teacher and theorist at the École Nationale des Ponts et Chaussées from 1778 to 1788, where he developed an inimitable abstract style, which he developed to grand proportions, but was always borne by the idea that the building must fulfil its function. It is during this period that he also produced a design for the National Library, which applied his earlier idea for a public library to an elongated rectangular volume. Boullée's visions would have a strong influence on later generations' ideas about the design of library reading rooms.

Etienne-Louis Boullée, initial design for a public library in Paris, 1784. The cross section shows a domed central space.

Etienne-Louis Boullée, design for the reading room of the National Library, 1785

Henri Labrouste, French National Library, Paris, 1868.
The domed construction of the large reading room.

Henri Labrouste, Bibliothèque Sainte-Geneviève, Paris, 1850. The reading room totals 1,780 m^2 and is a cast iron construction.

The French National Library, designed by Henri Labrouste in 1862, completed a section of the Louvre on the Rue Richelieu resulting in a coherent ensemble. The tall arcades of the central oval reading room are made of slender iron columns that carry a shallow vault with its large oval skylight. The bookshelves line the walls behind the arcades from the floor to the height of the main cornice. The reading room – which Labrouste also realized in a similar linear arrangement for the Bibliothèque Sainte-Geneviève (1843–1850) – exploited the possibilities offered by the introduction of iron as a building material and became a model for many later reading rooms until well into the 20th century.

This brief historical overview shows clearly that, unlike other kinds of buildings, no single typological model has developed for the library over the ages. The reading room – as a repository for books as well as a place for study – remains the central pivotal space of a library and its formal elaboration has always dictated the design of libraries. Consequently, libraries have always been developed from the inside outwards.

References

1 Marcus Vitruvius Pollio, *The Ten Books on Architecture*, Book VI, Chapter IV, Sec. 1, translated by Morris Hicky Morgan. Oxford: Oxford University Press, 1914. http://www.gutenberg.org/ebooks/20239

2 Leon Battista Alberti, *On the Art of Building in Ten Books,* translated by Joseph Rykwert, Neil Leach, Robert Tavernor. Cambridge, MA: MIT Press, 1988, p. 153.

3 Leon Battista Alberti, *On the Art of Building in Ten Books,* 1988, op. cit., p. 287.

4 Walter Horn, Ernest Born, *The Plan of St. Gall: A Study of the Architecture and Economy and Life in a Paradigmatic Carolingian Monastery*, 3 vols. (California Studies in the History of Art 19). Berkeley and Los Angeles: University of California Press, 1979, vol. 1, p. 147.

5 Konrad Rückbrod, *Universität und Kollegium. Baugeschichte und Bautyp.* Darmstadt: Wissenschaftliche Buchgesellschaft, 1977, p. 87.

6 Leon Battista Alberti, *On the Art of Building in Ten Books,* 1988, op. cit., p. 379.

Karl-Heinz Schmitz

Form and Function in Library Design

A history of the library often begins with the observation that the word library refers to both the building and the collection. Given modern-day technological developments, one might ask if there is then a future for libraries. This question is made easier to answer if we extend this definition: libraries *are* collections, and libraries *are* buildings, but above all they are an image of a well-ordered world. It is by ordering the books that libraries become places where we can find what we are looking for, and where we can study what we are interested in. Today, in a world that we perceive as being increasingly complex and in which the flood of information seems ever more boundless, professional navigation is more important than ever. Few institutions are better placed to channel the flood of information than libraries – they have, after all, been ordering knowledge since the days of Callimachus. But how should libraries be structured in future and what should they look like? A short review of the history of the last 200 years can be instructive.

From the 19th Century to Modernism and the Present Day

"The exterior of a building should suggest, as much as possible, its designation and interior function. The distinguishing features of its exterior, in accord with the interior, express most expediently and most directly the characteristic of a building,"[1] wrote Friedrich Weinbrenner in 1809 in a treatise on theater buildings. J. C. Loudon expressed it as follows in 1833: "Every building should appear to be what it is, and every part of a building ought to indicate externally its particular use."[2] The belief that the exterior form of a building should express its function therefore has a long tradition. At the turn of the 20th century, Louis Sullivan expressed this even more succinctly in his declaration in 1896 that "form follows function", which would later become a central tenet of Modernism. Le Corbusier wrote that, "The plan proceeds from the inside out; the exterior is the result of an interior."[3] Hugo Häring described what he called *Leistungsform* (performance form), meaning that the form is an expression of the function it performs.[4]

The pithy formula "form follows function" fails, however, to take into account that the relationship between space and function is often both complex and contradictory. We know too that architectural briefs rarely ask for nothing more than to fulfill the requested function.

In reality, the 20th century has been an endless search for a unique expression that only rarely relates specifically to the function of the building. In addition, buildings often last longer than the purpose they were designed for, later being altered to serve a different function. The Anna Amalia Library in Weimar, Germany, was originally a residence from the Renaissance period that was converted into a library by August Friedrich Straßburger in 1760, while the Ulmer Hof, a 17th century palace in Eichstätt, Germany, was converted into a library by Karljosef Schattner in 1976.

A further reason why the exterior cannot always be an expression of the inner function is that buildings stand in a specific context that often determines the form of a building. The Biblioteca Marciana in Venice was designed as part of the Procuratie in Venice, which defines the urban space of St. Mark's Square and the Piazzetta and does not express any of the functions it contains as individual buildings.

And there is another important reason why there cannot always be a direct architectonic relationship between form and function. The history of functions and the history of form, or of architectural space, are not synchronous. In the late 18th century and early 19th century, the function of public buildings changed dramatically but architectural space remained more or less the same during this period. And in the early 20th century, new spatial concepts changed the face of architecture although the underlying functional requirements changed little.

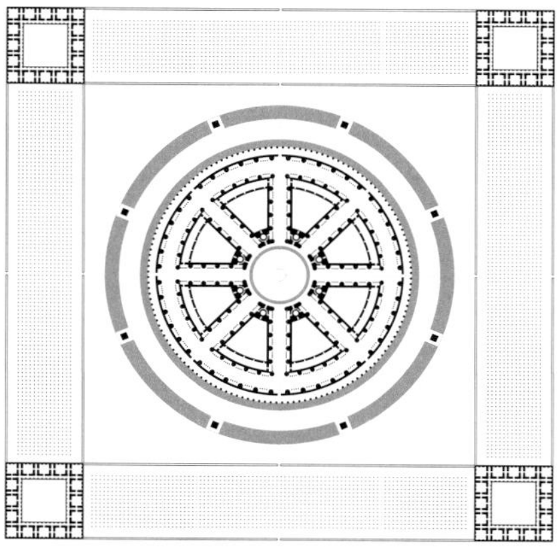

Designs for a library, Jean-Nicolas-Louis Durand, 1802–1809. The form of the building emphasizes its public character and accessibility.

Bibliothèque du Roi, Paris, Étienne-Louis Boullée, 1785. Entrance elevation

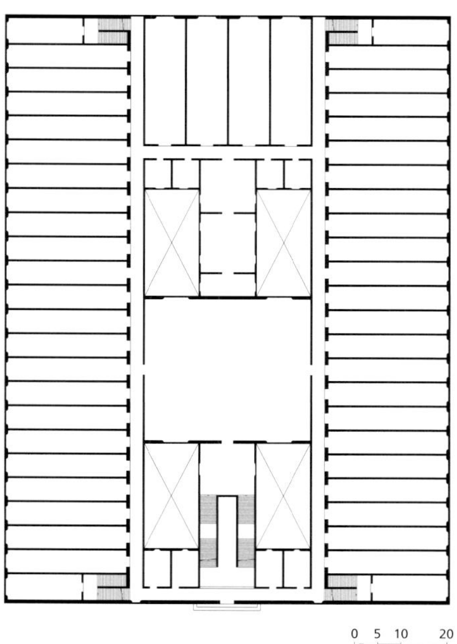

Design for a library, Leopoldo della Santa, 1816. The floor plan shows its division into three sections: reading (central reading room), book stacks (left and right), and administration (small rooms next to the four atria), an arrangement that is still common today

Libraries of the Enlightenment and the Bourgeois City of the 19th Century

The people who commissioned the libraries of the 16th and 17th centuries were kings, noblemen, popes, princes and bishops. Such libraries almost always housed a private collection and were an expression of an individual's preference: that of the king or nobleman. With the age of Enlightenment, and after the French Revolution in particular, there was a significant change in social systems throughout Europe. From the 18th century, and even more so in the 19th century, libraries were for everyone to use. From then on libraries were, "a sort of general archive [containing] all times, all ages, all forms, all tastes in one place ... a place of all times that is itself outside time and protected from its erosion",[5] as the philosopher Michel Foucault has written.

At the beginning of the 19th century, shortly after the French Revolution, the French architect Nicolas Durand articulated ideal plans for almost every kind of public building that a city in the new republic should have, including a library, museum, theater, hospital, school and law court. All of these are public buildings that for the most part did not exist in the cities of the Middle Ages, Renaissance or the Baroque. His design for a museum and his design for a library share two characteristic qualities: Durand designed them as free-standing public buildings, placing great emphasis on their public character and accessibility. Both buildings can therefore be entered from all sides.

Durand's teacher, the revolutionary architect Boullée, likewise emphasized the accessibility and public character of these new public buildings, as can be seen clearly in his design for an opera house and the entrance elevation of the new Bibliothèque du Roi in particular. The plans elevate the aspects of accessibility and public character to the most important feature of their designs. These plans were tantamount to a political statement: they were buildings for a new self-assured civil society, not just for a select circle of privileged people. The libraries and museums were no longer embedded in castles and palaces; they stood on their own in urban space and were open to everyone.

But while Durand's library plans from the year 1809 are an ideal plan in terms of public presence, they are not an ideal plan for a new library. Durand knew that libraries would no longer house just the collection of a king or prince. He also knew that libraries need spaces that are not only for exhibiting and reading books, but also for managing and storing them. But Durand had probably never spoken to a librarian. There are eight entrances, which means there are also eight exits through which one can leave the library with a book under one's coat. The book storage areas, located in the corners of the building, are far too small and neither they nor the administrative areas are directly connected to the other spaces in the library.

Leopoldo della Santa's design for a library in 1816 was the first to exhibit an ideal arrangement of functions. The library is divided into three areas that still exist in a more or less similar form to the present day: a space for reading, a storage area for books, and administrative areas. All of these areas are linked logically with one another and there is one single entrance and exit. Della Santa's tripartite library was an answer to the long-held dream of a universal library, one that could hold all the books in the entire world and which could be looked after by more than one librarian. The universal library of the 19th century was a library open to the people whose stock of books was organized and collected according to scholarly criteria. It marked the greatest functional change to the library since the age of Antiquity.

Design for Berlin State Library, Karl-Friedrich Schinkel, 1835. This tripartite library was never built.

During the same period, however, architectural space and architectural form remained largely constant. There were no revolutionary changes. New public buildings contained the same customary set of forms – rotunda, open hall and loggia –, a typology of spaces that we can see in almost all public buildings from the 19th century. The architects of the 19th century answered questions of function with the concept of spatial typology and spatial character, not with architectural form. These spatial types had been used for over 2,000 years and were simply adapted to meet different functions. The rotunda, for example, could be a sacral space, an exhibition space or a reading room. In the 19th century, the function was not expressed in terms of architectural or spatial form but by the character of the space. The building's form could remain the same for all three functions, although the spatial character differed in each case.

In 1835, Karl-Friedrich Schinkel drew up a design for a tripartite library, although it was never built. It is a very rational design and unlike his Altes Museum next to the Lustgarten in Berlin, which seems to be heavily influenced by the entrance to Boullée's design for the Bibliothèque du Roi, his library had a more modest entrance similar to that conceived by della Santa.

In 1868, Henri Labrouste took della Santa's sketch and translated it into a building that was to become an architectural masterpiece. Here too, the library is divided into three sections, with an area for reading, a storage area for books and administrative areas.

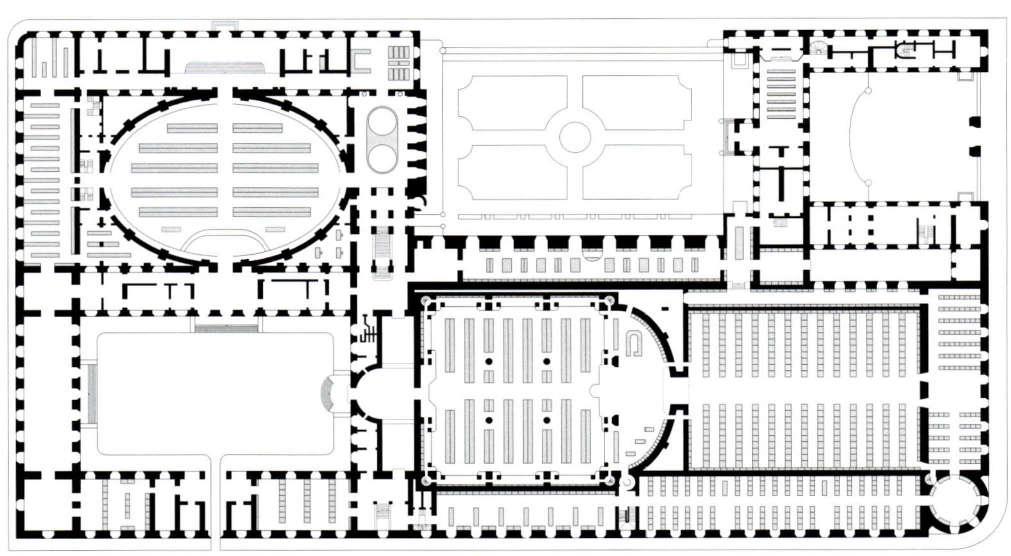

French National Library, Paris, Henri Labrouste, 1868. This library also has a reading room, book stacks and administrative areas.

City Library in Stockholm, Gunnar Asplund, 1928. Perspective

The Library of the 20th Century – New Spatial Concepts in the Age of Modernism

Towards the end of the 19th century and in the early 20th century, architectural space changed dramatically. Architects began developing new spatial concepts that were no longer compatible with the spatial principles of past epochs. Despite their respective differences, the Gothic, Renaissance, Baroque and Classical periods all shared the same fundamental notion of retained or enclosed space. The Modernist architecture of the early 20th century broke with this, positing a new spatial concept of open or flowing space. Never before in the history of architecture had there been such a radical shift in the development of architectural styles and architectural form. The old spatial typologies had no place in the new concept of open flowing space. A rotunda would be unthinkable. The pattern that had prevailed until the 19th century, in which an interior design and arrangement could exist within a wholly different exterior, was rendered impossible by the new spatial concept in which inside flowed into outside and vice versa.

How did this shift affect the design of libraries? Gunnar Asplund (1885–1940) was an architect who stood with one leg in the 19th century and the other in the 20th century. The history of his design for the City Library in Stockholm illustrates how Asplund's approach changed and this is visible in the design of the building and in one's experience of it. Paradoxically, this shift is best seen in the modern plinth. The main section of the building, the library itself, stands on a modern plinth that appears to float above ground. Here history is turned on its head: it appears as if the old grows out of the new and not the other way around.

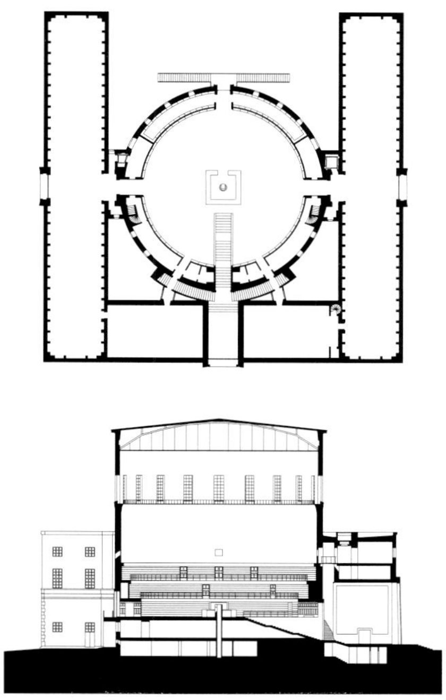

City Library in Stockholm. Plan and section

The succession of spaces that lead into the interior follows the concept of enclosed spaces. The stairs to the entrance on the modern plinth are firmly clasped by flanking walls. Thereafter follows a clear entrance situation – something that Modernist open space largely eradicated – from which one enters a dark corridor that successively narrows. At the end of the corridor is a large, brightly illuminated space in which the books are kept. The main room of the library is a metaphor for knowledge. This concept is again very much in the tradition of the 19th century, as Modernism is not receptive to expressing space in terms of metaphors. At the same time, the large, central space is very restrained and devoid of paintings and ornamentation: just books, white walls and light. Asplund therefore created a space that is in the tradition of the 19th century but can also be read as a modern space. Asplund employs a system of shelving embedded in the walls in order to give the central space the typical character of a library. The City Library in Stockholm is, however, one of the last great libraries of the 20th century to use such a system.

City Library in Stockholm. The central space is flooded with light and the books are stored in shelves embedded in the walls.

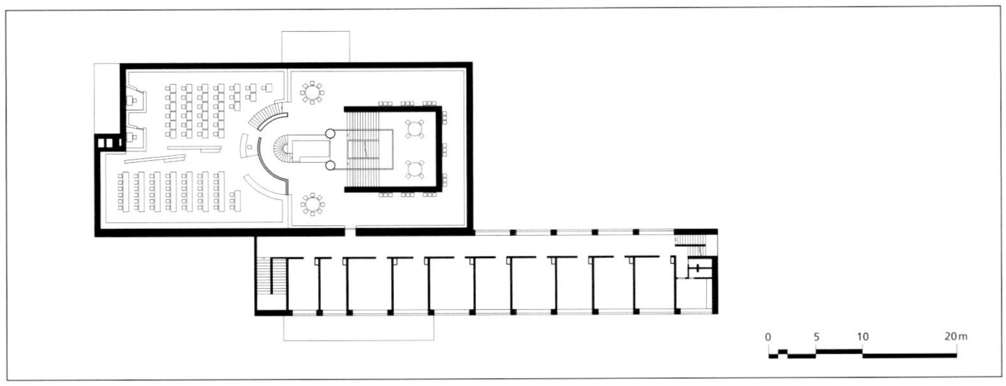

Library in Viborg, Alvar Aalto, 1935. General view and first floor plan. The volumes express the functions within: the narrow bar contains the administrative areas.

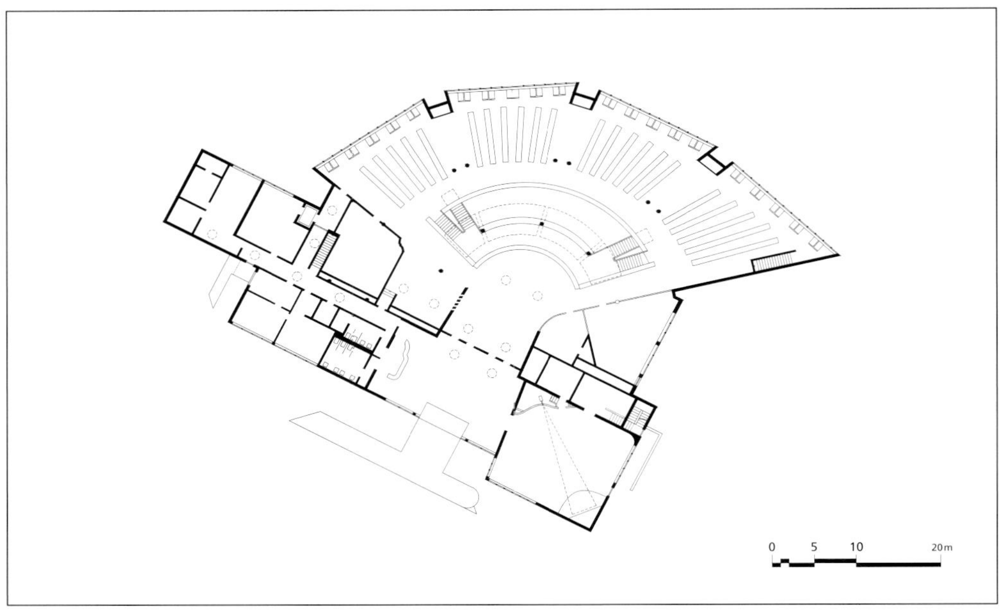

Library of the Mount Angel Benedictine College, Mount Angel, Oregon, Alvar Aalto, 1970. Atrium and floor plan. The public spaces and reading areas flow into one another. Only the lecture hall and administrative areas are enclosed spaces.

From 1930 onwards, the large enclosed reading room and embedded shelving fell out of use for two reasons. Firstly, embedded wall shelving was not compatible with the concept of flowing space. And secondly, the large central reading room was no longer able to accommodate the growing stock of books. The distance between the books and the reading space grew ever larger. In Stockholm, the reading rooms are already located elsewhere, namely in side wings of the buildings.

The Finnish architect Alvar Aalto designed a library for Viborg (Viipuri), Finland, previously in Russia, in 1927 as part of an architecture competition. The library, which was completed in 1935, stands on its own in a park and its different volumes do not relate to a specific external situation, only to its inner function. The administrative wing is located in a separate element. In Aalto's design the library floor plan is increasingly a flowing and open landscape. Nevertheless there are still echoes of the enclosed spaces of old in this library.

In a later concept for the Library of the Mount Angel Benedictine College in Mount Angel, Oregon, Aalto eradicated enclosed space entirely. In his design, almost all the spaces flow into one another and only the lecture hall and administrative areas remain as closed spaces. The library has no reading room at all: the reading areas are instead distributed throughout the library.

Staatsbibliothek in Berlin, Hans Scharoun, 1978. The library is a landscape of flowing space.

Hans Scharoun's design for the Staatsbibliothek in Berlin as part of the Kulturforum near Potsdamer Platz epitomizes the spatial concept of early Modernism. It manifests the ideas of Modernism by reconfiguring the library as an open landscape of spaces that flow into one another. But even when the library has a new spatial concept, it still reflects the basic functional concept of the early 19th century and the call of the Enlightenment for a boundless and open universal library.

Baden State Library, Karlsruhe, Oswald Mathias Ungers, 1989. The design makes reference to spatial structures in the urban context, especially the protestant church (left) designed by Friedrich Weinbrenner in 1816.

Developments since 1960

From 1960 onwards, the unconditional propagation of the new concepts of Modernist architecture began to wane. People called for a less radical form of Modernism that is receptive to the past, in which urban context is respected and enclosed spaces once again feature in interiors. The Baden State Library in Karlsruhe, Germany, is an example of this. Designed in 1989 by Oswald Mathias Ungers, it relates to the forms and spatial structure of its surroundings. In particular, the composition and formal vocabulary of the city's protestant church, designed by Friedrich Weinbrenner in 1816, influence the design of the library. In this project, the central reading room also makes an appearance. Like other library projects designed by Giorgio Grassi and Aldo Rossi, this project returns to the concept of enclosed space.

From the early 21st century onwards, new information and communication technologies started to influence how libraries are run and built: the type of media has diversified, and books are no longer the only media that libraries make available. The way in which media are stored also changes, because new forms of media no longer require physical space. Likewise, the library user's behavior and relationship changes because knowledge and information is no longer bound to a physical room in one particular place. Although some effects of these transformations are already evident and palpable, the true extent and effect of these changes remain uncertain. What we do know is that there are more publications, lectures and podium debates on the future of public libraries than ever before.

Enclosed and Flowing Space

Despite these changes, we can still find examples of both types of enclosed and flowing space in library buildings from recent years. Buildings such as the Jacob-und-Wilhelm-Grimm-Zentrum in Berlin (Max Dudler, 2009, pp. 232–237) are oriented around strongly defined spaces. The design emphasizes the presence and the specific character of the reading room, which employs a classical arrangement with tables following the pattern used in the 19th century. The implied assumption here is that fundamental shifts in the function will not entail fundamental changes to the building and its spatial arrangement.

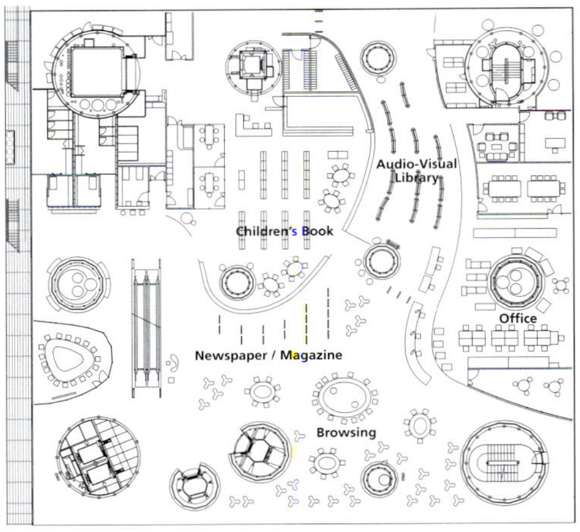

Sendai Mediatheque, Toyo Ito, 2001. First floor plan. The position of furniture is not fixed in this flowing space.

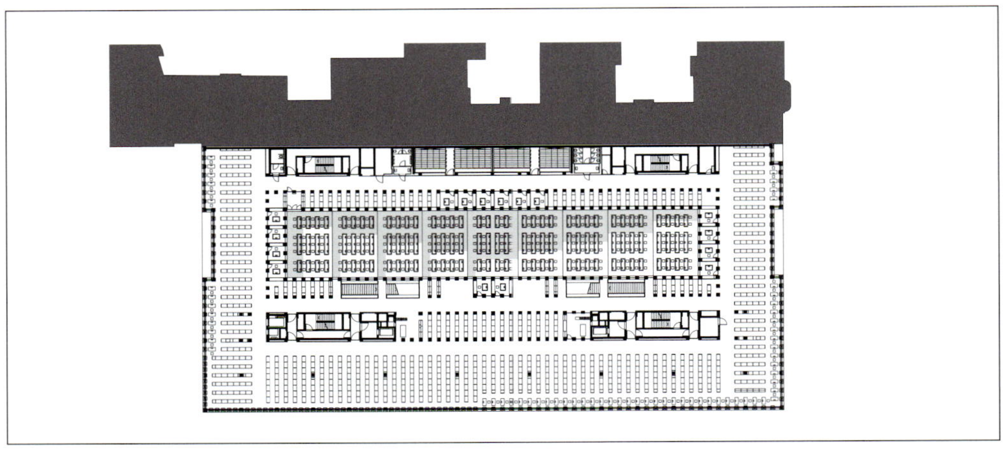
Jacob-und-Wilhelm-Grimm-Zentrum, Berlin, Max Dudler, 2009. Fourth floor plan. An orthogonal arrangement of reading desks and bookshelves defines the space.

Other library buildings such as the Sendai Mediatheque, designed by Toyo Ito, 2001, and the Rolex Learning Center in Lausanne by SANAA (2010, pp. 238–243) employ a concept of flowing space. Here the presence of the books is not emphasized and furnishings are designed to be movable and non-intrusive, so as not to create boundaries. Both buildings employ a free arrangement of tables that are not necessarily dedicated to working in peace and quiet. The users are not forced to sit next to one another in isolated concentration but can take a seat at a small round table, making it possible to talk and exchange opinions. These open spatial landscapes emphasize seamless interconnection, whether between the parts of the space, between areas of knowledge or social contacts.

High-rise Libraries

Early Modernism not only saw new opportunities in open space; it also recognized the potential that high-rise buildings have for building an entirely new and modern city. High-rise buildings have had a greater impact on the traditional notion of public urban space than the open-plan configurations of the early modern period. But how has this development influenced the design of libraries?

Beinicke Rare Book and Manuscript Library, Yale University, New Haven, Skidmore, Owings and Merrill, 1963. The spaces are arranged vertically above one another.

In 1963, Skidmore, Owings and Merrill, who had designed high-rise buildings since the early 1950s, created a library building for Yale University. While it cannot be classified as a skyscraper, the arrangement of spaces within is clearly vertical and not horizontal.

Louis Kahn's library for the Phillips Exeter Academy in Exeter, New Hampshire, also arranges the reading areas on several floors stacked above one another. This arrangement presents the architect with a challenge, as the flow of space from floor to floor is interrupted by staircases, meaning that one cannot wander so freely from section to section. Kahn, who does not adhere to the early Modernist concept of flowing space, resolves this problem by introducing a vast central space that reveals the full extent of the library on entering the building: visitors take in the library as a whole in a single glance.

Steven Holl's design for a library in 1988 also takes on the challenge a multi-story library. It demonstrates that multi-story arrangements also open up new possibilities and that the concept of flowing space can help to gather a multi-story space.

The Bibliothèque nationale de France by Dominique Perrault was one of the first libraries to employ a high-rise configuration in a way that the vertical division of the floors does not present a problem. While many libraries arrange the public areas, such as the reading room, above the book stacks, Perrault reverses the typical pattern, placing the book stacks, which are not accessible to the public, in the four corner towers. Because the towers are simple storage areas, there is no need for the floors

Bibliothèque nationale de France, Paris, Dominique Perrault, 1996. The book stacks, which are not accessible to the public, are located in the library towers.

to be spatially connected. The public areas are located in the large plinth, arranged generously around a large forest-like courtyard garden. Perrault's design is, of course, not solely motivated by the desire to find a new logical way of resolving the problem of dealing with ever greater storage areas. The built mass of the book stacks serve as beacons visible from afar. The four towers represent four open books, communicating the purpose of the building to the outside world.

We can, therefore, conclude that the question of the future of function and form in library design needs to be addressed separately. Changes to the function do not automatically entail changes to the building form.

While most librarians agree that the function of libraries is changing drastically, architects are not convinced that architectural form is shifting to the same radical degree as it did during the period of early Modernism. Indeed, some recent examples have successfully demonstrated that classical spatial concepts can still be a viable option and offer potential for further development.

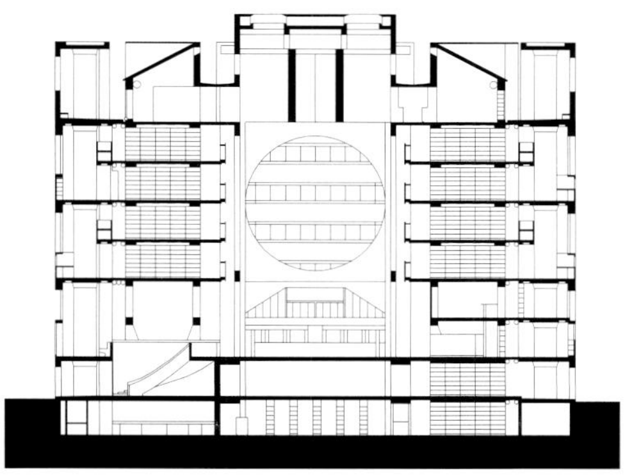

Phillips Exeter Library in Exeter, New Hampshire, Louis Kahn, 1971, section. The reading areas are stacked over several floors.

Design for an extension of the American Memorial Library in Berlin, Steven Holl, 1988. Diagram of the circulation and interior perspective. The multi-story space is structured as a flowing space.

References

1 Friedrich Weinbrenner, *Briefe und Aufsätze*, collated by Arthur Valdenaire. Karlsruhe: G. Braun, 1926.

2 J. C. Loudon, *An Encyclopedia of Cottage, Farm and Villa Architecture and Furniture*, 1833.

3 Le Corbusier, *Vers une architecture*. Paris: G. Crès, 1923 (English: *Towards a New Architecture*. London: J. Rodker, 1931; and Jean-Louis Cohen (ed.), *Toward an Architecture*, new translation by John Goodman. Los Angeles: Getty Publications, 2007, p. 214.)

4 Hugo Häring, "Form der Leistungserfüllung", *Innen-Dekoration*, October 1932, p. 361.

5 Michel Foucault, *"Different Spaces"*, trans. R. Hurley, in Michel Foucault, *Essential Works of Foucault 1954–1984*, 2 vols., London: Penguin, 1998, p. 182.

Nolan Lushington

Public Libraries in the United States

Early American Libraries: The 18th and 19th Centuries

In 1776, the year of the Declaration of Independence, when the United States was home to a population of an estimated 2.5 million, there were 15 publicly accessible libraries in the colonies, located primarily in Pennsylvania, New York and New England. Only 24 years later, in 1800, there were already 64 public libraries in the United States with a total of 50,000 books. In most cases the libraries were housed in buildings designed for other purposes, churches, local societies, residences. By 1876 there were 3,674 public libraries in the United States, holding a total of over 12 million volumes. By the middle of the 19th century the rapid spread of free public education in the United States created large new reading populations who understood the opportunity to better themselves through access to books and magazines. Innovations in printing – most notably the invention of the rotary printing press by Richard Hoe in 1847 and the mass paper production – made books affordable to a rapidly growing middle class. These two factors also advanced the development of freely available library service for all citizens, an idea that captured the imagination of the public during the second half of the 19th century.

Typical New England small village library in Bedford, New Hampshire. The public library is an important feature in the community.

New England Libraries

In New England, the legislation enabling communities to tax all their citizens for the benefit of creating public libraries, led to a flowering of library construction. With the assurance of public funding for operations and a rapid increase of wealth from factories and railroads many wealthy New Englanders chose the building of a public library as their way of giving back to the community. In most small New England towns today one can quickly spot these outstanding buildings for their classic and iconic design.

This rapid success story had reverberations for the design of the buildings as well. In 1876, Justin Winsor (1831–1897), librarian and head of the Boston Public Library, gave the following advice to architects: "We come to change the character of the library to that of a great collection to which multitudes have access and but few are personally known to the librarians. Such a state of affairs ... involves the shutting out of the public from the shelves ... The main idea of the modern public library building is ... compact stowage to save space and short distances to save time."[1] Winsor gave detailed instructions on how the shelves should be made and arranged. He also already envisioned a library of one million volumes[2] with compact storage to save space.[3] By 1896 the Boston Public Library was circulating 1.5 million books a year to 716,000 annual visitors.[4] These new public libraries were often envisioned by their governing bodies as a means to assimilation and the Americanization of the mass of immigrants coming into the country. Political leaders thought of libraries as places where people could be acclimated to a civic culture and uplifted.

By 1899 there were 10,000 libraries with 40 million books. 5,000 of these had at least 1,000 books. This building boom did not necessarily yield functional buildings. In 1879, the outspoken librarian William Frederick Poole (1821–1894), for instance, told an audience of his colleagues at the Fourth Annual American Library Association convention to "avoid everything that pertains to the plan and arrangement of the conventional American library building."[5] Poole was referring to the alcoved book hall libraries with several stories such as Henry Hobson Richardson's Romanesque design for the Winn Library in Woburn, Massachusetts (1879). The book stack was closed to the public, so staff had to climb a precarious spiral stair and clamber up high bookcases to retrieve books for users waiting at the delivery desk. It was next to impossible to heat the galleried book hall to a comfortable temperature without overheating its upper levels and damaging the books. The book stack capacity was minimal and much of the space was unusable for library purposes. Nonetheless, the Winn Library is a glorious cathedral-like space considered a monumental achievement by architects and much beloved by many library users.

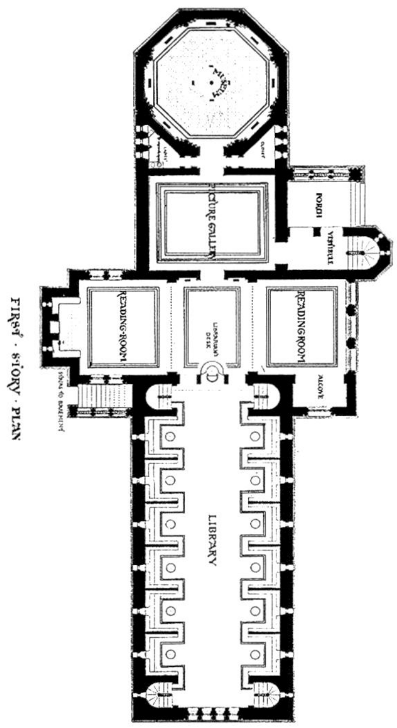

Woburn Public Library (Winn Library) in Massachusetts, Henry Hobson Richardson, 1879. Exterior view and ground floor plan

In a similar way, H. H. Richardson went on to design a number of public libraries, among them the Ames Free Library in North Easton, Massachusetts (1877) and the Thomas Crane Public Library in Quincy, Massachusetts (1880). All followed the traditional style by encasing the reading room in book-lined alcoves. In 1874 the Cincinnati Public Library opened with five levels of alcove stacks and a ceiling skylight. In the words of Justin Winsor, these traditional libraries were "planned to produce the largest rather than the smallest distance of books from the point of delivery" and exhibited the "inability of architects to recognize the paramount demands of administrative uses over the meretricious attractions of vista of books and displayed alcoves." Librarians called for a plan based more on function than form.[6]

Carnegie Libraries

Starting in 1886, Andrew Carnegie made funds available for constructing libraries throughout the United States and Canada. Under the influence of the Carnegie grants, which poured money into library building, the paternalistic social attitude of the 19th century gave way to a more open and egalitarian spirit.[7] From 1901–1910, 450 public library buildings were constructed while from 1911–1920 180 more were added. Andrew Carnegie's private secretary, James Bertram (1872–1934) had been put in charge of distributing the Carnegie library building grants. From 1904 onward Bertram reviewed plans. By 1911, when most of the Carnegie grants had already been allocated, Bertram thought the designs were often so grandiose and dysfunctional that he wrote a guideline titled "Notes On the Erection of Library Buildings" that offered to potential designers some advice on library design.

Bertram insisted on the functionality of the design and required "to obtain for the money the utmost amount of effective accommodation, consistent with good taste in building." His emphasis was on economy of space. He especially disliked wasted space at the entrance. "Too valuable space allotted to cloak rooms, toilets and stairs."[8] The site should admit natural light and be large enough to allow for expansion.[9] Bertram's notes focused on layout configuration and the organization of the building program but did not establish a specific style for the exterior design. The result was that the 1,689 Carnegie Libraries that were built in the United States exhibit a wide variety of architectural fashions, such as Classical Revival, Italian Renaissance, Beaux Arts, Spanish Revival and others.[10]

The Monumental Urban Library

In 1897, the influential librarian and library innovator John Cotton Dana (1856–1929) pointed out that the decreases in book costs made the concept of a library as a storehouse of treasures obsolete. The new open library allowed readers to enjoy "the touch of the books themselves, the joy of their immediate presence."[11] Libraires increased their book capacities and opened their stacks so that anyone could browse the entire collection.[12] Earlier designs that placed the book shelves around the walls of the reading rooms (wall stacks), were replaced with free-standing stacks (stall stacks) requiring reinforced floors to support heavy 2.1 m high stacks to meet the new requirements for thousands of volumes. These libraries were perceived as the "People's University", intended for the uplifting of all citizens. Whether they were funded by private money, as was the New York Public Library, or by city funds as in Boston, the concept reflected the great civic pride of the time.

The Library of Congress 1897

Ainsworth Rand Spofford (1825–1908) was responsible for the copyright law of 1870, which required all copyright applicants to send to the library two copies of their work. This resulted in a flood of books, pamphlets, maps and prints. Facing a shortage of shelf space at the Capitol, Spofford convinced Congress of the need for a new building. It was designed by John L. Smithmeyer and Paul J. Pelz, and the construction was devised by General Thomas Lincoln Casey, chief of the Army Corps of Engineers, assisted by engineer Bernard Green. The library, soon known as the Thomas Jefferson Building, opened in 1897. Reference book stacks radiated out from a centrally located immense card catalogue with thousands of drawers. The majority of the multi-million volume collection was housed in self-supporting stacks and located outside of the reading room. The stacks included open shelving and floor openings for the circulation of air.

Boston Public Library, Charles McKim, 1895. Main reading room

The Boston Public Library 1895

The Boston Public Library, established in 1848, was the first library to allow people to borrow books and take them home. The collections developed rapidly in response to demand and the book stacks outgrew two buildings before the end of the century. It was considered necessary to separate the reading rooms from the book stacks, and a new and much larger building was planned. Designed by Charles McKim of McKim, Mead and White, the new library opened in 1895, a milestone in public library architecture. The influential librarian William Warner Bishop wrote: "It is a beautiful and inspiring structure and houses a very wonderful collection. But its following of palatial architecture results in a very small main door, narrow windows on the ground level, a great amount of space devoted to the magnificently conceived and decorated staircase well ... and a courtyard which forces books to travel around three sides of a square to be delivered at one side."[13]

The New York Public Library 1911

In 1902 the design for the New York Public Library by Carrère and Hastings, one of the most outstanding Beaux Arts architecture firms in the United States, sought to remedy some of the criticism of the Boston library by building seven floors of bookstacks that sat directly underneath the grand reading room with book lifts and pneumatic tubes to facilitate sending messages to the stacks for the quick delivery of books. By the 1970s, the collection began to outgrow the available space and new library facilities were created underground by excavating the space underneath adjacent Bryant Park.

Library of Congress, Thomas Jefferson Building, Washington, DC, 1897. Exterior view and main reading room

New York Public Library, Carrère and Hastings, 1911. Main reading room

The Move Toward More Functional Design

Already in 1897, the great library innovator John Cotton Dana addressed the conflict between monumental design and functional requirements: "The free public library building ... so constructed as to serve thoroughly well the purposes for which it was intended exists in theory only." Dana went on to plead for greater ease of access and speed in intercommunication. He emphasized accessibility to the delivery and information desks near the entrance to the building. "The delivery counter should be so constructed as to serve as an aid in the transaction of business – as a means of communication, not as a barrier – between the assistants and the public."[14] Dana believed in the new open-access designs that were just beginning to replace the closed stack designs that had been common up to this time. He advocated special rooms for children "so arranged that the children may make their own choice"[15] – a revolutionary idea at that time.

He offered the following advice to the architect: "Make your building adaptable to new conditions. ... Avoid permanent partitions. ... Stairs are bad in any library. The smaller the library the worse they are. ... This working library of the future ... is in a building which is well lighted and can be easily readjusted, rearranged and extended to meet new conditions."[16]

The Enoch Pratt Free Library

In 1926, Joseph L. Wheeler became director of the Enoch Pratt Free Library in Baltimore, Maryland. His emphasis was on immediate accessibility of materials. He moved the books out from closed stacks. He saw the library as a kind of department store for distributing books. Wheeler felt that the structure should be a thing of beauty and that there was no conflict between a nice appearance and convenience and economy in plan and operation. When the new library building, which was to replace the original Romanesque Revival structure from 1886 designed by Charles L. Carson, was being planned he held a special meeting in which 25 librarians of other large cities gave their criticisms of the plans of the new building.[17] The replacement building was designed by Alfred M. Githens (1876–1973) and opened in 1931.

Enoch Pratt Free Library, Baltimore, Alfred M. Githens, 1931. Central hall

Wheeler and the architect Githens created a revolutionary library design. The large open book collection of 150,000 volumes was organized in subject matter departments that surrounded a central hall. The main floor was accessible directly from the sidewalk with the entrance at ground level instead of via a monumental pedestal at the top of a long flight of stairs. Street level show windows attracted users, comparable to a downtown department store. An information desk was located right at the center with selective popular and new materials nearby. All in all, the library was characterized by openness and hospitality instead of presenting a prison house of books.[18] Although the Baltimore library was a great improvement over the monumental staircases and massive reading rooms of earlier big city libraries, the disadvantages of this arrangement were inflexible staff distribution, difficult access to the books on floors below and expansion limitations.

Wheeler and Githens later collaborated on the book *The American Public Library Building* that became a standard for public library design for many decades. In Wheeler's opinion, a library should be "neither a storehouse for books nor a refuge for the idle; neither is it a civic monument. ... friendly in its expression of welcome to all, not aloof nor cold, nor trite and commonplace in its architecture."[19]

The Modular Library

Angus Snead Macdonald trained as an architect at Columbia University in 1915 just as it was making a major transition from the traditional Beaux Arts curriculum to a modern and technical curriculum.[20] He became president of Snead and Co., a distinguished manufacturer of steel book stacks. Snead and Co. installed the book stacks for the Library of Congress and the New York Public Library and they held many patents for book stack innovations. In 1933, Angus Snead Macdonald wrote in *The Library Journal* a two-part article entitled "A Library of the Future", suggesting some new ideas in public library design, chiefly the modular flexible design. He described a flexible library layout based on column modules spaced 2.74 m (9 ft) apart to hold up the heavy 732 kg per m² (150 lb per ft²) live loads required for books. Within the column grid Macdonald envisioned furnishings that could be changed easily. He emphasized flexibility, economy, informational comfort, and a reliance on artificial illumination and ventilation. Snead and Co. were integral in the move of the American library system from one of closed, structural stacks, to open stacks that allow for adjustability. Macdonald focused on the construction of modular libraries even to the extent of constructing a sample furnished module at his factory so that he could demonstrate its virtues to major library clients.

Here is how he described this new library: "We have provided over fifty special departments in which books on particular subjects are collected in close proximity to those on related subjects ... In both exterior and interior architecture we wanted a feeling of homelike intimacy rather than monumental impressiveness. To every department where our readers may go they will find a specialist ready to advise them authoritatively on whatever phase of a subject may be of interest. ... The ... departments ... are all in a constant state of growth and adjustment made possible by the fact that there are no permanent vertical divisions ..."[21] Macdonald envisioned public libraries as the center for public learning for the entire community. The library would not only provide the materials but also the expertise for learning a wide array of useful professions – truly becoming the People's University. During the Great Depression of the 1930s American public libraries became citizen learning centers despite limited resources. People desperately flocked to libraries to learn new trades and acquire competitive skills for the job market. National per capita library circulation reached its all time peak in the Great Depression.

The Flexibility Fallacy

In the 1950s and 1960s modular flexible design advocated by Angus Snead Macdonald was introduced with minimal bearing walls and a column grid gradually increasing from Macdonald's original 2.74 m (9 ft) to 7.62 m (25 ft) or more. Library planners presumed that expansions would occur at 20 year intervals. These modular libraries were an effort to design flexible open spaces for a variety of functions. Architects searched for the perfect column spacing module. Michael Cohen of The Architects Collaborative, the firm founded by Walter Gropius in 1945, suggested a 9.14 m (30 ft) column spacing that could be altered for book stacks spaced 1.83 m (6 ft) apart to stacks paced 1.52 m (5 ft) apart for increased book capacity. However, the problem with flexible design was that specific library uses have different functional requirements. Converting a book stack into a reading room requires more than just moving furniture. It is often unpleasant for readers to be in spaces originally designed for books. Sitting in a converted book stack space with its oppressive low ceilings and artificial light may be an unattractive experience.

The use has structural implications as well: While a book stack requires a floor loading capacity of 732 kg per m^2 (150 lb per ft^2) reading rooms require only half of that capacity. Further, the 2.13 m (7 ft) tall stacks require column spacing that matches the aisle spacing so that columns do not end up in the middle of the aisles. The lighting must be designed to reach the books on the bottom shelves while lighting for readers needs to be focused at tabletop height. Heating and cooling in a reading room for long-term comfort is crucial for seated readers, but less important for books. Natural light is healthy for the user but may be destructive for books.

National Plan for Public Library Service

In the post-war period the American Library Association began to develop library standards. In 1948 the ALA published "A National Plan for Public Library Service", which included "Essential principles in planning library buildings". It postulated that library buildings should be easily accessible to its potential clientele and established that location is all important if the library is to achieve its maximum usefulness. Further, standard types of library buildings should be developed to be used in typical situations such as the large city branch, the county library branch or the small-town library. Many public library buildings should be adaptable for expanded service in county or regional library systems. The public library building of the future should be planned and equipped as a modern educational center, providing rooms for meetings and conferences of organizations. It will need audio-visual facilities, projection rooms for films and soundproof listening rooms.[22]

A standard that became controversial had to do with how many people a public library should serve. 50,000 people was thought to be the minimum adequate tax base for a library facility. By 1950 this had been raised to 100,000. Many library systems were created grouping smaller independent libraries into larger systems. In the 1950–1970 period American Library Association planning guidelines evolved and established empirical standards for the size of public libraries based on population. It was assumed that 0.09 m^2 (1 ft^2) of space and three to five books per capita and five seats for every 1,000 people served would be adequate. As collections grew they occupied almost 50 % of the usable space in the building. These newer libraries had book lifts and even high-density storage for materials. Technical spaces were designed for efficient flow of materials.

References

1 Justin Winsor, "Library Buildings", in: U.S. Bureau of Education, *Public Libraries in the United States of America; their History, Condition, and Management. Special Report,* Department of the Interior, Bureau of Education, Part I. Washington: Government Printing Office, 1876, p. 466. http://digital.library.wisc.edu/1711.dl/History.PublicLibs

2 Justin Winsor, "Library Buildings", 1876, op. cit., p. 472.

3 Justin Winsor, "Library Buildings", 1876, op. cit., p. 467. Cf. also: Albert Predeek, *A History of Libraries in Great Britain and North America,* Chicago: American Library Association, 1947, p. 121.

4 Lucy Salamanca, *Fortress of Freedom.* New York: J. B. Lippincott, 1942, p. 28. Cf. also: *Public Libraries in the United States of America; their History, Condition, and Management. Special Report,* 1876, op. cit., p. 1053.

5 William L. Williamson, *William Frederick Poole and the Modern Library Movement.* New York: Columbia University Press, 1963.

6 Kenneth A. Breisch, *Henry Hobson Richardson and the Small Library in America.* Cambridge, MA: MIT Press, 1997, p. 88.

7 Abigail A. Van Slyck, *Free to All: Carnegie Libraries & American Culture, 1890-1920.* Chicago: University of Chicago Press, 1995, p. 28.

8 James Bertram, "Notes on the Erection of Library Buildings", 1911. Reproduced in: Abigail A. Van Slyck, *Free to All: Carnegie Libraries & American Culture, 1890–1920.* Chicago: University of Chicago Press, 1995, p. 35.

9 Theodore Wesley Koch, *A Book of Carnegie Libraries.* New York: H. W. Wilson, 1917, Chapter XVII "Library Planning", p. 207.

10 Theodore Jones, *Carnegie Libraries Across America: A Public Legacy.* New York: John Wiley & Sons, 1997.

11 John Cotton Dana, "The Public and its Public Library", *Popular Science Monthly,* June 1897, pp. 242–253, here p. 245.

12 John Cotton Dana, *Library Problems.* New York: H. W. Wilson Company, 1902, p. 26.

13 William Warner Bishop, "The Historic Development of Library Buildings", in: Herman H. Fussier, ed. *Library Buildings for Library Service.* Chicago: American Library Assocation, 1947.

14 John Cotton Dana, "The Public and its Public Library", 1897, op. cit., p. 248 and p. 249.

15 John Cotton Dana, "The Public and its Public Library", 1897, op. cit., p. 250.

16 John Cotton Dana, "Library Problems" (1902), in: John Cotton Dana, *Libraries Addresses and Essays,* 1916, op. cit., p. 31.

17 Philip Arthur Kalisch, *The Enoch Pratt Free Library: A Social History.* Metuchen, NJ: Scarecrow Press, 1969, p. 134.

18 Joseph L. Wheeler, *A Great Library in the Making. Annual Report of the Enoch Pratt Free Library.* Baltimore: Enoch Pratt Free Library, 1928.

19 Joseph L. Wheeler, Alfred Morton Githens, *The American Public Library Building: Its Planning and Design With Special Reference to Its Administration and Service.* New York: Charles Scribner's Sons, 1941. p. 1

20 Charles H. Baumann, *The Influence of Angus Snead Macdonald and the Snead Bookstack on Library Architecture.* Metuchen, NJ: Scarecrow Press, 1972.

21 Angus Snead Macdonald, "A Library of the Future", *Library Journal,* December 15, 1933, vol. 58, no. 22, p. 971.

22 Carleton B. Joeckel, Amy Winslow, *A National Plan for Public Library Service.* Chicago: American Library Association, 1948, p. 126.

Rebecca Chestnutt

Towards the Design of Libraries

Luisenbad Public Library, Berlin-Wedding, Chestnutt Niess, 1996. Sketches played a central role in the design process and in establishing a connection with the historical situation.

Few building types offer architects as much scope to explore spatial ideas as the design of libraries. But changes in the library system and a shift in the role libraries play in society have redefined the basis on which this building type is founded. For architects, this can serve as a starting point for reconsidering the design of libraries.

At the most basic level, libraries are a collection of books, or the rooms in which these collections are stored and read. For architects, libraries also conjure up a whole range of associations: the book = a store of knowledge; the written word = a vehicle for transporting knowledge; and the library = a place in which we are surrounded by knowledge, a sanctuary for studying, a place of debate, and so on. In the design process, these archetypal images feed the architect's creative imagination. But of the impressions that we associate with libraries, most have remained unchanged with one exception: the medium. The variety of different forms of data storage devices has expanded vastly, and continues to do so. Likewise, the spatial surroundings in which we seek information and broaden our knowledge is diversifying ever more. It is, perhaps, for this reason that the importance of libraries as actual places is growing.

In the libraries we have designed over the years, this aspect has always played a central role. The architecture of the library must not only fit into its urban context, but also strengthen the respective local situation. The library spaces themselves must provide a range of different spaces for meeting, relaxing and for working and concentrated study. The fact that libraries generally have large, spacious interiors makes them enjoyable places to be in and also enjoyable spaces to design. The building typology offers architects comparative freedom in developing spatial compositions that respond to the programmatic and functional requirements. This marks the beginning of a design process in which architectural ideas are successively distilled into a final concept. Although the end result may seem logical, or even quite natural, the final design is the product of an iterative process in which the architect has explored various avenues and weighed alternatives in the search for an appropriate solution. One factor that influences the course of the design process is the way in which the dialogue between the architects, the client and the end users is conducted. This may entail using certain tools for the design process – for example, sketches, diagrams, models or collages –, and these in turn have an impact on the development of a concept and the final design.

To illustrate the range of possible outcomes and different design approaches, we will take a closer look at three library buildings that we have designed, the first in 1988, the last completed in 2015. All three buildings were public commissions and each involved incorporating listed historical building substance, which made it necessary to evaluate different strategies and approaches. Each design has a fundamental conceptual idea and the three projects therefore each illustrate a different thematic focus and a different design process, which can serve as inspiration for other design tasks.

Thematic Principle: Path

The Gesundbrunnen district in Berlin originally grew around a mineral spring that was discovered in 1748 and became the focus of a health spa. From the mid-19th century onwards, it became a popular destination for outings and recreation outside the city. The Bibliothek am Luisenbad is a city library first designed in 1988 and completed in 1996. It is situated in a large, peaceful courtyard space in the interior of an urban block and has a total of 1,800 m² usable floor area. The building ensemble comprises three parts: two historical structures, namely the "Comptoir", extended by a corridor housing the administrative offices, and the "Vestibule", including the library foyer on the ground floor and a separately usable event space on the upper floor, were complemented by the third part, a demonstratively modern semi-circular addition housing the reading areas and bookshelves. The round building is surrounded by a courtyard with sculptures.

The design was the result of an open architecture competition, which meant that we had to rely largely on our own interpretation of the design task. (In competi-

Luisenbad Public Library, the rear facade. The historical facade of the entrance and the semi-circular section housing the subterranean reading area and bookshelves.

tion design briefs, contradictory requirements often remain unresolved). We began, as described above, with an associative exploration of the formal imagery of the architectural typology, using sketches to conduct an internal dialogue on the nature of the library. At the same time, we explored the fascinating potential of the site, again using sketches as a means of reproducing its structural characteristics, its location in the urban realm and to develop an urban figure for the site.

Spatial Concept and Composition
The idea of creating a clear pathway through the site around which the design could be based emerged relatively quickly. The original historical route in what was then the environs of the city leads between two remaining sections of the original building fabric but was barely visible to all but those with good local knowledge. It nevertheless exerted a strong influence which needed to be partially revised: the location of the Luisenbad needed reconfiguring, while at the same time making its history legible.

The design sketches from the conceptual exploration phase show various ways of determining pathways and the definition of the courtyard. The sketches attempt to partially clarify the relationship between the two historical buildings, the entrance building to the demolished theater hall, the vestibule and the former administrative building, the "Comptoir", and the public space between them. One of the first ideas was to bury a large part of the library spaces under ground, thereby respecting the integrity of the courtyard and the experience of the remaining historical relics of the original complex. For the library itself, the idea of a large space emerged, reached via a path that should not follow the historical route, but instead follows the road alongside the River Panke that ends in the park, and leads via the courtyard to the existing entrance hall. From there, the motif of a ramp leading downwards was explored in various configurations. Together with the other objects in the space – a stair, a large meandering counter and the volumetric footprint of the entrance hall – the path is turned into a series of small events.

Architectural Means and Tectonics
The initial concept for a library submerged below ground already embodied the fundamental phenomenological attitude of the later design with its prominent semi-circular shape. It is a product of the tension between here and there, and the orchestration of the path between them. The boundaries and the individual parts of the interior are defined using clearly legible architectonic elements – an archway, the ceiling, a column, compartment, ramp, bridge and tower – as well as spatial situations such as niches, gaps, thresholds and islands.

The space between the historical buildings was conceived as a plateau from which one can look into the library interior and the bookshelves within. At the same time, the path directs one's view out into the park, establishing a connection between the place and its surroundings. The ramp marks the transition from the realm of the old buildings to the new building, leading the visitor along a winding path that provides glimpses into the different parts of the library. This library space was not formed through a succession of spaces, nor a subdivision into rooms; rather it was created through a gradual process toward becoming the large interior semi-circular arc of the building.

Thematic Principle: The Aura of History
The new university library in Wildau, a small town southeast of Berlin, opened in 2007 on the campus of the Technische Hochschule Wildau, which is part of the historical site of the former Schwarzkopf factory complex. Built around 1900, the site comprised production facilities for manufacturing locomotives as well as housing for the workers. The program of spaces for an information, communication and media center was to be housed in one of the existing buildings, hall 10, located on an urban frontage delineated by the railway lines and defined by the characteristic gable-fronts vis-à-vis the housing estate. Together with the former director's house, it forms a gateway situation at the Wildau train station. The original plans for hall 10 drawn up in 1920

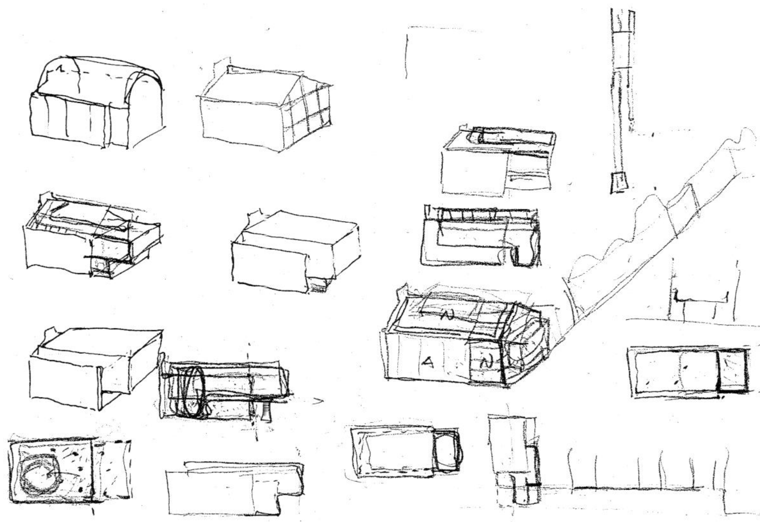

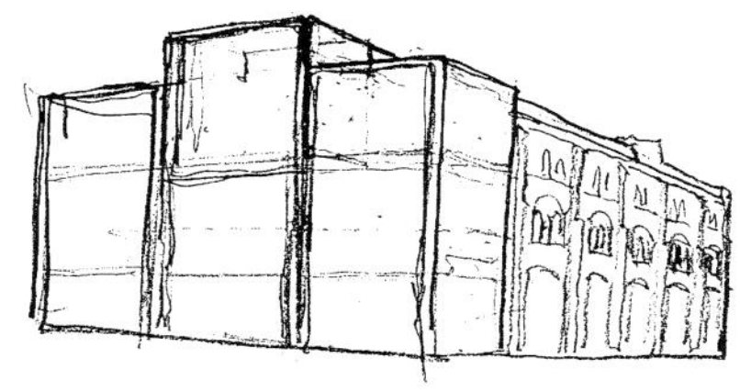

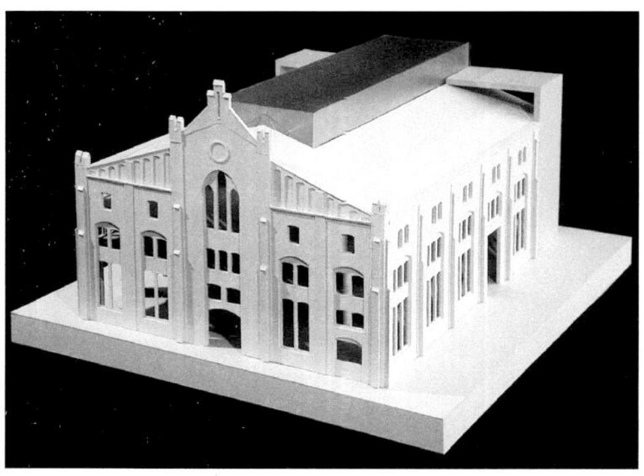

University library, Wildau, Chestnutt Niess, 2007. Models and sketches were used to develop the final concept.

show a building with seven bays, but the final building lacked the eastern-most bay. A temporary wall was built to keep out wind and weather and this building, unlike its neighbors facing the housing estate, thus lacked a representative gable frontage.

The design for the media center was developed in direct dialogue with the client and the end users. A fundamental part of the problem was the need to accommodate two primary functions of equal importance within the envelope of hall 10: the library on the one hand and the refectory and cafeteria on the other, together totaling 2,320 m². Both functions needed to be arranged on a single level, ideally with ground floor access, but neither the total area of the refectory and cafeteria nor that of the library fitted within the footprint of the historic hall 10.

Spatial Concept and Composition

The existing building has an industrial-utilitarian flair, but because it was never completed it also has an element of mystery to it that provided a starting point for the design concept. Although several stories high, the interior was always one large open space, lit by windows along the sides and a long skylight along the ridge that gives the space a particular, almost sacred feeling.

Usually, initial design explorations begin with the floor plan, but in this case we took the section as our starting point along with conceptual figurative sketches and a large-scale model. Our intention with the design concept was to complete the unfinished building and we therefore made a series of illustrations exploring different strategies for extending its form: should the building extension read as a drawer inserted into the building, a jacket that wraps around the end of the building, a reshaping of the existing building or a straightforward extrusion of its profile? Similar explorations followed for the configuration of the interior, including a free-standing framework, a series of terraces within the existing outside walls, or a house-in-house arrangement.

Of all the different strategies, the idea of a special space was judged most important. This has the capacity to serve as an emblematic space that signifies the university, and a favorite space for students who will remember it long after graduating. That meant converting the space – including introducing new levels – without compromising the overall impression of the fantastic, 15 m high historic interior, or detracting from its specific aura. The result is a complex composition of newly inserted floors that, depending on their direction and orientation within the space, stand apart from the outer walls, framing either a succession of loggias or large gallery spaces, or else extend right up to the walls where the spaces are more intimate. The focus of this large spatial constellation is the central atrium of the library beneath the distinctive skylight roof construction.

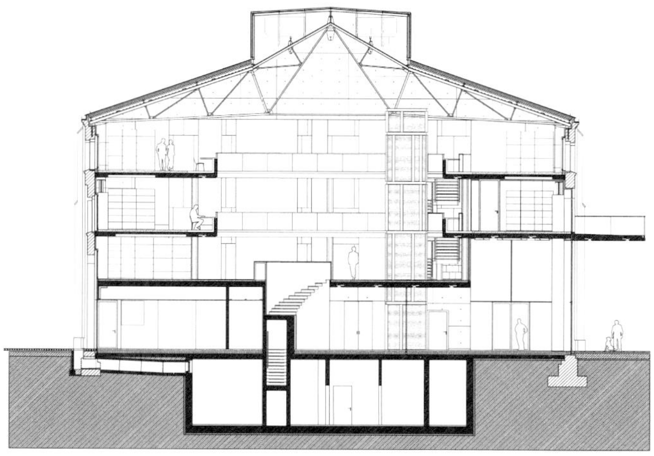

University library, Wildau. View of the converted industrial building of the new library. The transverse section shows the new floor levels.

Architectural Means and Tectonics
In developing the architectural design, we concentrated on approaches to dealing with the unfinished envelope of the historic structure. Both the building's tectonic structure and connotation as well as its urban position as one of a row of gable-fronted factory buildings along the railway line opposite the housing estate, proved relevant for the design process. In the context of its historic surroundings, the dimensions of the new building could not exceed the originally planned volume of the structure. In the end, we opted to extend the historic form of the building, continuing its structural pattern, proportions and fenestration in an abstracted form. The new gable at the east end of the building was given an iconography of its own that reflects its contemporary function as a university library in the context of technological development and its history.

Thematic Principle: Composition
A former fire station, now a listed building in the historically predominantly industrial district of Niederschöneweide in Berlin, has been converted and extended to serve as a district library with a total usable floor area of 2,300 m². It opened in 2015. The key factors influencing the project design were the need to make maximum use of the site, its location on a busy road and the emblematic character of the fire station building, built at the turn of the last century.

After an initial rational analysis of potential massing alternatives and corresponding volumetric forms, two sketches were taken forward for further exploration using a model. A new building would have to respond to the eclectic expressionism of the historic building. The design of the new extension therefore focused on ways of creating an ensemble together with the existing building and its expressive roofscape.

Spatial Concept and Composition
The difficult shape of the plot quickly determined the direction of the design process: the new building would take the form of a dynamic spiral with the historic tower as its point of origin. At the other end of the spiral, the building meets the road at a right angle so that it encloses a contemplative courtyard between the existing and new buildings. The sculptural articulation of the building volume as a modern continuation of the roofscape of the existing building was studied in numerous model variants. The roof line descends from back to front, lowering the eaves line around the courtyard so that it matches the scale of the existing buildings, linking the two.

To maximize the use of the site, the building mass is pushed as close as possible to the edge of the site, enclosing the courtyard in the center, while the staggered slanting roofscape of the old building is continued in the articulation of the roof of the new spiral-shaped extension. The form of the spiral is primarily a product of the building

District Library, Berlin-Niederschöneweide, Chestnutt Niess, 2015. The architectural form of the new extension, developed using a model, acts as a counterpoint to the expressive roofscape of the old fire station.

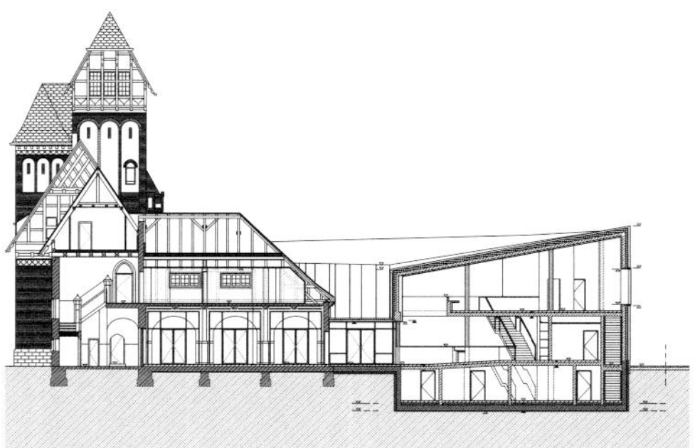

District Library, Berlin-Niederschöneweide. The section illustrates the conversion and extension of a historic listed fire station.

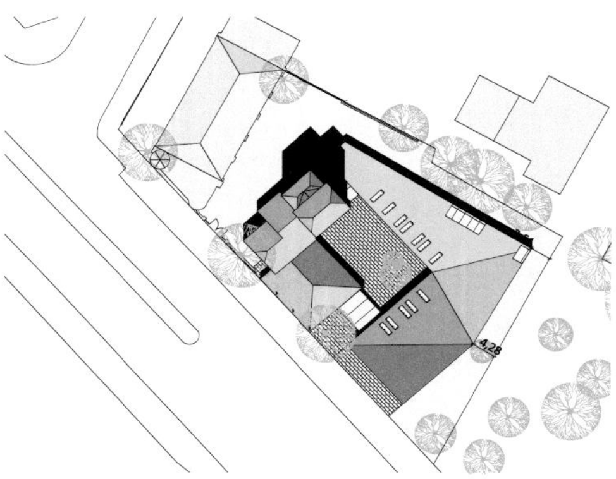

District Library, Berlin-Niederschöneweide. The site plan shows the short distance between the building and its neighbors and the location next to a busy road.

height in relation to how far away it must be placed from the plot boundaries: the lower the building height, the nearer it can be placed to the boundary. The overall composition continues the architectonic principle of the historic building, which comprises individually articulated volumes joined together to form a sculptural whole.

The spatial link between the existing building and the new extension, both within as well as outside the building is achieved by creating reciprocal views into and out of the large glazed areas and across the courtyard. The fire engine garage, the balcony and projecting bay as well as the different roof forms of the former fire station, which was originally built for fire practice purposes to train for emergency situations, are made visible from the ground and lower ground floors. Likewise, one can see directly from the fire station's garage into the new building.

The interior of the new library has three levels, the top two of which – the ground and upper floors – are set back as gallery levels. Cut-outs in the ceiling, clerestories and large sections of glazing in the facade steer the flow of space and establish an interplay with the building's immediate surroundings. For example, one has a view of the historic pump house and the large school building and fencing gymnasium, which were built around the same time as the fire station. The spatial interplay between the levels and between the new and historic parts of the complex respects the different parts of the building and allows each to achieve their own specific identity.

Architectural Means and Tectonics

In terms of how the new and old buildings form an ensemble, the materiality of the new extension is an important aspect. The use of pre-patinated zinc sheeting for the external skin inverts the physical mass of the roof of the existing building and lends the new extension a sense of sculptural solidity that sets up a dialogue with the tectonic structure of the fire station. The large glazed surfaces are arranged like cut-outs in the external skin, structuring the building form and lending it a sense of lightness. The sculptural articulation of the new extension allows the solid red brick building of the fire station to take center stage.

The Search for a Central Design Theme

The three projects described above show different approaches to the question of how important a strong underlying thematic idea is for the success of an architectural design. For us, this is very important. In the design process – that slow process of translating an architectural idea into something concrete – architects not only need to satisfy the requirements of the brief but also, in their efforts to invest their work with an individual character and location-specific identity, to identify a defining theme and to make this apparent to the building's users and visitors.

District library, Berlin-Niederschöneweide. Clerestories provide lighting and establish a connection to the outside.

Liliane Wong

Plan Configuration and Layout

The library is a centuries old institution. With the advent of digital technology in the 1990s, trend forecasters prophesied the end of the book and the close of an era. This has not, like so many extreme pronouncements, proven true. Rather, this technology has greatly enhanced and improved the global dissemination of information, expanding the reach of the library as an institution.

The 1990s were a defining moment for the layout of libraries. The ability to store large quantities of data on microchips and to access information in digital format led to far-reaching implications for the planning and growth of the library. The single salient fact that information no longer necessarily resided in a physical location within the library but in infinite and virtual locations had major impact on the library program itself. Long-standing program elements were made obsolete as new ones were introduced. At the level of books and equipment, card catalogues, microfiche readers, newspaper collections, archived periodicals, referenced indices and even many reference collections were downgraded in importance and some eventually eliminated. While the overall relationships between core library functions remained relatively stable, these changes rendered some specific adjacencies undesirable and, in some cases, unnecessary. For example, the required adjacency of the card catalogue to circulation and reference areas became moot with the replacement of the card catalogue by the many computer search stations placed throughout the library.

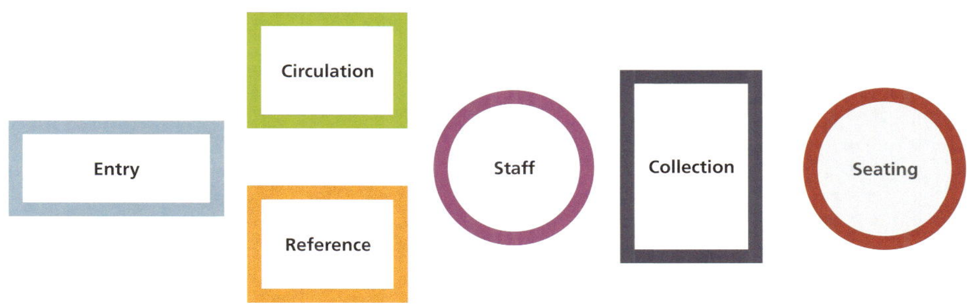

Each library accommodates the core programmatic functions of entry, circulation, reference, staff, collections and seating.

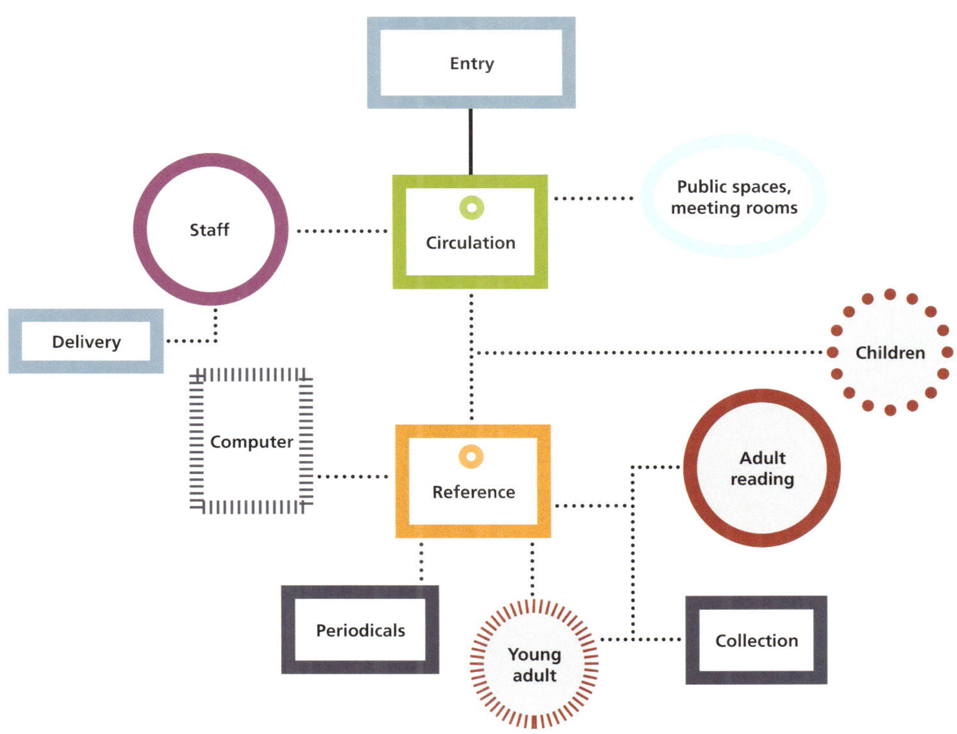

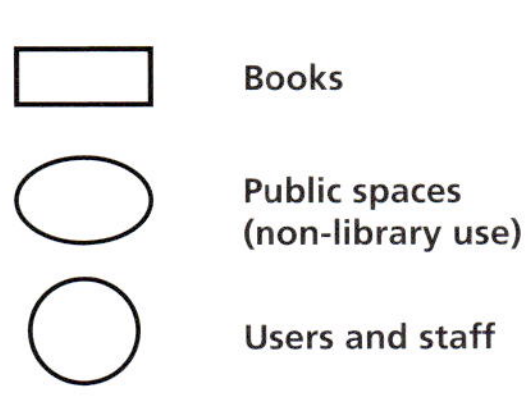

Typical adjacencies of core function elements

The layout of the modern library is defined by the core programmatic functions of entry, circulation, reference, staff, collections and seating. These functions continue to define the operations of all libraries without differentiation of size or mission. In public libraries these functions have additional components such as auxiliary collections and reading rooms that reflect its mission to serve many diverse users. The incorporation of digital capabilities has required changes but despite modifications in library services these functions have remained relatively constant. They reflect universal values for the working of the library; efficient movement of materials, clarity of travel for the different users, separations between different user groups and security for all users and equipment.

The layout of the library requires planning at two levels; the positioning of each core function element and the physical plan adjacencies of one core function element to another. Entirely interrelated, the elements of entry, circulation, reference and staff areas define a set of primary relationships within the library that are augmented by each element's secondary relationships to other less essential functions. Dependent on the type of library, these additional functions comprise reading rooms, children and young adult services, rare books, maps, newspapers, current periodicals and public spaces that can include classrooms, study rooms, meeting rooms, auditorium as well as auxiliary function spaces such as a theater or a café. The layout of stacks and seating, in contrast, is less strictly governed by group relationships than by parameters specific to themselves.

Each core function element has both an overall relationship within the library as an autonomous whole and a specific relationship to its immediate neighbors. The placement of these elements amongst the many other program elements of the library varies somewhat from library to library with resultant adjacencies that affect and often dictate the flow between the different parts. The flow of movement between the core elements, however, is well-established since there are only minor variations between the daily operations of most libraries.

The entry area serves as the primary connection to the different components of the library, in particular, the circulation area and the public spaces. It also acts as a bridge between the library functions and the public and more social ones. In some libraries, for instance the OBA – Openbare Bibliotheek Amsterdam (Jo Coenen, 2007, pp. 158–163) with its many public spaces, the flow from the entrance is further complicated by issues of opening hours, safety, size and prominence. The entry often has relationships to other elements, both primary and secondary, that are satisfied through a visual connection. Examples of these elements are the reference area and the many different types of public spaces.

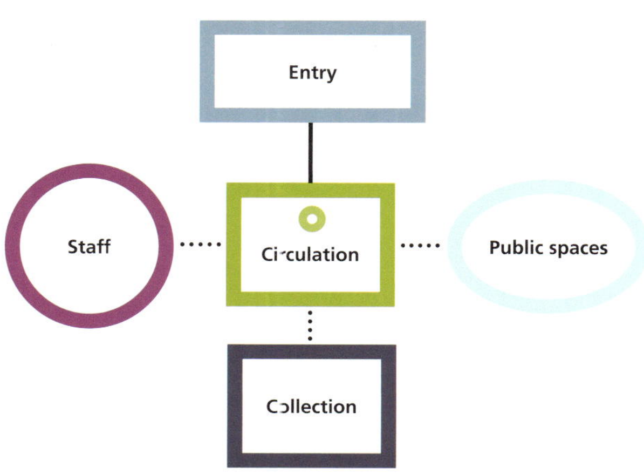

The circulation desk serves as a connector between the different sectors of the library.

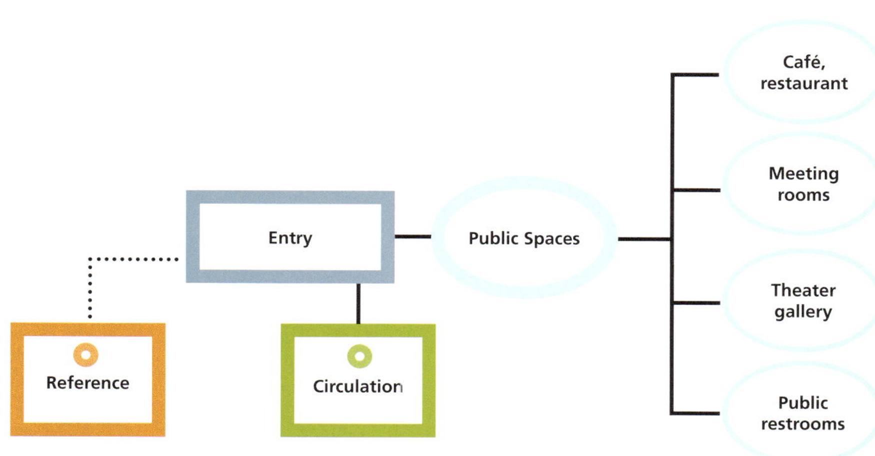

Typical movement flow in entry area

The circulation area is the central point of control; physically, in terms of check-out and book processing, and, visually, between the entrance and the other parts of the library. The circulation desk is the focal point although its importance as an ultimate "check point" has been somewhat diminished by the advent of self-check stations. At the Arabian Public Library in Scottsdale, Arizona (Richärd + Bauer, 2007, pp. 190–191), the circulation desk has been completely eliminated and replaced by self-check facilities. Circulation typically also holds a primary relationship with staff work areas and many secondary relationships including those with the new books and media areas.

The reference area is critical to information research requiring both physical and digital access. It may include a central point at a reference desk or, in some cases, multi-points with roving librarians called "information specialists" who are not place-specific. It has primary relationships with circulation, reference collections and computer areas dedicated to information searches. It may have secondary relationships with the young adult area, the general collections and public spaces. Due to its function, clear sight lines with computer terminals are important. The staff area houses the office space for the staff and the common space required for all technical work related to book processing as well as information technology and computer support. It has a direct relationship to circulation, a staff entrance and a delivery entrance. The staff area also contains the offices and the common spaces of the librarians, spaces typically accessed from the staff entrance.

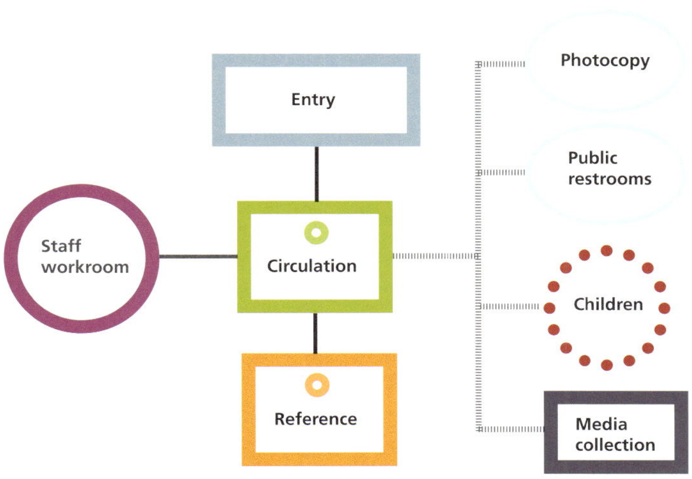

Typical movement flow in circulation area

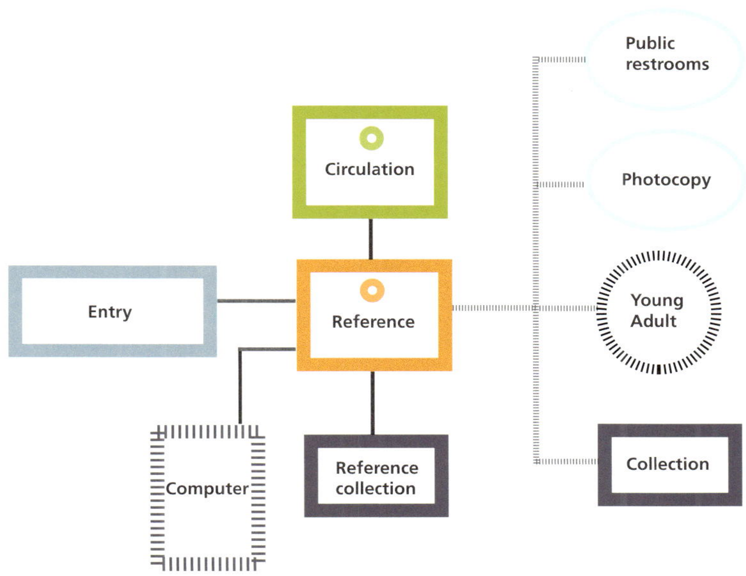

Typical movement flow in reference area

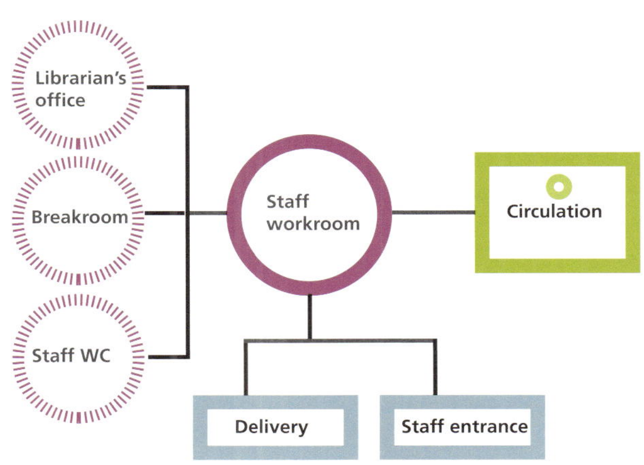

Typical movement flow in staff area

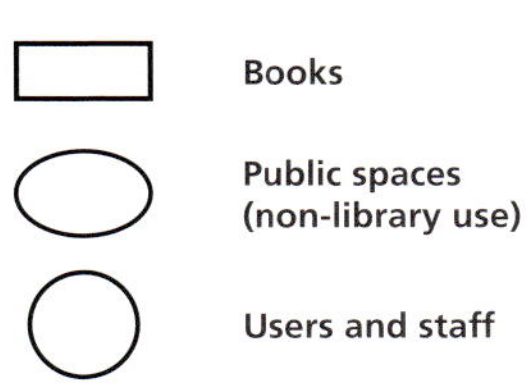

_BOOKS	VOL/CM	VOL/FT
_Fiction	.26	8
_Non-fiction	.33	10
_Large print	.26	8
_Paperbacks	.055	16
_Reference	.20	6
_Public documents	.16	5
_Textbooks	.26	8
_Legal	.23	7
_Medical	.16	5
_Young adult	.39	12
_Children's picture books	.66	20
_Children's reference	.26	8
_Juvenile	.43	13
_Juvenile paperback	.155	6
_MULTI-MEDIA		
_CD	.98	30
_CD ROM & DVD	.98	30
_Audio cassette	.62	19
_Audio cassette with book	.66	20
_Video cassette	.33	10

Shelving capacity factors for cifferent types of books and media

Collection

The collection, a core function program element, consists of many types of objects: books, periodicals, paperbacks, CDs, DVDs, and most recently, electronic books. With digitization, some collections are now virtual, existing as electronic or scanned documents. The requirements for housing the physical items have remained relatively constant with the changes of the digital age. Some evidence of the larger role of technology is discernible, for instance in the incorporation of electronic search monitors into shelving end panels.

The space required to accommodate a collection is media-dependent. The capacity of a shelving unit, defined by its width, depth and height and whether it is single-faced or double-faced, is characterized by the dimensions of the type of media it is designed to hold. Each shelf within a unit accommodates different quantities of books/media items depending on the type of material (fiction, reference, art, history, etc.). The able lists shelving capacity factors indicating media-specific multipliers for determining the capacity per linear centimeter or foot of shelf. (Capacity here assumes a shelf filled by approximately 80 % so that a growth factor is built in.)

Space requirements for accommodating a given collection can be calculated using "rule of thumb" formulas to determine the shelving capacity for a particular type of book or media item. The capacity of one shelf of materials can be calculated using the following formula:

Shelf capacity = length of shelf × media-specific shelving capacity factor (vol/cm).

For example, by using the value for fiction of .26 volumes per centimeter, one can determine the length required to accommodate a desired number of volumes. With a known height or number of shelves per unit, the shelving capacity of a whole unit can be calculated using the following formula:

Shelving unit capacity = shelf capacity × number of shelves

For double-faced shelving units, this number is multiplied by two.

Shelving Layout Principles

General shelving layout is based on the shelving capacity of entire ranges of shelves. Once the single shelving unit is established, it is relatively straightforward to calculate capacities for ranges within a bay as a measure of book capacity in a design. Calculations combining the different space requirements for the varying types of media yield a rough estimate of total space requirements for an entire collection. Variations will occur in different libraries because of different shelving policies and combination of materials.

While the reading room at the Jacob-und-Wilhelm-Grimm-Zentrum at the Humboldt Universität in Berlin (Max Dudler, 2009) recalls the monumental great reading rooms of an earlier era, the reading area at TU Delft Library (Mecanoo, 1997) has a more informal character.

Shelving layout is premised on a typical shelving system of a standard shelf width of 30 cm (while in the U.S. the standard shelf width is 3 ft.). Shelving units are based on 30 cm increments resulting in standard units of 60, 90 and 120 cm width. Shelving height depends on the numbers of shelves per unit with seven shelves high at typical stacks and two to three shelves high in reference areas. A stack is a specified number of shelving units in a line. Stacks, that is repetitive groups of shelving, are organized in ranges. Double-faced ranges are ones in which two lines of shelves are placed back to back, providing book access aisles on each side. Single-faced ranges are typically attached to a wall and accessed from one side.

In general, the planning of shelving layout continues to be based on several key factors such as the shelving system, the building's structural system and the building code. Universal layout principles typically refer to cantilever style and case style shelving. High-density and automated retrieval types have individual requirements specific to their system (see "Shelving", pp. 102–105).

Seating

Seating, another core function discussed here, has evolved with the use of computers and electronic books. Reading within a library has an ancient history; already in the Celsus library at Ephesus from the second century AD it is thought that scrolls were dispensed for use in an east-facing reading space. This precursor of the modern-day reading room exemplifies the relationship of the reader to the text as one that is defined by a spatial ceremony.

Today, the accessibility of books and information in digital format has made a further impact on the act of reading itself, forging new developments on the seating in modern libraries. Today's public libraries emphasize their hospitality rather than their formality. The formal reading room has given way as libraries re-envisage their identities as community "living rooms". While most public libraries retain their reading areas, they are small and informal. Table seating, previously located chiefly in the reading room, is found throughout the library, mirroring the ubiquitous quality of electronic information. Seating is located also in study carrels, computer banks, individual study rooms and cafés. However, in contrast to reading rooms of public libraries, the formal notion of reading and studying is still very much present in university libraries. The main reading room at Jacob-und-Wilhelm-Grimm-Zentrum at the Humboldt Universität in Berlin (Max Dudler, 2009, pp. 232–237) with its modern monumentality recalls the earlier formal concept of seating.

Burton Barr Central Library, Phoenix, Arizona, Will Bruder, 1995. All table seats are equipped with Wi-Fi for use of personal computers.

Seattle Central Library, OMA, 2004. The four-person lounge chair with its non-directional cruciform divider is highly versatile.

At the OBA – Openbare Bibliotheek Amsterdam, Jo Coenen, 2007, different types of seating accommodate various types of use; the white seats and the table seats are in the multi-media space, the red chairs are in the children's section.

Seats

With the incorporation of digital technology into the library, the monitor and the personal computer have become an integral part of library seating. Many tables are fitted with OPAC (online public access computers) stations and/or designed as electronic workstations. These seats have specific requirements of lighting and ergonomics, especially for intense use. Important issues of adjustability and flexibility affect the seating, the surface and the placement of the monitor itself. With the availability of Wi-Fi in most libraries, the function of the general table seating, too, is expanded for laptop use. In some libraries such as Will Bruder's 1995 Burton Barr Central Library in Phoenix, Arizona (pp. 146–149), this type of table seating has become the new reading room.

The advent of various electronic devices within the library has also led to new seating types associated with such use. While specific ergonomic and lighting requirements are integral to computer stations, seats incorporating the casual and multiple uses of digital devices, from research to shopping, from gaming to music, are less limited. Traditionally found only in the leather wingback lounge chairs of newspaper or periodicals reading rooms, informal library seating has proliferated as a new library seating type. The lounge chair at the Seattle Central Library speaks to a multiplicity of use in its design. The four-person chair with its non-directional cruciform divider is highly versatile. The OBA – Openbare Bibliotheek Amsterdam, designed in 2007 by Jo Coenen, with its extensive range of available media is exemplary of this endeavor. The library contains a wide array of new seating types. Designed for the hybrid activity of relaxing and studying, the lounge chairs all have bold forms, varying color and moldable material that conform to more than one task and one sitting position. At the Rolex Learning Center in Lausanne by (SANAA, 2010, pp. 238–243) the concept for informal seating is simply resolved by the use of bean bags that may be configured, individually or in groups, to each user's needs.

Carrels

The concept of studying and the seating requirements for it have also evolved in response to the changes of the digital age. Adapted from the monastic scriptorium, the traditional study carrel accommodates the needs of an individual for private study. Optimal attributes of natural lighting, ample work surface and privacy characterize the study carrels at Louis Kahn's 1971 Phillips Exeter Library in New Hampshire. Kahn's design integrates the exterior and the interior in a seamless weaving of facade to furniture. Today, the common use of the personal laptop computer has altered the design criteria of light and lighting as well as the requirements for the work surface. Present-day issues of security have raised also questions regarding privacy and the walls of the classic study carrel.

The built-in carrels at Louis Kahn's Phillips Exeter Library (1971) in Exeter, New Hampshire, have natural lighting and privacy. At the Mixing Chamber of OMA's Seattle Central Library (2004), the carrels are equipped with low dividers for semi-privacy and form a hybrid between group tables and the study carrel.

Traditionally, lines of study carrels were placed at the end of stack aisles and against a wall – an arrangement occasionally still found today, chiefly in academic environments. The current trend, however, is for placing of carrels, in groups, and in less remote settings. At the OBA – Openbare Bibliotheek Amsterdam, the security issues are resolved by the object-like nature of the carrel/pod, placed in an open environment, simultaneously providing privacy and security. At the Mixing Chamber of the Seattle Central Library, the study carrels, equipped with low dividers for semi-privacy, are a hybrid between group tables and the study carrel. Counter-style seating is another alternative. Built into walls and half walls at many libraries, the counter seat provides uni-directional focus for studying while remaining part of a larger group setting. At the Philological Library at the Freie Universität in Berlin (Foster + Partners, 2005, pp. 226–229) the counter seating is designed in undulating waves along the diffused light of the curved membrane roof while at OBA counter seating lines the edges of the multi-floor atrium.

Planning for Size and Growth

Assignable spaces are those serving a particular library function. These are divided into four categories: user space (reading, including computer use), accounting for approximately 20 % of all assignable space, meeting space 10 %, public service/staff areas 20 % and collection space 50 %. The core function elements of each library are assignable spaces. Non-assignable space is in addition to that and includes building service, circulation areas and mechanical spaces, supporting the building's general operation[1] and comprising 25–40 % of the total floor area. The percentage of non-assignable space is determined by spatial efficiency with a lower number indicating a higher efficiency. Extraneous circulation is a crucial factor impacting the percentage of non-assignable space as are architectural features without specific function. The ratio of assignable to non-assignable space is an assessment of overall spatial efficiency. One should, however, be cautious in using this ratio as a absolute indicator of efficiency as larger buildings can yield a higher ratio due to their size and ability to distribute the non-assignable space over a greater area.

User space

In a public library, user space is typically proportional to the population of the community served by the library. The number of seats provided in any public library in the United States is based on its user population, demonstrating the democratic principle of equal access. For communities with a minimum population of 10,000, user seats for reading and computers are calculated using the formula of 1 seat per 200 users. For smaller populations, the formula of 1 seat per 100 users is used. These general assumptions make it possible to determine rough overall sizes for user space that can be further subdivided by seating types. Recommendations for spatial requirements by seat type, derived from American Library Association publications, are: table seats require 2.7 m^2 per seat, carrel seats 3 m^2, lounge chairs or electronic work stations 3.5 m^2.

Meeting space

Space requirements for public programs, individual tutorials and group study vary widely between public and university libraries. In public libraries, additional variations exist depending on service priorities. There is, however, a trend towards an increase in these areas to serve the different needs of the community. These spaces, at a minimum, include one large program space seating 50–300 people, depending on the community, as well as group study rooms of varying sizes.

Collection

The space for the collection has traditionally been calculated based on the size required to accommodate the existing materials plus that for a 20-year growth.[2] However, with the integration of scanned texts and e-books into the library, the issue of designing for future collection growth has changed, since it does not equate to additional space. These include new ways of storage, virtual storage, elimination of archives through digitization, availability of another library's digital materials. While this process of digitization is a positive development in terms of space, many scholars are still better served by printed matter.[3] New methods of storage acknowledge this need, such as the automated storage and retrieval system at the Mansueto Library (Helmut Jahn, 2011, pp. 244–247) at the University of Chicago or the robotic stack system at the Chicago State University library. With the use of technology such as radio frequency ID chips (RFID), they can accommodate larger numbers of volumes in a fraction of the space required in conventional storage.[4]

Influence of Recent Changes on Layout Principles

The traditional library and its core functions have remained relatively intact in the modern library. In academic and research libraries changes have not been dramatic and the advancement of digital technology supports and enhances rather than detracts from their mission. One result of this shift is the introduction of a new program element; the "Learning Commons" is an environment dedicated to assist students in research and information needs through collaborative learning. With student learning as its major objective, the "Learning Commons" combines individual and group user spaces, information technology, reference services and instruction on

The Alan Gilbert Learning Commons at the University of Manchester, designed by Sheppard Robson and completed in 2012, offers a surrounding where students can get together and learn, either on an individual basis or working collaboratively in groups. There are 30 group study rooms of varying size, ranging from 2 to 12 people. The rooms are furnished with a whiteboard and a PC connected to a media screen. The Wi-Fi available throughout the building extends to the space outside and to the ground floor café. Although managed by the library, this state-of-the-art facility does not have any books inside it.

both technology and the responsible use of information. It is distinguished from the "Information Commons", which primarily provides technology and digital services.

Changes in public libraries comprise a wider range of responses. Efforts towards maintaining relevance in the digital world differ from library to library and are dependent on the specific issues of the community served. The addition of new program elements – from cafés, stores, exhibition spaces, theaters, etc. to health clinics, secondary schools and daycare facilities – affects the existing relationships and adjacencies of core library elements, altering the layout and flow of the library.

These new program elements often bring about an increase in the size of the overall library. In library planning, traditional formulas used to calculate space requirements do not account for these new elements; rather, such additions impact the library's efficiency and the ratio of assignable space to non-assignable space. The incorporation of these areas into the already complex program is often resolved by establishing new vertical relationships within the library. The traditional organization of repetitive floor plans of stacks and reading spaces was vertically arranged from "noisy" interactions on lower floors to "quiet" study above. The introduction of the new program elements in public libraries – many involving social interaction – has resulted in pluralistic approaches.

At the OBA in Amsterdam, the café, the skyline bar and the theater are interspersed between the entry levels and the top levels of the 13-story library. Access to the theater or bar at the OBA requires the user to traverse the levels of book collections and reading spaces. Such placement recalls retail design strategies that locate desirable items in remote locations so as to require travel through the entire establishment. The design for the Danish Royal Library in Copenhagen (Schmidt Hammer Lassen, 1999, pp. 122–125) with similar program elements takes the opposite approach by placing all public and social program functions on the ground and below ground. These public amenities are purposefully separated from the library functions and are accessible without entry into the library itself. At the Biblioteca España in Medellín (Giancarlo Mazzanti, 2007, pp. 194–197), the library functions are deployed horizontally as three separate buildings united by a plaza. The new functions of childcare center, community center and auditorium reside in buildings separate but adjacent to the library.

This pluralism confirms Rem Koolhaas' comments from OMA's 1999 proposal for the Seattle Central Library: "New libraries don't reinvent or even modernize the traditional institution; they merely package it in a new way."[5] "Unless the Library transforms itself wholeheartedly ... its unquestioned loyalty to the book will undermine the library's plausibility at the moment of its apotheosis."[6]

References

1 "Facilities Inventory and Classification Manual", National Center for Education Statistics, Section 3.2.3, May 2006.

2 At the Seattle Central Library, the Book Spiral was designed to accommodate such growth. Each Dewey Decimal section was calculated with additional room for the equal growth of each section. The design of the signage corroborated this strategy with Dewey Decimal numbers stenciled into the floor at the ends of certain stack ranges. While well-intended, this did not account for the actual uneven growth in certain subjects which, in future, may impact the accuracy of the signage.

3 An installation at the Rhode Island School of Design's Fleet Library titled "500 Books – a Measure of Absence" addresses the trend of libraries towards purchasing fewer books each year. The 2010 installation, the work of librarian Ellen Petraits, illustrates 500 books that will not be purchased and will be absent from the collection.

4 High-density automated storage uses only $1/7^{th}$ of the space required for conventional shelving while high-density non-automated storage uses $1/6^{th}$.

5 OMA/LMN Architects, "Concept Book", Seattle Public Library proposal, December 1999, http://www.spl.org/prebuilt/cen_conceptbook, p. 4.

6 Ibid. p. 6.

Liliane Wong with
Nolan Lushington

Library Spaces for Children, Teens and Young Adults

In the history of the library as an institution, the provision of dedicated space for non-adult readers is a 20th-century phenomenon. Since its inception in the early 1900s the planning of space for young readers has developed with evolving social mores. Today's library design concepts for children and teens reflect a mix of current interests, among them style, contemporary child development theory, education and community building. Together these ideas have led to the creation of library spaces for young readers that are unique to the 21st century.

Children's room in Boston Public Library, Copley Square, c. 1930

Youth section of the OBA – Openbare Bibliotheek Amsterdam, Jo Coenen, 2007. While retaining the overall color concept of white surfaces, the use of playful, geometric forms such as the curving bookshelves distinguishes the youth area.

Hennepin County Library, Maple Grove, Minnesota, Meyer, Scherer & Rockcastle, 2010. Bold colors emphasize the interactive wall panels in the children's room while a neon green ramp acts as a unifying element.

Children in the Library

The Boston Public Library was first to establish a space specifically designated for children in 1895 with more than 3,000 children's books.[1] Children's rooms in other public libraries followed with spaces intended primarily for book perusal and quiet reading, plainly furnished with tables, chairs and shelves. Children's rooms through the third quarter of the 20th century evolved from this standard with adjustments of scale, décor and style. Into the 1970s, children's rooms were often shelf-lined spaces with diminutive furniture, finishes in primary colors and wall art of juvenile literary characters from Maurice Sendak to Dr. Seuss. Digital technology in the library is, of course, a hallmark of the 21st century although its presence in the children's room is relatively unobtrusive outside of the requisite search monitors. Today's guidelines for the design of children's libraries focus instead on learning through physical experience. This goal is achieved through the provision of multi-layered space that allows for infinite permutations of use. In a 2008 interview, Gonzalo Oyarzún, director of the Santiago Public Library in Chile, indicated that "A children's and young adult library serves as a public square ... where they can feel free to choose, explore and know."[2] This vision is applicable for children and teens as well as their caregivers, offering a unified goal for the design of this space.

Interior Design Options

The stylistic evolution of today's children's libraries is a consequence of such a vision. The reliance on primary colored accents and pictures of literary characters that presume a prescribed concept of childhood has given way to a spirited use of architecture and design to provide a complex and stimulating environment. There is no longer a tacit adherence to bright colors for creating a stimulating children's environment, as demonstrated at the OBA – Openbare Bibliotheek Amsterdam (Jo Coenen, 2007, pp. 158–163). In the simple palette of white that characterizes the library as a whole the children's area is distinguished through the use of playful, geometric white forms such as the curving bookshelves and jack-like light fixtures. Intermittent accents of color provide a bold contrast to the otherwise monochromatic background. Similarly at the Hamilton Grange Library in Harlem, New York (originally designed by McKim, Mead and White and opened in 1906), the Teen Center (Rice+Lipka Architects, 2012) is a primarily black and white space accented with bold abstract murals/walls. The use of colors, too, is part of the architectural enhancement rather than a finish accent. At the Hennepin County Library in Maple Grove, Minnesota (Meyer, Scherer & Rockcastle, 2010), a building envisioned as a "pavilion in the park", without any internal separation or signage, color is a key component that provides visual cues for the patron. The bold color emphasizes minimally detailed interactive wall panels in the children's room while the neon green ramp is a unifying element in the teens' study space. Graphics are also used to engage the youthful visitor. At the Children's Library Discovery Center in Jamaica, Queens, New York (1100 Architect, 2011), a consistent signage concept invites observation and conjecture. At the Picture Book Library in Iwaki, Japan (Tadao Ando, 2005), the architectural elements of stair and guardrail are not only part of the space but become the picture book display shelving and seating. Finally, the multi-functional structural ribs of the Vennesla Kulturhuset serve as book shelves, small rooms, tables and lounge chair (Helen & Hard, 2011, pp. 202–205).

Learning through Play

Beyond issues of style, the design of children's libraries posits the space itself as an educational tool. Previous activities within the children's room catered to the very young typically in the form of storytelling in which the space served simply as a container. In a departure from this trend more recent designs of children's spaces focus on them as learning spaces. This attitude embraces the notion of learning through play – a concept derived from child development theories of the late 1970s – resulting in late 20th century children's rooms that sometimes resemble playgrounds/theme parks. Using shelving units of different heights as stepladder, the children's library at Ordrup Bibliotek in Copenhagen (Søren Robert Lund Arkitekter, 2007) encourages users to explore by physically climbing over the books. At greater cost, the children's room at the Cerritos Millennium Library (Charles Walton Associates, 2002) is a learning space inspired by the entertainment industry. An entrance made of gargantuan books leads to a room-sized aquarium, a replica tyrannosaurus rex and a banyan tree, all of which are tools for introducing children to ocean life, prehistoric creatures and rainforests. A different approach attempts to engineer experience by emulating the interactive museum. Interactive displays and activities are used to ignite curiosity about subjects from math and science to gardening and astronomy. Design experts from children's museums such as the Exploratorium in San Francisco, the New York Hall of Science and the Brooklyn Children's Museum serve as consultants. A collaborative public library and theater, the ImaginOn of Charlotte, North Carolina (Holzman Moss Bottino, 2005, pp. 182–183), offers multi-media interactive stations for exploring the art of narrative as well as an animation/sound studio for teens. The Children's Library Discovery Center, part of the Queens Central Library in New York, is characterized by interactive math and science displays dispersed throughout the library and the stacks.

At the Children's Library Discovery Center in Queens, New York, 1100 Architect, 2011, museum-like exhibits and "discovery stations" address children aged 3–12 and introduce them to topics such as weather, music and nanotechnology. The wayfinding concept is by Lee Skolnick, Architecture + Design Partnership.

Literacy for All

Today's children's library service most often includes community outreach in recognition of "literacy for all". The effect of this outreach varies from equal access to information in the form of computers to community centers and childcare facilities based within the library itself. For parents and older children, English proficiency resources, after school homework help, summer reading programs and parent education are examples of such service. For the very young, a new focus on "emergent literacy" serves to emphasize "the natural reading and writing behaviors exhibited by preschoolers before formal instruction begins."[3] This outreach has inspired many, from educators to artists and architects, to contribute their expertise. These efforts result in uncommon works of art as at the Library Initiative, a collaborative effort of the Robin Hood Foundation and the New York Department of Education to reverse low literacy in underserved neighborhoods. Participating artists have created memorable murals and art installations specific to the neighborhood children and culture – art with purpose and relevance for the users. The 21st century children's library is a curious amalgam of change, at once introspective and altruistic. Its complexity perhaps mirrors the uncertainty of our global economies in which the well-being of children remains nevertheless unquestioned.

The Emergence of "Young Adults"

At the Picture Book Library in Iwaki, Japan, Tadao Ando, 2005, the architectural elements of stair and guardrail become both display shelving and seating.

The teen or "young adult" in the library has come of age only in the 21st century. Children, teens and young adults historically shared a single open space. While there was recognition of the different reading needs of those under and over 12 years of age, there was little spatial differentiation other than designated shelving to identify the various users. The term "young adult" applied to a category of books specific to a span of years was only officially recognized in the United States with the 1957 founding of the Young Adult Library Services Association (YALSA). The creation of this group formally acknowledged that within the library "young people" comprised two groups: children (up to age 12) and young adults (age 12–18). The recognition of these groups corresponds to a shifting demographic brought about by a post-World War II population boom. By the early 1960s in the U.S. alone, "the number of 10 to 20 year olds … increased from 30 to 40 million."[4]

Early young adult literature addressed, for the first time, issues of adolescence. The decades from the 1970s through to the mid-1980s have "been described as the

The children's room at the Cerritos Millennium Library, Cerritos, California, Charles Walton Associates, 2002, is a learning space inspired by the entertainment industry. The entrance is made of gargantuan books.

The children's library at Ordrup Bibliotek, Copenhagen, Søren Robert Lund Arkitekter, 2007, encourages users to explore by physically climbing over the books.

Vennesla Kulturhuset, Vennesla, Norway, Helen & Hard, 2011. The structural ribs provide cosy seating for reading.

golden age of YAL, when a highly intelligent and demanding literature was written for young people that spoke to them with particular directness."[5] In subsequent years the topics of young adult literature would broach issues such as drug use, drinking, teen pregnancy and eating disorders. By the 1990s interest in this category of literature waned.

In the 21st century, while the general publishing industry is in turmoil, the young adult book market is, instead, vibrant and enjoying exponential growth. In 1997, 3,000 young adult books were published in comparison to the 30,000 titles published 12 years later in 2009. What began with the now legendary Harry Potter series in the early years of the millennium has expanded into a highly profitable market, heralding a second "golden age of young fiction".[6] Books such as Stephenie Meyer's Twilight series of teenage vampire love or Suzanne Collins' trilogy of a dystopic society, *The Hunger Games*, are examples of this trend. *Breaking Dawn*, the final book in Meyer's series, sold 1.3 million copies in the first 24 hours.[7]

As in the 1950s when young adult books were introduced into society, the last years of the 20th century and the first decade of the new millennium witnessed a similar demographic shift. "Between 1990 and 2000, the number of persons between 12 and 19 soared to 32 million, a growth rate of 17 % that significantly outpaced the growth of the rest of the population."[8] Today young adults comprise 18 % of the population.[9] According to a recent Pew survey, "16 to 29 year olds are the largest group checking out books from their local libraries."[10]

As one applies the democratic ideals of the public library where numbers of seats reflect the demographics of the population these statistics translate spatially into the proliferation of teen spaces. Decades earlier the term "young adult" simply referred to a few dedicated book stacks located at the periphery of the children's area. Today, teen or young adult reading refers to a unique collection and space, fully equipped with digital technology. Located near the adults and a clear distance from the children's room it serves as a gathering zone for this specific age group.

Teen Spaces as Community Outreach

In 2008 YALSA's Board of Directors formally adopted the position that "user-centered environments are integral in attracting teenaged users and transforming the role and image of the library."[11] The décor of teen or young adult spaces, as with the children's rooms, has evolved to reflect a sophisticated contemporary style with super graphics, modern colors, playful patterns and "mod" pieces of furniture. Many libraries have updated their teen spaces accordingly with positive results. Teen space, in contrast to children's rooms, comprises areas dedicated to both study and interaction. Tables, computers and sometimes study carrels cater to individual study and research. Grouped lounge seating allows for collaborative studying as well as socializing. While the requisite hushed atmosphere of earlier decades is clearly no longer enforced, some librarians question whether the concept of teen space must be reinvented to dispel the implied need for quiet within even the updated rooms. As a response to such a challenge, the Hamilton Grange branch of the New York Public Library in Harlem that opened in 2012 with a new teen space was designed to encourage mayhem, loitering and even eating. In a departure from the norm noise is encouraged and acoustic separation eliminated. The 408 m^2 space is entirely open, occupied only by two low objects: an inhabitable, glass vitrine for playing video games and a set of bleachers that conform to a multitude of seating options. While seemingly free of rules to encourage frequent teen use, this wide open space provides full and constant visibility for ever vigilant librarians.

The community outreach mission is also evident in the young adults' section. The teen room serves, in many instances, as an afterschool "hangout", especially in neighborhoods where they would otherwise be on their own or on the streets. In addition, many libraries have created programs specifically for establishing a community amongst teens. For example, the New York Public Library offers a Teen

The Teen Center at the Hamilton Grange Library in New York (Rice+Lipka Architects, 2012) is a primarily black and white space accented with bold abstract murals/walls.

Club, Teen Homework Lounge, Drawing workshops, Teen Author reading night, and TeenLIVE programs that "feature thought-provoking conversations, real debates, and exciting spectacular performances with ... favorite authors, artists, filmmakers, musicians, fashionistas. ... These programs address current cultural trends and important mainstays that inform the lives of today's teens."[12]

The richness of recent young adult culture, especially fiction, has caused an increasing "crossover" trend of adults reading young adult literature, creating fluid boundaries between young adult literature readers. In a 2009 contest, St Martin's Press searched for new talent of "... cutting edge fiction with protagonists who are slightly older than YA and can appeal to an adult," coining the term "new adult". Whether this term replaces "young adult" remains to be seen but the implications of such a term can bring revolutionary changes to the planning of the library. These shifts in defining the act of "coming of age" itself are defining – a society in transition.

With the hindsight of 20th century theories, immense efforts are placed on the design of children and teen spaces in 21st century libraries, efforts that address the educational and emotional welfare of the young. The fruits of these labors are twofold. Children of all ages have access to information and learning and consequently develop early on a life-long commitment to the library and its many services.[13] At a critical time in the history of the library, it is a sound investment for youth and for the institution.

References

1 Boston Public Library First Facts, Boston Public Library, http://www.bpl.org/general/firsts.htm

2 Sandra Feinberg , James Keller, "Designing Space for Children and Teens", *American Libraries Magazine*, March 14, 2010.

3 Donna Celano, Susan Neuman, *The Role of Public Libraries in Children's Literacy Development*, Pennsylvania Department of Education Office of Commonwealth Libraries, February 2010, p. 12.

4 Elizabeth Alderman, Jessica Rieder, Michael I. Cohen, "The History of Adolescent Medicine", *Pediatric Research* (2003) 54, pp. 137–147; doi:10.1203/01.PDR.0000069697.17980.7C

5 Mary Owen, "Developing a Love of Reading: Why Young Adult Literature is Important", *Orana*, Vol. 39, No. 1, March 2003, EBSCO Publishing, 2003.

6 "A Brief History of Young Adult Literature", CNN.com, October 17, 2013.

7 http://www.stepheniemeyer.com

8 Jen Doll, "YA for Grownups – What Does 'Young Adult' Mean?", *The Atlantic*, April 19, 2012. http://www.theatlantic.com.

9 United Nations, Youth: Social Policy and Development Division, http://undesadspd.org/Youth/FAQs.aspx

10 "A Brief History of Young Adult Literature", CNN.com, October 17, 2013.

11 Kimberly Bolan for YALSA, "The Need for Teen Spaces in Public Libraries", YALSA's National Guidelines and Position Papers, American Library Association, January 2008.

12 New York Public Library, http://www.nypl.org/kidslive-teenlive

13 For a survey of various types of children's libraries cf. Nolan Lushington, *Libraries Designed for Kids*, New York: Neal-Schuman Publishers, 2008.

Klaus Ulrich Werner

Dialogues: Client, Librarian, Architect

Most librarians are only ever confronted with the problem of "how to survive in the world of architects and building departments"[1] when they become involved in the building or conversion of a library, something that happens perhaps once, if at all, during their career. It is an exciting task, but one that very few librarians are prepared for. For most architects, the building of a library is likewise often a once-in-a-lifetime project. The key to optimizing the design and functionality of the building is to actively consult the library's eventual user – who is in most cases not identical with the commissioning client – but this is an opportunity that is all too often neglected.

A Meeting of Two Generalists

Of all the many people involved in the complex process of planning and building libraries, what singles out the architect and librarian is that they are the only true generalists among the many specialists: both of them have an overview of the entire project at every phase of it, and both have a good understanding of the broader context. Everyone involved in the planning and construction is, of course, interested in achieving the best possible result, but it is the architect and the librarian who, more than anyone else, are most interested in the building as a whole, in its long-term sustainability, in ensuring that it remains functional and durable. Not even the client, despite their vested interest in the later operation of the building and in particular in minimizing future running costs, has such a global and all-encompassing overview and interest in the end result. All of the other participants are specialists in their respective fields, with a defined scope of action and a set time horizon for their involvement. The architect and the librarian, on the other hand, are involved for the entire duration of the building project. The active participation of the librarian – as a collaborator and contributor – is assumed from the outset. For both roles, their respective unique qualities as generalists provide a strong basis for establishing an intensive and productive collaboration – and for developing a specific working relationship. That said, the various roles of the architect (master builder, creative designer and technician) correspond rarely to the tasks of the librarian, who represents the needs of the later users and is – hopefully – responsible for successfully ensuring the smooth running of the future library. The librarian is neither the client nor the sole representative of the client or the library operator but rather "just" represents the library user.

To a certain extent, both generalists are encumbered by their respective reputations, which at first glance do not seem conducive to productive communications and finding compromises. Architects are supposedly maverick artists who as non-conformists attempt to push through their design ideas in the face of resistance, and who believe they know what is best for the client and the users. Librarians, in Germany at least, have a reputation as being erudite custodians of books, although at present, their actual profile is more akin to that of a manager attempting to steer an educational and cultural institution through a process of transition. To establish a espectful and productive dialogue based on trust, both partners need to recognize what they have in common and to put aside any prejudices they may have of one another.

Establishing an Interdisciplinary Dialogue

Communications between architects and librarians are challenging in several respects because each is a professional in their own field – one albeit rather an artist, the other a manager – and a layperson in that of their counterpart.[2] At the beginning of a project, each typically has only a vague understanding of the other's field, their way of working and thinking, and their convictions and attitudes. To complicate the matter, librarians do not regard themselves as laypeople in such building projects: when it comes to library projects they naturally see themselves as competent and professional partners, and wish to (and should) conduct themselves accordingly.

From the viewpoint of the architect, on the other hand, architecture is not something that has to be explained, or even needs to be understood! The problem is that architects are not always able to anticipate how laypeople react to and perceive architecture.[3] For librarians, the process is challenging at several levels: project communications are conducted in an unfamiliar vocabulary and they find themselves having to adapt to an entirely new role in an environment that is familiar to everyone but themselves. The architect in turn may not view the end users as the most important factor for the design of the building, and so on. All these inherent communication problems can obstruct the development of what should be a productive and ideally strategic partnership. Instead, questions need to be formulated so that the respective communication partner can understand them. Architects need to get to know how the organism of the library works, its systems and logical relationships, the institution's self-perception – all of these endeavors promote understanding between the two disciplines and their respective ways of thinking and working.

For architects, design plans are self-explanatory, but most laypeople require further supporting visual material to understand them. When building a house for oneself, one would typically look at other buildings built by the architect selected for the task and talk to other clients. The same strategy can be helpful here too: librarians can familiarize themselves with the oeuvre of their architect to get to know their particular architectural approach and formal language.

Similarly, librarians can familiarize themselves to a degree with relevant background knowledge and terminology to improve their competency as a communication partner. Conferences, training courses and extensive background literature are provided on the topic of library building and equipment. Institutionalized work groups such as the Library Building and Equipment Section of the International Federation of Library Associations (IFLA)[4] or the Architecture Group of the Ligue des Bibliothèques Européennes de Recherche (LIBER – Association of European Research Libraries)[5] organize conferences and produce publications. Handouts such as the German DIN Fachbericht 13 "Bau- und Nutzungsplanung von Bibliotheken und Archiven"[6] (Building and Functional Planning of Libraries and Archives) or the ISO Technical Report "Information and Documentation – Qualitative Conditions and Basic Statistics for Library Buildings – Space, Function and Design"[7] are not only excellent sources of information for architects and librarians alike but also serve as a common basis for communication. The Freie Universität in Berlin organizes a professional development seminar entitled "Bibliotheken bauen und ausstatten"[8] on building and equipping libraries, aimed primarily at librarians and decision-makers in library construction projects. After repeated reports of communication problems with architects and other construction partners, the FU Berlin devised an additional course module on strategic communications in building processes. The intention is ultimately to qualify library representatives as competent and valuable communication partners in library planning processes. The seminar includes a day-long workshop run by an architect that explains to librarians how architects work, the planning process and how solutions are found.[9] The course focuses on understanding the approach of one's communication partner.

Understanding One Another's Vision

Although the self-image of architects as soloists who give little consideration to the "unqualified aesthetic judgement" of laypeople is thankfully no longer commonplace,[10] it has still not become standard practice to consult the building's users.[11] Librarians, in heir role as partners as well as as laypeople, must in turn recognize the architect and their respective aesthetic categories, philosophy and artistic expression and take the architectural design and its aesthetic concerns seriously. This becomes much easier, and more productive for both parties, if the librarian also has a vision of their own and can formulate this clearly for the architect.[12] For example, if a librarian objects to the architect's choice of a red floor, his or her response may be perceived as interfering with the architect's aesthetic concept if no adequate reasoning is provided.

The librarian may actually be worried that the color concept does not harmonize well with the functional, organizational and physiological requirements of the library's operation. The librarian's concerns have to do with functionality and durability: a muted color may be more conducive to the calm atmosphere and acoustics of a library, and a bright-colored carpet is harder to keep clean than a dark anthracite-colored carpet. It is possible to communicate productively if the partners understand each other's reasoning and are able to openly voice their underlying concerns.

Architects are primarily visual thinkers while librarians think in terms of functional processes and workflow procedures. Librarians can assist architects by visualizing their own thinking: functional plans for the use of the new library can be visualized diagrammatically, as can administrative procedures, user behavior, services and

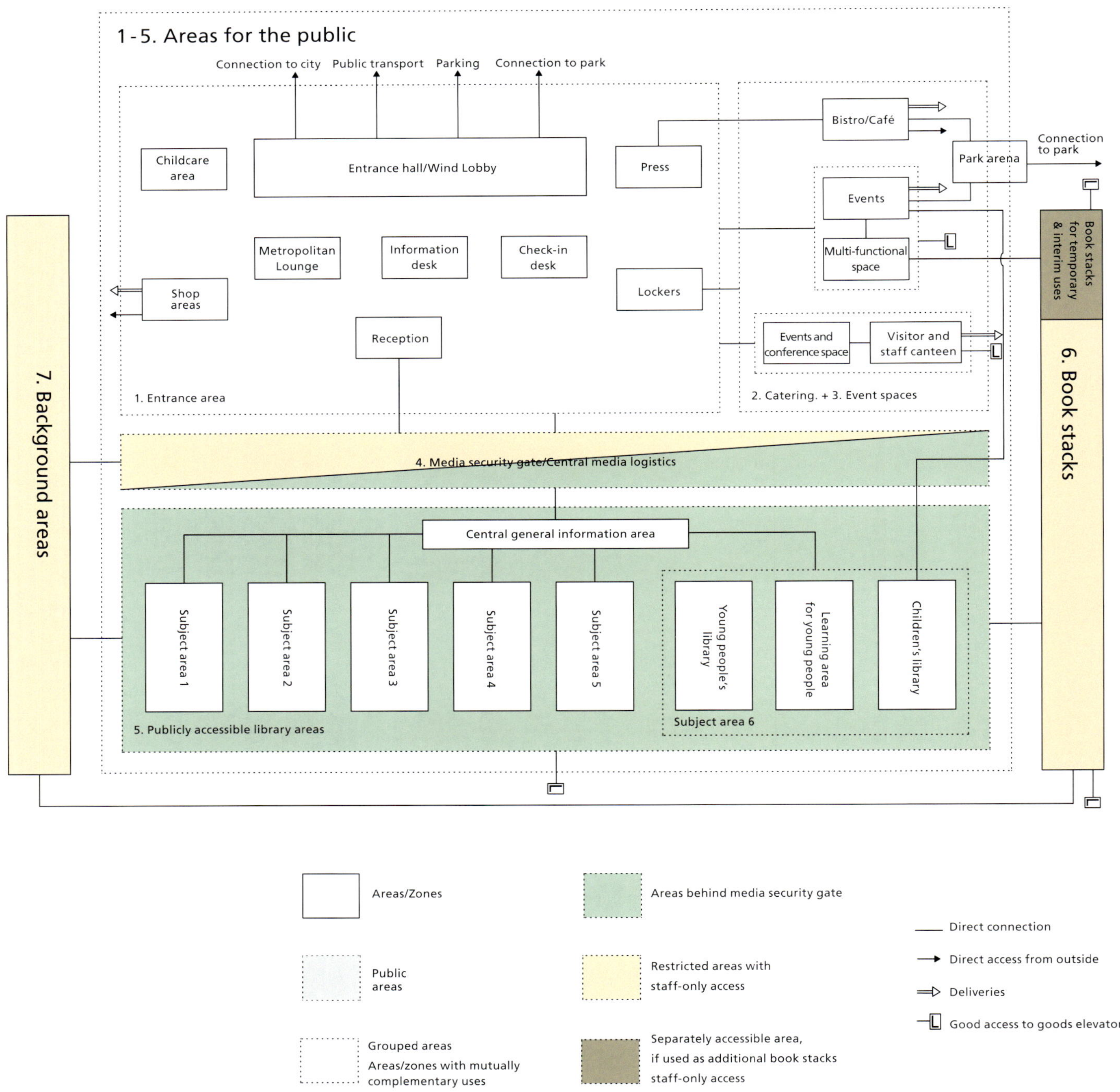

A visualization of the functional processes within a library produced by a librarian is a valuable source of information for architects during the design process.

interactions between library staff and visitors. Architects can ask: "What happens here, who comes here, when and why, and what are they looking for?" Detailed user scenarios and typical patterns of use in the library can help architects translate these functional requirements into three-dimensional spatial designs.

Librarians must also be aware that architects may have surprisingly conservative ideas about libraries, and the resulting imagery of the design may be more evocative of a museum: the library as a repository of knowledge, a place for reading and intellectual study in which the user sits immersed in thought surrounded by walls of books from floor to ceiling, or alternatively vast reading rooms with domed roofs or other similarly traditional images. The librarian will need to communicate that library information desks are complex workplaces that serve as a primary point of interaction and that the reading room with its individual study spaces is just one specific part of a modern library. Librarians need to convey how modern libraries are used, and what the current and future requirements for a contemporary and user-oriented library are in today's digital age. For the architect it is therefore useful to be able to refer to a detailed vision of the library from the viewpoint of the library visitors and guests[13] – a vision that outlines the diverse functions and usage of the building and not just the managerial aspects of running a library and its administration.

Architects are increasingly bringing in external consultants during the design phase of library projects, especially where they have no prior experience of similar projects. This helps to break down the boundaries between architectural design and the world of the library from an early stage during the design phase in the architecture office. As such, a competition entry can already benefit from the input of an expert on library design. Such external consultants are a boon for the entire project, and also for the librarian. Nevertheless, less experienced architects without their own specialist consultants can still always benefit from a librarian's advice and assistance in the later elaboration of building details.

Joint visits to libraries during the planning phase are a common means of promoting understanding, and one that can also be indispensable in later stages of the project: inspiration from other libraries can inform the project in all phases and the process of jointly looking and discussing promotes constructive dialogue between both partners.

Once in a Lifetime: The Planning and Building Process

For many architects as well as many librarians, the chance to build a library is a once-in-a-lifetime opportunity. This explains the special attraction of such projects and why they are given such intellectual consideration – and why they demand such particular care and attention from both parties.[14]

Certain aspects cannot be planned solely on the basis of a functional brief and schedule of rooms but require more detailed consideration: rooms and functional areas with particularly complex requirements such as the library foyer or the service and information desks are best addressed through workshop-like discussions between the architect and librarian including viewing of material samples and joint discussions with firms and suppliers. This kind of workshop is similar to that of working in an architecture office and enables the librarian to explain complex relationships in detail and to contribute to finding an appropriate solution. Intensive meetings of this kind lead to more well-considered solutions and contribute to a better understanding between the participants and trust in their respective competences.

Common areas of conflict are almost always the fittings and furnishings, in particular the furniture, shelving and workspaces. For architects the task does not end with the exterior of the building: the interior is just as much part of the building's design. However, when architects elect to design new shelving, librarians are invariably less willing to compromise. Shelving systems produced by established library suppliers are the product of decades of experience with the needs of libraries. Individual solu-

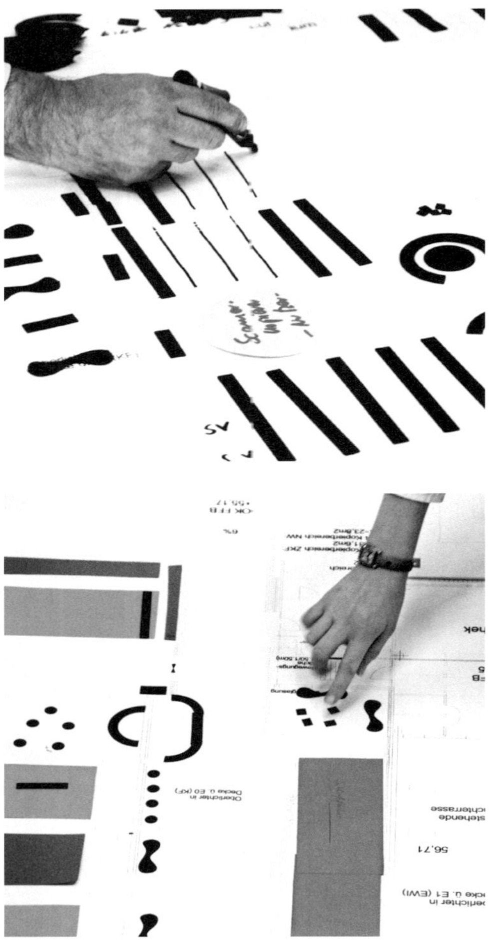

In a workshop with architects, the seminar participants develop alternative plans for an existing library project.

tions for the study areas and workspaces, on the other hand, can be both a more cost-effective and more satisfactory solution than off-the-shelf furniture systems for both the architect and librarian, providing the two work together. When it comes to the seating, librarians usually lack the necessary arguments for or against a particular chair: while the chair design proposed by the architect may look wonderful, the librarian is more concerned with how well they fulfil the functional needs of a place for study and learning so that a student can sit comfortably for five hours at a stretch when learning for an exam. These conflicts are best resolved by actively including the building's later users: allowing the users to help determine the choice of seating is a valuable option in many respects and is a compromise that can reasonably be expected of the architects. The simplest way of canvassing the opinion of library users is to present the alternatives for the proposed seating in an existing library for people to try out.

Even when the architect and librarian have established a good working relationship, the librarian will inevitably need to seek outside advice from participants not directly involved in the building process: a doctor or occupational physician can provide advice on questions of ergonomics, and administrative personnel at the institute, faculty or university will need to be consulted, not to mention user committees and equal opportunities representatives. A danger is that these changing strategic alliances can upset the balance of trust when working with the architect and it is important to avoid undermining their authority. Nevertheless, like the architect, the librarian may consult specialists on important aspects, for example inviting the equal opportunities representative to comment on the architect's choice of rectangular instead of circular handrails for the stairs. The librarian is acting here on behalf of the library's elderly users, and should be open and clear about his or her motives.

Librarians are generally unused to the typical discontinuities that commonly accompany planning and building processes:[15] The input of the different people involved in the project changes and the tempo of the individual sub-processes vary. To librarians, the simultaneity of the planning and construction processes seems chaotic, not least because they need to keep pace alongside their regular activities and responsibilities, while responding to ad hoc requests for input on requirements, facts, numbers or possible objections!

In addition, the long duration of planning and construction processes introduces further problems. Libraries are constantly adapting to rapid developments in information technology, their users' changing expectancies and not least the fundamental changes afoot within the educational system. The design for the library project may, however, already date back several years. Should the librarian wish to adjust the project to cater for new developments, it will entail making alterations that were not planned for in the specification nor in the cost calculations. And as it is not always possible to immediately provide additional funding to compensate for such changes, which are understandably widely unpopular. The more frequently this occurs, the more it can create the impression that the librarian did not think things through adequately to start with, or that the librarian is indecisive, not fully competent or is otherwise simply a "difficult customer". But the librarian's requests may in fact simply be a response to the rapidly changing context in the library environment. Librarians usually only have a limited understanding of the impact of changes and the costs they may incur, but they may rightly feel obliged to ensure that important innovations or new requirements are incorporated into the new building while still possible. A library renovation project is about more than giving a new face to the library; it is also an opportunity to make changes: to revise its administrative structure, to realign the library as a customer-oriented service, to strengthen its communicative potential and its social function in its context. While it is much easier for the architect to develop a new design for the library as it stands, it is a missed one-off opportunity to actively manage its transformation to meet new demands.

Librarians should not at any time assume that they will automatically be invited to attend planning meetings or other relevant discussions: it is rarely formally agreed and they may find themselves needing to assert their position. The architect can, however, make it his or her task to emphasize the importance of the role of the librarian as the representative of the library's users vis-à-vis the other participants. It is in their own interests and in the interests of achieving the best possible result: a well-designed library that also functions optimally. As a layperson among numerous building specialists, the librarian may similarly find themselves sidelined in professional discussions. The architect should insist and ensure that the librarian is comprehensively involved in all aspects of the building process and is present as a matter of course at all important meetings. It will show in the final result when the architect and librarian work together successfully over the course of the entire planning and building process.

References

1 Karl Krarup, "The Royal Library – the Library's Role in the Building Process", *LIBER Quarterly,* 14, no. 2, 2004, p. 232. http://liber.library.uu.nl/index.php/lq/article/view/7774/7878

2 Riklef Rambow, *Experten-Laien-Kommunikation in der Architektur.* Münster, New York: Waxmann, third edition, 2011, p. 13. (Internationale Hochschulschriften 344)

3 Riklef Rambow, *Experten-Laien-Kommunikation in der Architektur,* 2011, op. cit., p. 21.

4 http://www.ifla.org/en/library-buildings-and-equipment

5 http://147.88.230.242/liber-lag/

6 DIN, Deutsches Institut für Normung (ed.), *DIN-Fachbericht 13:2009-11. Bau- und Nutzungsplanung von Bibliotheken und Archiven,* third edition, Berlin: Beuth, 2009. A new, revised edition is planned for 2016.

7 ISO TR 11219, 2012.

8 "Bibliotheken bauen und ausstatten" – the 12-day international seminar takes place once a year at the Freie Universität Berlin. http://www.fu-berlin.de/sites/weiterbildung/weiterbildungsprogramm/bib/bibbau/

9 The workshop was run by Marina Stankovic and Tobias Jortzick (Marina Stankovic Architekten, Berlin).

10 Riklef Rambow, *Experten-Laien-Kommunikation in der Architektur,* op cit., 2011, p. 181.

11 Cf. Klaus Ulrich Werner "'Muss der Direktor immer dabei sein' Gedanken eines bauenden Bibliothekars", *Libreas. Library Ideas,* no. 1, 2005. http://www.ib.hu-berlin.de/~libreas/libreas_neu/ausgabe1/pdf/direktor.pdf

12 Cf. Andrew McDonald, "The Top Ten Qualities of Good Library Space", in: Karen Latimer and Hellen Niegaard (eds.), *IFLA Library Building Guidelines.* Munich: Saur, 2007, pp. 13–29.

13 See Jonas Fansa, *Bibliotheksflirt: Bibliothek als öffentlicher Raum.* Bad Honnef: Bock + Herchen, 2008. http://edoc.hu-berlin.de/oa/books/reOk3GeXGKXw/PDF/28XaSCmGsBFzY.pdf

14 Cf. "This desire for place, space and dignity...", Interview with the architect Robert Niess, in: Petra Hauke and Klaus Ulrich Werner (eds.), *Second hand – aber exzellent. Bibliotheken bauen im Bestand.* Bad Honnef: Bock + Herchen, 2011, pp. 1–35.

15 Marie-Françoise Bisbrouck, "From Concept to Commissioning: The Library – Scheduling, Programming, Phasing", *LIBER Quarterly,* 14, no. 2, 2004, pp. 218–231. http://liber.library.uu.nl/index.php/lq/article/view/7773/7877

Liliane Wong

Funding Options

Libraries are costly endeavors, not only to construct anew but also to maintain and to refurbish. The procurement of funding for these efforts, both in the public and private domain, is therefore a crucial aspect of library planning.

The planning of private libraries and public libraries differs widely with respect to issues of funding. Funding is divided into government and non-government sources, private funds being part of the latter. Non-government sources include foundations, both private and community, corporations, and professional associations. Libraries funded by private monies and gifts are subject to stipulations of the individual donor but are otherwise free from the constraints of governmental or public funding regulations. Examples of private libraries include research libraries of private institutions, royal libraries, and libraries of corporations such as businesses and law firms. Notable privately funded libraries include the Bodleian Library at Oxford University and the Vatican Library.

By definition, a public library is established under government regulations to serve a particular community and is supported, in whole or in part, by public funding.[1] Government funding occurs at many levels and depends, in great part, on the structure of the individual government. The processes for funding vary and are particular to the many types of government.

Funding for operational use differs from funding for new construction or special programs. Depending on the scale, upgrade and refurbishment may be considered under either new construction or operational use. In the U.S., for example, funding for operations occurs at federal, state and local levels. Government funding comprises federal money, which accounts for less than 1 %, state money for less than 10 % and local money for over 80 % of library expenditures.[2] Funding for European libraries occurs on two levels; individually, through the structure of each country, and, collectively through the support of the European Commission for joint endeavors. In the former, each country provides funding through its own regulatory processes. For example, in Finland, the library is part of the citizen's right to information, a right protected by the legislation, and the state has subsidized up to 40 % of all library expenditures.[3]

The process for a new library begins with a preliminary design and the selection of an architect. In Europe, this process is mostly conducted through an international competition. The design is subsequently used for fund raising. In the U.S., the planning process often begins with a needs assessment conducted by a library building consultant working closely with the library governing body and organizations within the community to define library programmatic needs. The cost of the preliminary design for a new library is often an operational expenditure. Financing for the construction of new libraries falls outside of operation costs and typically includes funding sources such as grants, donors and loans in the form of government bonds. In the U.S., new public libraries are usually funded through the issuance of treasury bonds that are paid for through the taxes of the community it serves. This type of funding requires public approval based on the preliminary design. A majority vote is required without which a project may not advance beyond this phase. In the case of OMA's design for the Seattle Central Library (2004, pp. 154–157) the citizens of Seattle voted overwhelmingly to approve the U.S. $ 196.4 million bond measure for the new facility, whereas in the case of Mario Bellini's winning competition entry for the Turin Central Public Library, this financing did not materialize and the project did not continue beyond the preliminary design. The continued development of the library typology will most likely lead to new and unique resources for the funding of future libraries.

In the U.S., alternate funding opportunities exist for specific programs or special services within the library. Organizations such as the National Endowment for the Humanities (NEH) awards grants for projects specific to the humanities while the National Endowment for the Arts (NEA) supports programs in arts and literature.

Legislation, too, has created funding opportunities for special services. For example, the American Library Services and Technology Act (LSTA) with its focus on access to information technology has created flexible funding resources within the library to promote certain priorities. In American school libraries, funding opportunities may be found in Federal grants such as the Elementary and Secondary Education Act (ESEA), originally enacted in 1965, that provide funds to schools in areas of high poverty or for schools focusing on bilingual education.[4]

In Europe, the structure of the EU affords additional funding opportunities through the European Commission, for library projects promoting the sharing of information between the EU countries. For example, the Telematics for Libraries Program began in 1990 with the objective of unifying information access for European nations. Funded projects were TESTLAB, a project for visually handicapped readers, and CHILIAS, a project to develop multi-media applications for children's libraries. Recent opportunities include the European Commission's support of the EDL project to integrate the bibliographic catalogues and digital collections of the National Libraries of 47 European countries and the ICT (Information and Communication Technologies) Program to develop a single European information space.

The concept of the digital library and information space has also spawned new funding possibilities. Within one country, projects such as Harvard University's plan for the Digital Public Library of America redefines the boundaries of public and private libraries in the U.S. With their global reach, projects for digital libraries are not confined to even a particular country or region and have enabled a new accessibility to funding opportunities. For example, the American Andrew Mellon Foundation awarded a grant for an international non-profit organization based in Europe to create the National Library of Mongolia.

Recent trends in new projects include libraries that co-exist and share facilities with another institution. In Denmark, the Gellerup Library shares facilities and functions with the Gellerup Community Center. In London, the Idea Store (Adjaye Associates, 2005, pp. 184–187) combines the library with a learning center/educational facility. These collaborative efforts present different types of financing outside the realm of typical library funding. The continued development of the library typology will most likely lead to new and unique resources for the funding of future libraries.

References

1 Early in the history of the public library movement in the U.S., however, library buildings were often funded by a single wealthy benefactor – chief among these was Andrew Carnegie, who funded over 1,600 library buildings from 1886 to 1919.

2 Based on data from 2007–2009, *Public Library Funding*, http://www.educationbug.org

3 Wigell-Ryynänen, "Finland's Public Libraries – Visited and Valued", *Information Today Europe*, February 25, 2011.

4 Title VII of the Elementary and Secondary Education Act.

Wolfgang Rudorf

Structural Concepts

The structural approach to libraries is tightly intertwined with the overarching programmatic and aesthetic building notion. The quintessence of any structural analysis is the consideration of all static and dynamic loads acting on a building and the comprehension of the resulting reactive forces within the structural members. Optimization of the frame considering actually occurring load conditions and load combinations, limiting excessive deflections and respecting material characteristics to resist the acting forces, and to consequently transfer the loads into the bearing soil is the objective of the structural design. Extending the contemporary structural systems beyond the traditional frame, for example by assigning structural tasks to envelope components, paired with the availability of complex analytical tools, and an integrated project delivery process where interdisciplinary knowledge and risks are shared among team members transforms the historic typological parameters of libraries. Freed from load-bearing walls and limited spans necessitating a compartmental design approach, contemporary concepts dissolve the boundaries between interior and exterior, and create fluid space configurations within envelopes of exceptional complexity and the ability to communicate the building's purpose.

Acknowledging that there is no standard formula for structuring a library building, this chapter will focus as a point of departure on the engineering aspects framed by the mathematical constraints of loads, building code regulations, material properties and construction systems leading to the design of the load-bearing skeleton expressing the highest degree of structural economy. Considering the typical book as a three-dimensional unit of a particular width, height and depth, associated with a particular weight, the organization of library material can be numerically comprehended and translated into spatially and dimensionally anticipated arrangements. A direct link therefore exists between the module book, the shelving unit, the array of shelving units, and the structural grid of the building. At the same time the number of volumes per linear foot corresponds to the loads the structural frame is required to support.

Designing for flexibility and further expansion of a collection or archive, often a programmatic prerequisite, constitutes a challenge to the structural project economy and requires a careful analysis regarding the number of volumes, their anticipated location and organization within the given envelope. In particular the concept of transforming parts of an open-access shelving system to high-density, compact shelving to accommodate collection growth requires an initial design response regarding floor load capacity and is usually not retroactively achievable. Similarly, future relocation or expansion of a collection to a different part of the building demands consideration early in the planning process.

From a structural perspective libraries are designed for their various components – reading areas, study spaces and administrative functions have to accommodate far smaller life loads than stack areas or spaces equipped with compact shelving. However, not only the structural integrity of the building's superstructure is relevant, shelving units and storage systems themselves require resisting gravitational and lateral loads and, depending on the library's location, withstanding code-regulated seismic loads.

The following paragraphs will explore in greater depth the relationship between collection layout and structural grid, applicable load requirements, and the selection of structural systems with respect to material choices and constructability. Advantages and disadvantages pertaining to plan flexibility, building quality and performance characteristics, as well as the interface with mechanical systems will be discussed on a theoretical level. Various case studies will be referenced to illustrate actual solutions and to document their particular structural concepts in the context of a holistic design approach.

Structural Analysis in the International Building Code

It is beyond the scope of this publication to provide inclusive information on standards, codes and regulations applicable to particular jurisdictions. We will use the International Building Code, IBC, regulating construction in the USA,[1] as one base reference. The IBC was first published in 1997 and establishes quite detailed and user-friendly minimum requirements for new construction. It emphasizes safety, especially in terms of fire protection. Constantly integrating new research and experience, it is updated every three years. It takes various climate zones and seismic conditions into account and is therefore also a useful reference tool in other parts of the world. Within this context, we will also use imperial dimensions. Determining occupancy classification and the relevant construction type defined by materiality, a stringent parameter of a library's permissible height and area, are a prerequisite to any structural analysis and hence also applicable elsewhere.

Occupancy

Chapter 3 of the IBC classifies structures with respect to use and occupancy. Libraries are listed in Assembly Group A-3, pertaining to spaces for the gathering of persons for civic purposes.[2] If a program includes occupancies that differ from the assembly use, for example a library as integral part of a shopping mall or an educational facility, further analysis as to construction type, area and height limitations is required to determine the need and rating of fire separation between occupancies.[3]

General Building Heights and Area

The IBC regulates height and area of a library in correlation to the type of construction. It defines five construction types, Type I through Type V, with decreasing fire resistance rating of structural frame, bearing walls, floor assembly and roof construction. Representing the highest fire resistance rating, Type I and Type II construction require the use of non-combustible materials; reinforced concrete and steel respectively. Type III and Type IV both require exterior walls constructed of non-combustible materials. Any code-compliant material, including combustible materials, is permitted for interior building elements of Type III construction, while interior building elements of Type IV, also referred to as heavy timber construction, are of solid or laminated wood without concealed spaces. Type V, the most vulnerable type of construction, permits structural elements, exterior and interior walls composed of combustible materials. If exposed to fire, a structural member manufactured of a non-combustible material such as steel would lose structural integrity through deformation, increasing the potential for the collapse of the larger system. Vice versa, a combustible structural member constructed of wood, for example, could be protected against the destructive forces of a fire by gypsum wallboard encasement. Consequently, the IBC introduces for each construction type (except for Type IV) a subcategory A and B prescribing the fire resistance rating measured in hours of withstanding exposure to fire of the exterior walls, the structural frame, the floor/ceiling assembly and the roof construction.

A library constructed according to Type I A construction with a fire resistance rating of three hours for the structural frame, the exterior and interior bearing walls, a two-hour rated floor construction and a 1 ½ hour rated roof construction could be of unlimited height, number of stories and floor area while a Type II A construction with one-hour fire-rated building elements would limit the height to 65 ft (19.8 m), the total number of stories to three and the area to 15,500 sq ft (1,440 m²) per floor (ill. 1). Type V A with a one-hour protection would limit the allowable height to 50 ft (15.2 m), the number of stories to two and the plate area to 11,500 sq ft (1,068 m²), while a Type V B construction would limit the height to 40 ft (12.2 m), the number of stories to one and the floor area to 6,000 sq ft (557 m²). If the building is equipped with an approved automatic sprinkler system, the code grants a height increase by 20 ft (6.1 m), an increase of the maximum permitted stories by one story and an area increase of 200 % for multi-story buildings and even 300 % for single-story structures.

Group	v	Type of construction								
	v	Type I		Type II		Type III		Type IV	Type V	
		A	B	A	B	A	B		A	B
Group	Height	Unlimited	160 ft (48.8 m)	65 ft (19.8 m)	55 ft (16.8 m)	65 ft (19.8 m)	55 ft (16.8 m)	65 ft (16.8 m)	50 ft (15.2 m)	40 ft (12.2 m)
	Stories (S) Area (A)									
A-3	S A	Unlimited Unlimited	11 Unlimited	3 15,500 sq ft (1,440 m^2)	3 9,500 sq ft (883 m^2)	3 14,000 sq ft (1,300 m^2)	2 9,500 sq ft (883 m^2)	3 15,000 sq ft (1,394 m^2)	2 11,500 sq ft (1,068 m^2)	1 6,000 sq ft (557 m^2)

1 Allowable building heights and areas for libraries[4]

	International Building Code	
	Uniform	Concentrated
	psf (KN/m^2)	lbs (KN)
Reading rooms	60 (2.8)	1,000 (4.45)
Stack rooms	150 (7.2)	1,000 (4.45)
Compact shelving	250 (12)	1,000 (4.45)
Corridors above ground floor	80 (3.8)	1,000 (4.45)

2 Minimum uniformly distributed and minimum concentrated live loads for library floors

For obvious reasons new library construction is generally executed as Type I and II construction, allowing large floor plates with high load capacities on multiple stories. The adaptive reuse of a multi-story building of a construction type with a higher content of combustible materials and a lower fire rating can prove difficult with regard to the allowable size of the floor plate and the location within the building – for example in a Type III B construction with non-combustible two-hour rated exterior walls and interior building elements of any material assuming zero-hour rating, a library floor could not be established above the second floor (first floor in Europe) since the code-regulated story limitations are shown as stories above grade plane.

Structural Load Assumptions
The use and occupancy of a building produces live loads encompassing people, collected materials and furnishings. Location-specific environmental loads include snow, rain, wind and seismic loads. Dead loads are comprised of the self-weight of the structure including all building-integral components.

Books, periodicals, archival documents, microfiche and audio-visual collections establish within a library building the most critical load conditions closely interrelated to their organization, display and storage. The uniformly distributed live loads for library stack rooms and compact shelving are based on the average book weight of 65 lbs/cu ft (10.2 KN/m^3) and are listed in ill. 2.[5] Centered on a typical U.S. double-faced shelving unit organized in ranges spaced 3 ft (0.91 m) apart, the following computations regarding weight of books and number of volumes for the purpose of load calculation and collection layout can be performed.[6]

Load and Volume Calculation for a Typical Library Collection
To give a calculation example, we assume a double-faced shelving unit (DFS) 2 ft (0.61 m) deep with a shelf depth of 12 in (0.3 m), 3 ft (0.91 m) wide, and 90 in (2.29 m) high, on a 4 in (10 cm) base and with six adjustable shelves spaced 12 in (0.3 m) on center for maximum book storage capacity on seven tiers between base and canopy. If we further assume a 100 % working capacity,[7] one DFS would store about 35 cu ft (1 m^3) of books weighing a total of 2,275 lbs (10.12 KN) based on the code-regulated book weight of 65 lbs/cu ft (10.2 KN/m^3). Converted to a uniformly distributed load, the actual floor load based on linear rows of shelving, separated by 3 ft (0.91 m) aisles, thus allocating 15 sq ft (1.39 m^2) of space per DFS, would compute as 150 psf

(7.2 KN/m^2) – equivalent to the minimum uniformly distributed live load specified by the building code for library stacks.

High-density or compact shelving of books and archival material as well as the storage of microfiche cabinets require floors of far higher load capacity. Typically, library compact shelving reduces open aisle space by half or even a third depending on the size of the installation, demanding a minimum of 250 psf (12.0 KN/m^2) floor capacity while microfiche usually constitutes a concentrated load covered by the listed 1,000 lbs (4.45 KN).

The average shelf capacity based on volumes per linear foot is in agreement with the code-specified minimum uniformly distributed live load for stack areas. Legal volumes with a spine width of 2 in (5 cm) and bound periodicals with a spine width of 1¾ in (4 cm) usually constitute the highest shelving loads due to their large format, uniform size and density. The same DFS unit used for the calculation of the load-accepting area would accommodate 252 volumes, equivalent of about 30 cu ft (0.84 m^3), and thus staying well below 150 psf (7.2 KN/m^2). Eight volumes per linear foot (0.3 m) for textbooks, fiction or classics and a working capacity of 80 % resulting in 336 volumes[8] per DFS are assumed standard for common stack areas. Despite the high number of volumes, typical variations in book formats and weight assure that the permissible live load is within limits.

Both the forward high reach of the average user and the advantage of organizing oversized volumes within the running order of the collection (requiring greater spacing of the shelves) typically limits library ranges for public access to a maximum of six shelves. Maintaining sight lines in collection areas may reduce the height of shelving even further. Due to the reduced number of tiers paired with the decreased book volume density per DFS shelf to provide for organizational flexibility and future growth of the collection, the load capacity thresholds stipulated by code are usually not reached.

Structural Grid

The structural bay size is a direct function of the stack layout and overall structural economy. Again based on a conventional linear shelving concept, a 2 ft (0.61) wide double-faced shelving range and a 3 ft (0.91 m) wide aisle would generate a grid dimension perpendicular to the rows of shelving derived from multiples of 5 ft (1.52 m). The preferred aisle width referenced in the Americans with Disabilities Act (ADA)[9] is 3 ft 6 in (1.07 m),[10] the minimum required width is 3 ft (0.91 m), requiring a 40 in (1.02 m) clear perimeter aisle, and often aisle widths of 5 ft (1.52 m), equivalent to the turning radius of a wheelchair, are requested for circulation and browsing. The grid dimension parallel to the rows is a multitude of the 3 ft (0.91 m) shelf unit plus the space required for the column. Economical structural grid dimensions vary between 25 ft (7.62 m) and 30 ft (9.14 m). A grid of 30 ft (9.14 m) is preferred since it allows the organization of five 2 ft (0.61 m) wide double-faced shelving ranges separated by 4 ft (1.22 m) wide aisles or six double-faced shelving ranges separated by 3 ft (0.91 m) aisles respectively.

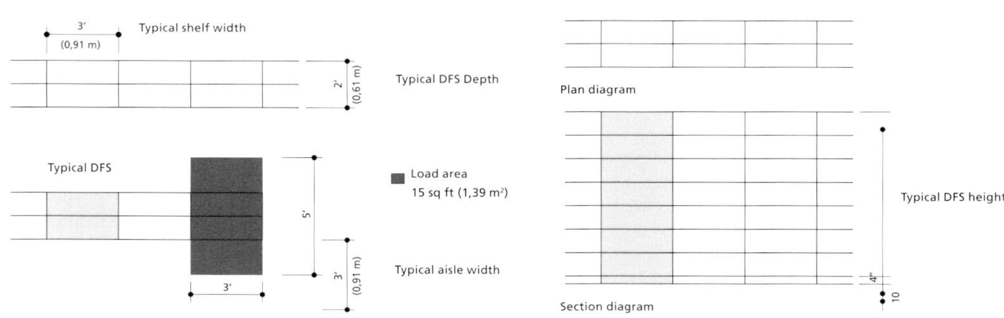

3 Calculation of load accepting area per DFS for typical library stack area based on 2 ft (0.61 m) deep DFS units and 3 ft (0.91 m) wide aisles. The DFS load of 2,275 lbs (10.12 kN) is uniformly distributed on 15 sq ft (1.39 m^2).

Structural Economy

Accommodating the book collection will always remain the primary aspect of library construction. Total number of volumes, book formats, collection organization, anticipated growth and overall flexibility as well as floor area efficiency and the density, width and height of stacks – wider aisles encourage browsing while lower shelves increase overview and consequently heighten safety within the collection area – constitute some of the parameters impacting the selection of the structural concept.

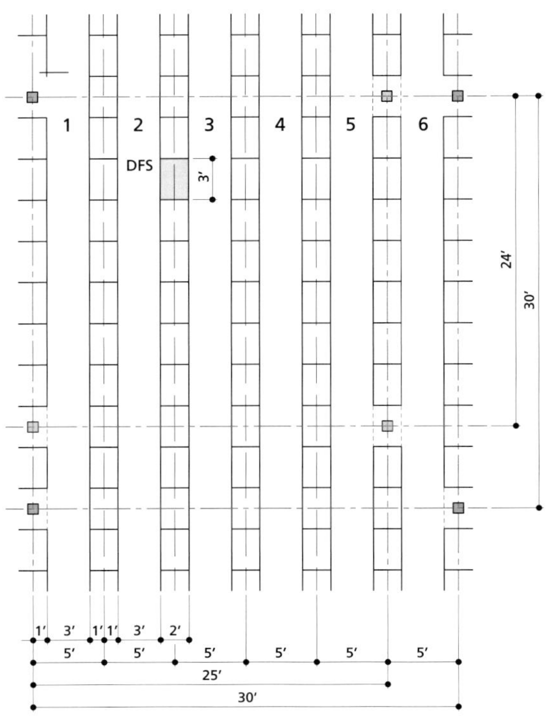

4 Typical grid layouts in the imperial system: 25 × 24 ft and 30 × 30 ft column grid based on 3 ft aisle and 2 ft deep DFS units accommodating five or six DFS ranges respectively

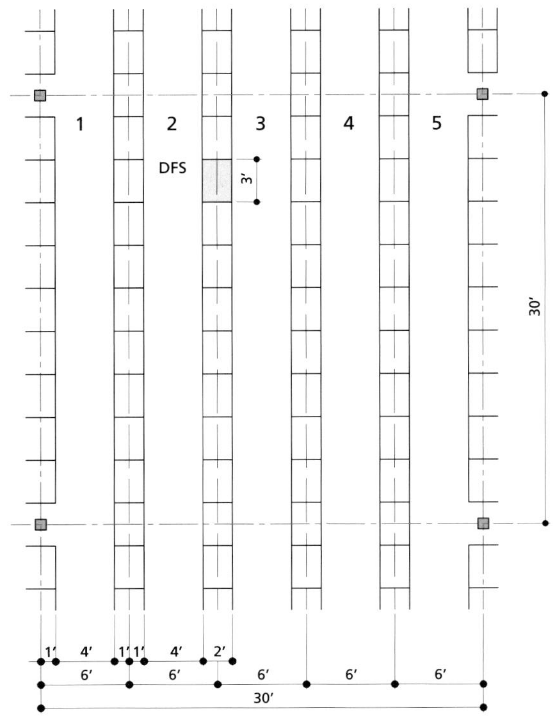

30 × 30 ft column grid based on 4 ft aisle and 2 ft deep DFS units accommodating five DFS ranges

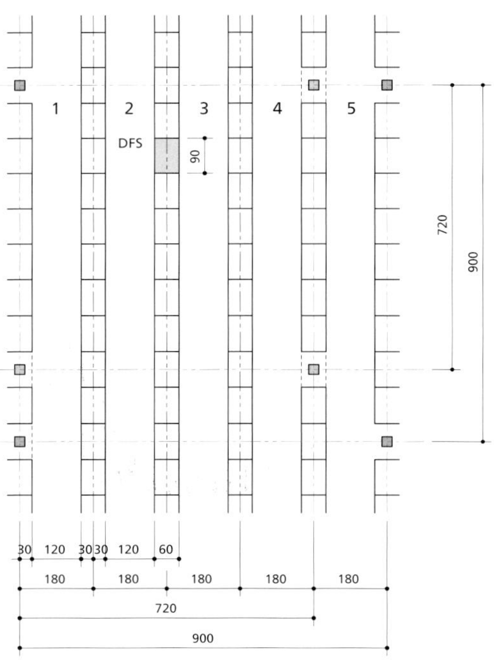

5 Typical grid layouts in the metric system: 7.2 × 7.2 m and 9 × 9 m column grid based on 1.2 m aisle and 60 cm deep DFS units accommodating four or five ranges respectively

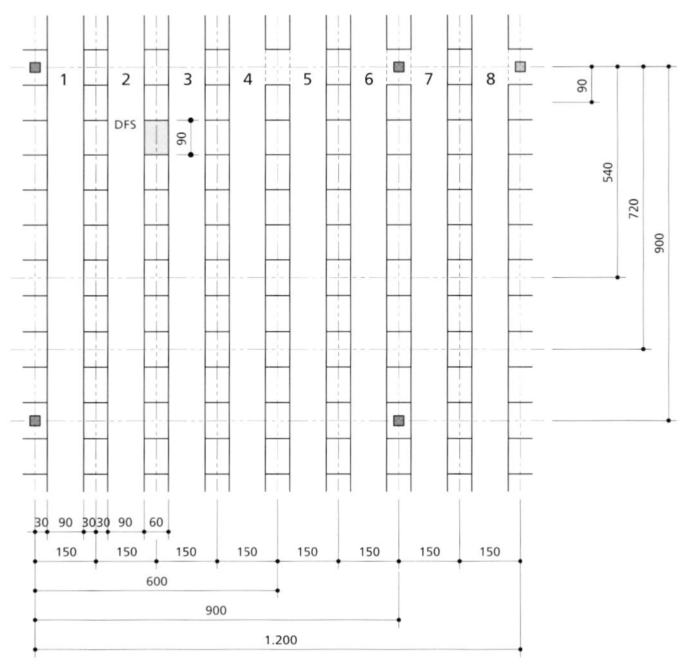

9 × 9 m column grid based on 0.9 m aisle and 60 cm deep DFS units accommodating six ranges. The shelving grid provides the possibility of a 12 m span accommodating 8 ranges. Generally, the column spacing along the centerline of the ranges is more flexible.

6 Jacob-und-Wilhelm-Grimm-Zentrum Berlin, Max Dudler, 2009. The sub-grid of 1.5 m is reflected in the rhythm of the envelope fluctuating between window openings aligned with the stack aisles and sandstone wall panels. Along the perimeter load-bearing columns are spaced 6 m apart.

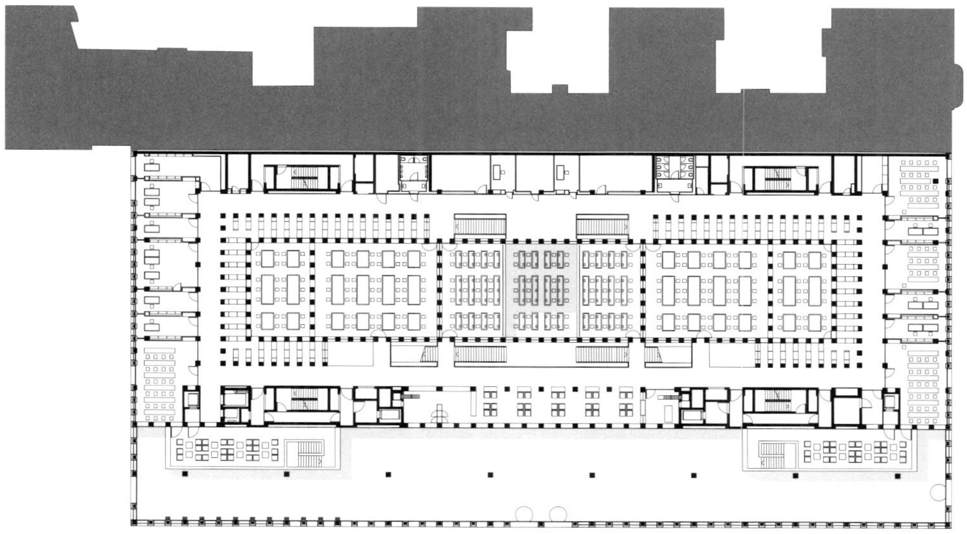

7 Jacob-und-Wilhelm-Grimm-Zentrum. The organization of the DFS units on a 1.5 m wide sub-grid generates the library's design concept. Depending on load requirements column spans alternate between 12 m, 6 m and 4.5 m in the stack bays.

Various strategies to achieve structural economy and spatial quality exist. The Jacob-und-Wilhelm-Grimm-Zentrum (ill. 6–7) in Berlin (Max Dudler, 2009, pp. 232–237) submits to an orthogonal grid and celebrates the book as the basic construction module. DFS units, 0.6 m wide and separated by 0.9 m aisles, arranged perpendicular to the perimeter of a typical library floor plate, generate the 1.5 m wide sub-grid defining the placement of structural columns, load-bearing walls and shear walls, the rhythm of the building envelope, the sequence of the intermediate non-load-bearing interior pilasters, the structural grid of the skylight above the central reading room and the width of the custom-made worktables.

Toyo Ito's 2007 Tama Art University Library in Tokyo (ill. 8–9) pursues a very different approach: it is a library building with a seemingly random grid composed of intersecting elliptical arches with varying spans. The sloped entry floor plate and the tilted roof plane require the steady increase of the rise of the arches. Constructed of concrete-clad steel plates, the spring points of the arches are placed at the intersections or rhamphoid cusps of alternating concave and convex curves. Low, three shelves high, seamlessly constructed, meandering double-faced stacks are interwoven with the archways conveying the curvature of the structure into the horizontality of the floor plate.

8 Tama Art University Library, Tokyo, Toyo Ito, 2007. The non-linear structural grid is formed by the confluence of elliptical arches.

9 Tama Art University. The sinuous form of the display cases is a reinterpretation of the structural form in the horizontal plane.

Structural Systems

Large spans, open uninterrupted floor plates, multiple stories and the requirement for high load capacities promote steel and concrete or a combination as the most likely construction materials for a library. Inherent to the various systems are advantages and disadvantages regarding floor assembly depth, structural spans, lateral stability, layout flexibility, vibration control, system integration, fire protection and aesthetics. Furthermore, striving for structural economy demands attention to constructability, construction schedule and market parameters like the availability of technical know-how, labor force and lead times.

Both structural systems, i.e. steel and concrete, as well as their amalgamation allow for highly innovative solutions. Ill. 11 will provide an overview of selected structural systems. Maximum span requirements dictate the selection of the structural system, and consequently determine the depth of the floor assembly and the achievable floor-to-ceiling height as a function of the interface between building systems and the superstructure.

10 Overview of selected gravity load systems and their properties (all dimensions are approximations)

GRAVITY LOAD SYSTEM	DIAGRAM	PROPERTIES
Two-way Concrete flat plate	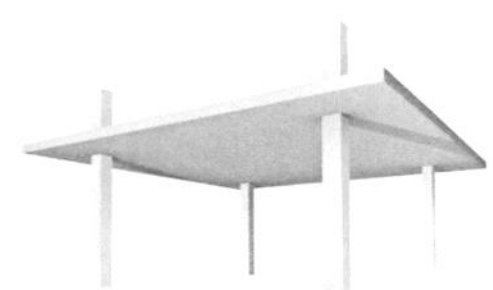	Column grid 7.2 × 7.2 m Slab thickness 25 cm Camber to compensate for dead load deflection
Two-way Concrete flat slab with Drop panels	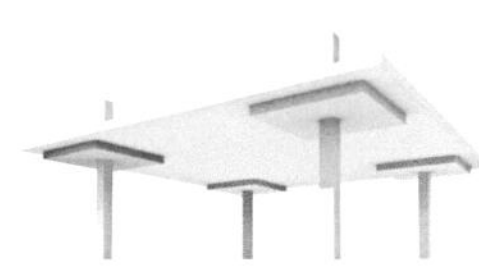	Column grid 7.2 × 7.2 m Slab thickness 20 cm Drop panel 18 cm Overall depth 38 cm Column grid 9 × 9 m Slab thickness 25 cm Drop panel 28 cm Overall depth 53 cm
Two-way Concrete waffle slab		Column grid 7.2 × 7.2 m Slab thickness 10 cm Ribs 25 cm Overall depth 35 cm Column grid 9 × 9 m Slab thickness 10 cm Ribs 30 cm Overall depth 40 cm Camber to compensate for dead load deflection
Slab on metal deck Steel beams	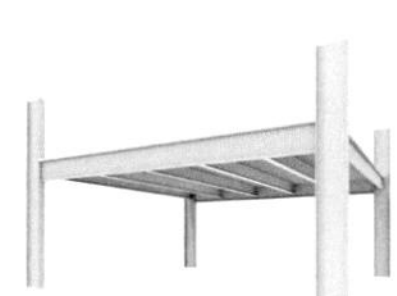	Column grid 7.2 × 7.2 m Filler beam w 14 (ipe 360) Girder w 18 (ipe 450) Composite slab 8 cm Leightweight concrete on 5 cm deck Overall depth 58 cm at girder Column grid 9.1 × 9.1 m Filler beam w 16 (ipe 400) Girder w 24 (ipe 600) Composite slab 8 cm Leightweight concrete on 5 cm deck Overall depth 75 cm at girder Camber to compensate for dead load deflection

11 Advantages and disadvantages of frequently used structural systems

STRUCTURAL SYSTEM	ADVANTAGES	DISADVANTAGES
In-situ concrete	Shallow structural depth Good vibration characteristics Good acoustical properties High degree of fire protection Good thermal properties Short lead time	Slower construction Heavier constuction Less flexibility with shaft locations Difficult future modifications Expensive winter construction
Post-tensioned concrete	Shallowest structural depth Good vibration characteristics Good acoustical properties High degree of fire protection Good thermal properties Short lead time	Slower construction Heavier constuction Less flexibility with shaft locations Most difficult in terms of future modifications Expensive winter construction
Steel	Light weight Speed of erection Flexible Easy future modifications Shaft layout flexibility	Greater structural depth Long lead time Fire-protective treatment required Poor thermal properties

Structural Innovations

Interdisciplinary dialogue, building information modeling, system computational analysis and the employment of an integrated project delivery concept with the objective to share knowledge and responsibilities throughout all stages of the design and construction process allow the realization of structures outside the conventional realm of library construction. The structural framework becomes an intrinsic part of the building's spatial qualities and material expression as documented in Toyo Ito's Sendai Mediatheque, the Seattle Central Library by OMA and the Rolex Center by SANAA. All three libraries challenge the common typology by radically reinterpreting the structural super-frame.

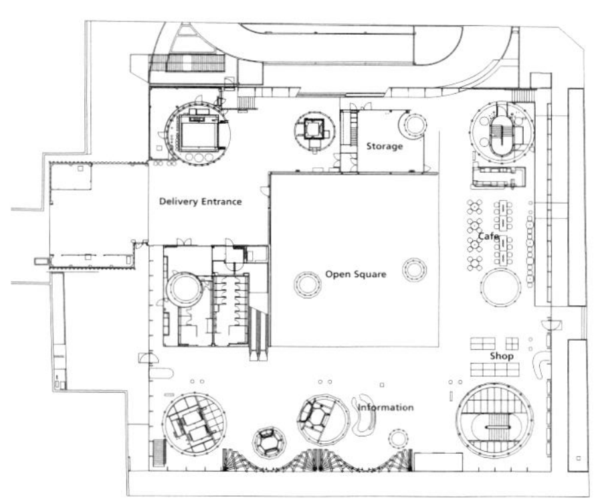

12 Sendai Mediatheque, Toyo Ito, 2001. Ground floor plan

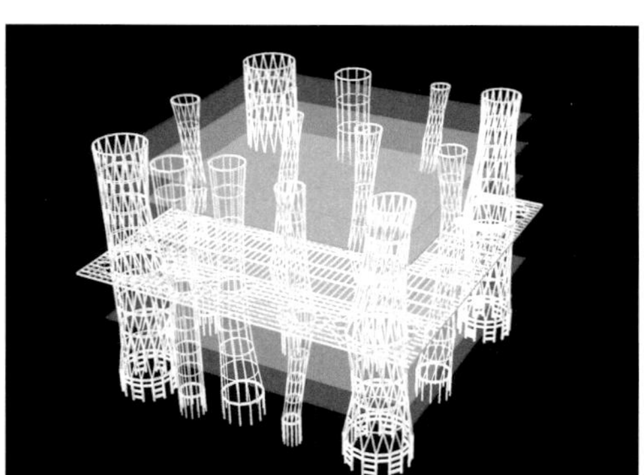

13 Sendai Mediatheque. The axonometric shows the engagement of the tubular towers with the floor structure.

Sendai Mediatheque: Tubular Towers

The multi-story Sendai Mediatheque (Toyo Ito, structural design Mutsuro Sasaki, 2001) is of interest in the structural context (ills. 12–13) because of its ingenious substitution of a conventional column grid for a complex array of circular towers constructed of a lattice of round tubes. The towers organize the volume in a non-hierarchical fashion both horizontally and vertically without curtailing program flexibility or transparency.

Thirteen round towers varying between 2 and 9 m in diameter placed on a sinuous grid inside a 50 m square footprint constitute the vertical superstructure of the Sendai Mediatheque. Constructed of a multitude of inclined, round steel tubes ranging from 12 to 25 cm in diameter, encompassed at floor levels and between plates by horizontal circular rings of steel, each tower generates a uniquely configured "hyper shell" supporting the gravitational loads of the seven-story library. From plate to plate the circular floor penetrations both shift eccentrically and vary in diameter, forcing the individual steel tubes to directional deviations generating scissor-like juxtapositions and a complex three-dimensional spatial experience. At the same time the meandering pattern of the floor plan is conveyed into the verticality of the structure. Only the four triangulated corner towers are designed to absorb the lateral forces transported in the floor diaphragms. Below grade the truss structure of these towers changes to a ductile rigid frame providing the energy dissipation capacity required by seismic design standards.

A composite floor sandwich constructed of a network of narrowly spaced steel ribs changing in depth and orientation depending on the prevailing load conditions and a 20 cm thick concrete topping slab spans between the ring beams of the tubular towers. The skin of the building is suspended from the slab edges cantilevered beyond the perimeter towers, thus greatly enhancing the transparency and dematerialization of the building by blending the inside with the outside. The net-like structural concept of vertical tubes interconnected with the steel grid of the composite floors eliminates the need for vertical shear walls enabling the realization of flexible program space throughout the media library.

Seattle Central Library: Exoskeleton

The organizational concept of the Seattle Central Library (OMA with LMN Architects, structural design Arup Structural Engineers and Magnusson Klemencic, 2004, pp. 154–157), comprised of three distinct rectilinear cuboids forming programmatic clusters (termed Assembly, Book Spiral, Headquarter) floating within a multi-faceted transparent skin above a two-story concrete base, demanded a highly complex engineering approach (ills. 14–15). The basic structural objective to resist gravitational, lateral and seismic forces is partially met through the unconventional employment of building components functioning in both the architectural and structural realm, such as the glass skin engulfing the stacked program elements.

14 Seattle Central Library, OMA, 2004. A diamond-shaped exoskeleton and mullion system support the glass envelope.

The multi-story Book Spiral is centered between the cuboids. The dislocation in space of the three rectangular cuboids generates extensive cantilevers. A system of skewed columns along their perimeter counterbalances the cuboids and transfers proportionate gravity loads into the in-situ concrete base levels where the resulting thrust forces are channeled into the floor diaphragms and accepted by concrete columns. On the interior of the rectangular volumes an orthogonal column grid supports the stacked floor plates and connects the three cuboids. A vertical, 60 m tall rectangular concrete core contributes to the support of the floating cuboids and their structural stabilization. Perimeter cross-braced trusses located in the sidewalls of the rectangular volumes resist lateral forces and carry gravitational loads.

The cuboids are woven into a structural skin, an inclined exoskeleton, deviating between 20 and 45° from the horizontal, and extending along the street elevations over the entire height of the building. The diamond grid formed of thousands of individual rhombi constructed of 30.5 cm wide-flange steel members with 1.2 m wide and 2.1 m high diagonals is continuous within the individual facets, bending at horizontal seams. The steel diagrid of the envelope opposes exclusively wind and seismic loads (but not gravity forces) and for this reason was permitted by code to remain unprotected against fire. Structurally the diagrid and the cuboids are connected with slip joints, allowing the skin to stabilize the platforms against lateral loads without absorbing gravitational forces.

15 Seattle Central Library. A 60 m tall rectangular concrete stair tower and mechanical shaft contribute to the support of the floating cuboids.

At the slanted envelope planes, the lattice-like seismic steel frame directly supports a shallow glass mullion system. Contrary, at the vertical facades due to the lack of such a seismic framework, deep floor-to-floor-spanning mullions sized to withstand lateral curtain wall loads, not only resemble the geometry of the diamond grid but also emulate the profile of the seismic I-beams, thus creating a coherent appearance.

Rolex Learning Center: Ultrathin Free-form Shells

Realizing the Rolex Learning Center in Lausanne (SANAA, structural design SAPS and Bollinger + Grohmann Ingenieure with Walther Mory Maier, general contractor Losinger Marazzi, Lausanne, 2010, pp. 238–243) as topographic architecture with the intent to create space for a highly experimental learning atmosphere demanded exceptional structural expertise and creativity (ill. 16–17). The floor structure of the single-story undulating volume, pierced by 14 curvilinear openings or patios, is comprised of two shallow, irregularly shaped concrete shells of different size and varying curvature; both shells are structurally tied into the roof plate of the basement, congruent in shape with the rectangular 162.5 × 121.5 m perimeter of the Learning Center above.

16 Rolex Learning Center, SANAA, Lausanne, 2010. The large shell under construction.

The slender shells, exposed to significant bending moments in addition to the in-plane forces, are strengthened by highly reinforced concrete arches located along the perimeter and in the zones between patios. Seven arches, spanning between 55 and 90 m, are

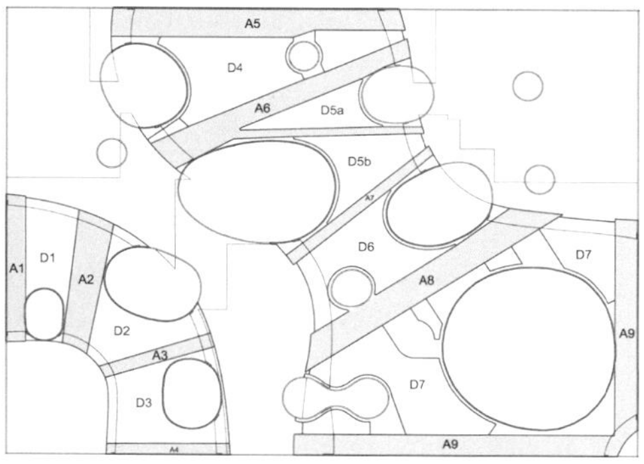

17 Rolex Learning Center. To stabilize the shell slabs, seven arches were embedded into the large shell and four arches into the small shell.

embedded into the large shell, and four arches, with spans between 30 and 40 m, into the small shell. Horizontal outward thrust forces are resisted by post-tensioned cables in the roof slab of the basement. Coplanar with the underside of the shell surfaces, the arches and patio edge beams, designed with greater structural depth than the adjacent slabs, project up to 20 cm above the top of the shell slabs.

Pouring the sloped shell slabs, even in zones up to 15 %, without the need of counter formwork was achieved by adding plastic fibers into the concrete mix, providing the necessary viscosity for the oblique installation while facilitating pumping. The reinforcement steel in the arches, reaching a concentration of up to 470 kg/m^3 for the transfer of stresses induced by the bending moments, necessitated the use of bars of up to 50 mm in diameter, to assure space between bars for correct installation and consolidation of the performance concrete. The reinforcement also reduced long-term deflections due to creeping and shrinkage, thus minimizing the tolerances required for the execution of the glazing system. The roof plane follows the fluidity of the floor slab. Executed as a membrane roof over wood decking and supported by a 9 × 9 m grid of steel beams with laminated wood filler joists on slender steel columns, it provided sufficient lateral stiffness.

References

1 International Code Council, *2012 International Building Code (IBC)*. Washington: ICC, 2011, p. iii, Preface.

2 International Code Council, *IBC*, chapter 3, section 303, Assembly Group A, p. 41.

3 International Code Council, *IBC*, chapter 5, section 508, Mixed Use and Occupancy, p. 101.

4 Based on table 503, Allowable Building Heights and Areas, *IBC*, chapter 5.

5 Paragraph 1607.3 of the IBC states that "the live loads used in the design of buildings and other structures shall be the maximum loads expected by the intended use or occupancy but shall in no case be less than the minimum uniformly distributed live loads."

6 Uniformly distributed live loads for library floors are also listed in other codes such as the German *DIN Standard 1055-3, Einwirkungen auf Tragwerke*, Part 3, Eigen- und Nutzlasten für Hochbauten, 2006, and DIN, Deutsches Institut für Normung (ed.), *DIN-Fachbericht 13:2009-11. Bau- und Nutzungsplanung von Bibliotheken und Archiven,* third edition, Berlin: Beuth, 2009, and the National Standard of the People's Republic of China GB 50009, Code for the Load Design of Buildings.

7 Working capacity defines the percentage of open space on a shelf, also referred to as fill range. The management of a collection (re-shelving and adding new acquisitions) requires a working capacity below 86 %.

8 Volumes per linear dimension vary by the type of collection (a complete listing of spine dimensions for the calculation of shelf capacity is included in the section on Shelving, pp. 102–105).

9 American with Disabilities Act, Accessibility Guidelines, ADAAG, 8.0 Libraries, 8.5 Stacks.

10 By comparison, the German Institute for Standardization declares a 1.2 m wide aisle as accessible, resulting in a shelving grid of 1.8 m. Cf. DIN, Deutsches Institut für Normung (ed.), *DIN-Fachbericht 13:2009-11. Bau- und Nutzungsplanung von Bibliotheken und Archiven*, 2009, op. cit.

Wolfgang Rudorf

Climate Control

Most libraries are designed for public access and house primarily modern books and media collections that are not irreplaceable from a historical point of view. Hence, climate control is more concerned with human comfort aspects during hours of operation than maintaining an absolutely stable environment, as required for purely archival purposes. Nevertheless, many libraries are also guardians of rare documents and unique materials that demand a different level of safekeeping with respect to temperature, relative humidity, air quality, and control of light, often requiring the installation of separate systems for collection and non-collection spaces. In other words, climate control always needs to reconcile the requirements of user comfort on the one hand and conservation issues on the other hand.

Methods to achieve indoor thermal comfort and relevant conditions for artifacts in a public access library vary between climate zones. Human thermal comfort standards, prevailing microclimate, energy codes and standards, environmental issues, available energy sources, and sustainability concerns are all parameters shaping the system design with options ranging from mechanical, to passive and hybrid heating, ventilation and air conditioning concepts. Yet, the system approach is primarily determined by the type of library, its content and program, by operational aspects, the library's size in terms of volumes, area and number of users. Interdisciplinary creativity, dialogue and sharing of information are crucial in achieving a synergetic interface between architecture, structure, and building systems.

The effectiveness and success of natural ventilation and cooling, and other alternative energy concepts, entails the owner's commitment to understand not only the operative system aspects based on the seasonal, daily temperature differentials and hours of operation, but also the basic thermal and air quality parameters to provide occupant comfort and appropriate collection conditions. This is in particular true for systems that are not entirely automated, but are either semi-automatically, or even manually activated.

Thermal Comfort
Cutaneous thermoreceptors are instrumental in regulating body temperature, and consequently are a critical determinant for human thermal comfort, a state dependent on variables reaching from non-quantitative individual differences to measurable non-environmental personal factors, such as activity levels expressed as metabolic rates and the insulating value of clothing to quantifiable environmental factors, including air temperature, thermal radiation, humidity and air speed. There is also a cultural factor at work: what may be perceived as comfortable in one part of the world, might be gauged as too hot or too cold elsewhere. To a modest degree, the boundaries of thermal comfort zones are elastic; modifications of the variables, for example, increasing the air speed, intensifies, in turn, evaporation coolness of the skin, thus expanding the acceptable temperature threshold, or contrary, a higher clothing insulation value is effective in countering a lower temperature setting.

Thermal comfort zones are defined in the context of energy codes and standards specific to varying energy strategies, reaching from entirely mechanically controlled buildings to fully free-running (i.e. not heated or cooled) buildings, taking advantage of beneficial climate conditions promoting the employment of passive thermodynamic processes for heating and cooling. In principle, there are two models for determining thermal comfort: 1. the static comfort model relevant for buildings equipped with mechanical heating ventilation and air conditioning (HVAC) systems that ensure constant indoor temperatures all year round and 2. an adaptive model for determining acceptable thermal conditions in occupant-controlled naturally conditioned spaces, primarily through the operation of windows only supported by mechanical ventilation using unconditioned outside air. Finally, there are mixed-mode buildings (often in use in Europe's temperate climate zones) where the refrigeration equipment for cooling is only temporarily activated.[1]

Recommended inside design conditions for HVAC-controlled public, non-archival libraries are typically 20–22° Celsius, 40–55 % relative humidity with air movement at 0.13 m/s and 8–12 air changes per hour. However, certain climate zones will achieve appropriate comfort levels and conditions just by providing for heating and natural ventilation, while other zones will require only cooling and dehumidification, or the seasonal or year-round operation of full-scope heating, ventilation and air conditioning systems. In non-archival libraries, HVAC systems may operate only during opening hours, or cycle on/off with thermal satisfaction alone. Archival libraries, and rare book collections, discussed later in this chapter, require strict climate control without relative humidity fluctuation and temperature set points relevant to the collection material. In general, uncontrolled high humidity levels and lack of ventilation facilitate mold growth (65 % relative humidity is considered borderline), a devastating threat to book collections. Systems operating within the above-listed boundaries provide not only thermal comfort for the occupants, but also reasonable protection for the contents stored and displayed in a non-archival library.

In the context of energy conservation and sustainability, the acceptance of climate parameters and meteorological variables, as a contributing form-giving force and the basis for a project's energy program, are of critical importance. Building envelopes, conceptually reaching from sealed to semi-permeable and from transparent to opaque, as well as the form factor, the ratio of the envelope's surface area to volume, are by far the most influential parameters impacting energy consumption. Solar and wind exposure, thermal transmittance and air leakage rates of envelope components, such as roofs, walls and fenestration, the ratio between opaque and transparent areas, the intensity of insulation and choice of construction materials, paired with the internal heat emission generated by occupants and equipment, determine the overall load profile of a building. In addition, changes in use patterns and occupancy numbers during operating hours, variations in the operating schedule as such, climatic shifts relative to time of day and season trigger significant load fluctuations to be considered and analyzed for the design, sizing and spatial organization of mechanical equipment.

Energy standards inform design requirements for building envelopes and HVAC equipment; paired with local meteorological records and site-specific air quality data, a comprehensive climate profile for a particular location evolves, offering fundamental information for the conceptual approach to indoor climate control, potential energy conservation, bioclimatic design and eligibility for green building certification.

Ventilation and Indoor Air Quality

Ventilation, the dynamic process of airflow within a building, is not only critical for achieving thermal comfort by controlling temperature and humidity levels, but also for assuring acceptable indoor air quality through the dilution of pollutants (grouped in odors and irritants) by both introducing outdoor supply air and exhausting stale air. In libraries, air pollutants are not only a health threat to the occupants but hazardous for rare book collections and archival material as well. Standards define acceptable indoor air quality, determining air change rates per hour (particularly critical for the protection of archival material), and quantity of ventilation air per occupant measured in liter per second, and prescribe compliance methods based on system design, reaching from mechanically to naturally conditioned buildings. A recommended value for libraries is 8.5 l/s per person, and the occupant rate for a reading room should not exceed 20 occupants per 100 m^2.

Reading rooms, closed and open-stack areas, archival storage, rare book collections, study spaces for individual and group work, multi-media labs, assembly spaces, internal data centers, administrative offices, food service and technical library support areas all require a specific system response to ventilation needs and thermal comfort based on project-specific parameters, such as occupant load, floor plate dimensions, space configuration, volume, location and adjacencies. For example, deep floor plates, often typical for libraries accommodating large stack areas, require a system approach capable of responding to skin and core loads. Stack lighting and user heat emission produce internal thermal loads that demand cooling, while the perimeter zones, depending on season and solar orientation, require either heating or cooling.

Concrete core activation utilizes the thermal storage capacity of concrete slabs for cooling or heating. Aluminum tubes are embedded into the neutral zone of the concrete slab.

Construction systems, in-situ concrete, for example, offering thermal mass storage capacity, mostly control system design and the integration of ventilation distribution. Climate parameters, however, are the most influential force in the design of ventilation systems. Moderate outdoor temperatures, substantial temperature swings between day and night time or notable temperature differentials between sun-exposed and shaded building surfaces, prevailing wind patterns and climate conditions characterized by low relative humidity increase the potential for bioclimatic concepts, such as free cooling, night cooling (night ventilation of thermal mass), passive cross ventilation and evaporation cooling (assuming control of contaminants). Arriving at a system design that conserves energy, while satisfying ventilation needs and achieving thermal comfort, requires a holistic approach and integrated process.

Ventilation Rates and Monitoring

In buildings equipped with complete HVAC systems or just mechanical ventilation, the rate of outdoor air ventilation and the degree to which the airstream is filtered prior to space infusion determines indoor air quality. Primary parameters are the outdoor air quality, the physical boundaries of the zone to be ventilated, the number of people occupying the zone, and the effectiveness of the air distribution system depending on type – both mixing or dilution ventilation systems and displacement ventilation systems are relevant for library installation.

For concrete core activation 10 cm diameter aluminum tubes with internal radial fins for optimized heat absorption are used.

Demand ventilation, based on carbon dioxide monitoring, allows substantial energy savings due to the reduction of conditioned supply air to zones that are not frequently used or fully occupied, such as assembly spaces, large conference rooms, semi-public stack areas or archival storage rooms. The sensors of the Seattle Central Library (OMA, 2004, pp. 154–157) are linked to the building's energy management system, modulating air intake dampers and air distribution volume to curb indoor CO_2 concentration to below 530 parts per million (by volume) or 0.053 %, and consequently increasing human comfort.[2] However, low CO_2 concentrations are only one aspect in achieving high indoor air quality; eliminating volatile organic compounds (VOCs) from the building process, isolating ozone-producing printers and reprographic machines from the library environment, using green housekeeping products, and the commissioning, monitoring and maintaining of systems are of utmost importance as well.

Maintaining balanced temperature and humidity levels on open and often intercommunicating floors is of great complexity and requires automated operation. User control may be exerted in staff work areas, small meeting rooms, administrative offices and certain auxiliary spaces. There, operable windows for natural ventilation, individually controlled shading devices and thermostats may increase personal comfort.

Systems

HVAC System

The tendency in modern ventilation and air conditioning engineering for libraries leans towards the use of dedicated outdoor air systems, DOAS, that handle all latent loads (and part of the sensible loads due to preconditioning of the outside air with energy recovered from the return air stream) and parallel systems comprised of optional all-air variable air volume systems, fan coil units, unitary water-sourced heat pumps or chilled beams satisfying the sensible load requirements specifically demanded by a particular use and space. First costs for DOAS tend to be higher in comparison to conventional all-air HVAC systems. However,

Sendai Mediatheque, Toyo Ito, 2001. In winter mode, the very narrow, south-facing double-skin facade creates a thermal buffer zone between the exterior and interior glass curtain walls.

the long-term energy savings, assuming total energy recovery, are substantial, and full compliance with indoor air quality and thermal comfort standards is achieved. With the elimination of condensation formation on parallel equipment, the risk for microbial contamination is greatly reduced, making the concept ideal for archival libraries. A prerequisite is the design of a sealed building envelope, minimizing uncontrolled outdoor air infiltration.

Free Cooling Mode

Libraries located in moderate climates, described by low average temperatures, have the potential of operating in reduced or free cooling mode during most of the year, or at least during the swing seasons, by supplying the building directly with filtered, but unconditioned, outdoor air, as is the case for the Seattle Central Library designed by Rem Koolhaas. In Seattle, maximum average outdoor temperatures below 21° Celsius for most of the year allow the library to operate for extended periods in free or reduced cooling mode.

Utilizing the thermal storage capacity of concrete slabs for cooling or heating is known as concrete core activation, a concept employed inside the extensive stack areas of the Jacob-und-Wilhelm-Grimm-Zentrum in Berlin (Max Dudler, 2009, pp. 232–237). There, 14° Celsius outdoor air circulates through a grid of 10 cm diameter aluminum tubes embedded into the neutral zone of the slabs, cooling the concrete floor. In absorbing the excess internal heat, the temperature in the stack area is lowered, while the temperature of the circulating air is raised to 21° Celsius, a suitable temperature for reintroduction into the space, satisfying ventilation needs.

Double-Skin Facade

A double-skin facade, as developed for the Sendai Mediatheque in Japan (Toyo Ito, 2001), creates a ventilation-controlled buffer zone between the outside environment and the building's interior climate. In winter mode, with vents closed, the static air volume detained between the single-glazed outer skin and the insulated inner glazing system heats up and creates an effective thermal barrier between the exterior and the interior environment, thus enhancing the comfort zone along the inner curtain wall; in summer mode, openings at the bottom and the top of the cavity (the space between the two glass skins) initiate stack ventilation, consequently reducing the thermal load inside the cavity and the thermal load of the adjacent library floor, respectively. Under low humidity conditions, the stack effect can support passive cooling by forcing cooler air from the sun-opposed building side across the floor plate. A dot screen etched into the exterior glass panels reduces sun infiltration and glare.

Computerized adjustable louvers, expandable and retractable shading devices, fixed canopies and lightshelves, treatment of glass surfaces, and the installation of specialty solar control glass are available measures in managing interior thermal loads and ventilation needs generated by expansive glass surfaces. Finding a balance between desirable visual indoor-outdoor connections, daylight optimization, and solar gain, while preventing overheating, excessive glare, and damage to the collection from overexposure to ultraviolet light requires an interdisciplinary approach. To minimize solar gains inside the glass enclosure of the Seattle Central Library, a triple-layered, krypton-filled glass pane, with a diamond-shaped expanded aluminum metal mesh suspended between glass layers, covers half of the envelope.

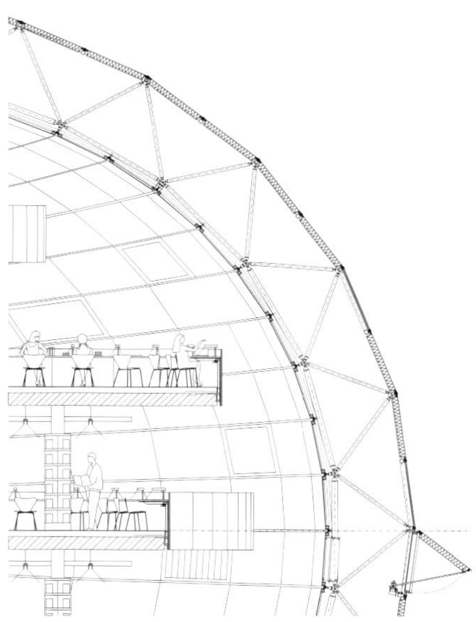

Philological Library, Freie Universität, Berlin, Foster + Partners, 2005. The envelope section shows the interstitial space between interior and exterior membrane that is utilized for ventilation.

The Philological Library at the Freie Universität in Berlin (Foster + Partners, 2005, pp. 226–229), offers a unique approach to ventilation. A tubular space frame in the shape of a prolate spheroid, clad on the exterior with alternating rectangular aluminum and glass panels, and on the inside with a translucent white fiberglass membrane, generates a double shell with an interstitial space utilized for ventilation. Similar to the concept of a vertical double-skin facade, computer-operated ventilation panels at the base and at the crest initiate or block airflow, thus regulating the temperature between the two membranes and the indoor climate respectively.

Inside the dome, a structurally independent, multi-story concrete structure accommodates stacks and workspaces. Concrete core activated slabs support space heating and cooling.

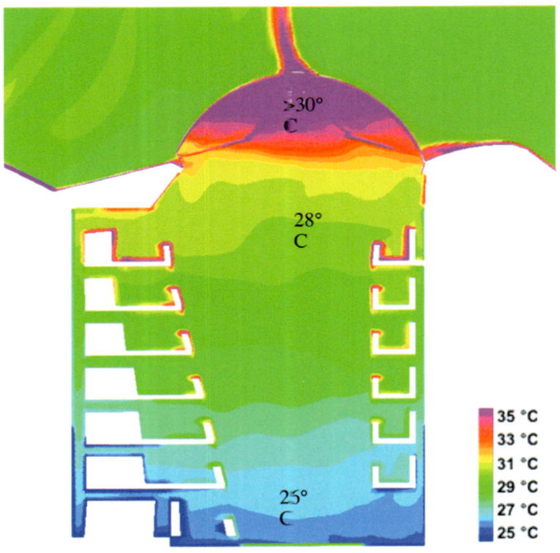

Law Library, Universität Zürich, Santiago Calatrava, 2004. Inside the elliptical atrium, the fluid motion analysis shows stratified air masses, with temperatures of above 30° inside the glass cupola and 26° Celsius at the entry level. This stratification avoids the need to condition the entire air volume of large open spaces.

Displacement Ventilation

A conventional mixing ventilation system supplies air at high velocity to rooms through overhead diffusers, inducing the existing air to mix and to achieve temperature equalization and uniform contaminant concentration. Exhausted air is returned through ceiling grilles or ceiling plena. Displacement ventilation systems, on the other hand, deliver air at low velocity, typically near floor level, into the space. Superior indoor air quality, containing high levels of outside air, is achieved by the unidirectional transport of conditioned supply air through buoyancy forces generated by heat sources – people, computers, lighting – right to the breathing zone of occupants. Contaminants are not diluted, but carried above the breathing zone by the rising air.

In cooling mode, supply air temperature in displacement ventilation systems is about 5.5° Celsius higher than required for conventional ceiling-supplied mixing systems, that is roughly 18° versus 13° Celsius. Energy efficiency is achieved by reduced conditioning needs and by being able to use outside air directly for more hours of the day. In employing a variable air volume system, the supply airflow can be modulated to allow for demand ventilation. Manipulating supply airflow and supply air temperature, or both, controls the temperature of the ventilated space.

The described buoyancy effect causes the stratification of air masses, permitting the creation of clean thermal comfort zones within 3 m above occupied floor levels, while air layers above this datum operate at temperatures and contamination levels outside the human comfort range, as explicitly reflected in the temperature profile of the University of Zurich Law Faculty Library (Santiago Calatrava, 2004, pp. 220–221). Stratification avoids the need to condition the entire air volume of large open spaces, such as the atrium in the Law Faculty Library, the central reading room in the Jacob-und-Wilhelm-Grimm-Zentrum, Berlin, or the large glass envelope of the Seattle Central Library, for human comfort, thus aligning architectural concept with energy conservation goals.

During spring and fall, based on temperature differentials between inside and outside air and actual weather data, computer-automated vents open at the bottom and top of the atrium, initiating a flow of unconditioned air through the core of the multi-story Law Faculty library. In winter mode, with all envelope vents closed, the building operates in mechanical heating mode, supplying conditioned air to the multiple levels of the atrium. In summer mode, with outside temperatures above 25° Celsius, linear automated vents along the base and ridge of the cupola, with a combined opening area of 14 m^2, provide cross ventilation, reducing heat build-up caused by solar gain, thermal load of occupants, lights and equipment.

During the summer months, conditioned air is supplied to the balconies through diffusers located in the base of the wall-encompassing shelving system to achieve acceptable thermal comfort. Vertical ground-source heat pumps are located around the perimeter of the building; with the earth acting as a heat sink in cooling mode and a heat source for preheating supply air in winter mode, the need for a cooling tower and chiller is eliminated.

Unlike ceiling-supplied mixing systems, displacement ventilation systems are less suited for projects requiring extended periods of heating. Consequently, in the case of the Jacob-und-Wilhelm-Grimm-Zentrum, the displacement system is limited to the central reading room. Both the 92 horizontal skylight units, glazed with highly insulated solar control glass and equipped with automated horizontal perforated shades, and the deep circumferential stack wings define the thermal envelope of the introverted space. Insulated vertically from exterior temperature conditions

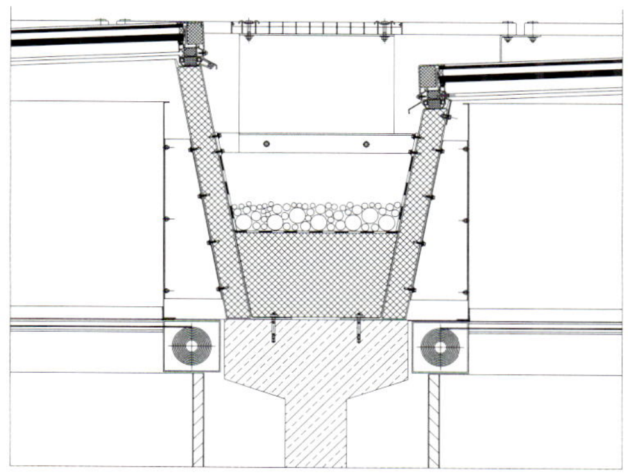

Jacob-und-Wilhelm-Grimm-Zentrum, Berlin, Max Dudler, 2009. Partial cross section of skylight units depicting the automated horizontal perforated shading devices.

Jacob-und-Wilhelm-Grimm-Zentrum. The roof of the central reading room consists of 92 horizontal skylight units. Highly insulated solar control glazing protects the space against passive solar gain while reducing glare on the interior.

and protected horizontally against extreme passive solar gain, the central reading room operates predominately in free cooling mode. However, under heating demand, the location of the supply air grilles above the reading tables generates an airflow pattern comparable to a mixing system. For indoor air quality, the stacks are equipped with a conventional mixing ventilation system, with diffusers integrated into the canopy of the shelving units.

Chilled Beams

Library-integrated data centers, in particular, but also multi-media and computer labs, and reprographic centers, often located in the core of the building, generate isolated, sizeable thermal loads that require cooling. To this end, ceiling-integrated, active, chilled beams tend to be a very effective application. Dehumidified, preconditioned supply air from a dedicated outdoor air system is forced through nozzles in the beam, inducing existing air from the space to pass through the cooling coil, delivering cool air to the space. Through grilles at ceiling levels, return air is ducted back to the air handler. By modulating the chilled water flow rate, the system reacts to sensible load changes in the space. Advanced design solutions for chilled beams combine cooling with other building systems, such as fire suppression systems, fire and smoke detectors, lighting and public address systems.

Jacob-und-Wilhelm-Grimm-Zentrum. Removable panels allow access to the building's vertical infrastructure located in the non-structural piers. Duct risers inside the piers feed into the concrete core activation system and into supply diffusers. The perforation of the panels contributes to the acoustical quality of the space.

System Integration

The interface between the building and its mechanical systems is not solely critical for reasons of functionality; rather, the selection and application of systems is often deeply intertwined with the architectural concept and expressed aesthetics. The vertical air distribution system requires strategically located shafts within the plan configuration, and horizontal distribution branches require ceiling plenums, or the construction of raised access floors, impacting the achievable clear floor-to-ceiling height within stories, and consequently, the overall height of the building – a critical cost factor. The placement of supply air intake and return air exhaust is directly related to the building envelope, the building's height, form and plan, as well as the environmental conditions, orientation and site context. Decentralized air handling systems offer flexibility in terms of building integration, allow reduced duct sizes and shorter runs, and the possibility of addressing specific thermal and air quality demands. Centralized systems, due to their size, often require mechanical penthouses. Cooling equipment usually is centralized or part of self-contained interior and exterior systems with external cooling towers.

In the Jacob-and-Wilhelm-Grimm-Zentrum, the structural column grid is divided into a much narrower grid with vertical, non-structural piers that allow the integration of air distribution risers and other building infrastructural components. Vertical duct runs feed into the pipe manifolds embedded in the concrete slabs for

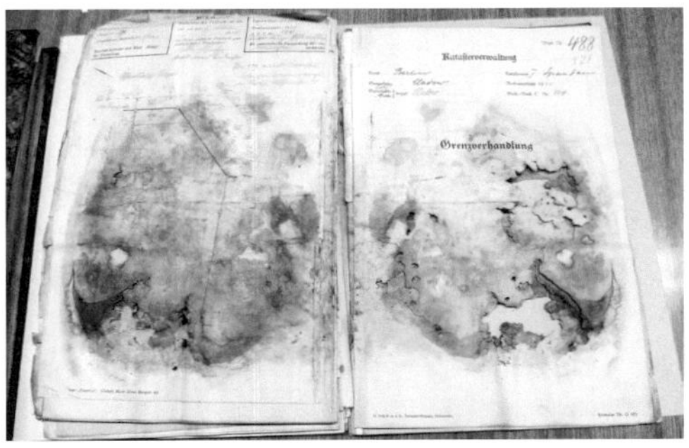

Mold damage in historical file

core activation, into the supply diffusers in the reading room, the air outlets along the perimeter of the building, providing thermal comfort at the window worktables, and into the diffusers integrated into the canopies of the stacks. The latter concept, paired with the collection of return air at selected points, eliminates horizontal duct runs or plenum space inside the collection area. Avoiding the need for suspended ceilings optimizes the efficiency of the concrete core activated floor slabs and reduces the overall floor-to-floor height in the stacks.

Archival Libraries

Preservation of special collections, comprised of rare books, unique and often irreplaceable archival documents of different media, and an unlimited variety of historical artifacts and artwork, demands the design of environmental control systems tailored to very particular needs. The obligation to provide public and scholarly access to collections, and the desire to display valuable pieces within the premises of a library, are to a certain degree counterintuitive to the concept of safekeeping and further complicate the organizational and building systems approach to housing and preserving collections. Finding a compromise between the ideal environmental conditions and the realistically achievable technical, operational and economical measures, paired with a collection-specific risk analysis, should be part of the pre-schematic design phase involving archival librarians, conservators, programmers and building consultants.

Book showing damage from insect infestation ("bookworms")

A number of threats can affect collections, among them (in decreasing order of seriousness): light, relative humidity, temperature, air pollution, pest infestation. Control of a library's indoor relative humidity, temperature and air quality is the quintessential prerequisite for the protection of the collection. It minimizes the risk of humidity-related decay processes, the deterioration of collections due to poor air quality, ventilation and the infestation by insects. Vibration-free installation of equipment and ductwork, the routing of pipes outside critical areas and the provision of emergency power supply for mechanical systems will eliminate mechanical risks to the collection caused by shock, vibration and leaking pipes and maintain climate control and system monitoring during power interruptions.

Air quality standards are achieved by complex filtration systems. The contamination of a system's internal components, such as cooling coils and supply lines, as well as dust build-up on fans and inside ductwork, is prevented by prefiltration, while fine-particulate filtration and gas-phase filtration provide protection to the collection material itself. It is recommended that archival and specialty collection libraries store chemically stable permanent collections at 50 % relative humidity and a temperature between 15 and 25° Celsius, maintaining the above-mentioned air movement speed of 0.13 m/s and hourly air change rates between 8 and 12. Chemically unstable library and archive collections should be housed in cold store, or cool store, with temperatures and humidity tailored to the specific objects.

THREAT		AFFECTED MATERIALS AND DAMAGES	CONTROL MEASURES
Light Permanent photochemical change Permanent photophysical change		Books, textiles	Architectural design Eliminating UV light Limitation of illumination density Limiting total illumination duration Operational procedures
Humidity Biological damage Mold growth Mechanical damage Expansion and contraction Increase of stiffness Chemical damage Acid hydrolysis Corrosion of base metals Chemical deterioration of organic materials		All paper objects Dyes (increase hydrolysis reaction of cellulose, thus weakening paper; increase fading of dyes)	Airtightness of building envelope (e.g. positive pressure environ-ment) Design of mechanical system
Air pollution	**Inorganic pollutants:** Sulfur dioxide, nitrogene oxide	Cellulosic materials Paper, historic wall papers, Historic textiles Animal skins Leather Parchment Photographs Dyes, e.g. in cloth binding	Air quality control Zoning Enclosure of materials Filtration
	Oxidizing pollutants: Ozone, peroxyacetyl nitrate, peroxide	Dyes and pigments (fading) Fabrics, textiles, cellulosic material Photographic prints Leather, parchment, animal skins	Location of office equipment (copy machine) Electrostatic air cleaners
	Organic carbonyl pollutants: Formaldehyde	Photographs Photographic film	
	Other pollutants: Fatty acids, particles	Yellow papers and photographs Books Textiles (Abrasion of surfaces; dust entraption; disfiguration of books and textiles by soot)	Filtration

Selected threats, at-risk materials, damages and control measures

References

1 Buildings in the U.S. are regulated by ANSI/ASHRAE standard 55-2010, "Thermal Environmental Conditions for Human Occupancy", while European buildings follow standard EN 7730-2005, "Ergonomics of the Thermal Environment", and EN 1525, "Indoor Environmental Input Parameters for Design and Assessment of Energy Performance of Buildings".

2 CO_2 levels in outdoor supply air typically range from 300–500 ppm. An outdoor air ventilation rate of 7.5 l/s per person will dilute bioeffluents in a building with sedentary activity patterns to an acceptable degree. Indoor CO_2 concentration should not exceed the outdoor concentration by more than 650 ppm and concentrations greater than 5,000 ppm may constitute a health risk.

Wolfgang Rudorf

Lighting and Illumination

Visual comfort is intrinsically related to light, to light's interaction with architectural space, the properties of materials employed in forming the spatial membrane, and the elements placed inside for human inhabitation. The complex physical properties of light and light distribution are to be balanced with the physiological sensation of light perception and interpretation, the psychological phenomena connecting light to ambience, and the functional aspects of providing the relevant level of illuminance for tasks to be performed within the space. Architectural lighting design is further complicated by the interaction of artificial light sources with the dynamic illluminance parameters of daylight.[1] The perception of objects in a space, and the ability to perform a visual task, diminishes with increased exposure to glare caused by unbalanced intensity of illluminance, a light source positioned in the field of vision and by reflection.

In general, the various tasks executed in libraries need values in the range of 200–2,000 lux.[2] Minimum illuminance levels averaging between 300 lux and 500 lux are recommended for reading rooms, 300 lux for active stacks areas and 50 lux for inactive stacks. Other activities as book binding and embossing require higher light levels, 500 lux and 1,000 lux respectively.

Reading, the primary seeing task in a library, is directly related to the reading material itself – font size (assuming a standard viewing distance of approx. 25 cm between eye and reading material), the chosen type face, contrast between text and display medium (commonly black ink on white paper), color contrast of illustrations (saturated colors achieve the highest level of contrast), graphic design concepts, and the sheen and texture of the paper, as well as the quality and method of printing. Visibility science distinguishes between seeing/reading tasks that demand a high level of mental activity, like the study of mathematical symbols or an unfamiliar language, which employ central or foveal vision (focusing on the task within the 2° cone of foveal vision), and conventional reading tasks, assuming familiarity with the material to be comprehended and, hence, allowing a far wider cone of vision suitable for scanning a printed page visually.

Tama Art University Library, Tokyo, Toyo Ito, 2007. Suspended fixtures with upward-pointing light sources provide an even luminous ceiling plane and a glare-free base illumination for the stack and reading space. Thus the level of light intensifies gradually from floor to ceiling.

The luminance of the reading environment, the contrast between the reader's immediate surrounding and adjacent spaces, and the color contrast between the object to be viewed and the surface on which it rests, are the primary factors controlling lighting conditions in the reading and studying areas of a library. Furthermore, the reader's general eyesight, determined by medical conditions and age and levels of fatigue, is, to some degree, linked to the illumination of the reading environment and requires design consideration and special accommodation. Individual visual comfort is often achieved by adjustable, user-operable supplemental task lighting at workstations and carrels. The concept, allowing a lower overhead lighting level, supports energy conservation, thus complying with energy standards regulating lighting power density and the control of lighting.

Luminance of a surface type task should be equal or marginally higher than the luminance of the background, although ratios of 3 to1 are acceptable in most circumstances. Consequently, the reflectance (defined as the ratio between incident and reflected light) of a worktable surface for reading material printed on matte white paper with a reflectance rate of 0.77 (i.e. 77 % of the light incident on the paper surface is reflected), yielding a luminance of 120 cd/m^2 under illuminance of 500 lux (as recommended for the performance of visual tasks of medium contrast or small size), should not exceed 0.25. Newspaper, less refined than white paper, has a reflectance rate of 0.68, while the reflectance of glossy white magazine paper is above 0.80. Reflectance is directly material-dependent, and although the human eye is not able to distinguish between a light-emitting source and a mere reflecting source, the distinction of the two is important for a successful lighting concept. Critical in reading tasks is the viewing angle in relationship to the incident light angle, the angle at which the illuminance is directed onto the paper. Light pointing straight

Jacob-und-Wilhelm-Grimm-Zentrum, Berlin, Max Dudler, 2009. The green tabletops provide a strong contrast to the reading material although within the wider field of vision the luminance of tables and wood-paneled walls seems well balanced, creating a serene space quality.

Philological Library, Freie Universität, Berlin, Foster + Partners, 2005. Contrary to the approach taken in the Jacob-und-Wilhelm-Grimm-Zentrum, the luminance of the worktables is congruent with the study material. The translucent white inner fiberglass membrane of the double-skin shell provides daylight to the space while avoiding glare.

down onto the reading material avoids reflected glare or veiling reflection, offering a well-balanced reading environment.

Luminous ceilings, achieved by suspended fixtures with solely upward-pointing light sources or by light sources installed behind a frosted glass or acrylic membrane, avoid the occurrence of glare while rendering the space in uniform light.

Browsing, locating and retrieving books from stacks, as well as the management of the collection, involve the visual task of reading book titles and identifying labels. Correct lighting levels across the vertical surface of the shelving unit, the spines of the books, is achievable by two conceptual methods; canopy lighting, i.e. linear lights parallel to the range cantilevered out from the shelf standards at the height of the canopy, and linear light fixtures, ceiling-integrated or suspended, centered on the aisle or perpendicular to the ranges. Canopy lighting offers the greatest flexibility with regard to changes in the shelving layout; while ceiling-connected lighting aligned with the aisles is considered the least flexible solution.[3] The task-specific distribution characteristic of canopy luminaires, directing light with high efficiency onto the vertical shelving plane, permits low-level luminance for the surrounding areas, ultimately conserving energy. In active stack areas, the recommended luminance level measured vertically at the floor is 80 lux.

Reading room	Option 1 General lighting supplied over the entire area Option 2 Low-level lighting supplemented by local task lighting	300 lux
Individual/Group study rooms		300 lux
Carrels	Task lighting depending on configuration and location	500–1,000 lux
Auditorium/Lecture halls	Adjustable to multi-functional program	varies
Class rooms/Computer/Media labs		300–500 lux
Arts and craft spaces	Daylight color rendering of light source recommended	300–500 lux
Children's program rooms	Ambience adjustable to activities ranging from reading to play and craft	varies
Collection areas: active stacks	Vertical surface illumination of stacks Canopy lighting Parallel/perpendicular lighting above ranges Spotlights for highlighting specialty books/themes 80 lux measured vertically at floor level	80–350 lux
Collection areas: inactive stacks	Measured at 75 cm above floor	50 lux
Archival collections/Rare books	Illuminance values collection- and object-specific	varies
Library circulation	Supplemented by local task lighting	300 lux
Offices		500 lux

Recommended illumination levels at table height

Sophisticated 3D rendering programs based on radiosity (representing radiant exitance or radiative flux of both reflected and re-radiated light) and ray-tracing techniques, offering great realism by taking into account absorption, reflection, refraction and fluorescence, support the virtual analysis and manipulation of lighting concepts and lighting effects prior to realization. Computer-based photometric calculation programs rely on the luminaire's candle power distribution curve, the geometrical relationship between luminaire and light-receiving surface, and distance between source and surface, while the lumen method provides information on illuminance at the light-receiving surface measured in lux and energy code relevant electrical power density measured in watts per square meter. Luminaire-specific photometric data and the integration of daylight, hours of operation, and the degree of sophistication of automated lighting control systems for both day and artificial light are additional parameters towards a balanced system approach.

References

1 Cf. Mohamed Boubekri, "Daylighting", pp. 90–95 in this volume.

2 Luminous flux is a human physiological unit describing the photometric power perceived by the eye as an object's brightness (not quantifiable), while illluminance measured in lm/m² (lumen per square meter, 1 lm/m² equals 1 lux) is an object's luminosity. The flux of 1 lm (lumen) emanates from a 1 m² surface of a transparent 1m-radius sphere surrounding a centered light source.

3 Within a 9 m column span, four or five rows of double-faced shelving units are achievable, depending on aisle width. Hence, a lighting concept parallel to the aisles would curtail flexibility regarding the layout of ranges while lighting perpendicular to the aisles would maintain illumination level.

Mohamed Boubekri

Daylighting

Modern libraries are places for learning as well as entertainment. Libraries demand sophisticated lighting systems that are of high visual comfort and flexible enough to respond to the numerous visual tasks taking place in libraries. The daylighting of libraries has some unique physiological requirements that differ from many other building types. The requirements relate to the quantitative and the qualitative aspects of visual performance defined by illuminance levels, distribution of light, glare and visual comfort.

Lighting in libraries is important because of many reasons. Sufficient light levels must be provided for the users to be able to write on horizontal and read on vertical surfaces such as bookshelves. Design consideration may include avoidance of all forms of glare, excessive sunlight penetration and too high or too low contrasts. The dynamic character of daylight must be taken into account in order to maintain the quantitative and qualitative aspects of illumination.

General Lighting Requirement for Libraries

Illuminance Levels

The goal of lighting in libraries is to facilitate the learning experience by providing adequate and comfortable light levels that can be endured for prolonged periods of time. The main visual tasks in libraries are reading and writing texts, differing in size, shapes and contrast levels. Reading tasks may vary from children's books printed in 10- to 14-point type on matte paper to newspapers printed in 7-point type fonts. Other tasks, such as studying illustrations and handwritten pages varying in contrasts are possible. An illuminance level of 300–500 lux is recommended for reading rooms.[1] Both the stacks areas and the general reading areas require toplighting. The stacks need toplighting because the book shelves block light coming from the sides. For the general reading area it is also recommended to have uniform lighting in order to allow for flexibility of use of the space.

Light Uniformity

Uniform light is the most widely used form of illumination in libraries. Such a strategy provides ideally the same illuminance level for the entire workplane where a specific visual task is performed. In practice this is not always possible and, inevitably, there is always variation in illuminance levels on the same workplane and between workplanes. To address this issue of light level variations, lighting standards in several countries prescribe maximum uniformity ratios (ill. 1), ratios between lowest light levels to average light levels in the room that should not be exceeded.[2]

Source document	Uniformity ratio across task area
CIBSE Code for Interior Lighting	0.8 minimum/average
Deutsches Institut für Normung. DIN 5035 Innenraumbeleuchtung mit künstlichem Licht (1979)	0.67 minimum/average
Standards Association of Australia. AS 1680 Code of Practice for Interior Lighting (1976)	0.67 minimum/average
Nederlandse Stichting voor Verlichtingskunde Aanbevelingen voor Binnenverlichting (1981)	0.7 minimum/maximum
CIE Guide on Interior Lighting (1986)	0.8 minimum/average

1 Recommendations for illuminance uniformity

While it is impossible to obtain uniform illumination through side windows, it may be possible to obtain more uniformly distributed natural light using a number of top daylighting strategies. Due to the dynamic quality of daylight, light levels are constantly changing according to the time of day and seasons. As a result, the distribution may be uniform but the daylight levels are never constant throughout the day.

2 Tall windows at the Grainger Engineering Library (Woolen, Molzan and Partners, 1994), on the campus of the University of Illinois at Urbana-Champaign allow deeper daylight penetration and improved visual comfort.

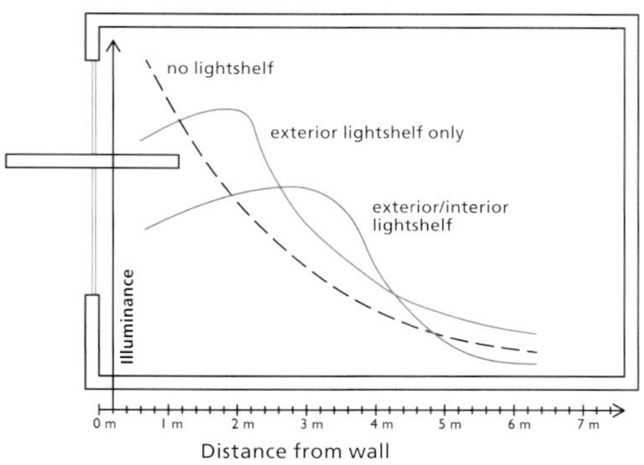

3 Lightshelves deflect light upward and deeper into a room.

4 Clerestories in the reading room of the New York Public Library, Carrère and Hastings, 1911

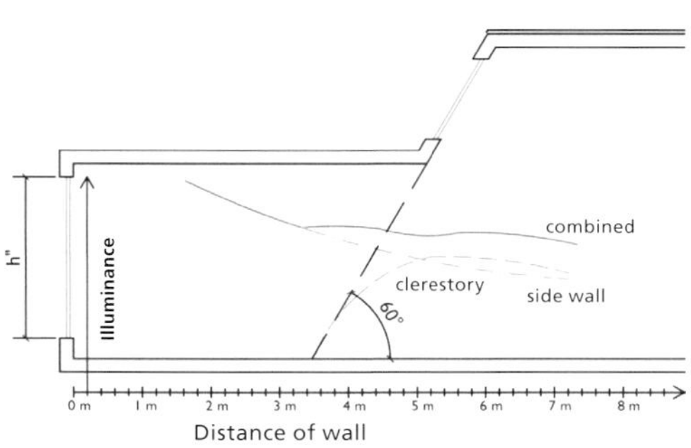

5 Clerestories combined with side windows provide a more balanced daylight distribution inside a room.

Daylighting Strategies

Sidelighting

The two available sidelighting devices are side windows and clerestories.

Side windows

Side windows not only supply daylight but also fulfill the other function of a window, i.e. views and often ventilation. As a result they are the most widely used type of fenestration. From a strictly daylighting point of view, side windows are, however, one of the most problematic daylighting strategies because of the rapid degradation of daylight levels as the distance from the window wall to the interior of the room increases. Daylight levels become very low beyond a distance of 4.5–6 m from the window. A well-known rule of thumb, which relates the size of the window to the depth of daylight penetration, suggests that the depth of the effective daylit zone where daylight levels are more or less significant roughly corresponds to twice the height of the head of the window starting from the floor. However, this rule of thumb in truth only applies to a curtain wall situation where the window extends across the entire width of the room and it does not refer to a singular small window within a wall. Beyond the issue of the depth of daylit zone, a problem that is often encountered with a singular side window is discomfort glare, i.e. discomfort caused by excessive contrast between the high brightness of a singular window and an interior object placed within the window range or an excessive contrast between the window and its darker surrounding surfaces. Tall windows allow for deeper daylight penetration and much improved visual comfort (ill. 2).

In order to overcome the problem of excessive contrast between the window and its adjacent surfaces, it is often recommended to harvest daylight from two different directions such as from two corner side windows. In doing so, the daylight coming from the second window reduces contrast by increasing daylight levels on the surfaces within the room.

Lightshelves may be used to capture some of the excessive daylight in the front of a room and deflect it deeper into the room by means of a highly reflective ceiling (ill. 3). In such a case both the upper side of the lightshelf and the ceiling need to be of high light reflectance. Lightshelves may be interior only, exterior only or combined. In addition to its role of balancing the daylight distribution across a room, a lightshelf may provide shading and cut on excessive glare by obstructing a portion of the sky seen from a certain vantage point inside a room.

Clerestories

Clerestories are side windows placed high in a wall resulting in a deeper daylight penetration within a room (ill. 4). Clerestories may be combined with side windows to provide a more balanced daylight distribution into the stacks area or the reading room of a library (ill. 5).

Toplighting

Top daylighting applications harvest daylight from the roof of a building and channel it inside, providing henceforth a better daylight distribution throughout a room. Under overcast sky conditions, the sky is brighter at zenith then it is at horizon. Consequently the amount of daylight on the roof of a building is much higher than the amount incident on the side facade of a building. Under sunny clear sky condition, the amount of daylight incident on a horizontal surface depends on the altitude angle of the sun and orientation of the facade. The higher the angle the higher the amount of daylight harvested on the roof. The amount of daylight striking vertical surfaces depends, in this case, on the facade azimuth angle, the angle between the normal to the facade and the projection of the sun on the ground.

Skylights
Skylights are the most popular and simplest of the toplighting devices. They consist of apertures within the roof of a building covered with a transparent material (ill. 7). In addition to the transmittance properties of the skylight cover, the efficiency of a skylight system depends largely on the geometric proportions of the skylight well and the light reflectance property of the walls of the skylight well. Given a certain size of the opening of the skylight at the top, a skylight with a splay angle of less than 90 degrees (ill. 6) is more efficient than a straight skylight of the same depth.[3]

In the event of multiple identical skylights, it is recommended[4] that spacing between skylights should not exceed the interior floor-to-ceiling height of a room for a more even daylight distribution throughout the room (ill. 8).

Roof Monitors
Roof monitors (ills. 9, 10) are openings with vertical glazing within a roof. The solid and opaque part of the roof monitor may be sized to block sunlight when it is not wanted. As such they allow for greater control of the daylighting condition. Roof monitors may be orientated in any direction to suit a particular need. If they are faced toward the north, only diffuse daylight may be collected. Toward the east and west, a low sun angle may be easily deflected in order not to create visual discomfort inside the room.

Sawtooth Toplighting System
Sawtooth roofs, in which opaque modular elements are combined with transparent surfaces, whether inclined or in various shapes, are especially popular in commercial, industrial or educational facilities such as gymnasia, libraries, museums,

7 Round skylights at Pierce College Library in Los Angeles, California, HMC Architects, 2013

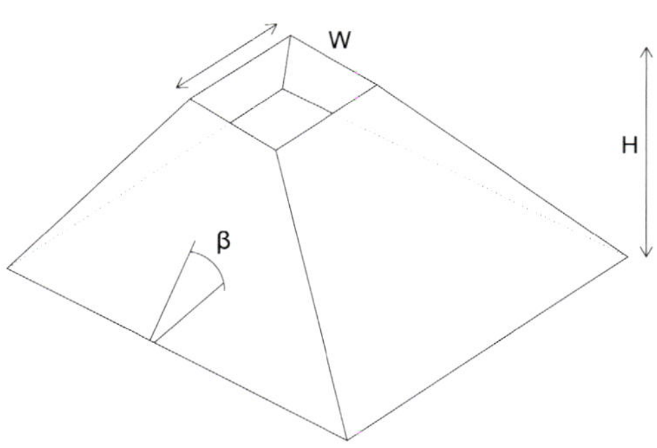

6 Splayed angle skylight

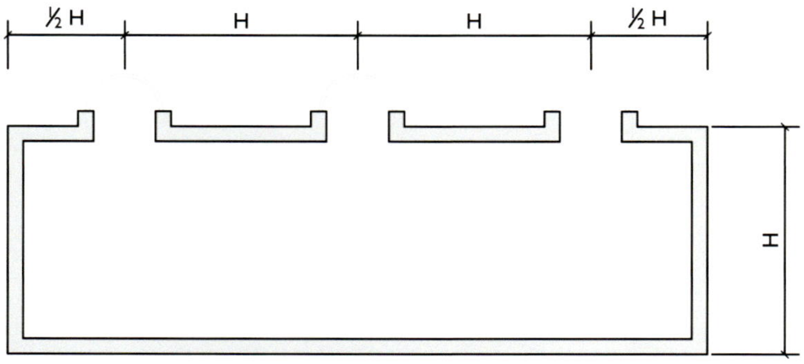

8 Recommended spacing between skylights for light uniformity

warehouses etc. (ills. 11, 12). Sawtooth systems generally harvest light from one direction, are suitable for large spaces and tend to provide a unidirectional daylight distribution. Similar to roof monitors, sawtooth systems may allow sunlight inside or may block it when it is not desired. The sizing of sawtooth systems involves daylighting and energy considerations. From a daylighting perspective, the spacing between the various openings of the sawtooth system is 2½ times the smallest height of the room for more uniform daylight distribution (ill. 13).[5]

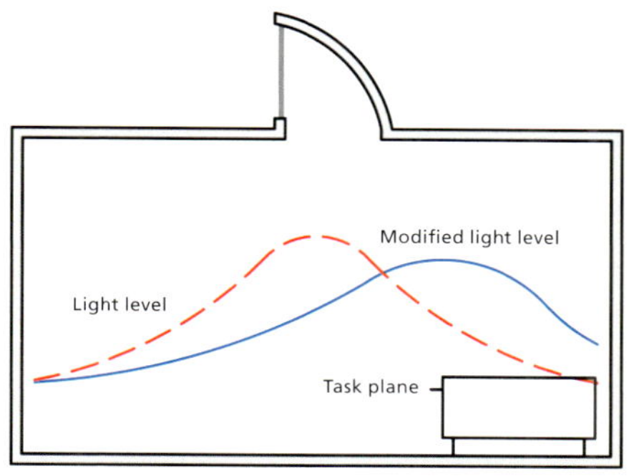

9 One-sided roof monitor

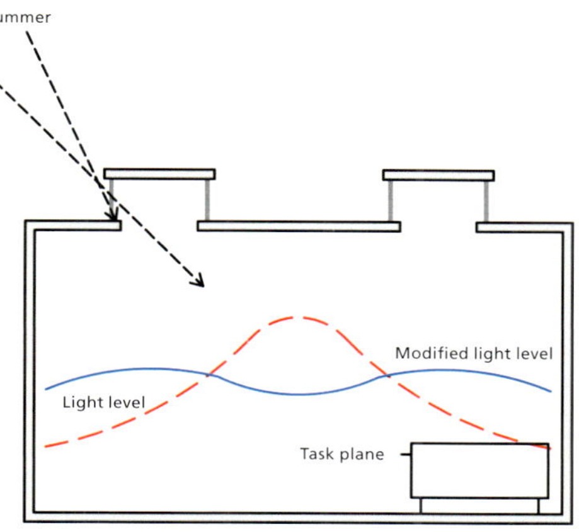

10 Double-sided roof monitor

11 Sawtooth lighting system from the interior at the Los Angeles County Museum of Art, William Pereira, 1965

12 The South Jamaica Branch Library in Queens, New York, Carl Stein and Elemental Architecture, 2010, is equipped with a sawtooth lighting system.

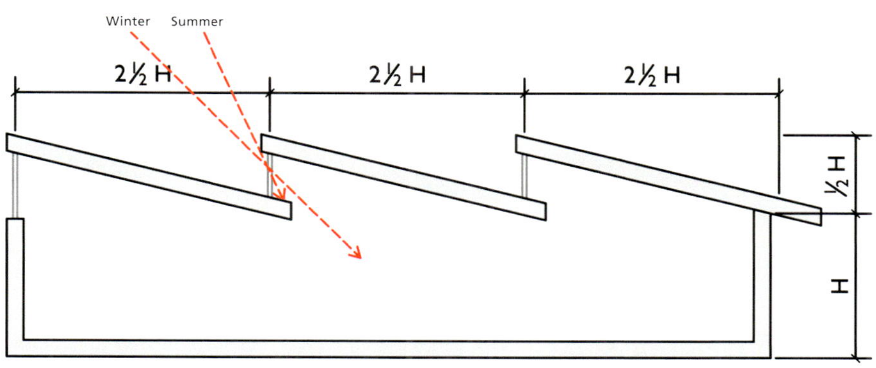

13 Recommended spacing for sawtooth systems

Contemporary daylighting solutions often involve sophisticated design strategies, addressing specific lighting and climate conditions. The following three examples present but a small selection from a wide range of options. They illustrate dramatically different approaches to library daylighting design from different regions of the world. The daylighting options presented in these three case studies range from an emphasis on ceiling height and solar control, to dramatic core daylighting using lightwells and a tensile fabric structure to shade an all-glass building skin. In each case the key aspect is control of daylight penetration and distribution.

Skylight and Daylight Controls

The Public Library in Champaign, Illinois, USA, designed by Ross Barney Architects and opened in 2008, has a total area of 12,260 m^2, seats 431 persons and includes 87 computer stations, five public meeting rooms and a collection of 285,000 books and AV materials. The building's 5.5 m ceiling height allows daylight to flood the entire first floor of the library. Daylight controls are incorporated within the overhead lights throughout the ground and first floors and turn off the electric lights when light levels reach 500 lux. A large linear overhead skylight above the stairwell floods the core area of the building with natural light throughout the day. The west side of the building incorporates brick pillars and copper mesh shades that block the sun while allowing diffuse daylight inside the reading rooms of the library.

The glazing on the south side of the building is fitted with a honeycomb structure, an angular selective technology that redirects light rays, providing high diffuse light transmission while keeping direct solar rays from entering the building (ill. 14, 15). This ray redirection technology provides both more light and better light. Up to 70 % light transmission can be achieved, depending on the insert and glass types specified, while reducing glare and improving visual comfort. The honeycomb structure performs like a series of very small louvers, but in cellular rather than linear form. This structure, combined with a proprietary polymer composition, provides the unique advantage of dynamic performance – increased solar heat protection at peak hours – without the dramatic reduction of invisible light that occurs with other dynamic technologies such as switchable glass. Angular selective glazings are designed to attenuate direct solar radiation, the main source of solar heat gains and glare, while transmitting a significant amount of diffuse daylight.

14 Public Library, Champaign, Illinois, Ross Barney Architects, 2008. The glazing on the south side of the building is fitted with a honeycomb structure to partially redirect light rays.

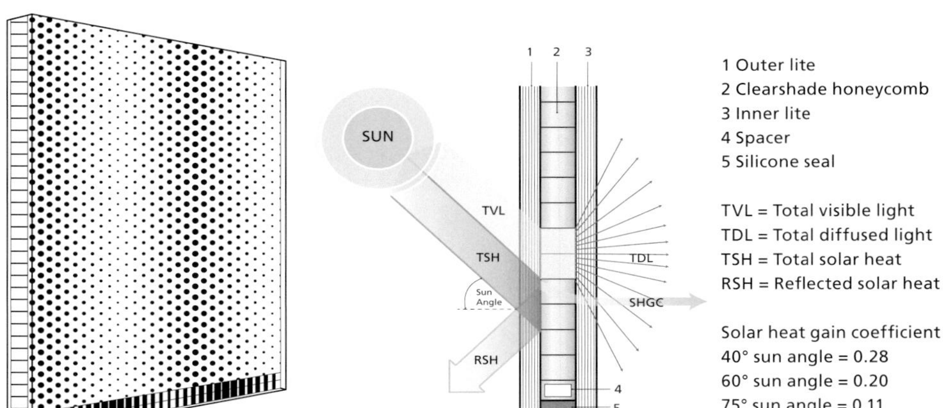

15 Public Library, Champaign. Diagram of glazing unit with inserted honeycomb layer.

17 King Fahad National Library, Riyadh, Saudi Arabia, Gerber Architekten, 2013. Textile awnings cover the facade and provide shade.

18 King Fahad National Library. The refurbishment and extension of the existing library involved a completely new lighting concept.

19 Central Library, TU Delft, the Netherlands, Mecanoo, 1998. The lightwell in the center of the building admits daylight to the core of the building, even reaching the lower floors.

16 King Fahad National Library. Interior of the new library space

Skylights with Customized Shading Membranes

The existing King Fahad National Library in Riyadh, Saudi Arabia, was refurbished and extended by Gerber Architekten in 2013. The cubic shape of the new building completely surrounds the existing building, thus presenting a new structure while preserving the old one (ill. 16–18). The original concrete dome of the old building was replaced by a steel and glass dome, allowing more light into the central portion of the old building. The former roof of the existing building now provides a reading landscape, and the open-access sections on the third floor of the new building can be accessed via bridges from the reading area. Everything is covered by a new roof, punctuated by skylights under which white membranes provide shade and gently distribute the light throughout the entire interior. The exterior of the new facade consists of customized cladding made up of concave and convex rhomboidally shaped textile awnings that filter and soften the harsh sunlight of the region.

Large Lightwell

Central Library, TU Delft, the Netherlands (Mecanoo, 1998, pp. 216–219), is the largest technical-scientific and the central library of the Netherlands. The green roof of the library makes the building a landscape feature, sloping gradually from the ground upward and bearing a cone-shaped structure. This structure provides cover for a large lightwell (ill. 19) that permits daylight to enter the middle section of the building. Daylight fills the building through the central lightwell and the glass walls on three sides.

References

1 Cf. also Wolfgang Rudorf, "Lighting and Illumination", pp. 88–89 in this volume.

2 A. I. Slater, "Illuminance Uniformity on Desks: Where is the limit?", *Lighting Research and Technology*, vol. 22, no. 4, December 1990, pp. 165–174.

3 Mohamed Boubekri, W. Y. Anninos, "Skylight Wells: A Finite Element Approach to Analysis of Efficiency", *Lighting Research & Technology*, vol. 27, no. 3, 1995, pp. 153–159.

4 Illuminating Engineering Society of North America – IESNA, "Recommended Practices for Daylighting", *IES-RP-5-99*, 1999.

5 For a comprehensive discussion of toplighting systems, refer to Mohamed Boubekri, *Daylighting Design: Planning Strategies and Best Practice Solutions*. Basel: Birkhäuser, 2014.

Aat Vos

Library Refurbishment

By definition, libraries will exist forever as every new day brings new information that needs to be organized, disclosed and stored. Theoretically, this means a library building should be built for eternity. In fact, however, buildings slowly fade away as time passes by, so maintenance is of the essence to keep a library operational during its average lifespan of at least 80 years. But maintenance alone will not guarantee this lifelong usage of a library. Customer demand and client behavior changes too. So besides the structural need for makeovers, there apparently is a commercial need. That is why library refurbishment is a necessity in order to keep the library vivid, visible and vibrant. In general, such a refurbishment takes place every 15 to 20 years. In some markets, especially where libraries compete with third commercial parties in leisure markets, libraries need to adapt faster. In the Netherlands, a small overhaul every five years is not uncommon. One can conclude that every library building faces an interior refurbishment at least four, and sometimes up to ten times during its lifespan.

A typical library refurbishment is initiated by the library itself or by the municipality. Interestingly, they both have different motivations. Generally speaking, the municipality will start such a process with the building in mind – the technical maintenance – while the library will be motivated by customer-related and content issues – the commercial maintenance. These different approaches are reflected in the financial discussions that usually occur when refurbishment is addressed, as the typical technical maintenance is part of a long-term scheme that is budgeted, where the commercial maintenance is usually not. These funding issues can result in refurbishment inertness, which is the main reason why so many libraries look outdated. Nevertheless, library refurbishment is an issue every library has to deal with.

When looking at healthy library development over the years, it emerges that the ability to refurbish without too many difficulties plays a key role in a library's long-term success. What is needed for a successful library refurbishment, what are key factors to take into account and how can a sustainable library interior concept be achieved that can adapt over the years?

The Three Library Faces

When talking library design, an interesting fact is that a library in general has three slightly different faces. It can be explained by the ancient Greeks, who already knew three meanings for the word βιβλιοθήκη (*bibliotheca*, library). Mentioning the library, the Greeks could address a building, a collection of books or the library organization. That seems logical, but becomes even more interesting when you think library design. It is all too often that an architect imagines a beautiful building, the interior architect suggests beautiful bookshelves while the library organization itself has detailed design ideas of the user interface based on its continued client contact. Apparently, a library has three faces. But do they work together well? Especially with large projects, this slightly different perception of what a library should be often causes mismatches during the lifespan of a building that could have been prevented, if this insight had been taken into account.

A building consists of several shearing layers.

The Shearing Layers

In his book *How Buildings Learn*,[1] American writer Stewart Brand elaborated the concept coined by architect Frank Duffy of the shearing layers. This concept views buildings as a set of components that evolve in different timescales; Frank Duffy summarized this view as follows: "Our basic argument is that there isn't any such thing as a building. A building properly conceived is several layers of longevity of built components."[2] Apart from the *site* as the geographical setting, the main element of the building is the *structure*. Exterior surfaces cover the structure with a *skin*, and within the structure the *space plan* with walls, ceilings and floors creates rooms. These rooms are serviced by all kinds of technical equipment and *services* in order to keep the structure warm, dry, healthy and so on. And, to complete the shearing layers, all kinds of *stuff* like furniture fill the room. The interesting thing about these layers is that they all have different timescales. In general, structures live for 80 years, skins for 40 years, the space plan for 20 years, services for ten years. Now, what has this to do with libraries?

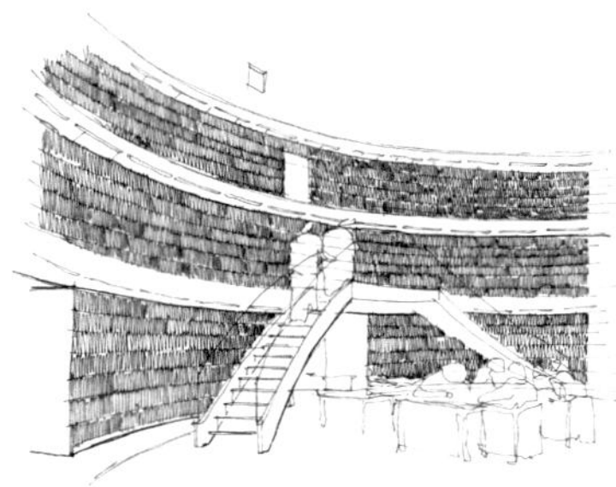

City Library, Stockholm, Gunnar Asplund, 1928. Its great rotunda is lined with circular wooden bookshelves.

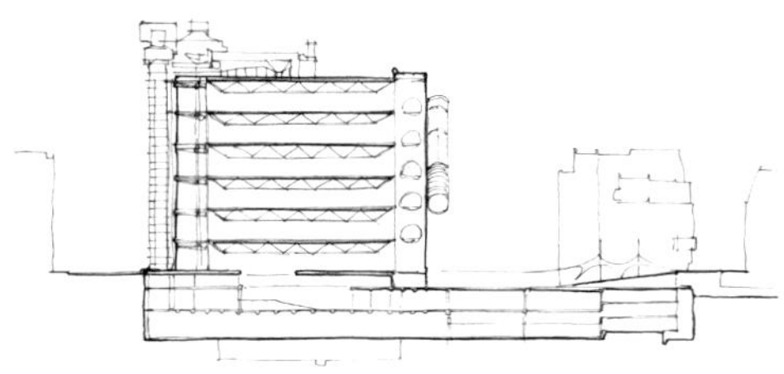

Centre Georges Pompidou, Paris, Renzo Piano and Richard Rogers, 1977. The open spaces without any columns allow for a flexible furnishing and shelving layout.

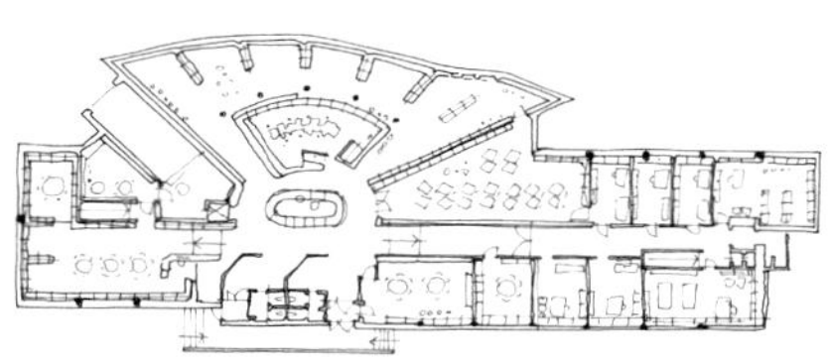

City Library, Rovaniemi, Finland, Alvar Aalto, 1965. The wall-like shelving creates the space plan.

Shelving: Structure, Space Plan or Stuff?

When designing a library, the question should be asked whether the shelving is part of the architecture (the structure or space plan layer in Duffy's terminology), or whether it is part of the layer of "stuff". A great example of shelving as part of the structure can be found at Gunnar Asplund's City Library in Stockholm, Sweden, 1928. Its great rotunda features many stories of circular wooden bookshelves, surrounding a huge open room. An example of a completely different approach, with shelving conceived as a temporary occupation of a room, can be seen at the Centre Georges Pompidou, Paris, 1977, designed by Renzo Piano and Richard Rogers. The Centre features entirely open spaces without any columns, thus enabling every possible furnishing and layout on its substantial 14,000 m^2 floor space. Somewhere in between these two extremes Alvar Aalto's City Library of Rovaniemi, Finland, 1965, can be found with its long wall-like shelving that acts as a space plan. Clearly, when shelves are part of the "stuff layer", a major makeover is far easier to achieve than when shelves are part of the "structure layer" or the "space plan layer". If they are, one might consider not changing the shelving at all during refurbishment processes, and turn to other improvements instead, thus leaving the architecture intact. Indeed, fixed shelving can be a restriction to future improvements. This leads to the question of the relation between a library building and a library interior – what are its key determinants?

A Library Is its Interior

The three faces of the library converge in its interior. Here architecture, books and the library organization meet, and are joined by, interior design. That is why shelving layout should always be designed with both the architecture and the user interface in mind. A library interior is completely different from an office interior or a domestic environment, the latter ones taking into account, to a larger degree, individual taste as a measure of their main design choices. A library interior is far more than just a collection of stuff and furniture brought together under an umbrella of individual design preferences: it determines fully the way the library is able to operate. A library interior that is not developed together with the library organization is bound to fail. To put it this way: when architects and librarians do not team up in designing the library interior, the architect's dream might become the librarian's nightmare. There is no way an architect is able to create a library interior without carefully consulting and understanding the third face of the library, and librarians should stand up and insist upon architects to do so. Workshops are wonderful occasions to discuss a necessary library refurbishment.

Emergence of Library Interior Design

In a way, the birth of contemporary European library interior design can be found in Germany, at the City Library in Gütersloh, Germany, 1984, designed by architect Wolf Hilbertz. This library was among the first to disassociate itself from traditional libraries, and introduced new elements to the library program such as a coffee bar, very fast book return logistics and different atmospheres to reflect special content. This forerunner was followed in 1993 by the Library of Münster, Germany, by architects Bolles-Wilson: a popular, active and open information center that featured a for that time innovative book collection divided into three areas, the so-called *dreigeteilte Bibliothek* (tripartite library): a background archive collection, a standard collection and a special highlighted part of the collection, all beautifully composed as a perfect example of a structure and space plan layer library. In the meantime, many Scandinavian countries built their *Kulturhuser*: buildings with many cultural, social and municipal functions combined.

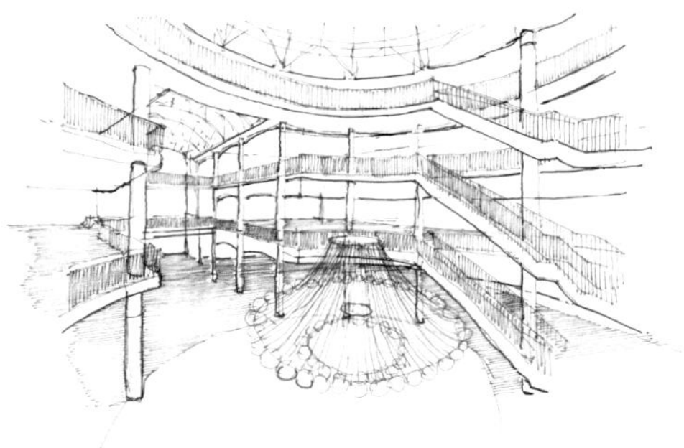

City Library, Gütersloh, Germany, Wolf Hilbertz, 1984, was one of the first libraries to introduce new elements such as a coffee bar to the library program.

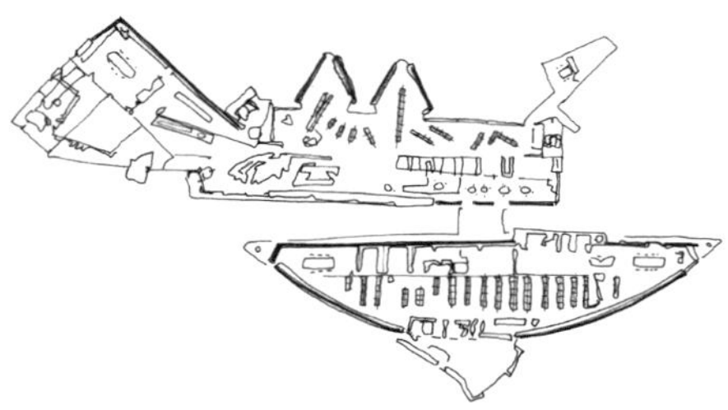

City Library, Münster, Germany, Bolles-Wilson, 1993, sketch of floor plan

In 1999, Joseph Pine and James Gilmore coined the term "experience economy", stating that the creation of an experience around a product had become an inevitable necessity in order to be able to reach customer satisfaction and achieve purchase.[3] The Library of Smallingerland, opening as the first Dutch "experience library" in 2001, quickly adapted this, as did many others, such as the Amstelveen Library, 2001, also in the Netherlands. These libraries added all kinds of different experiences to the library visit, introducing the first retail-like shopping windows, gathering areas and display stands to the library floor. When the Almere Library in the Netherlands in 2002 started to research and analyze client behavior, the connection between retail approach and library layout first became evident. This analysis, initiated by the Almere Library, stated that a typical overall library user does not exist. Instead, there are various types of users or target groups. For example, young mothers with children are mostly interested in easy-to-read literature, lifestyle cooking and picture books for their kids. Or middle-aged men are mostly interested in thrillers, traveling and success stories. Therefore, the library should be divided into various "mini libraries", each addressing one specific target group. These departments were initially referred to by the names of popular Dutch magazines, addressing the same profile as the library department. The name of one of these magazines, *Libelle*, targeting young mothers with children, then became the name of the entire concept. Is has evolved over the years, and the efforts made to investigate the needs of their client groups have reached almost scientific proportions. Later, this idea of various library departments resulted in a number of library formulas that have continued to shape Dutch libraries since the early 2000s. Most of these formulas were originally initiated by regional library organizations, followed by a national library initiative, funded by the state. Today, a Dutch library can decide to have its interior refurbished according to the rules of several ready-to-roll library formulas. They consist of (usually eight) different departments, all with a distinct look and atmosphere. The so-called "White Box" (design: Jos de Vries) features a rich variety of shapes and mainly uses the color white. The "Black Box" (design: SVT) features more basic shapes and is characterized – not surprisingly – by the use of black. As these formulas are quite expensive to implement, the interdisciplinary design studio aatvos recently designed an affordable "budget formula" called the "Blue Box".

As clients are used to a social and urban context that renews itself faster than ever, the need for library refurbishment seems to accumulate faster over the years as well. In a way, library design reflects retail or car design: the average lifespan of a shop or car nowadays hardly exceeds five to seven years, where it used to be seven to ten years a decade ago. Therefore the commercial maintenance becomes more important. What do these rapid makeovers mean for the way media are displayed?

The Book Collection: Four Quadrants, Tripartite or "Many Worlds"

In the old days, libraries were straightforward. The book collection was divided into four quadrants, and one could find fiction and non-fiction books, split into two age groups: adults and youth. The non-fiction is usually organized by a division system based upon content. As we have seen, since the innovation initiated at the Library of Münster other approaches have ensued. With the introduction of experience libraries, target group libraries and library formulas, the need for a new division system arose. In general, various systems can now be distinguished. The first, the traditional four quadrants, is still around. As is the second, namely the tripartite library that we have seen in Münster. A third system has been first introduced at the experience library in Smallingerland and developed over the years into various library formulas such as the White, Black or Blue Box. It evolved into a collection of "mini libraries" or "worlds". An average library that is divided into worlds usually contains six to twelve different departments. Each one of them contains a specific part of the library, either addressing a specific target group, or grouping media around a specific content profile, thus splitting the library into smaller parts that can easily be overseen. In a way, this third system reflects modern society, as people want to spend less time to find their way. So, in order to keep up with social change, libraries should consider implementing a new division system when refurbishment takes place. But of course, there is more to a contemporary library than just books.

A Third Place

With their first place being their home and their second place being their work, many people feel the need for a third place, that is a free, safe, cozy, available, accessible public space that is just out there and offers hospitality and a coffee to stay or to go. Think of a small business meeting on neutral ground, spending time with friends, charging a phone while surfing the web, or just taking a short break. The company that has really turned third places into a worldwide success is Starbucks. Starbucks sells coffee by offering such a third place, and they would not have achieved their enormous success without a deep understanding of the need for such a space and its special amenities in today's urban life. Many semi-public places like museums, hospitals or railway stations have followed their lead. However, at practically all of those third places one is expected to buy at least something. This is where libraries come in: they are able to offer such a place free of charge – and should do so, in order to ensure future customer connection and client satisfaction. Besides welcoming customers, what can libraries use those third places for?

New Functionality

Refurbishment is by definition initiated because library interiors no longer meet actual requirements and are no longer equipped for the job. Modern functionality, first introduced at the Gütersloh Library, continues to conquer library space. As books partly withdraw from many clients' main interest, and are becoming both function and decoration at the same time, new functionalities like courses, classes, seminars, places for workout and workshops, classrooms, room for debate and cultural events, music performances and so on enter the library premises at great speed. Libraries become places of social education, cultural encounters and meeting places for lifelong learning and co-creation. Libraries have come to play a key role in the social emancipation of minorities, a stepping-stone for the have-nots to develop a social life again. In order to accommodate these new functionalities, libraries need space. Space for classrooms, study places for individuals and groups, café-like areas for informal gathering, meetings, hang-outs, lots of places for display and studios for hands-on workshops. In a way, libraries turn into small-scale department stores with a blend of functions that are all attached to the low-key, free public library brand. These new functionalities reload the library brand. This is an opportunity for refurbishing libraries one should not miss.

Amstelveen Library, the Netherlands, 2001, accommodates a "poetry experience diner", created as part of the refurbishment by Aat Vos in 2012.

Digitecture

With smartphones being ubiquitous, libraries need to find ways to cope with the danger of a social-physical vacuum these all-around gadgets bring along. This occurs when the smartphone owner is more connected to his online social network than to his offline environment. Libraries need to come up with technical solutions to neutralize this vacuum. While the technology is still under development, it is important to conceptualize such a library environment and find ways to implement solutions when refurbishing a library. What about a library that notifies you when your friends are around, offers screen-like walls to swipe your timeline on, touch tables to share your latest pictures and the ability to co-create the public atmosphere in a game-like setting or adaptive rooms that visitors can make their own by chancing color, sound, images, acoustics and smell? In the near future we will see an increasing presence of digital technologies in architecture, followed by a merge of these two professions into digitecture. In this field, the classic difference between digital (communication) and architecture (space) disappears. We will see spaces with functionalities we have not experienced before, making it possible that people do no longer visit *the* library, but visit *their* library instead. RFID and iBeacon technology can be of a great help.

In the Netherlands, a number of "formulas", i.e. preconceived interior design solutions, make quick refurbishment of a library easier to achieve.
The "Blue Box", designed by aatvos, is an affordable formula that was used to refurbish Voorburg Library in 2013.

Public Library, Kerkrade, the Netherlands, Alex Talsma and aatvos, 2014. This refurbishment involved a holographic touch shopping window, RFID-operated display and signage elements,and media walls.

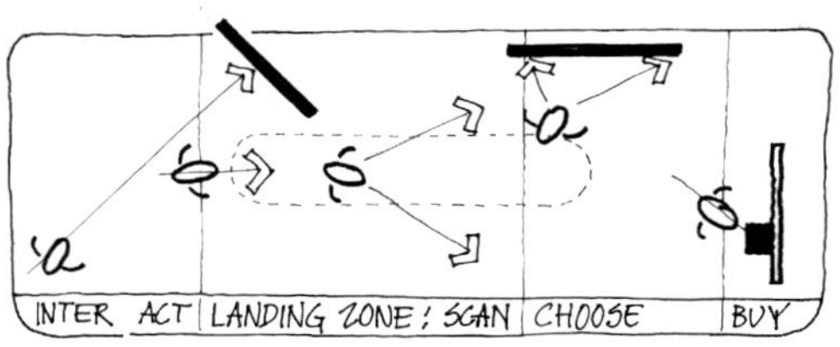

A customer or library user goes through four stages in order to make a purchase or borrow a book.

Use of RFID

As many books are already equipped with radio frequency identification or RFID chips, this technology can be used to do far more than just smoothening the lending process. When shelves and display tables are equipped with antennas, static furniture can become responsive to its content. As touch technology conquers the display world with great speed, the intuitive interactive library has become a reality. The first signs of this development can be seen in the work of Alex Talsma and aatvos for the Public Library in Kerkrade, the Netherlands, 2014, featuring a holographic touch shopping window, many interactive display and signage elements, media walls and so on. It is only a matter of time, before e-paper will be used for signage solutions, enabling the library to communicate in real time with its customers throughout the library. In many ways, the next stage of interior architecture has become more digital than ever, offering great opportunities for libraries to take the next steps towards client participation and co-creation when refurbishing the library. But how can we cope with all these new functionalities? How can all of this be brought together in a refurbishment project?

Why We Buy

When planning a contemporary refurbishment it is useful to start by considering the library layout and floor plan. As we noted earlier, it is important to distinguish the type of library one has to deal with. Is it the classic "structure layer" library or a more flexible "stuff layer" library? In both cases, similar challenges have to be faced. As the traditional library layout is no longer suitable for the job, a more intellectual approach is needed to get people to use the library. Paco Underhill[4] has described four simple stages every customer needs to go through in order to be able to purchase a good, or – in terms of a library – borrow a book. At first, one has to be attracted in order to enter the library. Secondly, once inside, a landing strip or decompression zone enables one to reduce speed and to open oneself for library content. This is facilitated by display furniture positioned in the lower part of the visual field; an overview across the library environment is simultaneously possible at the upper part of the visual field. The third stage consists of distinguishing library departments, the above-mentioned so-called "worlds". Display and graphic tools are needed to communicate a world's identity. And the last stage is the actual interaction with the product itself, in this case the library book. Note: it is only after traversing these four stages that the customer selects the book. A difficult part of a library as such is its content: books all look alike. In a way, an attractive and varied display is easier to achieve in a department store than in a library because of the greater product variety: a wheelbarrow has a completely different aesthetic than a lipstick, for instance. Libraries need to be able to draw attention to one specific book or a collection of books by employing non-book elements, such as visual communication.

Visual Identity

The traditional library interior usually has a consistently designed atmosphere, with one type of floor covering, a balanced color scheme and a lighting design throughout the entire space. When a library is to be refurbished, one might consider refitting this palette with just the latest materials and fresh colors. However, one might seize the opportunity to adapt to the new developments mentioned earlier, resulting in a more differentiated library interior design.

One of the main prerequisites is communication. The above-mentioned four stages every customer goes through imply that communication proceeds according to a sequence of different messages that all need to be designed for a specific task. For instance, the entrance communication has to be readable from a distance of 50 to 30 m, the names of the different departments from as far as 30 to 15 m, and one specific book promotion from approximately 3 m. This means that font size, word count and the dimensions of visuals vary due to their task within the library.

When a refurbishment is also used to change the way the collection is segmented, and various departments are introduced, the need for a distinguished look and feel might emerge. It is clear that a differentiation by color, texture or lighting helps to communicate different departments. And of course, colors themselves are able to communicate a message too, so that for example red is an obvious color for books on crime and passion.

Also, when new functionalities are added, the typology of the library interior changes too. While the traditional library interior includes shelving, seating elements and counters, new functionalities might introduce new elements to the library interior, changing its visual identity. The quality as a third place for instance brings lounge furniture, armchairs and espresso bars to the library, while the experience library brings along display furniture, exhibitions, shopping windows and props. Other options might be a television studio, music rehearsal rooms, meeting rooms, new digital functionalities or stages for performing arts.

The Next Refurbishment

One might gain the impression that, due to these complexities generated by the refurbishment, the library becomes inert to future changes, thus making the next refurbishment a complicated and expensive undertaking. That is not necessarily the case. If the design is carried out in a smart way, it consists of different layers. One can think of a layer of "necessities" that are usually expensive, like shelving systems, tables and chairs, and a second layer of visual identity that contains all visuals, graphics, color, textures and so on. These elements are usually cheap and easily changeable, so a next library makeover can be done at this level only and hence at minimal cost. For example, one might consider easy-to-replace carpets or wall visuals. By designing a refurbishment this way, library design becomes durable, and enables the library to adapt to future changes that, as we have seen, will occur with an increasing speed.

It is the interior designer's job to ensure that all of these different elements and different layers work together consistently. When this is accomplished, a refurbished library not only has updated looks, but – far more important – has been equipped with enhanced and increased functionality that will prepare the library for the next successful episode of its lifespan.

References

1 Stewart Brand, *How Buildings Learn.* New York: Viking, 1994.

2 http://en.wikipedia.org/wiki/Shearing_layers

3 Joseph Pine and James Gilmore, *The Experience Economy.* Boston: Harvard Business School Press, 1999.

4 Paco Underhill, *Why We Buy: The Science Of Shopping.* New York: Simon & Schuster, 2000.

Wolfgang Rudorf
Liliane Wong

Shelving

City Library, Stockholm, Gunnar Asplund, 1928, was one of the last large libraries to use perimeter shelving.

Historically, precious handwritten books were stored in boxes or chests and carried near the person of the owner. The printing press brought about an accessibility to books and with common book ownership book titles were written on the spine. Shelves were designed to display these spines. Early shelving was made of wood and often built into the walls of the room itself. This perimeter shelving, prevalent throughout many centuries, has become obsolete since the early 20th century, with Asplund's City Library in Stockholm one of the last prominent examples. With the introduction of cast iron and subsequently steel, shelves, both perimeter and freestanding, were fabricated of materials that could withstand the required physical loads. A special case were multi-tiered cast iron systems that supported not only the weight of the books but also the floor platforms and even the roof structure, thus making shelving part of the load-bearing structure. The introduction of digital technology in the 1990s unleashed conjectures of future bookless libraries. Despite such predictions digital technology has been integrated into the library without the elimination of the book. Today, the physical collection remains a critical part of the library and the accommodation of the collection a crucial part of library design.

Widener Library, Harvard University, Cambridge, Massachusetts, c. 1914. This construction view shows a portion of the fifth stack tier, carried by girders over the ground-story reading room. The lower part of the shelf supports are extended into the aisles to carry wide fixed bottom shelves.

Shelving Systems

Shelving system types are cantilever style, case style, high-density and automated-retrieval. Cantilever and case style are commonly used in all libraries and design requirements refer primarily to these types. High-density and automated-retrieval storage have individual requirements specific to their system. In the U.S., shelving systems are standardized and designs of libraries are based on the availability of pre-determined shelving sizes. In Europe, shelving is often custom-designed.

Shelving systems, be they cantilever or case style, are modular and consist of multiples of a single shelf unit. The dimensions of the single unit (SFU, single-faced shelving unit) as stand-alone or placed back to back with another unit (DFS, double-faced shelving unit) form the basis of the shelving system. Heights depend on the numbers of shelves per unit, with units seven shelves high at typical stacks. In reference areas shelving units may be two to three shelves high. The characteristics of these units impact the design of many different aspects of the library; book capacity, structure, layout, lighting, egress.

The Jacob-und-Wilhelm-Zentrum in Berlin (bottom) uses four-post case style shelving units, while the Seattle Central Library (top) has a cantilever shelving system. These are the two systems predominately used in library collections.

Stacks and Layout

A row of shelving units, single-faced or double-faced, makes up a range. Stacks consist of ranges of shelves and the aisles that give access to them. Aisle nomenclature specifies their locations within the shelving layout; side aisles run parallel to the stacks while cross aisles run perpendicular to the side aisles, providing breaks in the side aisles. End aisles are at the end of a group of ranges and may serve single-faced sections against a wall. Main aisles, also perpendicular to side aisles, are a part of major access routes.

As means of egress the characteristics of the aisle – width, height and length – affect the occupant's health, safety and welfare and must comply with building, safety and accessibility regulations. Optimal shelving layouts use ranges of six to seven double-faced shelving units, although practice permits longer ranges. The length of such a range maximizes the linear continuity of shelving while remaining within comfortable lengths of travel.

While book capacity is important, human comfort is of equal importance in shelving layouts. Repetitive shelving ranges are, in fact, densely positioned walls and, depending on the aisle width and shelving height used, they impact the psychological perception of the space. In heavily trafficked urban libraries, for example, a shelving aisle of minimum width could be perceived as less inviting than a wider one. Similarly, shelving ranges of more than six shelves in length (each shelf at 1.2 m) comply with travel distances but may be perceived as oppressive or even threatening in some situations. Shelving heights (or numbers of shelves per unit height) are determined as a compromise of volume capacity and the atmosphere created by such height. Seven-shelf high shelves are most efficient in terms of book storage, but their height renders the top shelves inaccessible for universal reach. Allowing also for the advantage of organizing oversized volumes within the running order of the collection (requiring greater spacing of the shelves), shelving height in publicly accessible libraries is typically limited to six shelves or even five shelves. While maximum shelving capacity is an issue of economics, the design parameters of aisle widths and shelving lengths and heights are determinants of the atmosphere of a stack area.

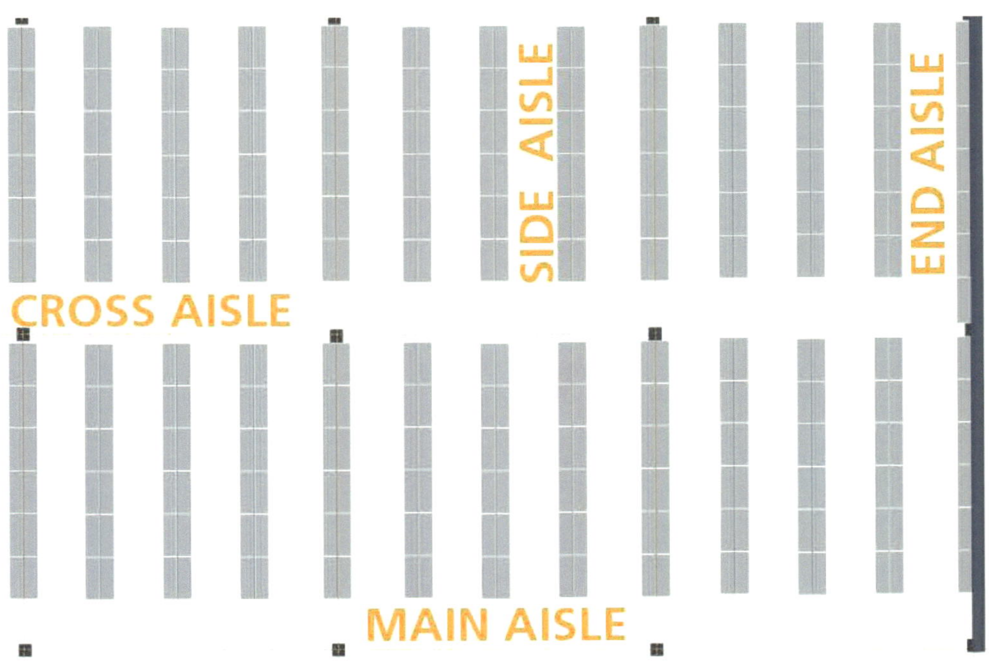

Typical shelving layout

Classification Systems

Determined by available space, structure, economy and efficiency, shelving layouts have an impact on the physical placement of books. The need for systems of book location originated in the second half of the 19th century with the introduction of the open-stack library. Since then, all books had to be identified through a library classification system. While the earliest systems were enumerative for book location, today's systems are distinguished by different types of order; classification through chronology, subject, geography, language as well as minute subdivisions of such classification. The predominant universal systems include Dewey Decimal Classification, Library of Congress Classification, Universal Decimal System. There are also some nation-specific systems such as Britain's Bliss Classification, Sweden's SAB Sveriges Allmanna Bibliotekforening, Germany's Gesamt-Hochschul-Bibliotheks-Systematik (GHBS), the Colon Classification, used primarily in India, Japan's Nippon Decimal Classification, Korea's Korean Decimal Classification, China's Chinese Library Classification (CLC) and the Russian Library-Bibliographical Classification (LBC). In addition, single subject fields have their own classification systems. For example, the MCS stands for Mathematics Subject Classification or PACS is the Physics and Astronomy Classification Scheme.

A widespread classification system is the Dewey Decimal Classification system (DDC), a system created by Mevil Dewey in 1876. It is most prevalent in the Anglo-American realm and in use in 85 % of all U.S. libraries, in particular public libraries and some smaller academic libraries. This system of classification consists of ten classes; 000- computer science, library and information science and general works, 100- philosophy and psychology, 200- religion, 300- social science, etc. Each class is further divided into divisions; for example, a book on European economy would be labeled 330.94 in which the 100th's place denotes social sciences, the 10th's place is specific to the subject of economics and the decimals reference geographical location, in this case, Europe. Most research and academic libraries in the U.S. use the Library of Congress (LCC) system of classification developed by Herbert Putnam in 1897 for the Library of Congress, or a similar universal system. Subjects are divided into broad categories that are enumerative. The system uses 21 letters of the alphabet to denote different subjects. For example; B is for philosophy, psychology and religion, K is for law, N for fine arts, etc. Each of these subjects is further divided into subcategories. For example, Class B is divided into B for general philosophy, BC for logic, BD for speculative philosophy, BF for psychology, BH for aesthetics, with each class letter followed by a number sequence. Books are stored and arranged in ascending order according to classification. Repetitive bays of double-faced shelving are conducive to sequential book numbering. LCC-classified books are optimally placed within a shelving layout that permits a consecutive order by section. The Book Spiral at the Seattle Central Library (OMA, 2004, pp. 154–157), where the DDC classifications were incorporated into the signage system on the floor, is an example of a system in which book classifications and sequencing were considered as part of the design and shelving layout. The use of single-faced shelving, typically placed on walls, maximizes the book capacity of a space but complicates the continuous flow of the numbering sequence.

At the Sendai Mediatheque in Japan (Toyo Ito, 2001) an orthogonal shelving layout is placed in a space without a repetitive structural grid.

Shelving Applications

In application, these general principles and dimensions can be and, in fact, are adjusted according to the collection and the user type. Multiples of densely placed shelving bays are most applicable for stacks where storage capacity is a priority and user access limited to book retrieval. This economy of repeated bays of rectilinear shelving cannot be overestimated and is confirmed by its use in the majority of libraries. At the Lewis Library at Princeton University (Frank Gehry, 2008, pp. 230–231) that is uniquely characterized by curving, sculptural forms, where nevertheless orthogonal floor plans and stack shelving plans prevail, providing repetitive and efficient rectilinear bays. Similarly, at Sendai Mediatheque in Japan (Toyo Ito, 2001) economical, orthogonal and repetitive shelving layouts are utilized in a library that is otherwise designed without a repetitive structural grid.

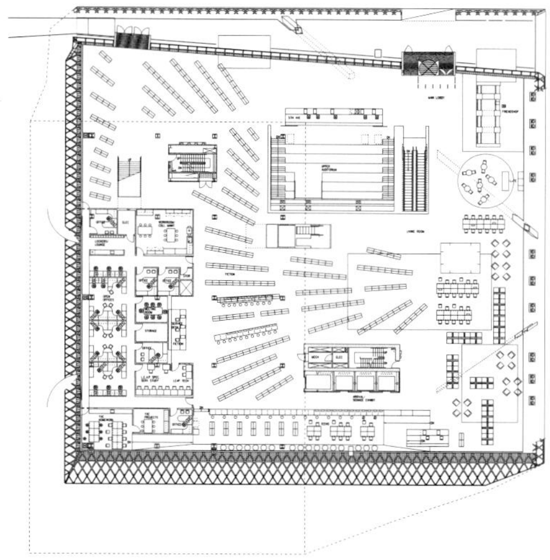

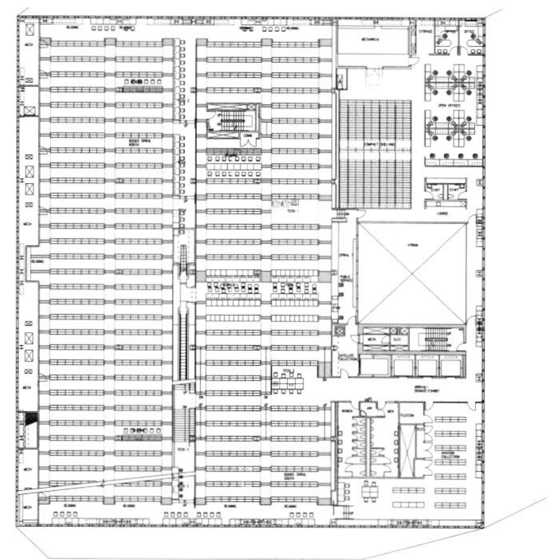

Seattle Central Library, OMA, 2004. The sixth floor plan (right) shows densely arranged stacks in repetitive ranges. On the second floor (left), repetitive shelving bays have ranges of different lengths and are arranged in a playful pattern, resulting in the less formal atmosphere of the Living Room.

Shelving layouts at TU Delft Central Library (Mecanoo, 1998, pp. 216–219) are based on the Pareto Principle, a theory that the majority of users use only a small percentage of all available books. With a total collection of almost 1 million items, the TU Delft Library shelving design accommodates the majority of the volumes, i.e. the "less used", in the closed stacks below ground, while the "most used", in this case 80,000 volumes, are on display in the general reading room on four-story high, suspended steel frame shelving.

The recommended shelving limits adjust to the needs of different collections and users by variations of range lengths and aisle widths. Stacks, with their storage function, may often be designed with longer ranges while other parts of the library such as the reference or new books area may be designed with shorter lengths and wider aisles suited to frequent use. The many uses of shelving at the Seattle Central Library illustrate this planning concept. At the Book Spiral on floors five to eight, the stacks are densely arranged and repetitive ranges of six and seven shelves (7.2–8.4 m) extend the maximum permissible length. The reference room shelving arrangement in comparison is a classic bay of a five-shelf (6 m) range with generous aisle space that is conducive to the frequent use characteristic of the reference collection. In the Living Room on the second floor, repetitive shelving bays are used in a less structured fashion with ranges of different lengths, arranged in a playful pattern. Such a configuration accommodates fewer books but provides a different atmosphere.

High-density shelving (compact shelving) layouts[2] differ from cantilevered or case style shelving primarily in aisle requirements. Based on the concept of moveable ranges, high-density shelving slides on a system of tracks. With this mobility, shelving ranges are placed immediately next to one another without individual aisles. Groups of ranges share a track system that includes the accommodation for a single aisle. When access is required at a particular range, the ranges move apart, manually or electronically, creating an egress aisle where needed. With this system, the space requirements are half that of regular shelving.[1] Due to the density of the shelves, however, the floor loads are doubled and require additional structural support (see Structural Concepts, pp. 70–79). The limits of the range lengths are the same as with cantilevered shelving. At Viana do Castelo Public Library in Portugal (Alvaro Siza, 2007, pp. 192–193) different lengths of ranges correspond to the different uses of the shelves from conservation to storage of periodicals.

References

1 "Description of Shelving Options", University of Chicago Library Shelving Additions, University of Chicago Board of Trustees, May 11, 2005, p. 3.

2 The alternate option of off-site storage is discussed in: Danuta A. Nitecki, Curtis L. Kendrick, *Library Off-Site Shelving: Guide for High-Density Facilities*, Englewood, CO: Libraries Unlimited, 2001.

Michael Franke-Maier

Orientation and Wayfinding Systems

All over the world, library staff are given to organizing their library spaces with an abundance of notices, stickers and signs explaining how to use the library facilities and the media within. One might, rather mischievously, suppose that this is a product of a professional compulsion to categorize, explain and inform. But it could also be shortcomings in the architecture that give rise to such behavior. The lack of adequate signage in a building – whether the product of excessive respect for the architecture or of a minimalist design aesthetic, whether because the converted building was not originally designed as a library or has not been modernized for a long while, or whether simply due to a lack of will to finance orientation and wayfinding systems – inevitably leads to precisely this phenomenon of improvisation, and it is therefore no surprise that literature for librarians invariably contains a do-it-yourself chapter.

The Swiss typographer Adrian Frutiger, an iconic designer of signage and orientation systems, has argued that "any ... movement has become almost unthinkable without directional signs and inscriptions."[1] Others, however, have demonstrated that a minimalist design approach is not necessarily incompatible, provided that the routes within a building are defined from the outset and the architecture concept facilitates intuitive passage through the building. In such cases, the wayfinding system is a product of the architecture and one needs no further orientation aids. The other extreme is the opulent use of conspicuous signage and wayfinding methods to achieve what Andrew McDonald calls a "wow effect",[2] or to give spaces a particular atmosphere that in addition to its functional purpose contributes to the architectural quality of the building.

Libraries as Urban Magnets

Orientation and wayfinding systems begin with the external skin of the building. the Seattle Central Library designed by Rem Koolhaas' office OMA (2004, pp. 154–157) or Zaha Hadid's design for the Library and Learning Center of Vienna University of Economics and Business employ integral dynamic lighting concepts to announce the presence of the library within its surroundings so that the library becomes a magnet in the urban realm.

But a conspicuous outward appearance does not tell us anything about the design of he internal orientation and wayfinding system. This could, for example, be realized using quite conventional means. So what makes the orientation and wayfinding systems of libraries different from those of fun pools, zoos or airports? And what do they have in common?

The Library and Learning Center (Zaha Hadid, 2013) at Vienna University of Economics and Business in the Leopoldstadt district: a fascinating form that attracts attention and invites one to actively engage with the building.

A typical element of bibliographic signage systems: aisle labels at the ends of bookshelves as seen in the ZLB – Zentral- und Landesbibliothek Berlin, American Memorial Library.

Wayfinding Principles

Libraries, if we consider them purely in terms of being repositories of books, do require special consideration: the book numbers of the bibliographic classification system are the final element of a chain of wayfinding signs and labels that lead the visitor from subject area to book aisle to individual shelf. Of particular interest is the transition from the architectural wayfinding system to the bibliographic classification system. The spiral layout of the Seattle Central Library, for example, employs a novel solution to this problem using flush-fitted mats emblazoned with the numbers of the Dewey Decimal Classification system – the most widely used system in the USA – to mark the aisles. These mats can also be easily removed and placed elsewhere, making it easy and straightforward to extend or reorganize the collection as needed.[3] This design solution is a direct response to a need for flexibility and easy adaptability. A permanent sign, either in the floor or on the wall, would be much more laborious to change.

But while books still play a central, albeit gradually diminishing role, modern libraries are now also comprehensive service centers that handle numerous other media and digital services. In this respect, orientation and wayfinding systems in libraries differ only marginally from those of other buildings and therefore follow the general principles of communication design.[4]

In airports and rail stations, for example, the signage is conspicuous and appears frequently to reduce the stress caused by "pressure of time or anxiety about taking the wrong flight or train."[5] In libraries, however, this may only be relevant for certain areas such as for textbook collections. In all other respects, libraries are much like any other public building where "orientation signage is an aspect that needs to be addressed for each individual situation" and "the need for a complex or a simple wayfinding system depends largely on how extensive the library space is."[6]

A key design consideration, especially with regard to the choice of wording, is the user group it is designed for, and the vocabulary used must be adapted accordingly. People are guided by the directional signage of the wayfinding system to a particular place or object.[7] The orientation system, on the other hand, shows the "topographical location of objects", for example on an overview plan, or "clarifies what one can expect to find where."[8]

Black rubber mats laid flush with the concrete floor mark the aisles of the Seattle Central Library (OMA, 2004), using the Dewey Decimal numbering system 000–999.

Mixed Reality: Space as a Social Network

Today, architects need to ask themselves how hybrid libraries that provide both printed as well as electronic media can mesh effectively with the virtual world of apps, with GPS, RFID, QR codes and NFC, with audio guides and in future also with data goggles. In the same way that architects collaborate at a certain point with interior designers, they will need to work with the designers of virtual worlds. At present, these virtual representations are usually made after completion of the building. Noteworthy examples include the online systems for the Basel University Library[9] or the Hamburg City Libraries.[10] These libraries have created visual guides to the structure of their buildings that show the location of books and services and make these available as smartphone-compatible apps to help users to find their way as well as what they are looking for.

The ZLB – Zentral- und Landesbibliothek Berlin has found a clever way of combining modern technology with the services it enables and the library's corporate design and corresponding orientation and wayfinding system. As part of a revision of its corporate identity, the library took the opportunity to redesign its orientation and wayfinding systems. It also introduced self-service book lending using an RFID-based system. All three of these elements come together at the book returns terminal: the logo – which depending on your viewpoint could be the outline of an open book or alternatively a laptop – precedes the wording of the signs, and at the returns terminal the RFID antenna forms part of the shape of the logo. The logo is used consistently as a key component of the library's branding concept.[11]

A System of Options

The existing literature on orientation and wayfinding systems for libraries generally covers the aspects of typography, material, form and color, signage typologies and pictograms, barrier-free access and more recently also Universal Design, as well as the elements to which these are affixed. For a comprehensive breakdown of the systematic design of classical wayfinding systems, it is worth consulting one of these informative publications, including some of the older publications. Here we will examine only some of the design options available. Focusing especially on the role of orientation and wayfinding systems as an atmospheric element of library design, we will present both classical approaches as well as some innovative and somewhat surprising examples.

Right: The online guidance system v:scout by arTec – visual solutions (here in use at the Bücherhallen Hamburg) offers a three-dimensional view of the library and facilitates locating services and specific items.

Left: Label on the front of the RFID-based book returns terminal in the facade of the ZLB – Zentral- und Landesbibliothek Berlin: at the top the library logo, in the center the RFID antenna in the same shape as the logo, and pictograms below that show how to use the terminal (graphic design: Von Zander Architektur & Design, Berlin).

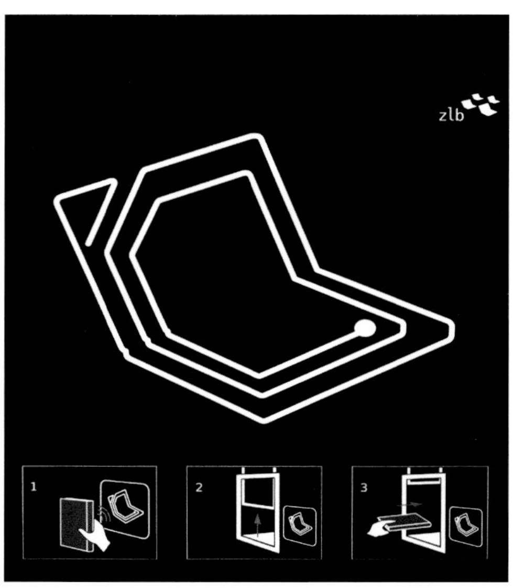

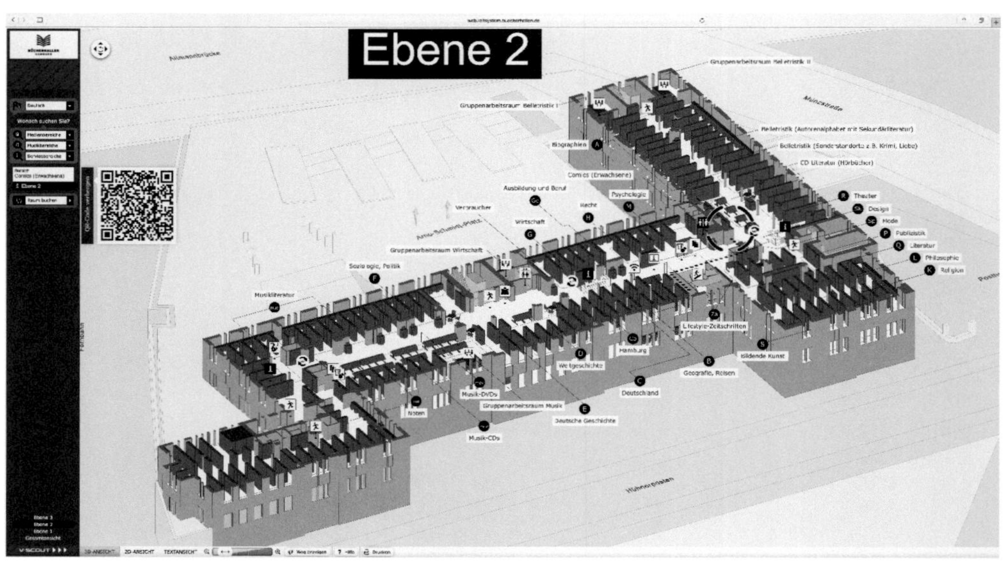

The identification sign for the conference room of the Médiathèque André Malraux in Strasbourg (Jean Marc Ibos, Myrto Vitart, 2008; graphic design: Ruedi Baur)

Hamlet, Miss Marple, Dracula: the names of literary figures make it easier to find one's locker in the State and University Library Carl von Ossietzky in Hamburg (graphic design: kirsch bremer artandarchitecture, Hamburg, based on an idea by the library staff).

Typography as a Mnemonic System and Tag Cloud

The typography of signage systems must be both clearly visible and legible: usually a sans-serif typeface such as Helvetica or Arial is recommended at a size appropriate to the viewing distance. It should be placed free of visual noise[12] and at right angles to the direction of movement.[13] For optimal visibility and legibility, signs should be mounted at a height of 1.63 m. As is the case with many rules, some designers choose to deviate from these principle guidelines: for example, the orientation and wayfinding system of the Médiathèque André Malraux in Strasbourg (Jean Marc Ibos, Myrto Vitart, 2008. pp. 198–201) employs a total of seven different typefaces, some of them in italics, and some serif faces. These have been given different colored backgrounds and the typeface denotes the genre of the books or the function of the respective place. When embedded in short passages of text, they form attractive "tag clouds" which are applied directly to the walls, columns, doors, counters and the floor without any "additional signage bearer".[14] Here the orientation and wayfinding system has been made an integral part of the building's interior design concept – despite having been implemented at a late stage in the building project.[15]

The redesign of the cloakroom lockers at the Information Center of the Carl von Ossietzky State and University Library[16] in Hamburg likewise employs a kind of tag cloud while simultaneously using it as a mnemonic device: electronic lockers, which although now superseded by modern RFID-based locking mechanisms are still widely used, require library visitors to memorize a PIN number and the number of the locker, one of which is invariably forgotten by the time the visitor returns to the lockers. The library conducted a survey inviting their users to name their favorite literary figures and these were then used to label the individual lockers. The resulting tag cloud of locker doors also serves as a mnemonic device, and because it is derived from user suggestions also helps users identify with their library – a design idea that has the potential to become a trend in library locker areas.

Material and Color Choices

When choosing colors, there are essentially only two primary restrictions that narrow down the possible spectrum of colors: firstly, colors that are reserved for specific purposes in national and international norms (such as the ISO norms), for example for emergency exit routes. These are not permitted for orientation and wayfinding systems. Secondly, colors and color combinations that are not discernible by people with color vision disorders. Here the principles of Universal Design apply. Other than these, designers are not limited in their choice of colors. It is important nonetheless to find an appropriate balance in the use of color with respect to the many other dimensions of an architectural concept: architects should be aware of the psychological effect of colors, their effect on the illumination of a space, the need for sufficient contrast between textual signs and background, and not least any corporate design guidelines that should be observed.

At the IKMZ – Informations-, Kommunikations- und Medienzentrum at Brandenburgische Technische Universität in Cottbus, Germany, the silver-gray text and silkscreen application method creates an immediately recognizable connection with the pattern on the building facade (Herzog & de Meuron, 2004; graphic design and typography: New Identity, Basel).

The potential choice of materials is seemingly even greater than that of colors, although cost, durability and adaptability are ultimately often defining criteria. Obvious candidates include materials that can be shaped or worked to accommodate text directly within the material, e.g. plexiglass, polystyrene, metal, wood, glass and other materials. In the IKMZ – Informations-, Kommunikations- und Medienzentrum designed by Herzog & de Meuron in Cottbus, Germany (Herzog & de Meuron, 2004, pp. 222–225), the graphic design concept for the wayfinding system mirrors the material quality of the building's external skin: the wayfinding system uses the same principle of silk screening and the same silver-gray color of the pattern of letters that adorn the facade.[17]

No food and drink, keep quiet and use pencils only: regulatory and prohibitory signs in the new reading room of the Staatsbibliothek Berlin on Unter den Linden (HG Merz Architekten, 2012; graphic design: Polyform, Berlin).

Sign and Message

From a typological viewpoint, there are many different categories of signs.[18] In order to achieve the desired effect, signs – whether in the form of words or a symbol – need to be carefully chosen so that they appear at the right time in the right place and within the users' field of view.

Symbols take up less space and are less language-dependent, but the choice of whether to use symbols or words depends on the complexity of what they need to communicate, the zone where they appear within the library and the wider context of the library as a whole. Symbol-based signs such as pictograms must be individually learned by users as there is no standard set of library-specific archetypes to draw on: "A widely used and generally applicable system of pictograms for library orientation and wayfinding systems does not exist."[19] Where symbols are no longer able to succinctly express more complex instructions or situations, words are a better choice for signage.

There are, for example, interpretative signs that help people to independently determine the purpose of an environment, and operational signs that provide instructions on how to interact within or at a particular place in the library. Directional signs, usually a combination of text and arrows or of text on an arrow-shaped sign, are a fundamental category of wayfinding systems that direct users to a particular destination. As they arrive, identification signs mark the location of their destination. Two further very similar categories are regulatory signs and prohibitory signs, and for the sake of completeness, one also often sees warning signs and honorific signs.

Formatting Space

To implement a wayfinding and orientation system, one should first establish the exact number of signage items needed, best done by considering the floor plans.[20] The rule of thumb is no more than absolutely necessary. The result is a detailed inventory of all the places where signs are needed, the type of signage items at each place and their composition in terms of typography, color, material and any other graphical elements. Lines that lead visitors through the building and connect entrances and exits can likewise be marked in the plans. The aim is to "format" a space with signage in such a way that visitors, on entering the library, can immediately and easily find their way to the central service and functional areas. A grid of anchors that mark main routes allows visitors to find their bearings from any point in the building. The elements of wayfinding systems are hierarchically organized, becoming successively more specific. Orientation systems, on the other hand, have a more informative function.

A common element is a plan of the building in the entrance area or a diagram showing the different stories at the main entrances to each level of a library. A particularly effective example can be seen at the Philological Library of the Freie Universität Berlin (Norman Foster, 2005, see pp.226–229): a red banner extends vertically next to the central stairway, adding a vivid stripe of color to the otherwise cool gray tones of the library building.

Wayfinding system for the Philological Library at the Freie Universität Berlin: a red band extends vertically from the lower ground to the third floor (Norman Foster, 2005; graphic design: The World as Flatland, Amsterdam).

Detail showing the clear presentation of information: at the top, text on the collection and services, in the middle a floor plan and at the bottom a pixelated face as an identifying element for each floor.

The potential options of creating signage are almost endless, limited only by what is available on the market and the overall composition: signage can take the form of panels or cubes hung from the ceiling, free-standing pedestals or stelae, panels mounted on walls and shelves, illuminated display cases, objects that project from the wall, letters (stuck) on walls, ceilings, columns on the floor, three-dimensional objects that catch the light and cast shadows, doorplates on carrels and back-office areas, notice holders and brochure stands on counters and tables, information monitors with a ticker showing library news, and so on.

The formatting of a space should also be inclusive for all users, including people with disabilities. Tactile strips on the floor allow people with visual impairments to orientate and find their way. Signage at key points can be augmented with braille lettering, and lifts can provide speech feedback.

Reclaim your Library!

Finally, not all libraries are the same: how do the needs of an academic library differ from those of a public library with respect to orientation and wayfinding systems? Although most academic libraries are part of public institutions such as universities and are therefore open to the general public, the typical user profile is more predictable and users are probably also well-educated. This may be reflected in the design, for example in the choice of wording, the use of specific terminology or more complex orientation processes.

Tactile lines glued to the floor of the Library and Learning Center of Vienna University of Economics and Business provide guidance for the blind and partially sighted.

Bart Simpson is used to mark the children's book area of the District Library in Berlin-Tempelhof, Eva-Maria-Buch-Haus.

Public libraries, on the other hand, need to be usable by people of all ages, social backgrounds and levels of education. Public libraries must therefore choose generally understandable wording and use clear design in order to cater for all its users. In library zones used predominantly by specific groups of users, the design can, however, deviate from this principle. In metropolitan libraries or in city libraries with a high proportion of multi-ethnic populations, signage may be needed in several languages. Likewise, where public libraries also include other public services, for example those provided by public departments, these should be incorporated into the overall concept – without sacrificing the recognizability of the corporate identity of these guest functions.

The public library system in its role as a democratic provider of human knowledge has the task of making its facilities as accessible as possible to everyone. To achieve this, public libraries can extend the existing orientation and wayfinding systems in the urban surroundings into the library interior, and make use of familiar patterns so that the transition from outside to inside is as seamless as possible and the interior is perceived as being a public space. The National Library of Technology (Projektil Architekti, 2009) in Prague – although not a model example of a wayfinding and orientation system – illustrates this idea through the use of urban art in architecture in order to define the library as a public institution and as a space for social interaction. The artist Dan Perjovschi[21] has created artworks on the concrete walls of the main atrium of the library that are akin to drawings, cartoons and graffiti and turn the interior into a "gigantic sketchbook",[22] and as such into a collective territory:[23] *Reclaim your Library!*

The atrium of the National Library of Technology in Prague: the drawings on the walls present a commentary on socially relevant issues.

References

1 Adrian Frutiger, *Signs and Symbols: Their Design and Meaning.* New York: Watson-Guptill, 1998, p. 223.

2 Andrew McDonald, "The Top Ten Qualities of Good Library Space", in: Karen Latimer, Hellen Niegaard (eds.), *IFLA Library Building Guidelines: Developments & Reflections.* Munich: Saur, 2007, pp. 13–29, here p. 14 and 25.

3 Andreas Uebele, *Orientierungssysteme und Signaletik. Ein Planungshandbuch für Architekten, Produktgestalter und Kommunikationsdesigner.* Mainz: Schmidt, 2006, p. 241.

4 For example Chris Calori, *Signage and Wayfinding Design. A Complete Guide to Creating Environmental Graphic Design Systems.* Hoboken, NJ: Wiley, 2007; Beate Kling, Torsten Krüger (eds.), *Signage. Spatial Orientation.* Munich: Edition Detail, 2013. For further information on wayfinding systems in public libraries see: Fachkonferenz der Bibliotheksfachstellen in Deutschland, "Handreichung zu Bau und Ausstattung Öffentlicher Bibliotheken", 2012. http://www.bibliotheksportal.de/fileadmin/user_upload/content/themen/architektur/dateien/Handreichung_11.pdf, accessed April 4, 2014.

5 Adrian Frutiger, *Signs and Symbols: Their Design and Meaning,* 1998, op. cit., p. 353.

6 Ulrich Naumann, "Leit- und Orientierungssysteme", in: Iris Dannenbauer et al., *Bibliotheksbau: Kompendium zum Planungs- und Bauprozess.* Deutsches Bibliotheksinstitut: Berlin, 1994. Digital revised edition, 2004, p. 160. http://www.bibliotheksportal.de/fileadmin/user_upload/content/themen/architektur/dateien/baukompendium.pdf, accessed February 23, 2014.

7 Ulrich Naumann, "Leit- und Orientierungssysteme", 2004, op. cit., p. 159.

8 Ulrich Naumann, "Leit- und Orientierungssysteme", 2004, op. cit., pp. 159–160.

9 http://www.ub.unibas.ch/rauminfosystem, accessed January 26, 2014.

10 http://web.leitsystem.buecherhallen.de, accessed January 26, 2014.

11 See also Torsten Krüger, "Epilogue – The Iconography of the Third Millennium: 'Signage Represents a Key Component of the Brand Image of Building'", in: Beate Kling, Torsten Krüger, *Signage. Spatial Orientation,* 2013, op. cit., p. 153.

12 Aaron and Elaine Cohen, *Designing and Space Planning for Libraries. A Behavioral Guide.* New York, London: Bowker, 1979, p. 207.

13 Volker Braun, "Leit- und Orientierungssysteme in Bibliotheken", *Bibliothek. Forschung und Praxis,* 28(2004), no. 3, pp. 327–333, here p. 329.

14 Philipp Meuser, Daniela Pogade (eds.), *Handbuch und Planungshilfe. Signaletik und Piktogramme.* Berlin: DOM Publishers, 2010, p. 57.

15 Cf. Ruedi Baur, "Integration of Signs and Space", in: Beate Kling, Torsten Krüger, *Signage. Spatial Orientation,* op. cit., pp. 68–81.

16 Rolf Duden, Stefanie Töppe, *Ein neues Informationszentrum für die Staats- und Universitätsbibliothek Hamburg Carl von Ossietzky.* 102. Deutscher Bibliothekartag, Leipzig, 2013, poster session. http://urn:nbn:de:0290-opus-13744, accessed February 23, 2014.

17 Katharina Bitz, "IKMZ – ein Modell für die Zukunft der Bibliothek?", master thesis at the Ludwig-Maximilians-Universität, Munich, 2012. Open Access LMU/Geschichts- und Kunstwissenschaften no. 41 (2012). http://epub.ub.uni-muenchen.de/17441/, accessed June 30, 2014.

18 See also Chris Calori, *Signage and Wayfinding Design,* 2007, op. cit., pp. 72–74.

19 Ulrich Naumann, *Leit- und Orientierungssysteme,* 2004, op. cit., p. 162.

20 See also Beate Kling, "Analysis and Systematic Specification of Information Requirements", in: Beate Kling, Torsten Krüger, *Signage. Spatial Orientation,* 2013, op. cit., pp. 96–101.

21 http://www.perjovschi.ro, accessed March 14, 2014.

22 See also Roman Brychta, Andrea Lhotáková, *Národní technická knihovna. 50°6'14.376"N, 14°23'26.613"E.* Prague: Národní Technická Knihovna, 2009, p. 142.

23 See also Jean Baudrillard, "Kool Killer, or The Insurrection of Signs", in: *Symbolic Exchange and Death,* London: Sage, 1993.

Frank Seeliger

Book Security and RFID

Loss rates

Despite the fact that, thanks to the invention of moving type by Gutenberg, books have become affordable for almost everyone, library books still remain an attractive target for thieves. In fact, the uninvited appropriation of these desirable goods from public and private libraries has, it seems, been *en vogue* since libraries first existed. Hamlin[1] wrote that the "most common and the most distressing enemy of books [is] homo sapiens." Shuman[2] even went as far as to draw up a typology of book thieves.

Libraries, unlike retailers, do not undertake regular inventories of their stock, and precise figures for loss rates are therefore comparatively rare. Nevertheless, libraries estimate an annual "perceived" loss rate of between 3 and 5 %.[3] Some estimates and analyses, such as that undertaken at the University Library in Magdeburg, Germany,[4] or at a branch library of the ETH Federal Institute of Technology in Zurich,[5] revealed much lower values in the thousandths of a %. By comparison, figures from German retail suggest an annual loss rate of around 1.1 %.[6] In 2010 and 2011, the theft rate for the sector "books/magazines/stationery" was given as 1.7 % of turnover, significantly higher than the overall mean value of 1.3 % for all sectors.[7]

Spectacular incidences of theft remain the proverbial tip of the iceberg.[8] One such example is the so-called Shinn Lists in the USA, an inventory of the book losses attributed to a certain James Richard Coffman, alias James Shinn. In 1982, a book was even written about this "most accomplished book thief" as was noted on the cover.[9] In Germany, too, there are anecdotes and cases aplenty that from time to time attract the attention of the media. A few years ago, the case of a caretaker at the Erlangen-Nuremberg University Library made the headlines in Germany. Over a period of 20 years, he stole and sold books with a value totaling over Euro 400,000.[10] No less spectacular is the case of a civil servant at the Federal State of essen Ministry of Culture who "procured" more than 13,000 volumes from different libraries with an estimated total value in the millions. Aside from the obvious financial motive, some perpetrators are motivated by a passion for collecting, as was the case with a geologist from Darmstadt.[11]

Aside from these special cases, which do however illustrate the potential extent of the problem, there are a few, mostly older studies of loss rates that were determined following an audit of library stocks. One reason for this, aside from the significant time and staffing resources they consume, is that – unlike in the retail sector – there is no obligation to conduct inventories. Bahr quotes examples from university libraries in the USA that registered loss rates in excess of 10 %, and an inventory undertaken at the New York Public Library in 1975 determined that some 15,000 books had been stolen.[12] Wegner[13] quotes another study undertaken in 1996 of a college library with a loss rate of over 8 %. The subject library for economics at the Justus Liebig University in Gießen, Germany, which has a stock of 50,000–100,000 media units, was able to determine a loss rate of approximately ten books every month by undertaking regular inventories between 1993 and 2002.[14] After the introduction of a book security system for some of the media, the mean loss rate fell from 10.3 to 2.5 books per month. Such loss rates nevertheless vary significantly from library to library.

An area in which little data is available is the loss rate of audio-visual media (DVDs and CDs), which are often especially desirable items in library collections. Kahn noted that, "Today, DVDs seem to be the item of choice for theft and damage. In the first two years that DVDs were introduced to libraries, more than 50 % of them were checked out and never returned."[15] This is one of the reasons why many information-provision institutions put covers, dummies or empty cases in their public areas, and only hand out the respective audio-visual media at the loans counter.

RFID gates in the entrance to Jacob-und-Wilhelm-Grimm-Zentrum in Berlin (Max Dudler, 2009) are difficult to reconcile with the structural grid.

The Scope of Book Security

Most people's idea of book security is an inked stamp in the pages of an actual book printed on paper that indicates that the book may not be removed from the library without permission. The item may be used in the specified part of the library, usually the reading room, and sometimes also borrowed for use at home once it has been checked out. In Germany, this aspect of book security is also detailed in the currently valid *DIN Technical Report 13*.[16]

But book security also encompasses three further aspects: firstly, various other non-book materials also need securing such as CDs, DVDs, games, maps, USB sticks or microfiches in academic libraries. As such, the term "media security" would be a more accurate description. The second aspect concerns the considerate use of media. The condition of loaned media is generally checked when they are returned at the end of the loan period, but it is not as easy to monitor how media are used within the library. In the TV episode "Mr. Bean at the Library", Mr. Bean manages, in his inimitable slapstick manner, to completely mutilate an antique book in the reading room. While humorous and exaggerated, it does portray a real problem.[17] An obvious way of preventing damage is to have staff on hand to supervise. Technical means such as camera surveillance[18] or closed-circuit television, as used in the British Library,[19] have been shown to reduce incidences of the mishandling of media in libraries. The third aspect is the inability to locate media, i.e. not the loss of the item itself, but of access to it. Media are usually organized by subject so that publications that belong together can be found in the same vicinity. In book stacks, which in some cases are made accessible to the public at a later date, media are often organized according to the *numerus currens* principle, i.e. consecutively numbered in the sequence of their acquisition. It is not uncommon for books on entirely different subjects to stand next to each other.

If a particular item is available but cannot be found on the shelf in the designated place according to the organizational system or the online catalogue, they are classed as lost, unless they happen to be in use at that moment. For example, of the 2.5 million books at Duisburg-Essen University Library, some 3,000 are classed as missing, but that does not necessarily mean they have been stolen.[20] Librarians are familiar with book hideaways, where individuals place books in a position known only to them to prevent other users from accessing and removing them. Few libraries have the resources to regularly undertake inventories or audits of their increasingly large collections. However, for the user misplaced media are just as unusable as stolen media. Some experts even maintain that the practice of deliberately misplacing books represents a greater problem than their theft.

The inventory or stocktaking of library materials is an area that librarians can expect to change in future. The comparatively recent introduction of RFID (radio frequency identification) systems can help reduce the effort considerably. The first libraries to be equipped with RFID are successfully using it to undertake inventories of their stock, for example the art library in Sitterwerk near St. Gallen in Switzerland. The location of the 16,000 items in their stock is polled several times a day using an automated RFID inventory tracking procedure.[21] Misplaced media are even tolerated for test purposes because the position of the item can be determined and visualized based on the automated inventory system.

An RFID-based inventory of over 61,000 media in the open-access area of the Technische Hochschule Wildau near Berlin, conducted in early 2013, took a tolerable 40 work days and resulted in a recognition rate of 99 % and a reading rate of 60 media per minute. A loss rate of 550 media was determined. The widespread use of this approach may make it possible to soon have more reliable data on loss rates in libraries.

The Introduction of Article and Media Security Systems

Electronic article surveillance systems (EAS) were first developed for the retail sector as a means of preventing the theft of articles for sale. This term encompasses various different technical systems, including electromagnetic security systems (EM) and radio frequency identification systems (RFID), both of which are used in libraries.

Such EAS systems have been used for several years in library environments. In most systems, a label or button-sized tag is attached to each individual item or article (the media item itself or the media box). Different sizes and designs are available. Using different methods of contact-less information transfer, the status of the tag is read or written (bought, borrowed, returned and so on). This information is written at the point of sale or loans desk. This fairly cost-intensive technology only makes sense if the articles in question have a certain sales price. As such, these systems are most commonly used in the electronics and clothing sectors. In the book sector, some examples of application scenarios already exist. The Boekhandels Groep Nederland has used RFID since 2006 in the UHF frequency band to secure books for sale with a value of at least Euro 5. Similarly the publisher Wiley & Sons have started using UHF labels to label their 500,000 non-fiction books, though their primary motivation is to be able to better track the flow of goods.

Electromagnetic Security Systems

Developed in the USA in the mid–1960s,[22] electromagnetic security systems were first used more widely in libraries in the 1970s in the form of "Tattle Tapes".[23] Shortly after, similar approaches also began to be used in Germany.[24] Each book or media is tagged with at least one strip of electromagnetic metal tape (EM), usually in an unobtrusive position near the spine between two pages. The Biblioteca Central at the Universidad Nacional Autónoma de México (UNAM) even secured each book or media with three such magnetic stripes. These stripes can switch between just two states: magnetized or non-magnetized. They cannot hold any other information. When active, the magnetic stripe sets off a visual or acoustic alarm signal as it passes through a suitably equipped barrier-free gateway or double-leaf doorway at the entrance and/or exit. To be able to pass through the gateway without triggering the alarm, the strip must be de-magnetized, usually at the loans counter or with a mobile scanner.[25]

EM systems are only used for security purposes. For other needs, such as self-service loan systems and semi-automated returns, a second parallel system is required, usually involving barcodes. EM strips are also available for audio-visual media and are sometimes used for securing a library's entire collection. The *German DIN Technical Report 13*[26] on book security notes that pathways in the library must direct users towards a central control desk that cannot be bypassed. This needs to be taken into consideration when positioning the entry and exit gateways, regardless of the type of technology used.

The entrance area at District Library Berlin-Spandau is secured by a RFID-equipped triple gate, consisting of four antennas and three accesses.

The experience of using EM strips seems to vary: on the one hand, there are many thousands of installations in libraries around the world, and on the other, it exhibits a number of security vulnerabilities in different areas. One example was a trial by students at Augsburg University in 2010 in which different test-thefts were undertaken at the library, revealing the system's patchy detection rate.[27] There has been no definitive conclusion as to the effectiveness of this theft-prevention system.

RFID Systems

Towards the end of the 1990s, RFID (radio frequency identification) systems began to be used more widely in library environments. This system employs high-frequency radio waves (868 MHz instead of the usual HF band with 13.56 MHz)[28] to enable the contact-less airborne identification of objects according to the open ISO 18000–3 Mode 2 and ISO 15693 Standards and does not require a line of sight. Using a credit card-sized label, it can even identify individual items in a stack of books. An RFID system consists of a transponder attached to an object that contains an ID code as well as a reading device to capture the ID code.

RFID transponders can be as small as a grain of rice and it is also possible, using a special printing method, to create stable circuitry made of polymers. The advantage of this technology is a combination of its small size, the inconspicuous retrieval of the RFID data and its low price (some cost in the range of a few cents).

In contrast to EM stripes, RFID tags, as the radio frequency labels are called, can hold more information, which can also be modified, making them predestined for other purposes in addition to security. The most common application is for self-service book loan systems.[29] The ability to combine media security with self-service loan and return systems, along with the added possibility of RFID inventory tracking, has contributed to its popularity, and RFID systems are used in more than 10,000 libraries around the world. The demand has in turn spurred development of RFID products, for example the 3D location sensing of RFID tags in security gates and open standards for the data models that determine the information stored on a tag and its structure.

Much has been written about RFID systems and their integration in library contexts,[30] for example on an internet blog by Mick Fortune,[31] who has become known as "Mr. RFID".[32] RFID systems require two components. The first is the RFID transponder as coupling element that is affixed to or within the media. It consists of a ring-antenna and a chip that serves as the data carrying and identification device. The second is the RFID reader, which serves as a reader and writer and employs inductive coupling, using the principle of a load-modulated resonant circuit to provide both an energy supply for the transponder as well as for the data transfer using electromagnetic waves. The distance between the two components – the reader and the tag – varies according to the configuration used but must usually be within 1 m. Metallic objects – like many of the shelving systems used in libraries – can impact on the efficacy of the system. The media-security gates placed at the entrance and exit of libraries – typically barrier-free gateways of just over 1 m wide – are to all intents and purposes indistinguishable from EM security gates. A security gate consists of at least two antennas embedded in the walls that flank the gateway and a reader for reading and writing radio signals, likewise concealed behind the side walls or fascia of the gate.

The RFID tag, as the coupling element, can contain modifiable information, whether protected or not, depending on the book's or media's loan status. The majority of high-frequency (HF) installations use 13.56 MHz store data according to the ISO-standardized Application Family Identifier (AFI) values, which use pairs of hexadecimal 8-bit codes to record the status, protection status and information in plain text format, i.e. unencrypted. The latter is a potential security flaw, especially given the wider availability of NFC-capable smartphones (near field communication uses the same radio interface ISO 15963 as RFID), laying it open to risk of manipulation.[33]

The entrance of Public Library Heerstraße in Berlin-Spandau (top) is equipped with a RFID single gate, while Ingeborg Drewitz Library in Berlin-Steglitz (bottom) has a RFID double gate.

An alternative form of electronic article surveillance using EAS bits has not yet seen adoption in library contexts. The EAS bit is not part of the ISO 18000 standard, leading to potential incompatibility problems between vendors of such RFID systems.

For recording the on-loan or in-stock status (item security status) of a book or other media item, three combinations of pairs of 8-bit hexadecimal AFI values are in use: initially 92_{HEX} (on loan) and 91_{HEX} (in stock), then from 1995 onwards, $9E_{HEX}$ and $9D_{HEX}$, and in conjunction with the Danish data model (ISO 28560 Part 3), the combination 07_{HEX} and $C2_{HEX}$. The security gates of RFID systems scan for these three pairs of codes and respond with a visual and acoustic alarm signal should a media pass through it without having been checked out. It is also possible to identify the media passing through the gate using a procedure called gate tracking.

Compared with EM technology in which the magnetic strip can be hidden from casual view by placing it close to the spine, the typically credit card-size RFID tags have the disadvantage that they are plainly visible and can potentially be removed mechanically.[34] It is also possible to disable the security mechanism without great effort: aside from direct manipulation using NFC-capable smartphones, the RFID tag can be blocked from being read while passing through the gate by shielding it with metal packaging. This has not had an impact on the continuing adoption of RFID-based book and media security systems around the world. The full potential of the available possibilities has not yet been exploited; for example, many of the applications that currently use QR codes could be replaced in future by NFC-based applications. Such developments will depend on whether NFC technology becomes a standard feature of smartphones.

Conclusion

Specific aspects of RFID applications, such as the cost of implementation and the security systems, the legal context (privacy), physical criteria (building structure), quality standards and norms, the design of entrance areas (so that staff can intervene or gates coupled with turnstiles), as well as possible health risks must be assessed on an individual basis.[35]

In Germany procedures were developed for EAS systems in the early 1990s, and were defined in the Association of German Engineers VDI–4470 and VDI–4471 guidelines, but a basis for systematically comparing the performance of conventional EAS systems and RFID systems has only recently been outlined in VDI–4478. Performance criteria include the maximum number of RFID tags that can be detected at once as they pass through the gate, or the detection reliability at different speeds of passing through the gate, with different tag orientation and different carrier materials (e.g. metal and other materials that affect the resonating frequency). A systematic analysis of the respective strengths and weaknesses of both systems (EM or RFID) is still lacking and would provide a useful basis for libraries to assess their specific needs.

References

1 Arthur T. Hamlin, "The Technological Revolution", in: Arthur T. Hamlin, *The University Library in the United States: Its Origins and Development.* Philadelphia: University of Pennsylvania Press, 1981, p. 217, quoted in: http://libraryhistory.pbworks.com/w/page/16964569/'tattle tape'.

2 Bruce A. Shuman, *Library Security and Safety Handbook: Prevention, Policies, and Procedures.* Chicago: American Library Association, 1999, pp. 30–31.

3 R. W. Boss, "Security Technologies for Libraries", *Library Technology Reports* vol. 35, no. 3, 1999, p. 275, quoted in: Britta Wegner, *Mediensicherung in Bibliotheken.* Berlin: BibSpider, 2004, p. 27. See also Marin Majica, "Wer nicht leihen will, der klaut: In Bibliotheken verschwinden regelmäßig fünf Prozent aller Bücher – trotz Sicherungsanlagen", in: *Berliner Zeitung*, 24 October 2008, p. 19.

4 See the interview with Jürgen Heeg, Vice-director of the Magdeburg University Library, in ZEIT-Online, 8 March 2012, http://www.zeit.de/studium/hochschule/2012-03/buecherdiebe-bibliotheken/komplettansicht, accessed December 7, 2013.

5 According to written records by Dr. Oliver Renn, a branch library director at the ETH Federal Institute of Technology in Zurich, a two-day inventory undertaken in November 2013 of 60,000 volumes in the Chemistry, Biology and Pharmacy Infocenter revealed a loss rate of 13 books.

6 See www.GlobalRetailTheftBarometer.com and *Das Globale Diebstahlbarometer 2012–2013*, published in October 2013, see http://www.checkpointsystems.com/de-de/news-events/CheckNews/2013/Germany/Nov/GRTB.aspx, accessed December 23, 2013.

7 See Centre for Retail Research, *Das Globale Diebstahlbarometer 2011.* Newark, Nottinghamshire: 2011, p. 41.

8 See the list with examples from the 1960s to the 1990s by Bruce A. Shuman, *Library Security and Safety Handbook*, 1999, op. cit., pp. 29, 38–43.

9 William A. Mofett (ed.), *The Shinn Lists.* Oberlin, Ohio: Oberlin College Library, 1982, quoted in: Britta Wegner, *Mediensicherung in Bibliotheken*, 2004, op. cit., p. 16.

10 See Spiegel Online, June 3, 2008, http://www.spiegel.de/unispiegel/studium/buecherklau-in-unibibliothek-bewaehrungsstrafe-fuer-dreistes-diebesduo-a-557526.html, accessed December 7, 2013.

11 See ZEIT Online, March 7, 2012, http://www.zeit.de/studium/hochschule/2012-03/buecherklau-uni/komplettansicht, accessed December 72013.

12 Alice Harrison Bahr, *Book Theft and Library Security Systems.* New York: Knowledge Industry, 1978, p. 3 and p. 109.

13 C. Foster, "Determining Losses in Academic Libraries and the Benefits of Theft Detection Systems", 1996, quoted in: Britta Wegner, *Mediensicherung in Bibliotheken*, 2004, op. cit., p. 22.

14 See Britta Wegner, *Mediensicherung in Bibliotheken*, 2004, op. cit., p. 24.

15 See Miriam Kahn, *The Library Security and Safety Guide to Prevention, Planning, and Response.* Chicago: American Library Association, 2008, p. 30.

16 See DIN, Deutsches Institut für Normung (ed.), *DIN-Fachbericht 13:2009-11. Bau- und Nutzungsplanung von Bibliotheken und Archiven*, third edition, Berlin: Beuth, 2009, p. 65.

17 For further information on the problem of damage to books, see: Marcel C. Obiagwu, "Library Abuse in Academic Institutions: A Comparative Study", *The International Information & Library Review*, vol. 24, no. 4, 1992, pp. 291–305.

18 See Britta Wegner, *Mediensicherung in Bibliotheken*, 2004, op. cit., pp. 54–55.

19 See http://www.bl.uk/aboutus/foi/pubsch/pubscheme6/cctv.pdf, accessed December 7, 2013.

20 Anna Müller-Heidelberg, "Diebesnester in Regalen", Spiegel Online, October 17, 2011, http://www.spiegel.de/spiegel/unispiegel/d-80784994.html, accessed December 7, 2013.

21 http://www.sitterwerk.ch/kunstbibliothek/dynamische-ordnung.html, accessed December 7, 2013.

22 Alice Harrison Bahr, *Book Theft and Library Security Systems*, 1978, op. cit., p. 111.

23 Arthur T. Hamlin, "The Technological Revolution", in: Arthur T. Hamlin, *The University Library in the United States: Its Origins and Development*, 1981, op. cit., pp. 217–219; and Miriam Kahn, *The Library Security and Safety Guide to Prevention, Planning and Response*, 2008, op. cit., pp. 29–30.

24 Britta Wegner, *Mediensicherung in Bibliotheken*, 2004, op. cit., p. 27.

25 Frank Gillert, *Entwicklung einer Methodik zur labortechnischen Abnahme quellengesicherter Produkte und Produktverpackungen.* Frankfurt am Main: Deutscher Fachverlag, 2001, pp. 53–55.

26 DIN, Deutsches Institut für Normung (ed.), *DIN-Fachbericht 13: 2009-11, Bau- und Nutzungsplanung von Bibliotheken und Archiven*, developed by the Standardization Committee on Information and Documentation (NABD) in collaboration with an expert committee from German Libraries Institute (DBI), 2009, op. cit., p. 65.

27 Eva-Maria Knab, "Test-Diebstahl in der Unibibliothek: Augsburger Studenten beanstanden Schwächen im Sicherungssystem an der Uni-Bibliothek. Ein Test zeigte, dass sich der Alarm nicht immer auslöst", *Augsburger Allgemeine*, February 7, 2011; see also Alice Harrison Bahr, *Book Theft and Library Security Systems*, 1978, op. cit., p. 111; and Miriam Kahn, *The Library Security and Safety Guide to Prevention, Planning and Response*, 2008, op. cit., p. 30.

28 Ultra High Frequency (UHF) applications are much less common. In Europe, only a handful of libraries have UHF installations, for example the Library and Learning Center at Vienna University of Economics and Business, opened in 2013, the University Library at Pécs in Hungary or the Bilkent University Library in Turkey.

29 See the results of Mick Fortune's annual online survey of RFID library users, for example http://www.th-wildau.de/fileadmin/dokumente/bibliothekssymposium/dokumente/Mick_Fortune_Vortrag.pdf, accessed December 23, 2013.

30 Christian Kern, *RFID in Bibliotheken.* Heidelberg: Springer, 2011; Frank Seeliger et al., *RFID für Bibliothekare.* Berlin: News & Media, 2013; Martin Palmer, *Making the Most of RFID in Libraries.* London: Facet, 2009; Connie K. Haley, *Radio Frequency Identification Handbook for Librarians.* Westport, CT: Libraries Unlimited, 2007.

31 http://www.mickfortune.com/Wordpress/, accessed December 23,2013.

32 See Richard Wallis' introduction to Library Gang 2.0, http://www.alatechsource.org/blog/2010/05/library-20-gang-0510-rfid-connecting-with-the-physical-world.html, accessed January 10, 2014.

33 Sebastian Krautz, *Entwicklung von Sicherheitskonzepten für bestehende RFID-Bibliothekssysteme, in Hinsicht auf die Möglichkeiten NFC-fähiger Smartphones.* Technische Hochschule Wildau, Master's Thesis, 2012.

34 DIN, Deutsches Institut für Normung (ed.), *DIN-Fachbericht 13:2009-11. Bau- und Nutzungsplanung von Bibliotheken und Archiven*, 2009, op. cit., p. 65.

35 Frank Seeliger et al., *RFID für Bibliothekare*, 2013. op. cit., Conferences are an opportunity for exchanging experiences, for example: http://www.bibliothekssymposium.de/, accessed December 23, 2013.

National Libraries

Enforceable legal deposit legislation, ensuring the acquisition, the recording, the preservation, and the availability of a nation's published heritage, is the prerequisite to the formation, existence and meaningful operation of a national or central archive library, metaphorically described in the deposit legislation of the German National Archive as a "nation's memory". The depository concept, initially expressed in 1537 in the "Ordonnance de Montpellier", issued by King Francis I of France, decreeing that a copy of each book to be sold in the country had to be deposited first in the library of the royal court, evolved into today's modern deposit legislation, applying to publications of any format and media produced in a particular country, often including foreign publications in the country's language(s) or publications with parallel language texts. The catalogue of publications and materials required for public deposit varies by country, but includes, in general, two distinct categories: conventional publications in tangible form and materials presented virtually in public access networks. Usually excluded from public depository requirements are materials described as "gray literature" – publications not intended for public distribution and materials not formally published. Subject to deposit are publishers, individuals or organizations, responsible for the creation and dissemination of content.

National libraries exist and function within the political, economical and socio-cultural context of a country and are considered vital instruments in promoting freedom of expression, stimulating diversity, supporting education and research, and fostering international exchange through national library services. As custodians of a country's heritage, national libraries are bestowed with the responsibility of not only encouraging awareness for heritage material, but also developing the sensitivity required for identifying such material.

The modern vision of scanning "all that is thought and known" (H. G. Wells, *World Brain*, 1938) into worldwide sharable databases, a vision challenged by current copyright laws and competing players with divergent philosophies, business interests, funding strategies, and alliances, applies to the heritage collections of national libraries as well, and requires firm legal and technical constructs, sufficient funding, and an interdisciplinary approach. For example, Gallica, an online platform established by the Bibliothèque nationale de France, provides access to works in the public domain, as well as to recent publications by forging an agreement between the national library, the French Publisher Association, the Ministry of Culture and Communication, and the National Center for the Book. Incorporation under public law endows national libraries with the appropriate authority to realize their mission statement, enforce deposit legislation, and secure funding, and to function as an independent organ. The latter assures meaningful and effective cooperation on the supra-national and international level.

A new building type, the national library, was first recognized in Great Britain when Sir Hans Sloane's bequeathal of his private collection, including 50,000 books, 23,000 coins and medals, and 1,125 artifacts, to the nation was accepted through an act of Parliament in June of 1753. Together with the Cottonian Library of Books and the arleian collection of manuscripts, Sloane's library formed the foundation of the British National Library, then part of the British Museum, originally housed in the Montague House in Bloomsbury, London. In 1823, with the decision of King George IV to leave the library of his father, King George II, to the nation, the architect Sir Robert Smirke (1780–1867) was commissioned to design a new building on the site of Montague House.

The central reading room, surrounded by vast stack areas, embedded in the extensive quadrangle formed by the impressive, Greek Ionic column-lined south front along Great Russell Street, flanked by west and east wings and closed off by the perpendicular wing to the north, was completed within the last phase of the project. The opening of the reading room in 1857 attracted 62,000 visitors during a week-long public viewing event. Linear reading tables, radiating out from two concentric rows of tables towards the book-lined galleries along the periphery of the rotunda, offered workspace for 336 people. The very center of the space provided a platform for the attending librarian. Daylight, filtering through a skylight in the crest of the dome and windows inserted between the ribs of the cupola and aligned with the ray pattern of the tables, illuminates the reading room. Beyond the walls of the workspace, multi-story cast iron stacks provided space for more than one million books.

Today, the King's Library, located in the east wing, and the central reading room are preserved in their original form, while the British National Library moved in 1997 to a new location. The reading room, now open to all museum visitors, contains 25,000 books and catalogues related to the exhibits of the British Museum and an information center. A column-free, triangulated glass roof, spanning between cupola base and the cornices of the wing buildings, encloses the freed-up quadrangle, creating the Queen Elizabeth II Great Court, which functions as a gathering space and a link between the surrounding exhibition spaces. Since 1753, the collection of the British National Library has increased to 57 million holdings.

In the current debate revolving around the position of libraries and the discipline of library sciences within the rapidly changing knowledge environment, the British National Library attempts to find positions, through critical analysis of present conditions, observation of trends and projections and the development of strategies aiming at the operation of hybrid collections, comprised of conventional print material and digital content. The vast amount of information available exceeds multiple times the extensive print collection of the Library of Congress, and users are increasingly reliant on information professionals, who manage and identify authoritative content. The preparation and organization of digital material, the adding of hyperlinks, the collection of data specific to disciplines, as well as the aggregation of data in response to interdisciplinary research are some of the concepts deployed by the British National Library, providing users with continuous value-adding services. To this end, the British National Library has introduced a market-facing approach, ensuring alignment of services with the needs of their five key audience groups: researchers; business; library and information sector; learners; general public. Knowing the user profile, understanding user needs and inviting user feedback are critical parameters, shaping the future of national libraries and allowing them to stay relevant in their role as the custodians of a country's heritage and the dissemination of knowledge.

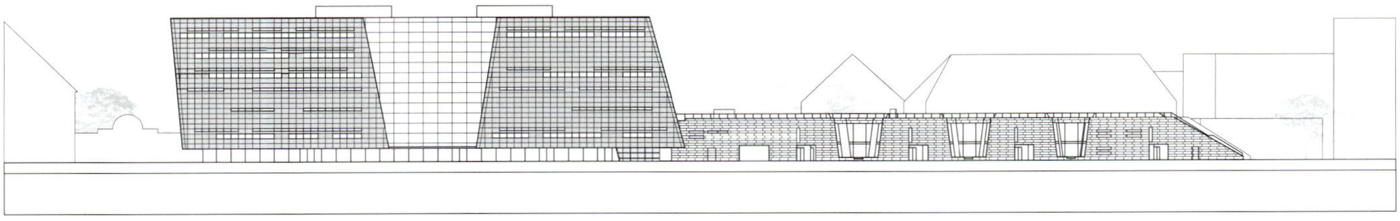

South elevation

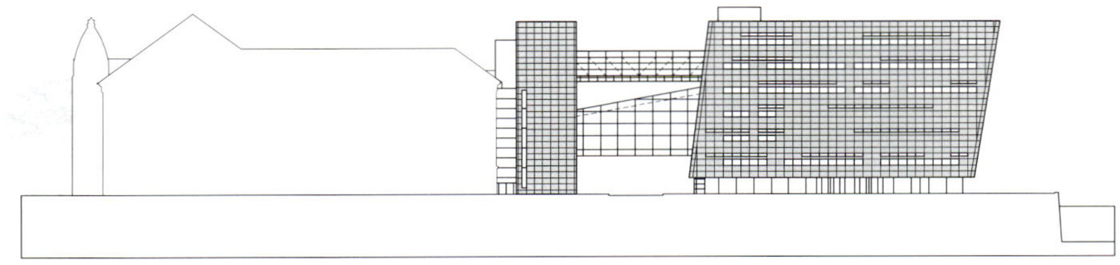

West elevation

Det Kongelige Bibliotek

Copenhagen, Denmark

Architect	Schmidt Hammer Lassen
Client	Dansk Kulturministeriet
Completion	1999
Floor area	21,000 m² (new); 7,000 m² (refurbished)
Number of volumes	200,000
Seating capacity	600 (hall), 300 (reading rooms)

More than a decade after its inauguration in 1999, the Danish Royal Library, universally known as the "Black Diamond", remains a significant landmark in Copenhagen, both as a public library and a part of the city waterfront. The work of the Danish firm Schmidt Hammer Lassen, the Black Diamond was the winning entry to an international competition in 1993. The competition, a product of several different governments, requested proposals for both the location and the design of an extension to the Royal Library on the Slotsholmen waterfront. There were long-standing issues of insufficient space and storage, already a problem in the 1906 Holm Library in the Danish Parliament and Archives complex.

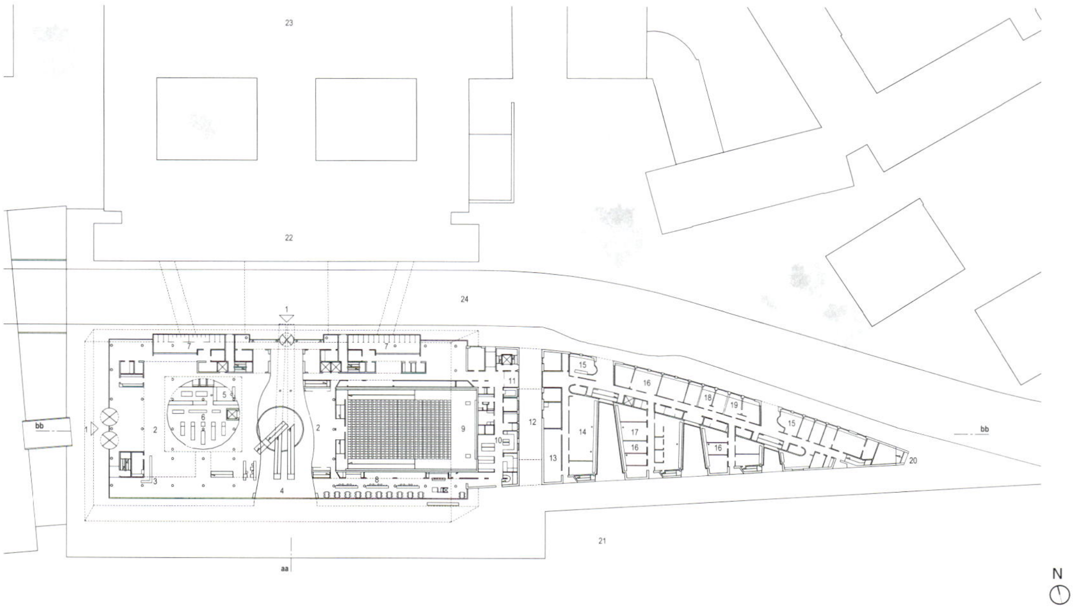

1 Entrance
2 Foyer
3 Café
4 Escalators
5 Ticket sales
6 Library shop
7 Audience toilets
8 Restaurant
9 Multi-function hall
10 Kitchen
11 Secondary entrance
12 Passage
13 Service booth
14 Course hall
15 Reception
16 Office
17 Catalogue room
18 Audio room
19 Sound/video facilities
20 External stairs
21 Harbor
22 Existing Hansen Building
23 Existing Holm Building
24 Christians Brygge Road

Ground floor

New plaza with a stairway of azobé wood leading to the water | Detail of structural glazed wall | View towards the waterfront of the "Black Diamond" and the "Fish"

These issues were not resolved by the 1968 Preben Hansen refurbishment, an extension ill received for its concealment of the brick facade of the original building. The proposal by Schmidt Hammer Lassen was selected for its creation of "a new building that appears as an independent work of architecture which through its masterly connection with the library, both separates itself from it while at the same time giving it prominence." (Source: "Udvidelsen af det Kongelige Bibliotek")

Addressing civic and urban issues through a new presence on the waterfront, one salient aspect of the Black Diamond project is the integration of the old library with the new building across the four-lane Christians Brygge Road. This process was initiated by the recognition of the formal procession on the east-west axis that begins in the historic library courtyard. This axis, on which the existing Holms entrance is located, becomes the primary axis of the new building. It culminates in a grand atrium with a spectacular view of the water through an enormous glass structure piercing the black mass of the library. On the exterior, the extension of the new vocabulary of black granite and glass to the facades of the Hansen addition across the Christians Brygge Road further unites the old and the new buildings. This gesture is enhanced by the assimilation of the thoroughfare through the addition of three glass bridges, high above the road, that connect the two buildings. Vehicles seemingly drive through the library complex.

The entrance of the new library on the south facade establishes a new north-south axis paralleling the waterfront. This sequence comprises a series of public and civic spaces that include a restaurant, a café, a bookstore, public restrooms, an exhibition gallery, an auditorium and the atrium/entrance to the library itself. This new axis intersects the east-west axis at the atrium and concludes on the north side in a low white building, nicknamed the "Fish", which houses four related research institutions.

View of atrium and travelators with the harbor beyond | Lecture hall/auditorium in the lower level of the library | Inclined travelators move users through the atrium and under the connecting bridges | View into the reading room from the atrium

A set of travelators moving in the east-west axis from the atrium lead to the formal entrance of the stacks and reading rooms on the third floor. These steeply inclined people movers create a ribbon around which the new library spaces are organized in curved, wavy forms. This light interior of organic shapes is in contrast to the orthogonal arrangement of the old library and the hard geometry of the external, black granite-clad form.

The simple geometric form of the library belies its structural complexity. Due to its proximity to the waterfront, the concrete column and deck system are set on a double foundation and are fixed by steel anchors to the limestone stratum 12 m underground. Four concrete towers containing stairs and core elements serve as horizontal bracing on the interior. The floating facade, in some instances hovering above the ground and inclined outwards, is cantilevered and requires a hung cable-stayed construction.

The library is most notable for its prescient awareness, in 1993, of the need to integrate new media in the library of the future. In providing a landmark that not only houses books but sets out to address new values that include the accommodation of different forms of media and cultural activities, the Black Diamond remains of great relevance in the design of libraries today. ***lw***

Birgitte Kleis, "Udvidelsen af det Kongelige Bibliotek", *arkitektur DK*, 9/1999, p. 468.

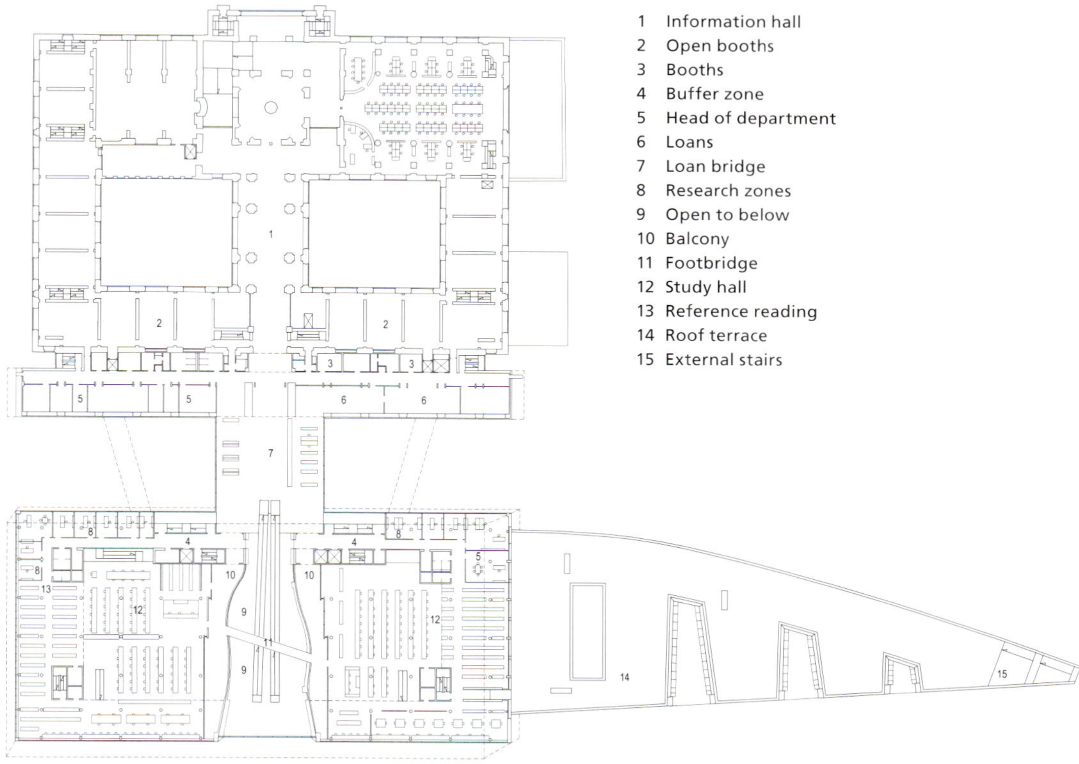

1 Information hall
2 Open booths
3 Booths
4 Buffer zone
5 Head of department
6 Loans
7 Loan bridge
8 Research zones
9 Open to below
10 Balcony
11 Footbridge
12 Study hall
13 Reference reading
14 Roof terrace
15 External stairs

Second floor

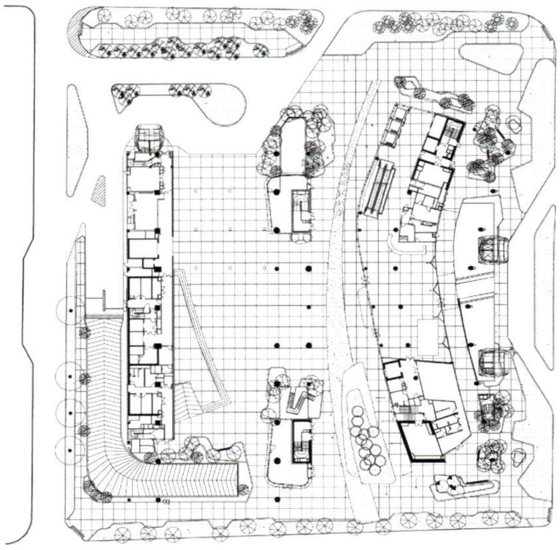

Ground floor

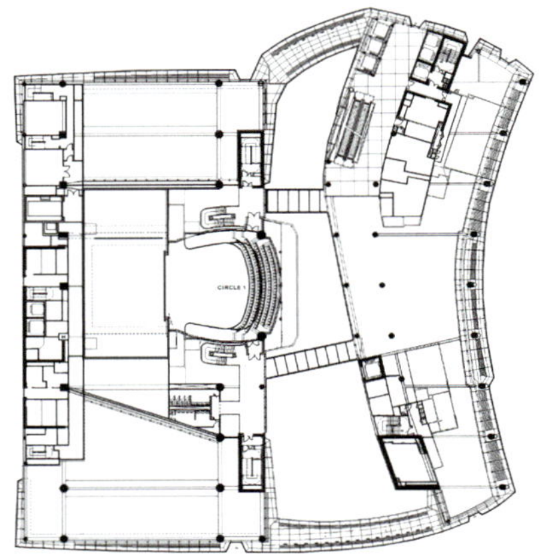

Third floor

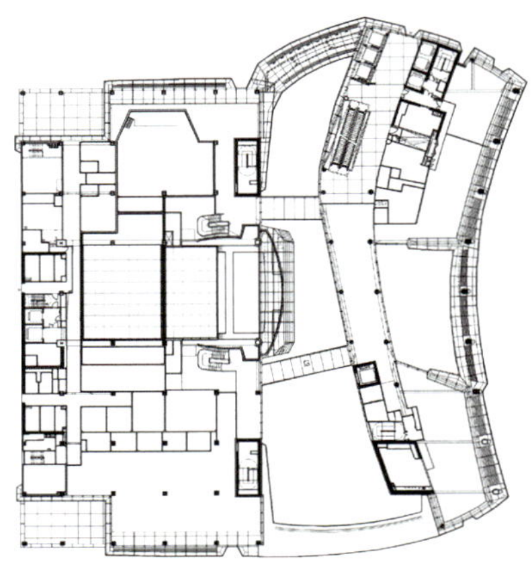

Fifth floor

National Library
Singapore

Architect	T. R. Hamzah & Yeang International
Client	National Library Board
Completion	2005
Floor area	79,000 m² (total construction) 59,000 m² (gross floor area)
Number of volumes	600,000 (reference)
Seating Capacity	190 (imagination room); 132 (pod); 615 (drama center)

A state-of-the-art white structure with an extensive array of curving blades, walkways and a rooftop pod-like pavilion, the National Library is the symbol of a present-day Singapore that has emerged as the world's fourth leading financial center. Selected from a competition, T. R. Hamzah & Yeang's design is a response to the government's initiative in 2000 to "lay the foundations for a 21st century knowledge based economy" (Source: *The Arup Journal*) enhanced by the advancement of technology.

The new library replaced a much-loved colonial brick building that embodied the history of the library system in Singapore, a history that paral-

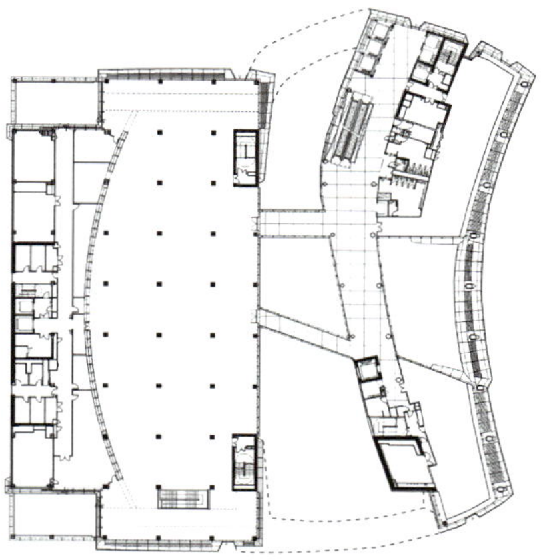

Eighth floor

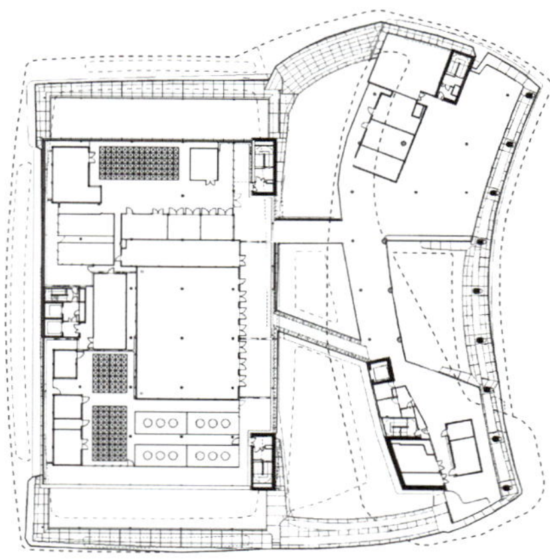

14th floor

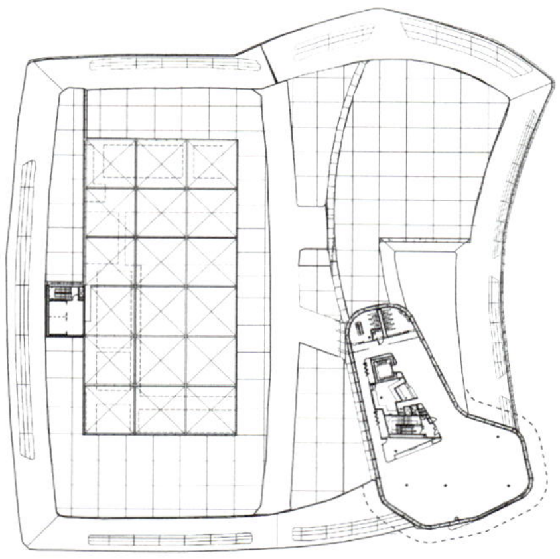

15th floor – roof plan

The library in its dense urban environment | View of the atrium | The Skycourt

lels the evolution of Singapore from colonialism to sovereign city-state. Initially a part of Singapore's 19th century educational system, the institution of the library progressed from a subscription library to that of library/museum, before becoming a free library for all Singapore citizens through an ordinance of 1957. Named the National Library, it is differentiated from Singapore's public libraries by its mission as the "nation's knowledge institution, preserving its cultural and literary heritage as well as providing trusted reference services." (Source: www.nlb.gov.sg)

This mission is architecturally realized in the form of two large 16-story volumes, one rectangular and one curved. Architects T. R. Hamzah & Yeang describe this strategy as a "juxtaposition of formality and asymmetry" (Source: www.trhamzahyeang.com) in which the differentiation of the volumes is coordinated with the various program elements. The rectilinear block houses the reading rooms and library collections – both the Lee Kong Chian Reference Library of over 600,000 items (floors 6–12) and the Central Public library (ground floor level, basement). The curvilinear and smaller structure houses the so-called "noisier" public, cultural activities including exhibitions, a 615-seat drama center and a multi-media space. These two separate structures are connected on the lower levels through the center by a semi-enclosed street/atrium and at the upper level through a series of bridges.

Also known as a "Library for the Tropics", the National Library is the first building in Singapore to be certified Green Mark Platinum by Singapore's Building and Construction Authority. This designation is due to the efforts of Ken Yeang and his studies in and application of bioclimatic principles. The facade is a primary example of these principles. The glass facades are double-glazed with low-E glass and include some of the world's largest sun-shading devices. These sun

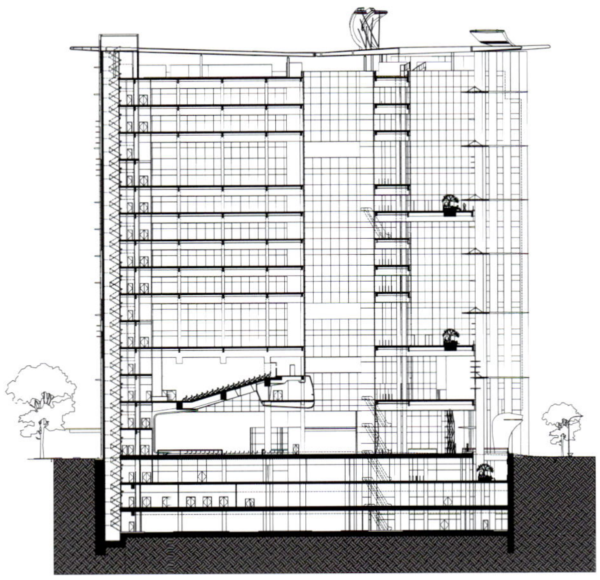

Transverse section

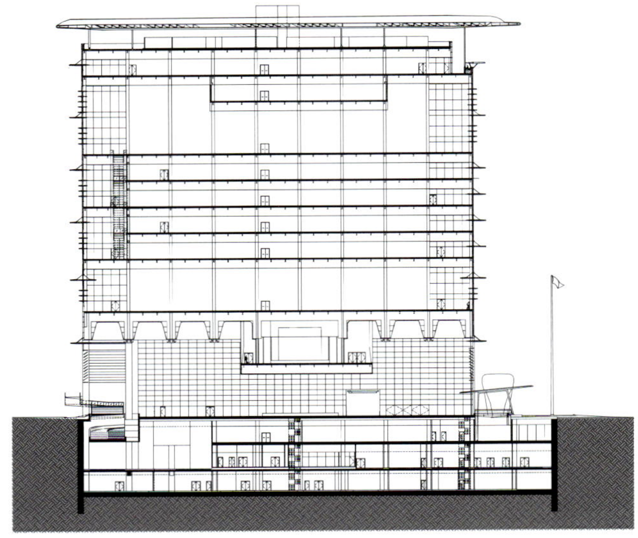

Section through internal street

Views of reading areas in the seven-storied Lee Kong Chian Reference Library | Collection at reference room | Upper level circulation overlooking the atrium | Views of entry lobby

shades/light shelves wrap around the building projecting into both the exterior and the interior, at some points 1.8 m from the face of the wall. Set at a 30° angle, they simultaneously control solar gain and glare while maximizing daylight. Other examples include the atrium, which is used as a "thermal stack" over the internal street. The wind tunnel effect cools the plaza and the transition space between the buildings, thereby lessening the demand for air conditioning. The list of sustainable features is long with highlights that include daylight control systems, rain sensors as part of an auto-irrigation system, start-stop elevators, CO_2 sensors in the air handling units, night setback in the air conditioning system, a series of "skycourts" as part of the gross floor area. These features together are responsible for an energy efficiency index (EEI) of 151 kW/hr/m^2 with measurable energy savings of 31 %.

With the design for the National Library, Yeang has created a civic icon for a Singapore that has shifted from its industrial past to a modern center of information technology and services. ***lw***

Russell Cole, Andre Lovatt, Mani Manivannan, Alan Newbold, Jim Read, "Singapore's New National Library", *The Arup Journal*, no. 2, 2006, p. 51.

"About the National Library Board Singapore", http://www.nlb.gov.sg.

"The New National Library Building, Singapore", http://www.trhamzahyeang.com/.

"National Library Building", http://www.AsiaBusinessCouncil.org/.

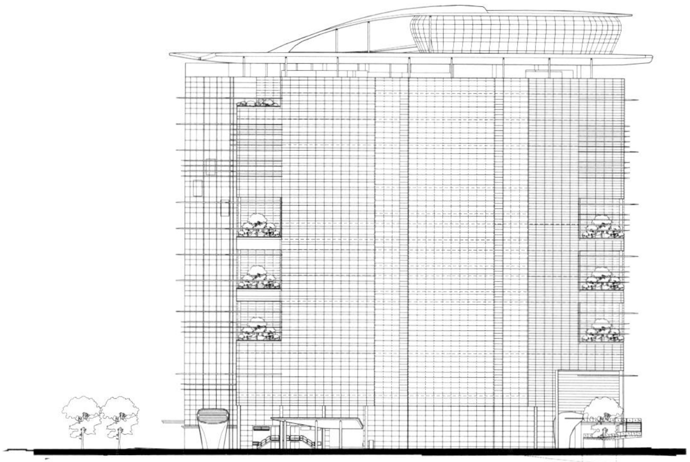

Bain Street elevation

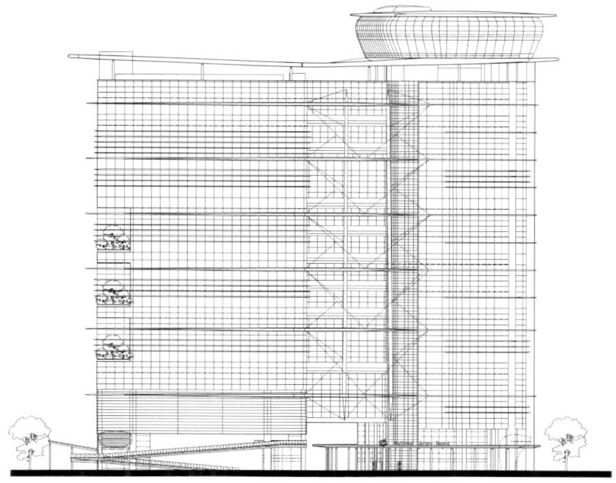

North Bridge Road elevation

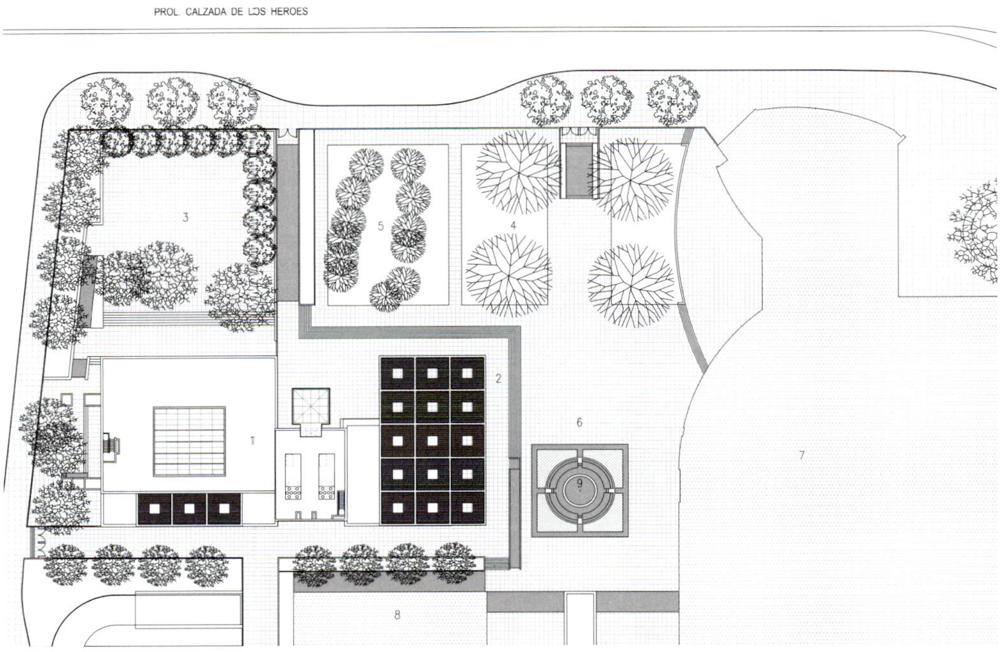

Site plan

1 Biblioteca Central Estatal de Guanajuato
2 Library plaza
3 Library reading patio with preserved trees
4 Plaza ficus with preserved trees
5 Plaza tabachine with preserved trees
6 Plaza
7 Museum of Art & History
6 School of Arts
9 Water fountain

Exterior glass wall and main stair at night | East facade from Laurel Garden | Main terrace under pergola | Library atrium from third floor

Biblioteca Central Estatal de Guanajuato Wigberto Jiménez Moreno

León, Mexico

Architect	Pei Partnership Architects
Client	Fundación Cultural Guanajuato
Completion	2008
Floor area	6,750 m²
Number of volumes	170,000
Seating capacity	1,200

Located in León de los Aldama, usually called Léon and one of Mexico's commercial and industrial centers, the Biblioteca Central Estatal de Guanajuato Wigberto Moreno Jiménez (Guanajuato State Central Library) serves the most populous city in the state of Guanajuato. The library was completed in 2008 as part the Forum Cultural Guanajuato, a 9.6 hectare complex for the promotion of culture, arts, entertainment and cultural tourism. The library was the first project to be built from a master plan of 2003 that also includes a performing arts center, an art museum, a new graduate-level art school and a commercial hub with a hotel, retail, cinemas and restaurants.

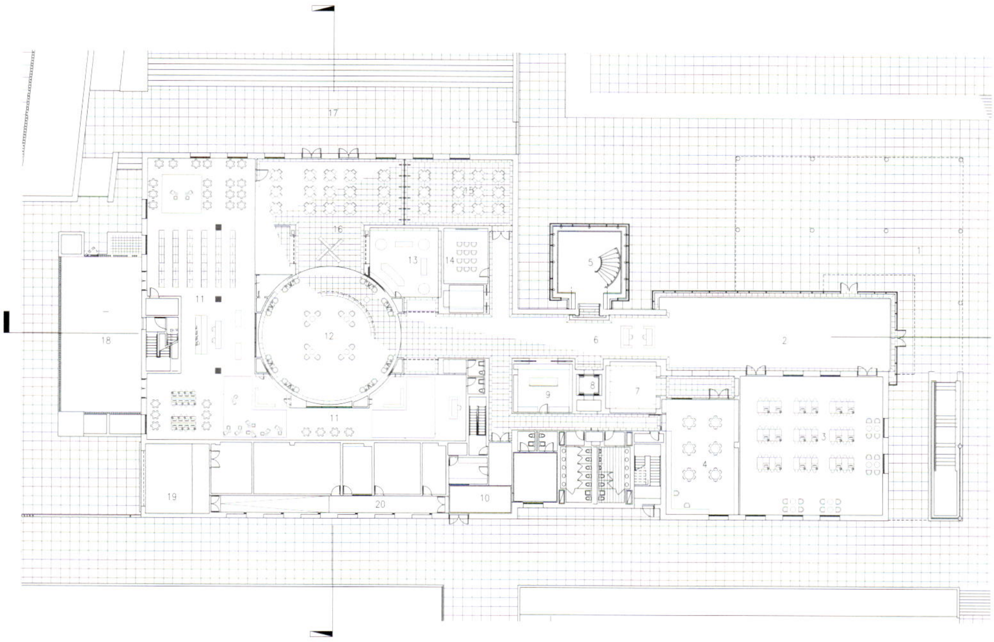

Ground floor

1 Library plaza
2 Entry lobby
3 Multi-media area
4 People with disabilities library
5 Main stair
6 Control area
7 Lockers
8 Elevator
9 Circulation desk
10 Staff entry
11 Children's library
12 Atrium
13 Bookstore
14 Bibliomedia
15 Multi-use room
16 Café
17 Library reading patio
18 Children's patio
19 Loading dock
20 Services

Previously housed in the Old Jail, the new 6,750 m² library consists of two stone, glass and steel volumes on an elevated terrace. These modern, rectangular two- and three-story structures are connected by a two-level glass gallery and served by a monumental staircase with views to the gardens. A three-story white steel pergola covering much of the elevated terrace and the lower volume provides an iconic element to the corporate exterior. The use of cantera, a local volcanic stone used for centuries for major civic buildings in this region, is an attempt to relate this modern building to the historic fabric of this 450-year old city famous for its leather manufacturing.

The library houses 170,000 volumes and accommodates up to 2,400 visitors daily. As Guanajuato state's public library, the primary spaces include a reading room, a periodicals room, an internet room, an audio-visual room with facilities for both private and individual viewing and other special dedicated spaces. The children's room includes the "Bebeteca", a special space dedicated to babies and children under the age of three. Intended to foster an early love of reading, this tiny space designed for a maximum of three small children and their parents uses color, texture and other visual and tactile means to achieve its goal. The Braille room for the visually impaired houses equipment such as talking calculators, tape recorders, relief maps, Braille printers as well as over 150 titles in Braille. A special collections room includes the book collection of Professor Wigberto Jiménez Moreno, an historian, linguist and anthropologist from León for whom the library is named, and the collection of Mary Esther, his wife. The Wigberto Jiménez Moreno Collection comprises 40,000 titles and includes a collection of New Testaments in 100 Mexican languages.

The notable spaces, a skylit atrium and the grand staircase, are variants of the same geometric concept – orthogonal spaces centrally occupied by a circular form. The site plan, too,

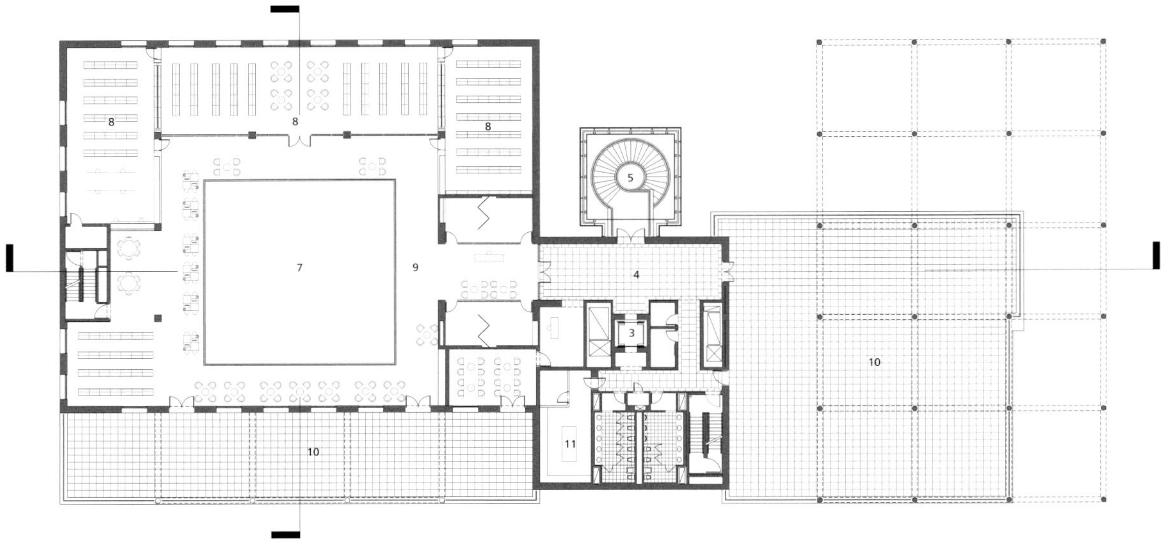

Second floor

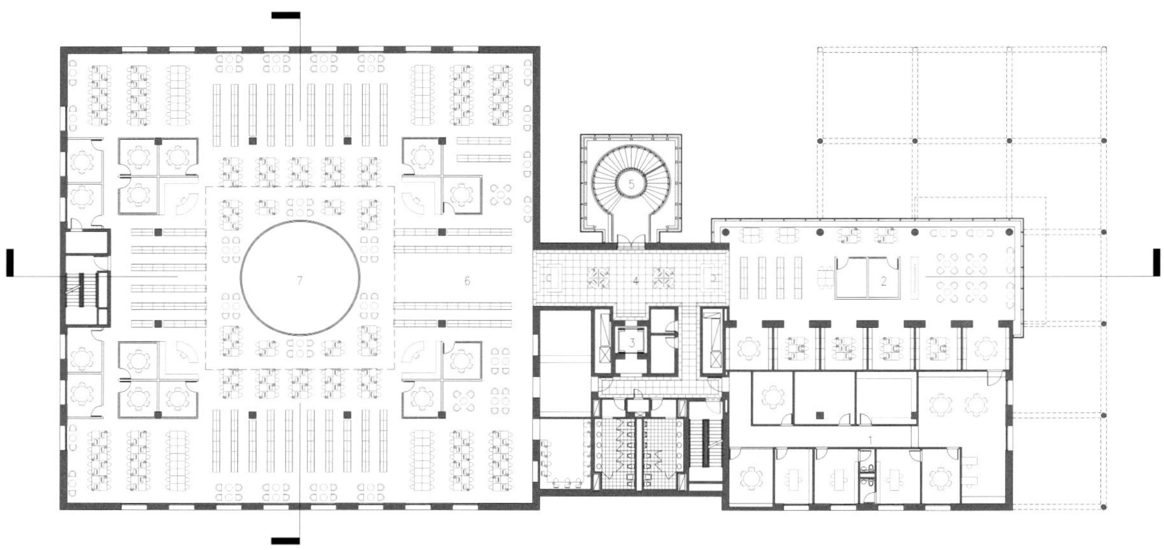

First floor

1 Offices
2 Young adults' library
3 Elevator
4 Lobby
5 Grand stair
6 Traditional library
7 Atrium
8 Special collection
9 Business and professions
10 Terrace
11 Kitchen

reiterates this idea in a set of circular, recessed steps sunken into a rectilinear field of geometric paving. This circle of steps, faintly reminiscent of the Greek *bouleuterion* (literally, a place for planning), holds a tenuous relationship to the library in its alignment with one of the columns of the steel pergola hovering over the building. While these circular steps seemingly have no relationship with the centralized forms of the building itself, their placement in the larger landscape and their alignment to gateways and pathways of buildings not yet built affirm their role to connect the library to the future Forum Cultural Guanajuato. As such, the prominence of the three-story pergola is clarified especially in light of the proposed design for the Performing Arts Center which, too, includes a high steel pergola of a similar vocabulary.

As Mexico's leading producer of leather and leather goods, León is a prosperous city. The civic leaders sought to enhance the city with this cultural center including the state library. As part of a larger complex, the public library assumes a different role. Often referred to as the "living room" of the community it serves, the library in this case must include in its mission the larger vision of the city's cultural initiative. In a departure from the iconographic facades of many public libraries, large and small, the Guanajuato State Central does not establish itself as an identifiable civic monument of learning. Rather, through a common architectural element of the master plan, a steel pergola, it becomes part of an extensive cultural whole for the city. ***lw***

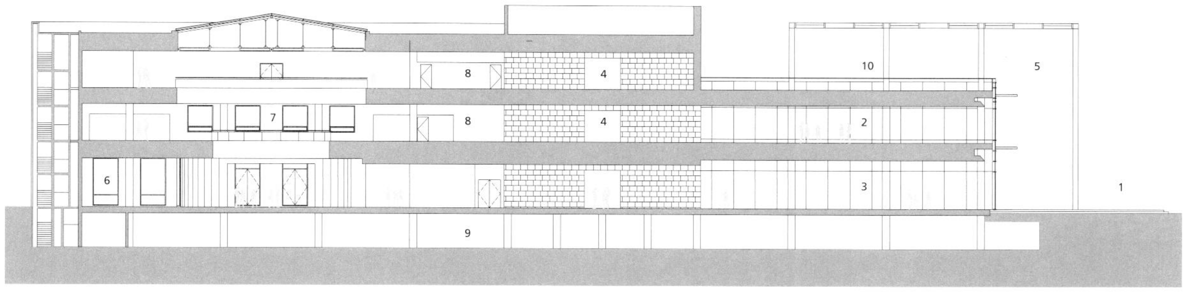

Longitudinal section

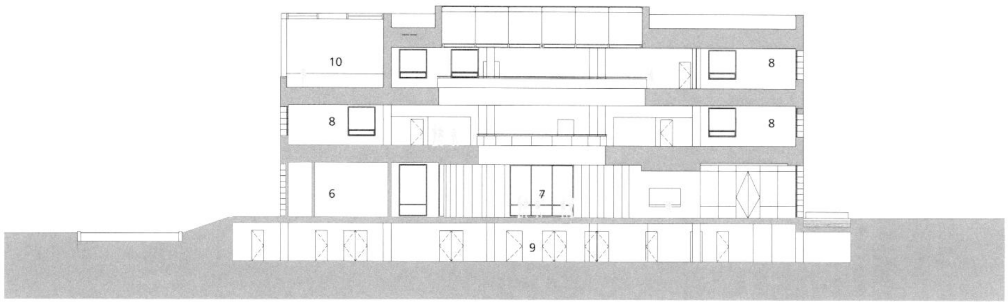

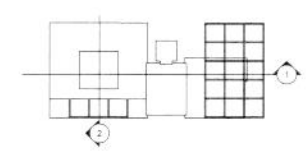

Cross section

1 Plaza
2 Young adults' library
3 Entry lobby
4 Lobby
5 Pergola
6 Children's library
7 Atrium
8 Library space
9 Parking
10 Terrace

East facade at night | East facade | North facade from plaza tabachine

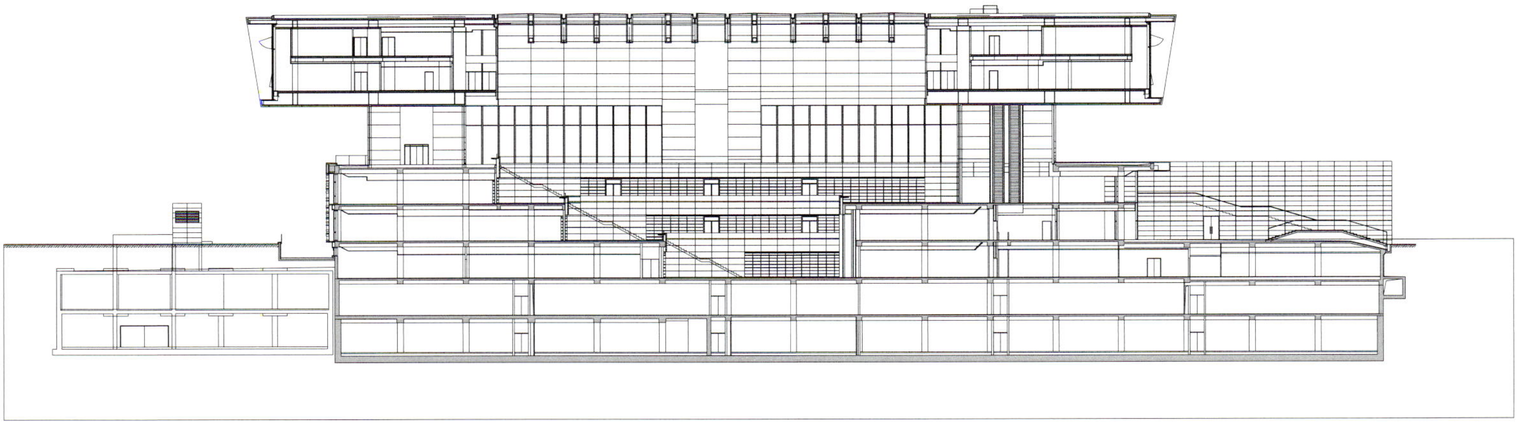

Longitudinal section

Detail of the metal-clad internal structure | The library in its highly trafficked context | The reading room from the basement level to the third floor

National Library of China

Beijing, China

Architect	KSP Jürgen Engel Architekten
Client	National Library of China
Completion	2008
Floor area	80,000 m²
Number of volumes	12 millions
Seating capacity	2,000

The design of KSP Jürgen Engel Architekten for the new National Library of China in Beijing was the winning entry in an international competition. Founded in 1909 in a Beijing temple by Puyi, the last emperor of the Qing dynasty, the library has transformed over the years in name, location, and size to rank today as the third largest national library in the world. Completed in 2008, today's National Library of China includes the new 80,000 m² facility with its capacity to hold 12 million volumes.

The tripartite design of the library, symbolizing the past, present and future, consists of a solid base, a glazed center section enclosing struc-

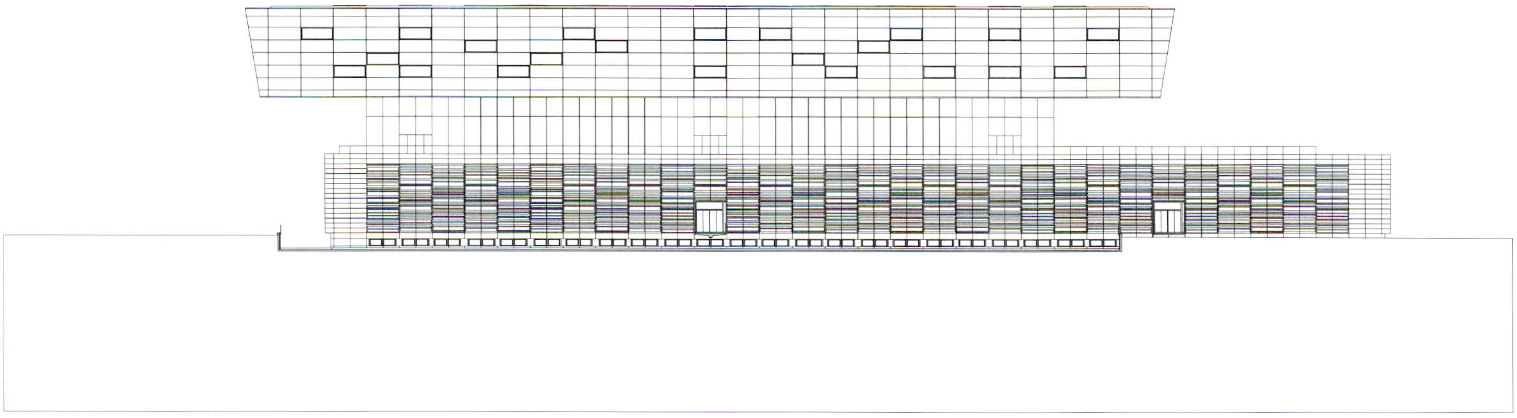

South elevation

tural cores and a steel-clad volume at the top. The stone-clad plinth houses the books and documents, representing China's rich cultural tradition. The glazed center section accommodates the public information area, access to reading rooms, foyer and cafeteria – all activities anchored to the present. The steel box at the top houses the digital library. Weighing 10,388 tons, the 120 × 105 m earthquake-proof steel of the roof structure is designed as a steel lattice framework. Six reinforced cores transfer this load to the base, thus enabling the column-free "floating ceiling" over the grand reading room. Based on the three traditional Chinese architectural components of building foundations, pillars and a floating ceiling, the form of the new library fulfills the "first function of the NLC" which, according to curator Zhan Furui, "is to pass on the culture of the Chinese nation." (Source: *Chinaview News*)

The collections of the new library also corroborate this function. Among its rich holdings are the Oracle Bones from the Shang Dynasty, the Dunhuang Manuscripts from the Jin Dynasty and the "Si Ku Quan Shu" or the "Library of the Four Branches of Literature", unparalleled manuscripts from the Ching Dynasty. These assets constitute the library's greatest treasures and are housed in a glass vault through which a visual connection is established between the three parts.

As in many libraries around the world, the NLC faces the challenges of readership in the technological age. Reading rates are steadily dwindling, from 60.4 % in 1999 to 54.2 % in 2001, 51.7 % in 2001 and 48 % in 2005 and 2007, as the Chinese use the Internet and online books with greater frequency. The creation of the National Digital Library is part of a strategy to combat this trend and to provide integrated services that include the availability of 10,000 e-books, mobile phone enabled library services and the use of RFID technology for the ease of locating items. Launched in 2005, the mission of the Digital Library Project (DLP) enhances that of the National Library to "serve as the complete and perpetual archive

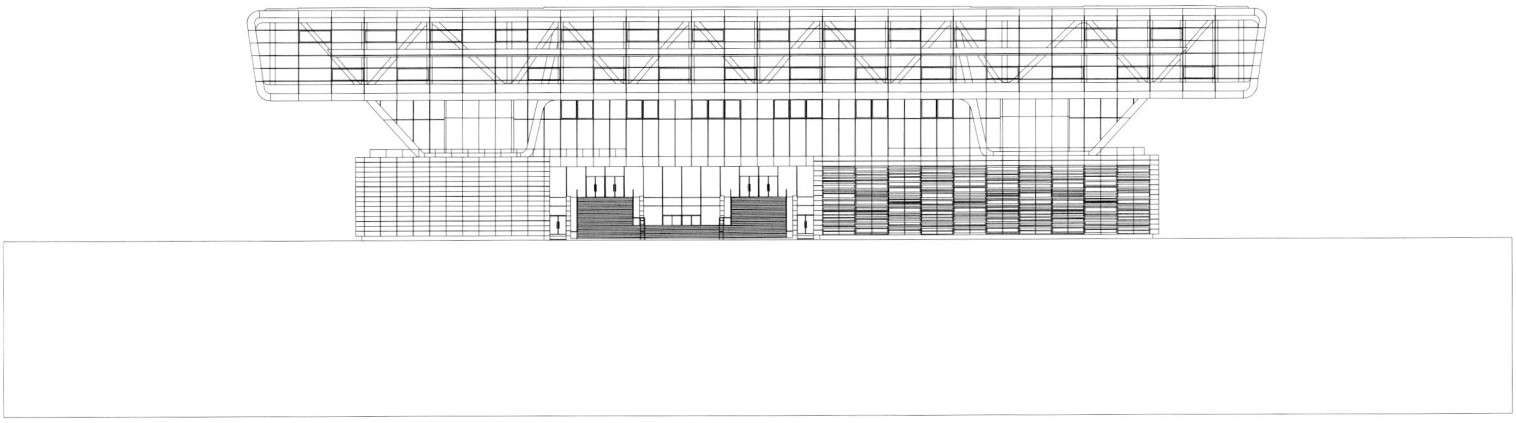
East elevation

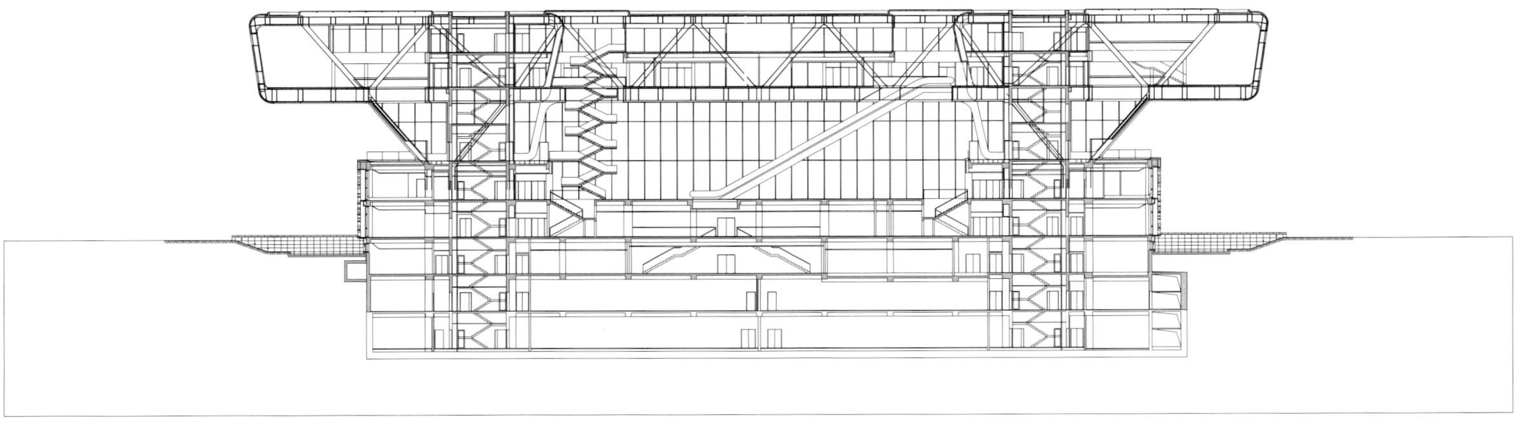
Cross section

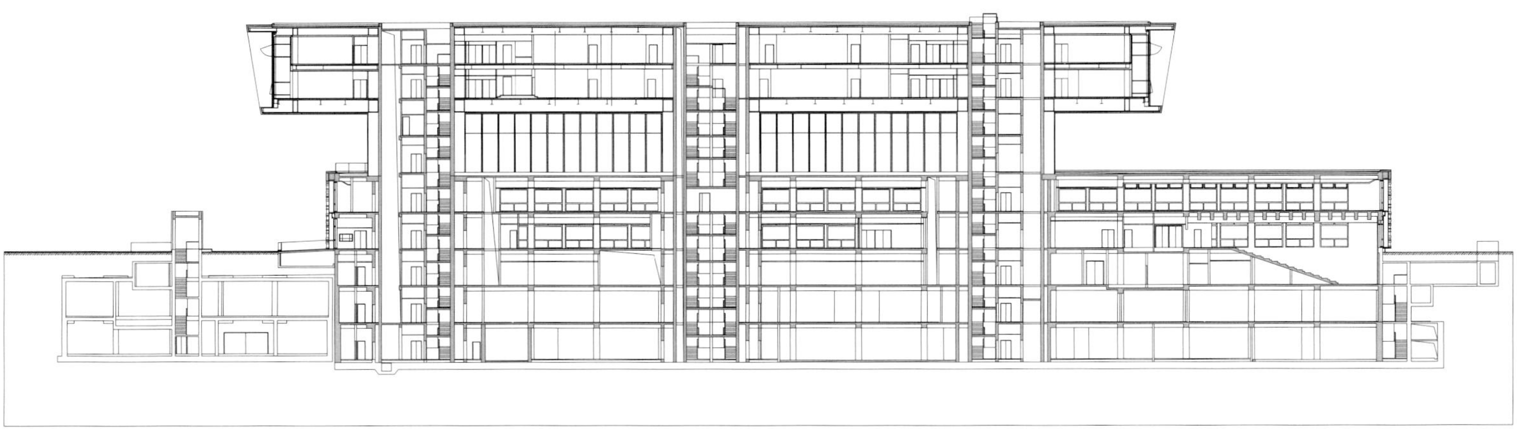
Longitudinal section

of all Chinese publications." The goals of DLP director Fu Ping are twofold: "first, to preserve in digital form manuscripts and books, many ancient and priceless, embodying China's history and cultural heritage; and second, to capture and preserve more ephemeral forms of today's dynamic Chinese culture. Web pages, e-journals, blogs and so on – that appear only electronically." (Source: *Library Connect)* With only 20 % of the National Library's holdings available to the public in digital form in 2008, the Digital Library will greatly increase the reach of the National Library. The work of KSP Jürgen Engel Architekten is part of the NLC's effort to make "use of all conceivable methods, including employing advanced technologies and ideas of administration, to maintain the leading position within the libraries in China and even the world." (Source: *Chinaview News*) ***lw***

"National Library of China: A Library of 100 Years Shoots for Future", *Chinaview News*, September 9, 2009. www.news.cn.

"From Tortoise Shells to Terabytes: The National Library of China's Digital Library Project", *Library Connect*, Elsevier Library Connect Publications, vol. 4, no. 3, August 2006.

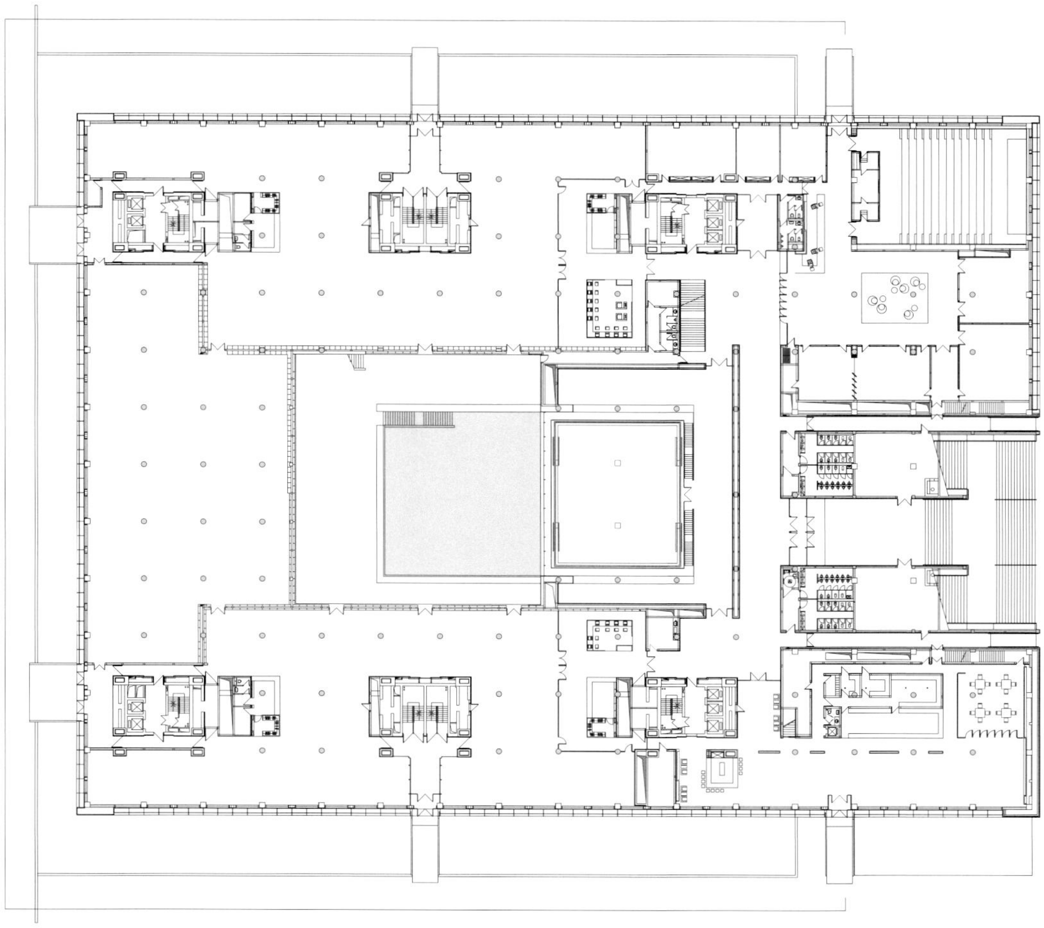

Ground floor

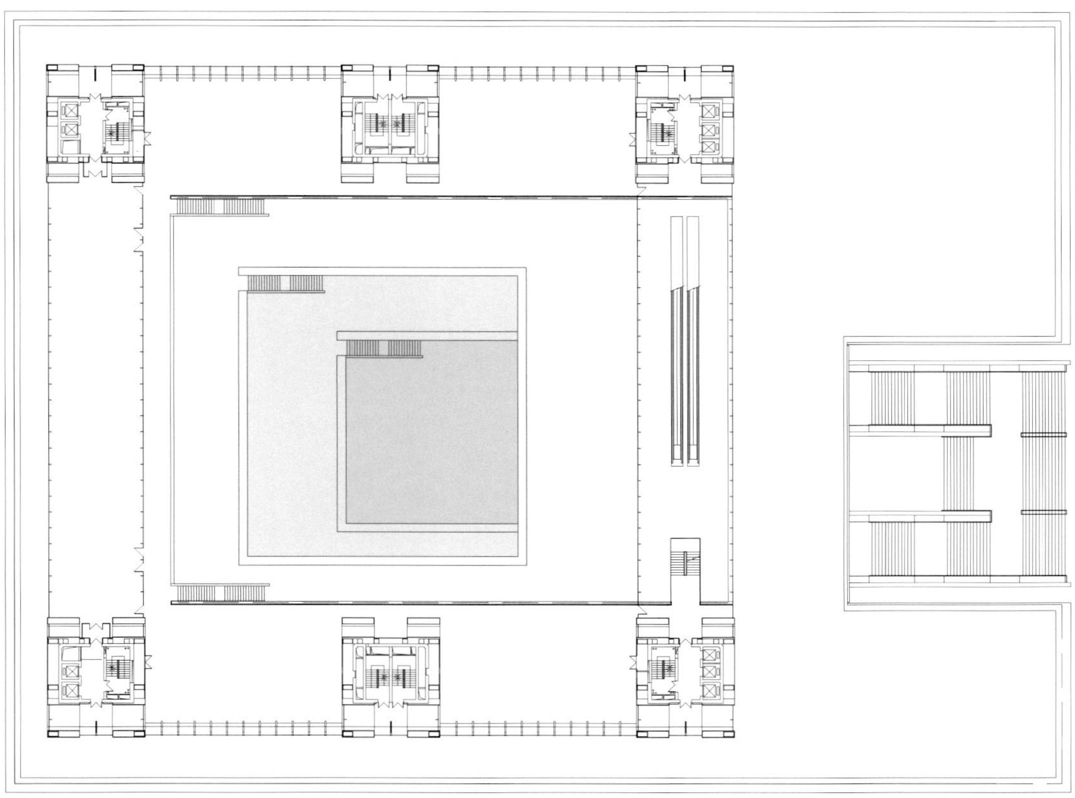

Second floor

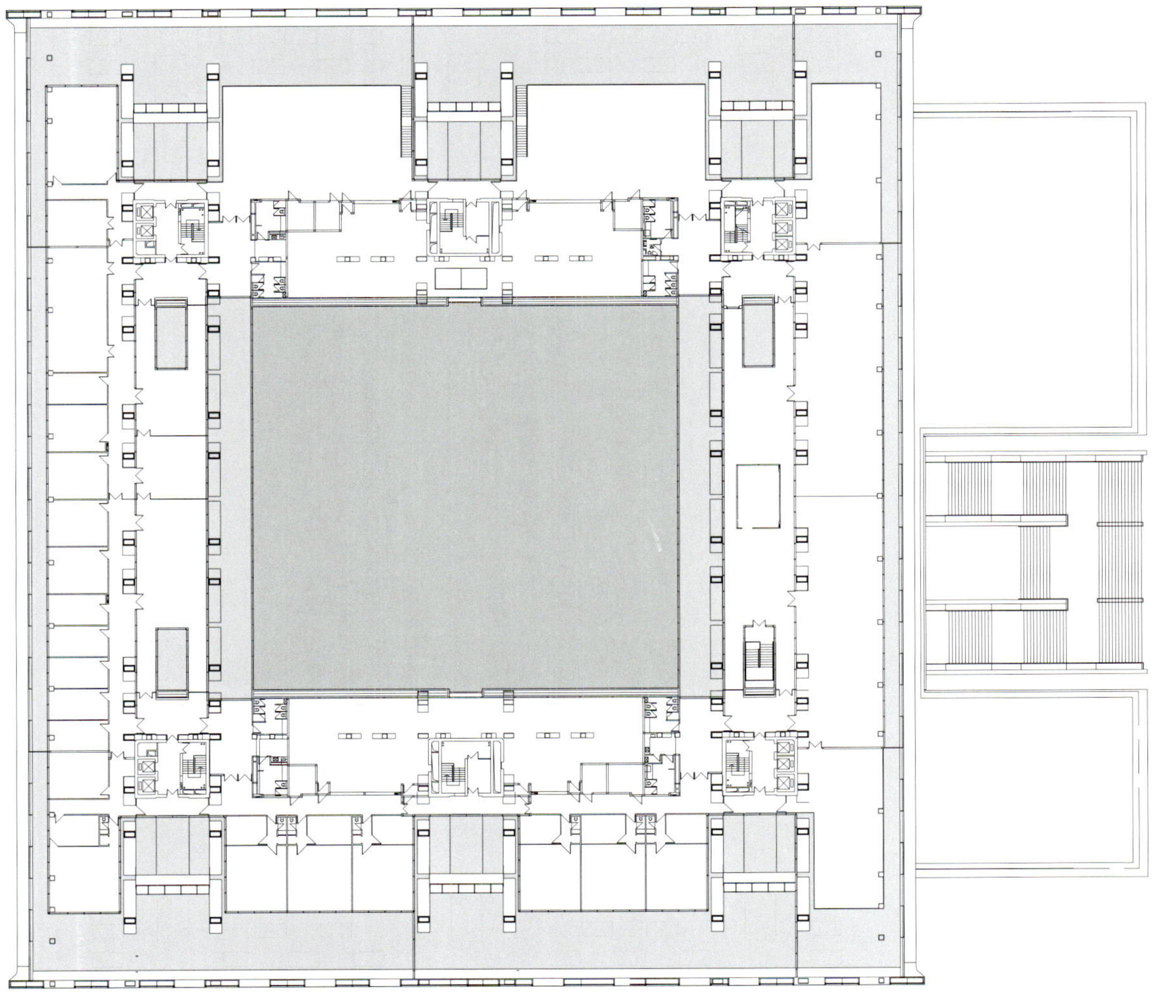

Fourth floor

The "Si Ku Quan Shu", holding precious manuscripts

The tripartite division of the building volume is most visible at night | Reading room | View from the garden

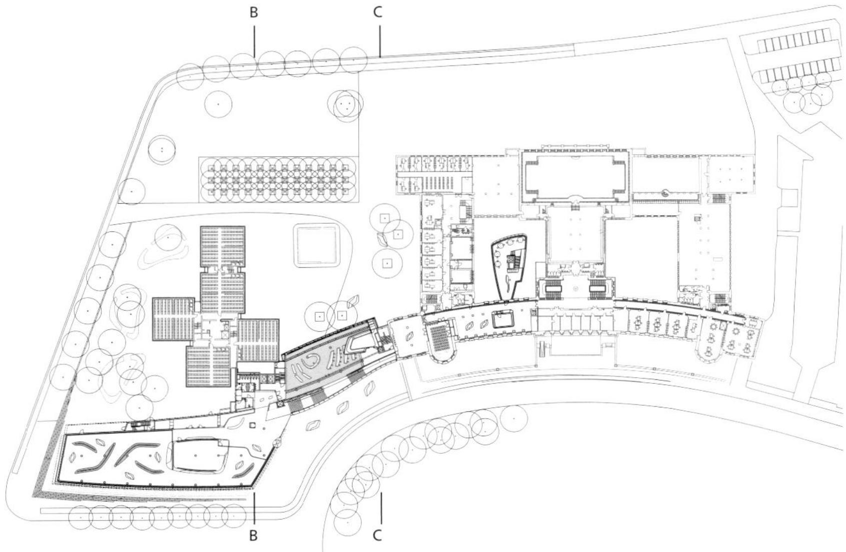

Staggered plan showing the public way from the ground floor (left) to the second floor (center), mediating between the new extension and the historic building

Deutsche National-bibliothek

Leipzig, Germany

Architect	Gabriele Glöckler Architektur
Client	Bundesrepublik Deutschland
Completion	2011
Floor area	100,000 m² (23,600 m² in extension)
Number of volumes	16.3 millions (media items)
Seating capacity	535 (40 in extension)

Located at the intersection of the trade routes Via Imperii and Via Regia, Leipzig, first named Lipiz, was bestowed city privileges as early as 1165. Since the Middle Ages, fostered by the founding of the University in 1409, the political events of the Reformation and Luther's translation of the bible in 1522, Leipzig's history and image in the world have been intrinsically interwoven with the book publishing and printing industry. Frankfurt, privileged by access to waterways and the close proximity to Mainz, where Gutenberg in 1450 had started the printing revolution, dominated the early book trading business until 1632 when trade restrictions, partially instituted in support of the Counter Reformation, started

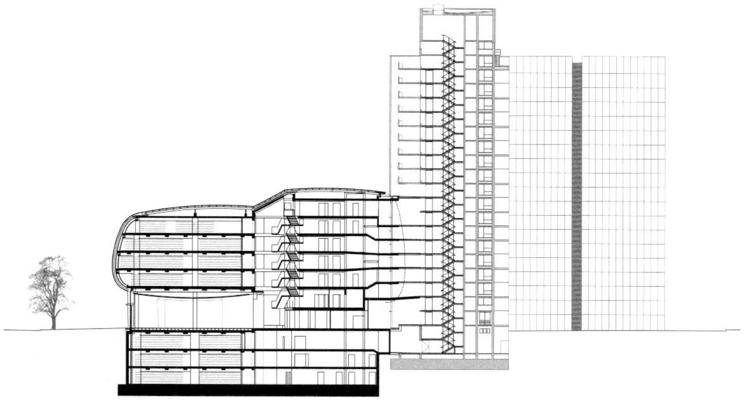

Cross section B–B

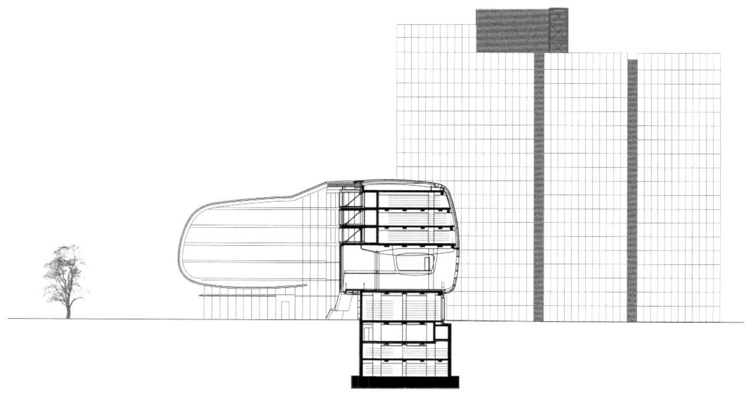

Cross section C–C

The library extension placed between the historic Neo-Renaissance building and the GDR-modern book tower | Facade on Deutscher Platz | The organically shaped reading and listening room of the German Music Archive floats within the 1963 courtyard

to render Frankfurt's book fair increasingly less influential. Through the financial commitment of the Kingdom of Saxony and the initiative of both the German Booksellers Association, founded in 1825, and the Leipzig Book Fair, the German Library was established in 1912. Its mission was to collect, archive, bibliographically document and make accessible all literature published in Germany. The library's first building, designed by Oskar Pusch, opened in 1916.

Increasing storage needs and additional space for the German Museum of Books and Letters necessitated the construction of the first (1936) and second extensions (1963), which were still undertaken under the auspices of the architect Oskar Pusch, consisting of two L-shaped multi-story wing buildings flanking the central reading room. The third extension (1982) by Dieter Seidlitz at the western edge of the site is comprised of five windowless square towers of varying height arranged around a central core. Above ground, this book high-rise was connected to the historic library only by a narrow steel tube encapsulating an automated book transportation system.

Gabriele Glöckler's 2011 addition to the German National Library is the fourth extension of the ensemble. The library master plan was laid out for an annual growth rate of 400,000 media items and thus reflecting a significant increase in book production and a broadening of literary topics.

The most recent extension consists of two distinct building segments, both extending outward from the foot of the tower, curvilinear in plan and section with reversing motion at their shifted interface. The building extends the concavity of the 120 m long facade of the Oskar Pusch structure, and then swoops into convexity outside the confines of the adjacent Deutscher Platz square. With its expressive architectural language, the addition negotiates spatially and stylistically

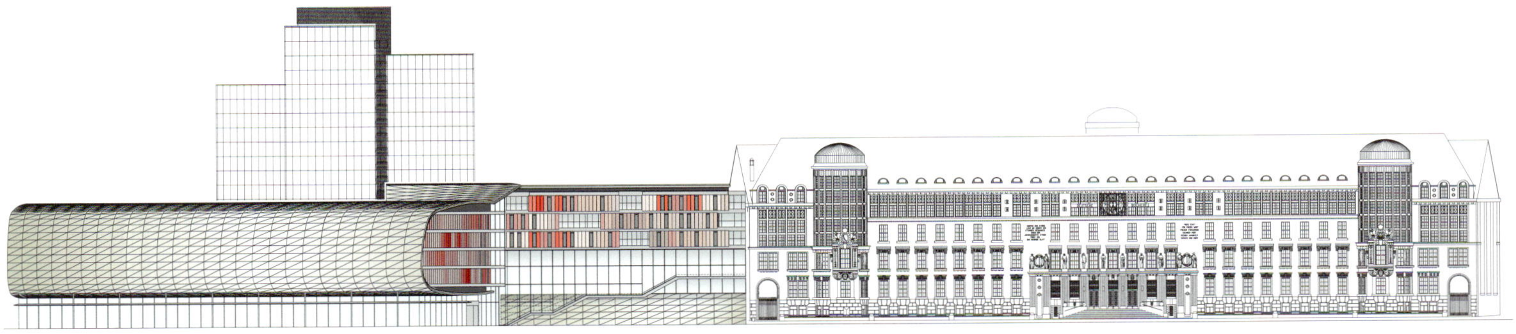

Elevation from Deutscher Platz

between the original historicist library and the tower as a symbol of past GDR modernity.

The formal language is derived from the shape of a book, comprising a book block and the book board. Shelved flat and hovering over translucent ground levels, the two volumes expose spine or fore edge respectively to the public realm of the street, as if to remind viewers and users of the changing method of organizing books on shelves. Historically, as book production expanded the marking of the book title on the spine prevailed over the tradition of writing the title with ink on the trimmed edge. As a result, the orientation of books on the shelf changed from fore edge facing out to spine facing out. Paying homage to Johann Sebastian Bach's life in Leipzig, Gabriele Glöckler transposed the auditory information of the *Goldberg Variations*, a work for harpsichord first published in 1741, into a visual sensory system by modulating the intensity of the spectral color red applied to the facade panels enclosing the magazine floors.

The entrance, located in the glazed shear plane created by the offset of the two new building volumes, marks the beginning of an interior public way. It weaves old and new building fabric into a new architectural amalgamation, while connecting areas of intensive public use. Beginning with the exhibition floor of the German Museum of Books and Letters, the passage subtly transits via a grand stair with a view onto the Deutscher Platz to the upper floor of the Oskar Pusch building. The exhibition space of the German Museum of Books and Letters is subdivided by circulation areas defining fluidly designed, organically shaped and climate-controlled showcases and a floating space for temporary exhibitions along the new reading room for the museum with a special suspended space – the vault – for light-sensitive exhibits.

Thoughtful interventions into the historic fabric allow the spatial and visual continuation of

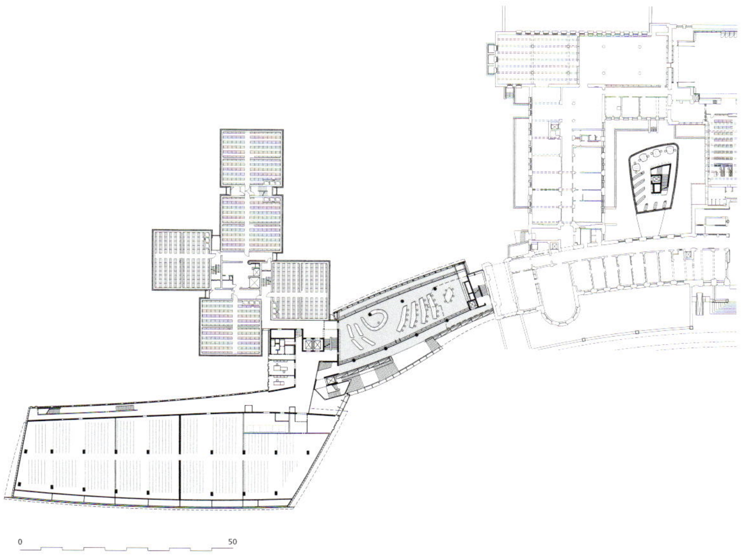

Ground floor

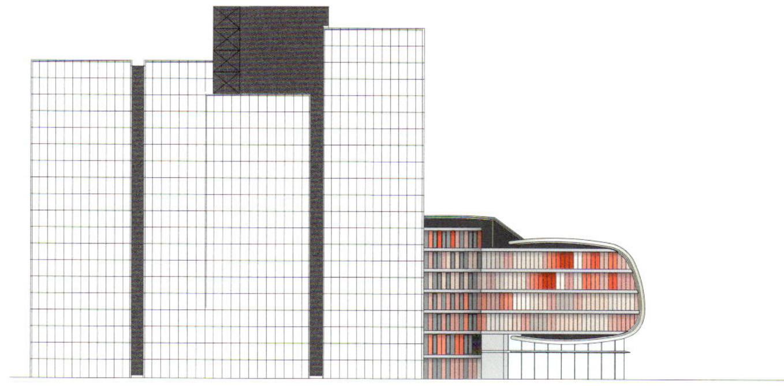

Elevation from Semmelweisstraße

Climate-controlled vitrines define circulation patterns and spatial expression of the exhibition area for the German Museum of Books and Letters | The sealed-off vault for the display of light-sensitive exhibits is suspended inside the reading room of the German Museum of Books and Letters | Grand stair

the public circulation spine, doubling as exhibition space along the courtyard-inserted, all-glass German Music Archive to the existing reading rooms.

An integrated climate control system with a highly efficient insulation, an active double skin roof membrane providing circulation air depending on the season and an array of energy-generating geothermal wells substantially reduce the energy consumption of the building. Conservation of the materials is a key objective and therefore a temperature of 18° Celsius (+-2) and a relative humidity of 50 % (+-5) is maintained throughout the closed stacks.

The collection is protected by a system of firewalls with automated fire doors and a highly efficient smoke exhaust system. In case of a fire, the infiltration of replacement air is thus regulated to keep circulation areas smoke-free. By circulating hot or chilled water through the window mullions, the window walls become part of the heating and cooling system. Triple-glazed window panels with sun protection coating provide optimal insulation values, offer even daylight density for the interior and reduced infiltration of ultraviolet radiation, while avoiding mechanical shading devices. All furniture and the exhibition architecture was designed by Gabriele Glöckler as well and forms an integral part of the complex. ***wr***

Large Public Libraries

In a world altered by digital technology – from e-books to robotic storage – the late 20th century public library struggled with an outmoded 19th century identity. Originally a place of reading and reference it sought a new relevance in keeping with change. Today, after more than two decades of self-reflection and reinvention, the public library is no longer in fear of obsolescence from a sole reliance on the commerce of physical books. The public library in the 21st century has emerged, regenerated by an expansion of its role within the greater community it serves.

Determined by the population they serve, public libraries differ greatly, ranging from one-room rural libraries for fewer than 1,000 occupants to multi-storied libraries catering to an entire metropolis. Large public libraries are typically urban and serve a core inner-city population in a central location accessible by public transportation. Small branch libraries serve the remaining metropolitan population outside the immediate center. With collections of up to 1.5 million volumes, large public libraries range in size from 25,000 m^2 to almost 40,000 m^2.

While public libraries of all sizes share similar missions and objectives, the realization of such mission differs between large and small public libraries. Once regarded as a formal civic institution, a revered book lender, a place of hushed reading and even an information center, the large public library has had to reinvent its identity in its quest for relevance. In the 21st century, the large public library has evolved as a type, often with architecture as a means.

As civic, urban monuments, a stately architectural language of classical elements imbued the grand public libraries of the 19th century with a formality that was recognizable from library to library and from city to city. Imposing reading rooms and closed stacks corroborated a formal concept of "knowledge through reading", a concept premised on the lendable book as a precious commodity. This concept became outdated with the easy accessibility of both printed and digital media. Today, large public libraries focus instead on an expanded concept of "knowledge through learning" – a broad mission that encompasses not only old and new media but also a vast range of programs centered on learning.

Serving extensive metropolitan communities, large public libraries today have outgrown the one-size-fits-all approach that made few distinctions between types of borrowers. Often in dense, urban settings with widely varied demographics, these communities now comprise a spectrum from the intellectually sophisticated to an underserved and barely literate population. Addressing the learning needs of these many different patrons creates the need for expanded programs and their attendant space.

Standard program elements of collection, reading spaces for children, young adults, and adults, reference, computer and Internet access are enhanced by cafés/restaurants, auditoria, meeting rooms, exhibition space, archives, business centers, multimedia facilities and theaters. In addition, less conventional programs include unique elements such as gift shops, drive-in book pick-up, interactive children's museums, health clinics, daycare centers and teen music-making facilities. This proliferation of program reflecting a multicultural, multidimensional user group has created opportunities both in exterior massing, with new elements, and in internal planning and layout, with new and complicated juxtapositions. This complexity is the generator of innovative forms and spatial relationships within the library that contribute to an evolution of the library typology.

Informed by numerous new programs, the form and style of new large public libraries are both less imposing and less formal. With a trend towards finding a new expression for the institution of the library, the architectural forms vary from modern glazed boxes to sculptural compositions enabled by new materials. Dependent on site and community, these complex programs are frequently resolved through a vertical configuration. In less dense settings, the lack of site constraints permits an array of massing options. With these possibilities, the singular formal style has given way to a pluralism of diverse yet distinctive architecture.

These numerous new elements have also created a complex internal organization, influencing the planning and layout. Once repetitive floors of orderly stacks and reading rooms have been replaced by floors of dissimilar program elements. Circulation through the library, previously based on call numbers of books to differentiate between the quasi-identical floors, is now one that traverses entirely different experiences, one after the next. Its similarities to large-scale retail establishments are apparent in which circulation assumes a crucial role. Commercial and retail design concepts often serve as precedents for organizing and connecting the many library programs.

The parallel to retail however lies not only in the design of the circulation. Many large public libraries with expanded programs have embraced the idea of the experience economy. As a retail establishment of knowledge it caters to patrons with offerings packaged as themed learning experience and entertainment. As a conduit between the arts and the community the library, with its exhibition galleries, auditorium or theater space, becomes a venue through which the community can gain access to performers, writers, musicians and artists. The public library as a knowledge mall is part of a successful transformation as it consolidates its position in a new era.

While emulating the successes of capitalism on one hand, public libraries, both large and small, are, on the other hand, deeply committed to community outreach. Early educational programs and afterschool activities are examples of common programs that are built into all public library budgets. But within communities of wider diversity, there exists a greater potential to use library design to ameliorate difficult political and social situations. The inclusion of programs such as a healthcare center, a secondary educational facility or a childcare center within the public library constitutes the shaping of a social agenda within the community. The public library as a platform for community engagement gains the institution a new legitimacy.

With the new wealth of possibilities large public libraries more and more employ architecture as a means of advertisement. As a modern civic monument, the architecture plays an important role in the creation of a positive and vibrant image within the community. Until the economic downturn, "starchitects" were sought for an architecture that would not only make the library's presence felt within the urban fabric but would also gain it status as an international icon. Architecture remains a tool of the new public library. It continues to play an important role in perpetuating a new perception of the public library, thereby attracting users and patrons through its innovative form and materials.

The many changes within the large public library are primarily user-based. While driven initially by a need to retain and gain patrons, the development of the large public library has grown from a product of necessity to one that enjoys a newfound significance. As an outcome of several decades of soul searching for a new raison d'être in the 21st century, the large public library has emerged with a rich, relevant and fulfilling mission. ***lw***

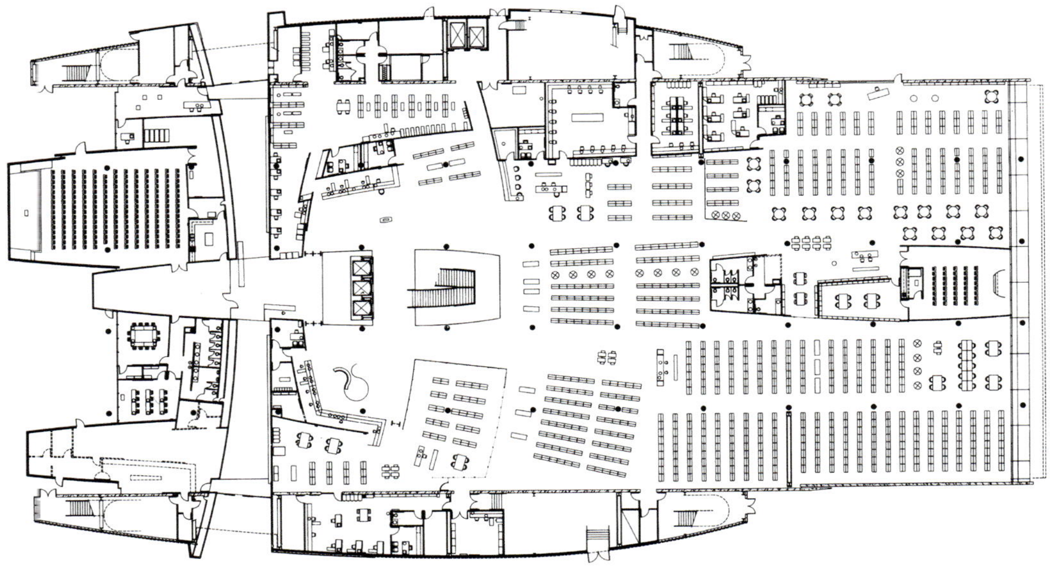

Ground floor

Burton Barr Central Library

Phoenix, Arizona, USA

Architect	Will Bruder with DWL Architects
Client	Library Advisory Board of Phoenix
Completion	1995
Floor area	26.000 m²
Number of volumes	705,000, up to 1 million
Seating capacity	1,300

Designed by architect Will Bruder in cooperation with DWL Architects, the Burton Barr Central Library, serving the community of Phoenix, captures a decisive period of change in library design in America.

The 26,000 m² Burton Barr Central Library opened in 1995, at the eve of the technological era. Inspired by Arizona's famed Monument Valley, the library takes its shape from the mesa, a flat-topped elevated landform of the Southwest. Clad in copper and enclosing a five-story atrium in its center, this volume is covered by a suspended tension structure. Housing some 705,000 items, this massive metal and glass struc-

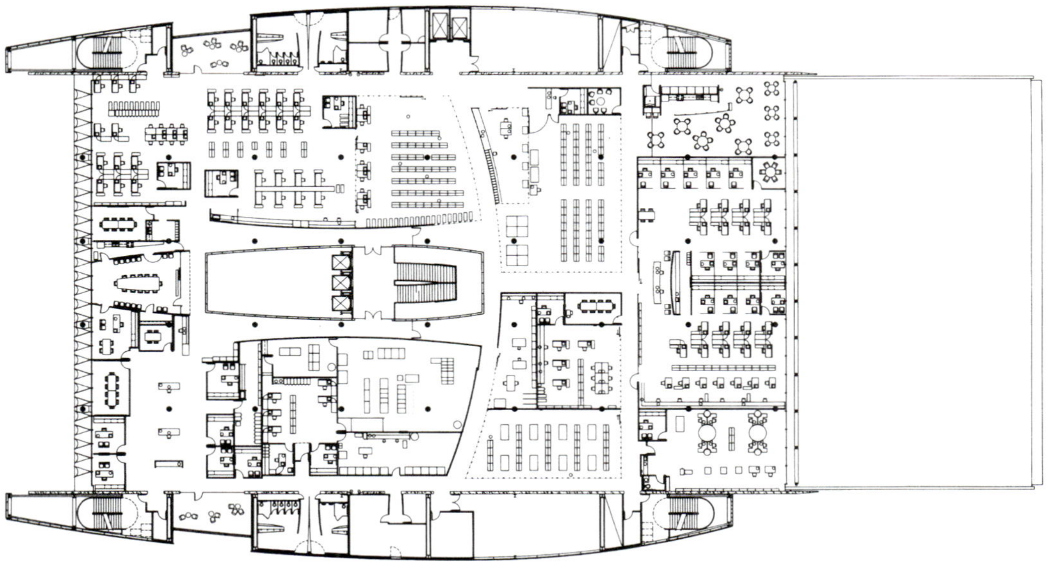

Second floor

Automated solar tracking louvers at south facade | View towards the collection | Library as "urban mesa" hovering above the road | The "Crystal Canyon" with elevator

ture, a landmark on the city's skyline, serves as the symbolic and administrative center for Phoenix's Public Library system. It also holds the largest reading room in North America, a vast 4,000 m² space situated in open plan on the top floor.

Designed at a time not yet submerged in the culture of sustainability, the building is notable for its environmentally focused features, both passive and mechanical, that include a computerized louver system on its south-facing facade, horizontal louvers, modular lighting systems, fixed light-deflecting sails and skylights that track the movement of the sun so as to provide consistent natural lighting. Its architectural orientation and features are designed to display sunlight alignment on equinox days with a "light show". Predating the LEED program by several years, the library received LEED Existing Building Silver designation in 2010. More recently, with funds from an Energy Efficiency Conservation Block Grant, the library invested in renewable energy through the installation of a solar-powered parking canopy consisting of 42 slanted solar panels, each of which produces power equivalent to that required for 0.6 homes while shading the car park.

The designs of Will Bruder for the city of Phoenix (he also designed the Agave branch library, which opened in 2009) are a barometer of the changing face of the American library in the digital age. Named one of Phoenix's Points of Pride, the library addresses the many needs of the community with its art gallery, program assisting new residents and immigrants, free full-service college planning and private space for teens. The Central Library posits the library as a stalwart but modern institution. Its outstanding features serve to promote the comforts of reading and studying. The magnificent reading room, too, corroborates the library as a place of books and reading. ***lw***

613-649
5
Restrooms
EXIT

Great reading room on fourth floor | View of lobby from reading room | View towards stacks

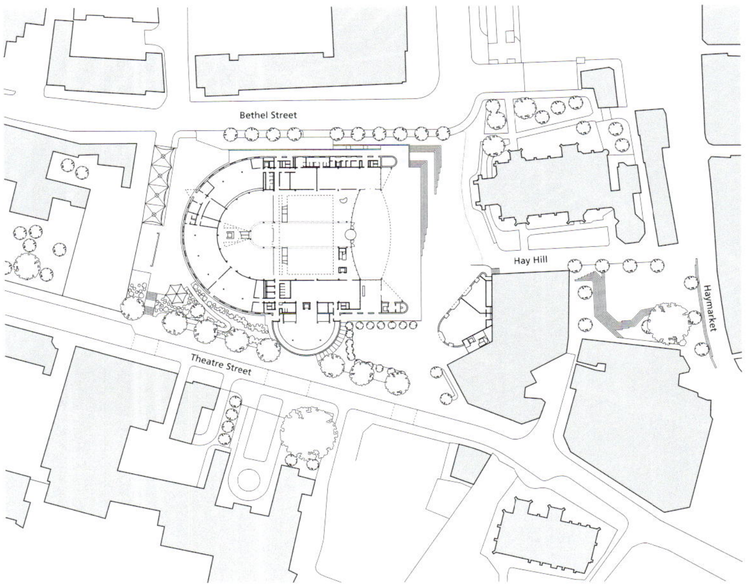

Site plan

Millennium Library

Norwich, UK

Architect	Michael Hopkins Architects
Client	Millennium Commission, Norwich City Council
Completion	2001
Floor area	4,621 m²
Number of volumes	450,000
Seating capacity	220

The Millennium Library, located in the center of Norwich, is a part of the complex known as the Forum. Built in 2001, it replaced the Central Public Library that was destroyed by fire in 1994. In the rebuilding process, the library sought to reinvent itself as a part of a larger institution, one that is described as "a cultural and recreational building for the whole community and is a dynamic center for information, learning and entertainment." (Source: "The Forum") In doing so, this 4,621 m^2 facility, a small public library by size, takes on the persona of a large public library through this extension of shared scope.

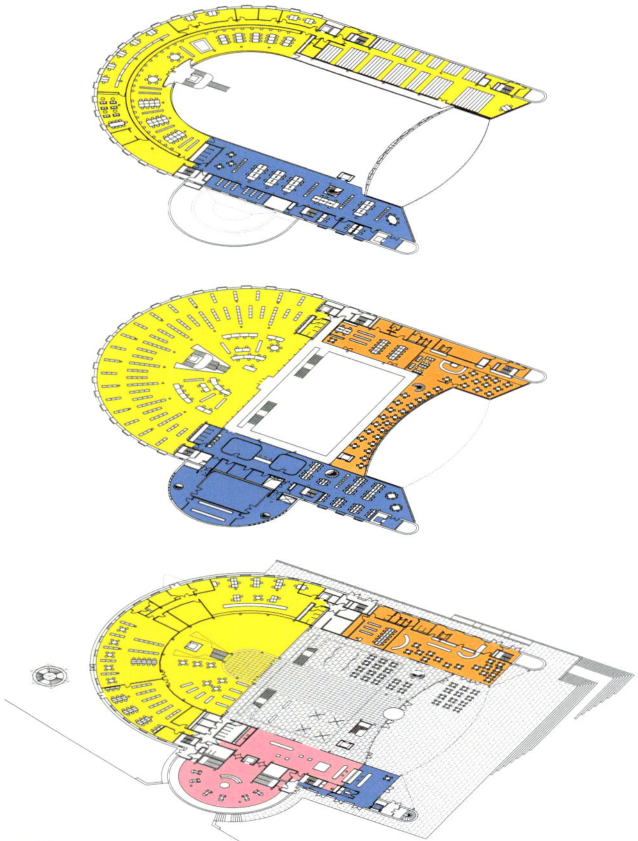

- Library
- Retail
- Public services (tourist information, BBC offices)
- Restaurants

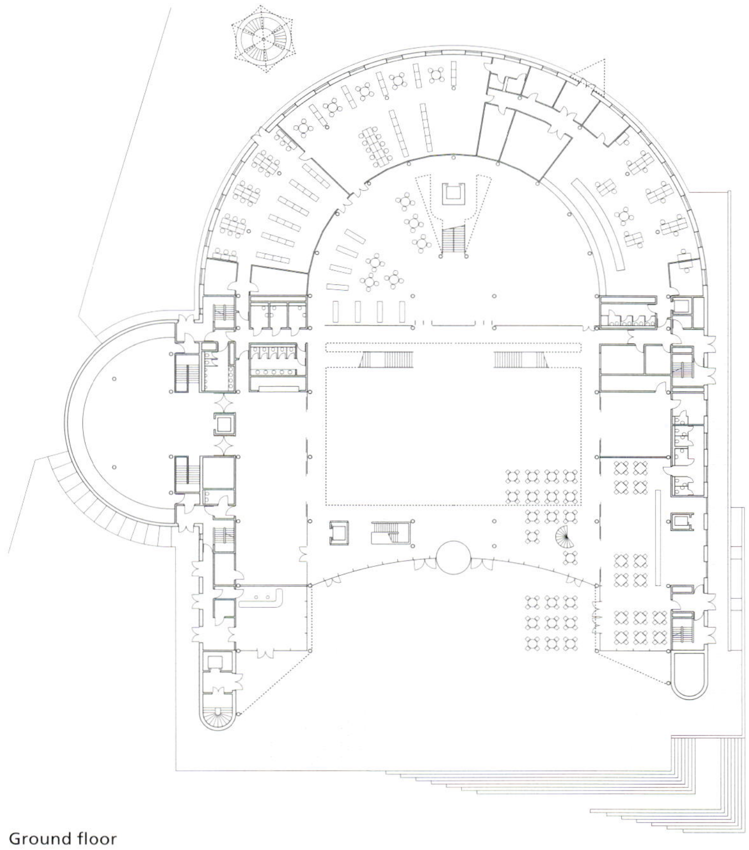

Ground floor

The characteristic bow-string trusses of the Forum | Restaurants across from the library | Library seating in the Forum atrium

Set in the heart of the medieval city, the Forum is a three-story horseshoe-shaped building surrounding a central space. Forming an enclosed courtyard, an exposed steel structure sits within curved U-shaped walls of handmade, load-bearing brick. The flat facade is fully glazed and provides visual access to the atrium with its glazed roof and bow-string, steel truss supports. The trusses form petal-shaped panels, alternately infilled with acoustic materials or glazing through which light enters the atrium. As part of an environmental strategy for a low-energy building, the building mass is used as a "'passive' environmental modifier" with the introduction of "'active' building engineering systems, which serve only to assist the fabric to recycle ambient energy." (Source: www.theforumnorwich.co.uk)

The Millennium Library is a state-of-the-art public facility serving a population of 800,000. It is noted for its special collections, an extensive picture collection of Norfolk, and a special collection in memory of the American Second Air Division USAAF, which served in Norfolk during World War II. As part of the Forum, a complex which houses not only the library but also the Norfolk Heritage Centre, the regional studios of the BBC, a tourist information center, learning shops and various cafés, restaurants and bars, the library has seen a dramatic increase in use – a byproduct of the millions of visitors and tourists to the Forum each year.

The decision to become an integral part of the Forum is the result of in-depth public focus groups and studies conducted in the process of rebuilding the library. The discussions established the need to reinforce civic life as a path towards "regeneration, education and lifelong learning." A reexamination of library goals to fulfill such a need concluded that while the provision of traditional information resources was important, access "to collective social spaces where communities can flourish" (Source: "Libraries Must Also

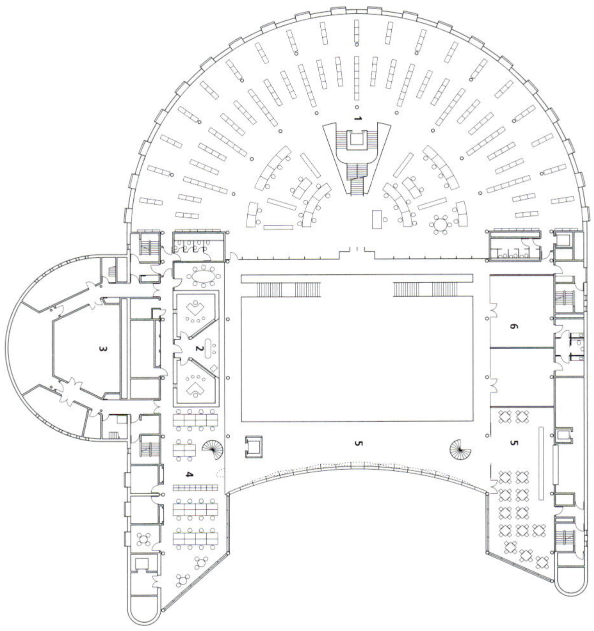

First floor

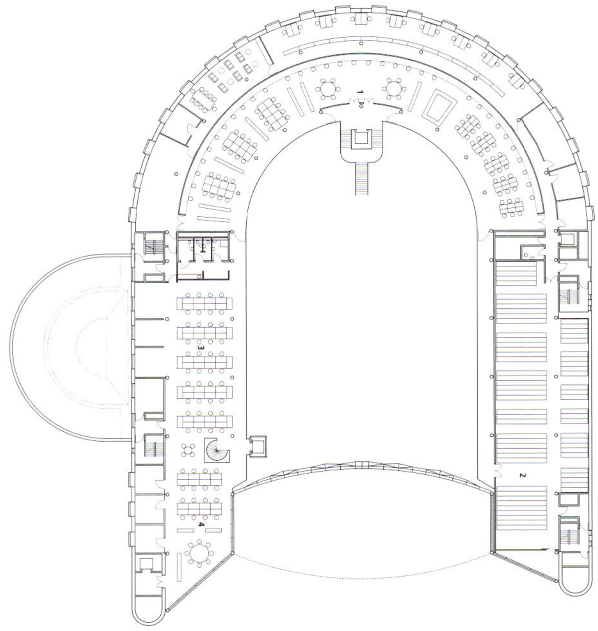

Second floor

View from the library down into the retail establishments | Internal circulation within the library | View from the medieval part of Norwich towards the library

Be Buildings?") was equally vital. As part of the Forum with its iconic horseshoe form, mall-like image and proximity to broadcast studios and pizza parlors, the Millennium Library is better able to accomplish this goal. But, in doing so, it relinquishes an identity, perhaps outdated, of the unique civic institution of the library. ***lw***

"The Forum", Norwich. Commission for Architecture and the Built Environment, 1 Kemble Street, London WC2B 4AN. http://www.cabe.org.uk/case-studies/the-forum

http:// www.the forumnorwich.co.uk

Jared Bryson, Bob Usherwood, Richard Proctor, "Libraries Must Also Be Buildings? New Library Impact Study", The Centre for Public Libraries and Information in Society, Department of Information, University of Sheffield, March 2003, p. 28.

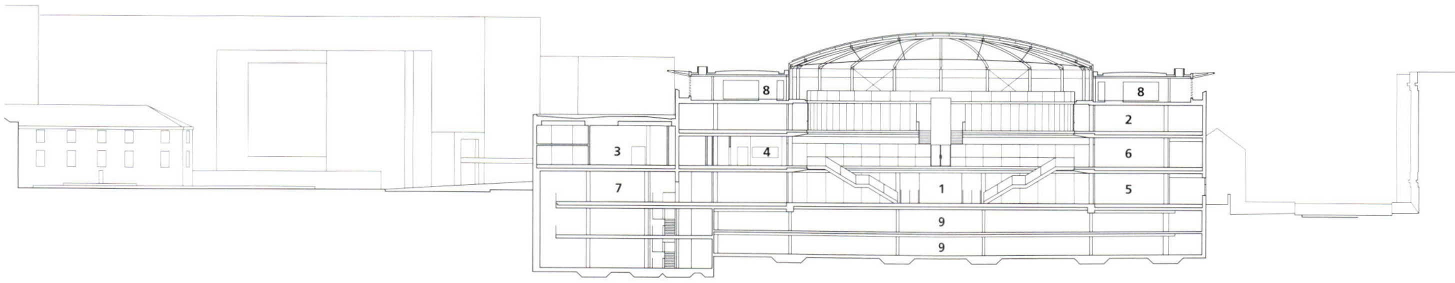

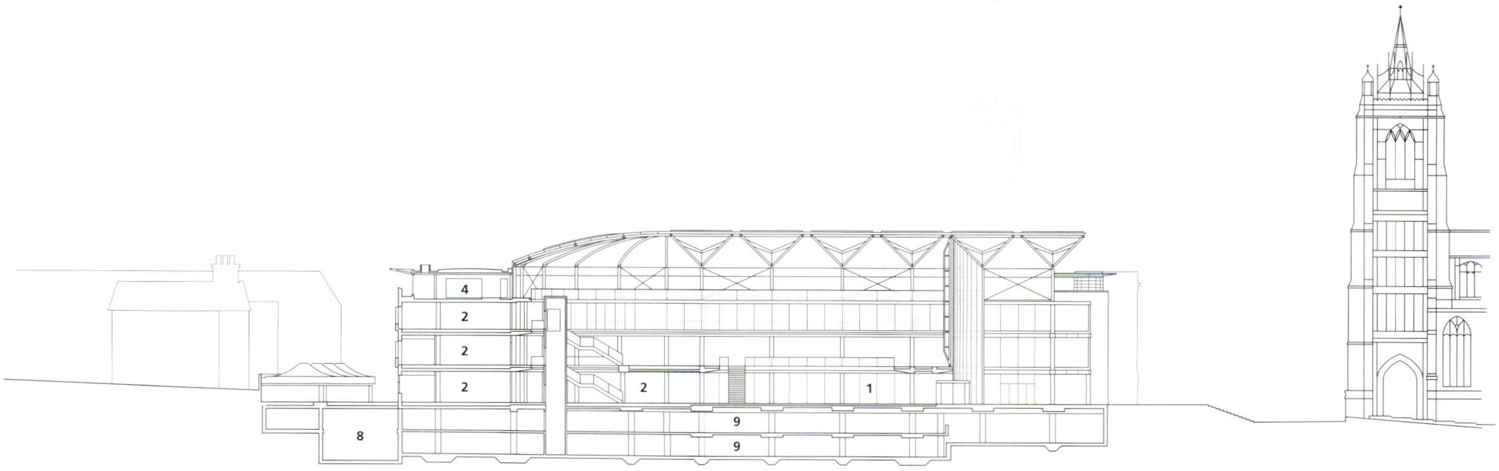

Sections

1 Atrium
2 Library
3 BBC television studio
4 BBC radio studio
5 Catering
6 Retail
7 Norfolk Heritage Centre
8 Services
9 Car park

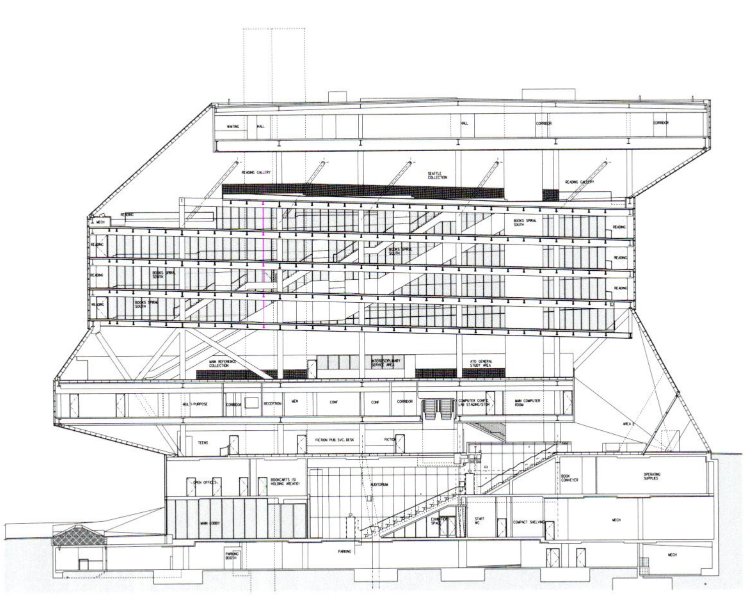

East-west section

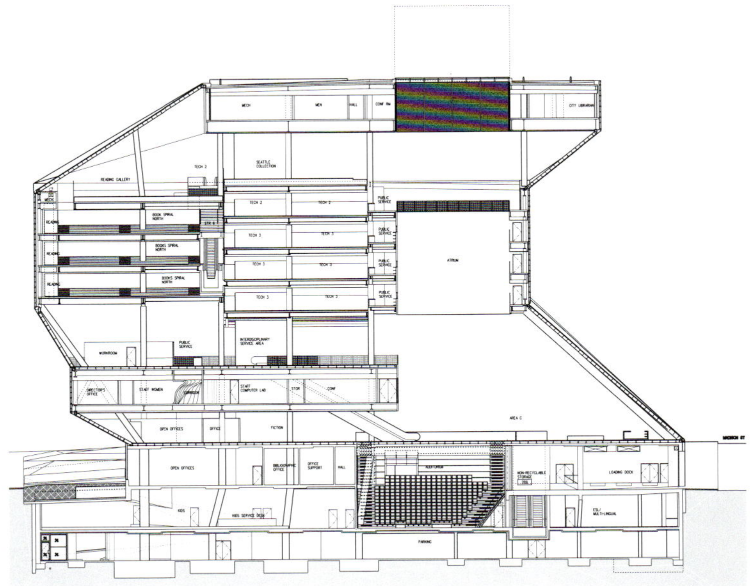

North-south section

Seattle Central's distinctive form in the surrounding urban context | The iconic neon yellow escalators to the reading spaces | Living room and auditorium

Seattle Central Library

Seattle, Washington, USA

Architect	OMA with LMN Architects
Client	Seattle Public Library
Completion	2004
Floor area	33,700 m²
Number of volumes	780,000, up to 1.45 million
Seating capacity	275 (theater); meeting rooms for 25–200; 400 public computers

Opened in 2004, the Seattle Central Library by the Office for Metropolitan Architecture (OMA) in joint venture with LMN Architects sets the standard for the library of the 21st century. At a moment in history when digital technology had brought about the need to redefine the library as an institution, the design of the Seattle Central Library is a bold work that embraces information in all of its various forms, resulting in a civic monument that is profound and became seminal for the building type.

Bounded by office towers and the federal courthouse, the library occupies a full city block on a steeply sloping site in downtown Seattle.

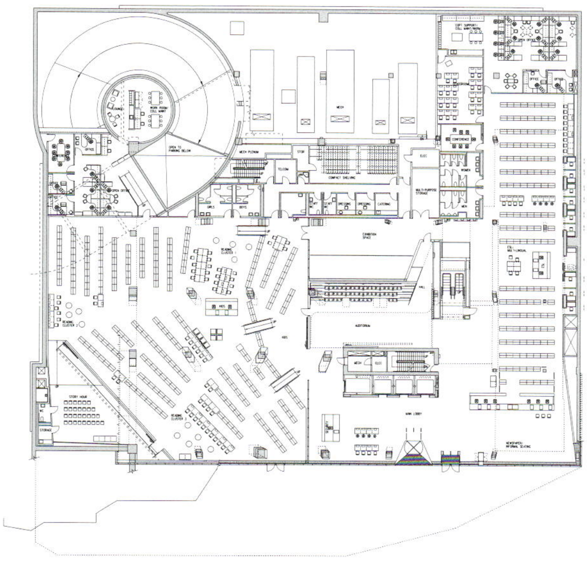

Level 1

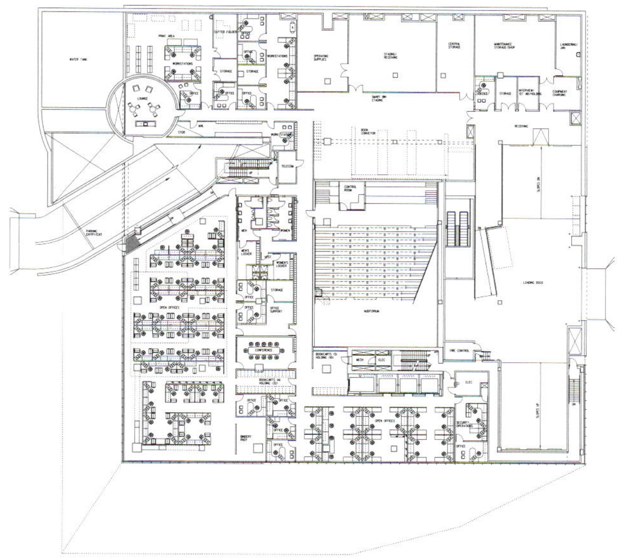

Level 2

The asymmetrical, exterior volume composed of angular, faceted planes of gridded glass and steel encloses the eleven-story, 33,700 m^2 building. The irregular profile created by these abstract geometrical forms is the result of OMA's novel approach to program as a means by which to reinvent the new library as a repository of information, "where all media – new and old – are presented under a regime of new equalities." (Source: "Concept Book", p. 8) Presented in 1999 as part of the design process, the "Concept Book" illustrates OMA's proposal in regard to the critical issues, common to many libraries adapting to the information age, resulting from the proliferation of information media.

OMA's concept is premised on the duality of the library experience of the 21st century as both real, through its physical structure, and virtual, through its internet site. Guided by the concept of the computing platform that includes, at a minimum, a computer's architecture, operating system, and programmatic languages, OMA reorganizes the library program into five so-called "platforms". Each of these platforms – parking, staff, assembly, books, and headquarters – is dedicated to its own purpose and occupies an autonomous volume designed and equipped for dedicated performance. Arranged vertically in overlapping fashion, these platforms are connected through four interstitial zones labeled as "trading floors" where the librarians and patrons "work, interact, and play" (Source: "Concept Book", p. 22). These zones constitute a "living room", a so-called Mixing Chamber, and a reading room. The abstract volumes of the exterior reflect the dissimilar needs of the platforms and zones in size, circulation, structure, interior mechanical needs, and solar orientation.

The platform dedicated to books addresses the common problem of flexibility in accommodating collections, housed in discrete rooms, as they unpredictably expand and contract over time. The solution is found in the Book Spiral, a continuous ribbon of books arranged in the

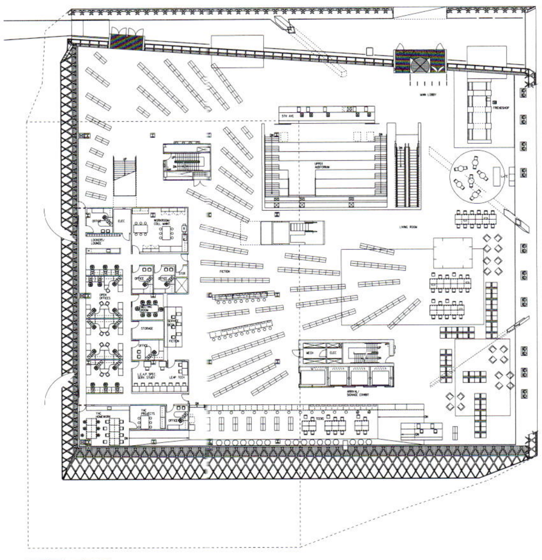

Level 3 (main entry level)

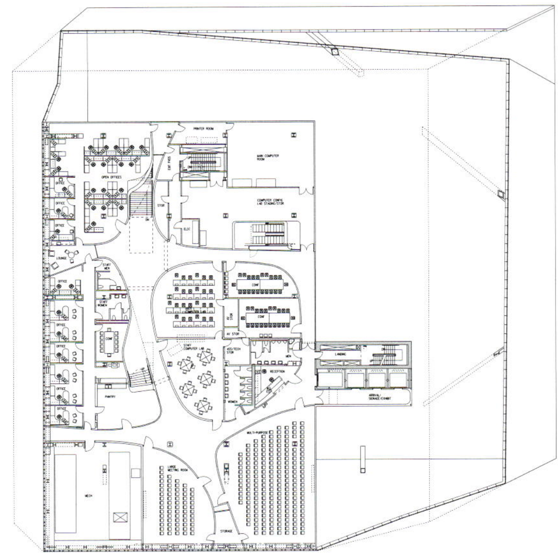

Level 4

Dewey Decimal System. The Book Spiral contains 6,233 bookcases which, at opening, housed 780,000 volumes but can accommodate up to 1,450,000 volumes without the addition of any bookcases in the future.

Additional features include the Mixing Chamber, an area dedicated to librarian and patron interaction that maximizes both human and technological intelligence, and the state-of-the-art book handling system that checks books through a conveyor belt into the library's circulation system using radio frequency identification (RFID) technology. Sustainable design elements included the recycling of 75 % of demolition and construction waste and resulted in the project's award of a Silver rating from the U.S. Green Building Council. ***lw***

OMA/LMN Architects, "Concept Book", Seattle Public Library proposal, December 1999, http://www.spl.org/prebuilt/cen_conceptbook

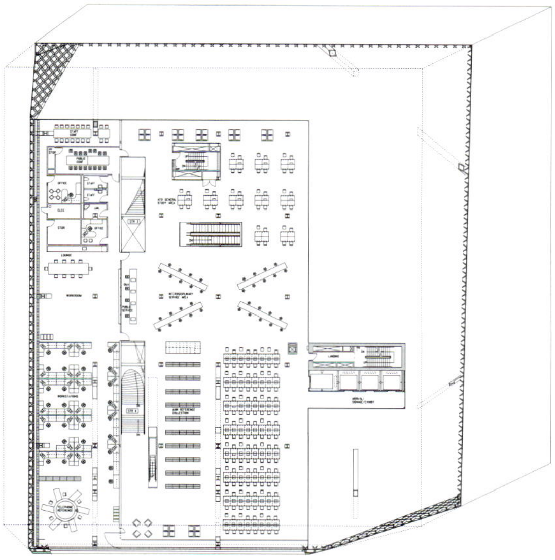

Level 5

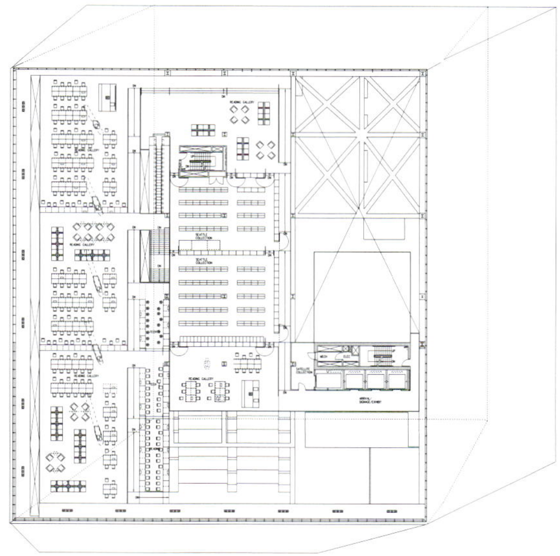

Level 10

Customized seating includes four-person lounge stairs | View of the Living Room at the main entrance lobby

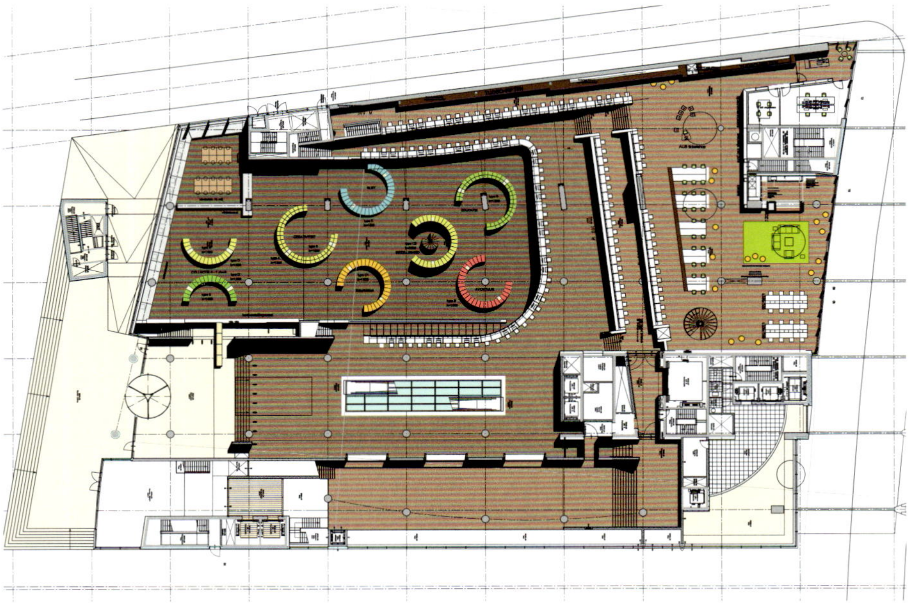

Ground floor

View of the OBA on Oosterdokseiland | Entrance as part of the "plinth" | Western red cedar and limestone facade | The escalators connect the library programs

OBA – Openbare Bibliotheek Amsterdam

Amsterdam, the Netherlands

Architect	Jo Coenen
Client	Amsterdam Gemeenteraad
Completion	2007
Floor area:	28,000 m²
Number of volumes	1.5 million
Seating capacity	275 (theater)

Completed in 2007, the Amsterdam Central Library or OBA – Openbare Bibliotheek Amsterdam, is currently the largest library in the Netherlands with 1.5 million books and 13 floors occupying 28,000 m². A replacement for the 1919 Prinsengracht library, a facility half the size, the OBA not only provides state-of-the-art library service but also public access to a theater, multi-media space, two cafés, and a restaurant. The OBA is situated on Oosterdokseiland, a new 200,000 m², mixed-use development planned to transform the IJ River bank into a dynamic work/live neighborhood. The master plan for restructuring this land adjacent to the Central Station, also includes office space,

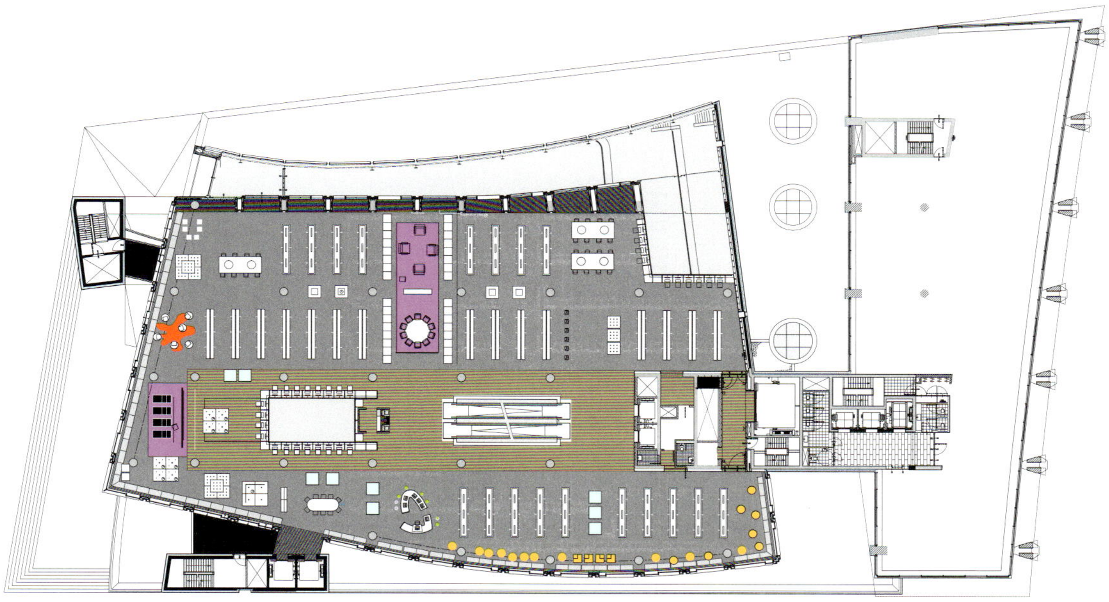

Second floor

a four-star hotel, a convention center, a variety of shops, restaurants, bars and a music academy. Architect Jo Coenen took advantage of this opportunity to incorporate aspects of urban life into the modern public library.

As the first project of Oosterdokseiland to be constructed, Coenen, known for his emphasis on contextualization, looked to design from inside out. The spatial sequence, derived from a unique view of the library program, is divided into three categories; "speed/haste", "rest" and "meet/relax/interact" – classifications that expand typical library functions and serve to attract a broader segment of users.

The classification of "speed/haste" refers to the entry levels and includes library programs such as the children's library, exhibition, periodicals, a panini bar/café and a multi-media space, all of which serve as a transition from the public urban space to the book stacks above. Designed for citizens of all ages from the young to the old, the entry levels act as a general living room for the city and offer a pause in the rhythm of urban life.

The classification of "rest" refers to the stacks that occupy five floors in the distinct and physically separated middle volume. These are spaces specifically designed to house the function of study and reading. The five floors utilize an architectural palette of black, white and wood and are centered around an atrium circumscribed by study desks built into the guardrails. White sculptural forms of molded plastic serve as iconic info points throughout the stacks. Plastic seating pods in different shapes serve as furniture.

The library's architecture helps visitors to orientate themselves. The escalators in the heart of the building, which also function as a light object, the large open space next to them, the connections of the different floors provided by the voids and the many different views to the

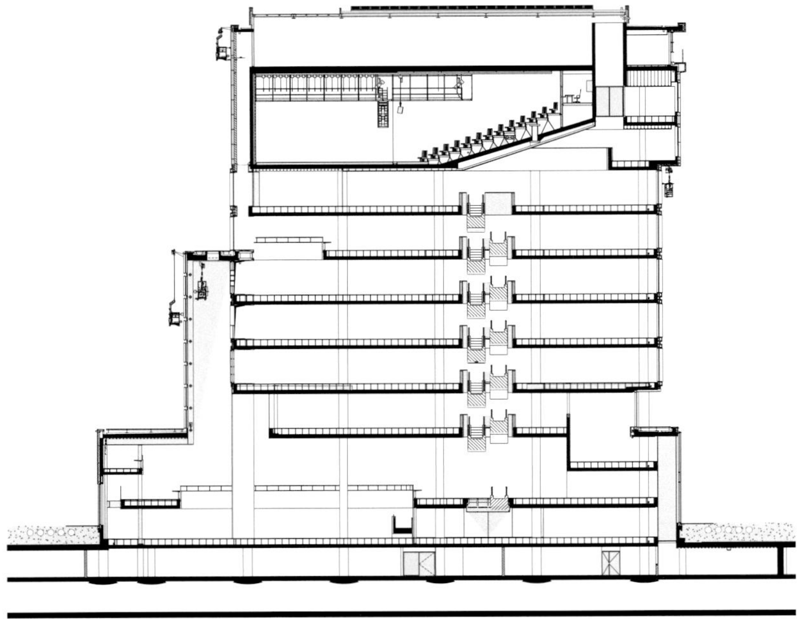

Transverse section

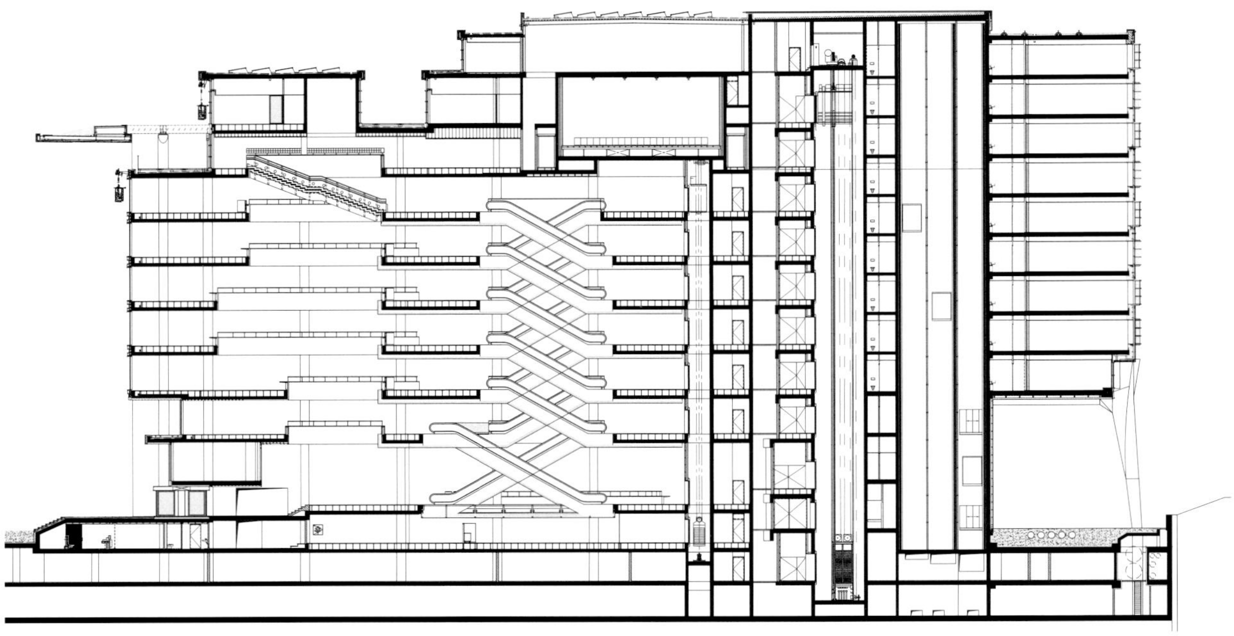

Longitudinal section

outside, all serve to help visitors find their way around the library. "Meet/relax/interact" refers to the top levels, which house a theater, bar, restaurant and a roof terrace with a panoramic view of Amsterdam. As an additional program that augments traditional library service, these functions are placed strategically at the top and draw the user through the many levels of study and book stacks dedicated to reading.

These three classifications are also used to divide the massing of the building into plinth, middle and top, in order to conform to building guidelines prescribed for the entire development. The entry levels or "plinth" align with required setbacks while the floors above are an intricate play of volumes that protrude and recede beneath an enormous stone canopy, 13 stories up in the air. This approach to meeting setbacks and building heights is accompanied by a use of glass that gives consideration to the availability of natural light for future, neighboring buildings. At an urban level, this massing recalls that of the temples of Antiquity and evokes a monumental scale that designates the entry plaza as a grand, civic meeting place. The upside-down L of natural stone at the front side of the building is an element that is clearly discernible from afar and the library has thus also become a visual landmark for Oosterdokseiland.

The success of OBA as a modern, public library is derived, in part, from its inclusion within the Oosterdokseiland development. Mirroring the goals of the development to create a unique urban live/work environment in the old harbor, similar strategies are utilized in the library to reinvent and redefine the role of the public library as a type. At a time when the role of books in 21st century life has been questioned, architect Jo Coenen embraces aspects of modern, urban life and incorporates them as library program. In doing so, he affirms the role of the public library as an active center of the modern city. ***lw***

The escalator creates a lit graphic element | Counter seating overlooking the children's room | Monumental stair to theater

Seating pods in the multi-media space | Counter seating wraps the edges of the multi-level atrium | Periodicals area | Interior volumes are set back to allow for an abundance of natural light

5
gezondheid
4
kunst
3
reizen
uitlenen
2
romans
1

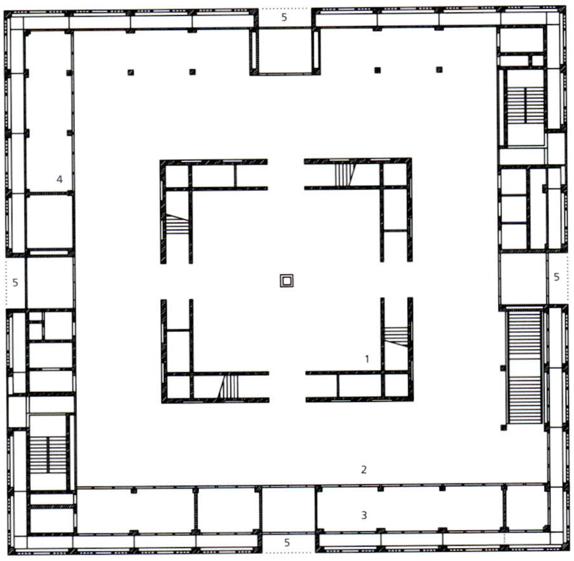

Ground floor

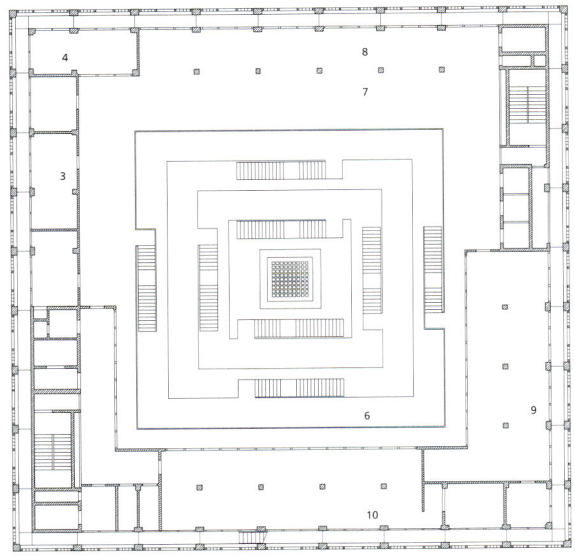

Eighth floor

1 Central space ("Heart")
2 Entrance hall
3 Offices
4 Sorting area
5 Entrance
6 Reading room
7 Media
8 Workspaces
9 *Graphothek* (library for art prints)
10 Café

Double-skin facade | A cube or hexahedron with an edge length of 45 m constitutes the volume of the library | View into the reading gallerias crowned by a large skylight; helically positioned stairs connect the multiple terraces | View of central space ("heart")

Stadtbibliothek am Mailänder Platz

Stuttgart, Germany

Architect	Eun Young Yi
Client	Hochbauamt Landeshauptstadt Stuttgart
Completion	2011
Floor area	20,225 m²
Number of volumes	500,000 (media units)
Seating capacity	400 (workspaces); 300 (assembly space)

The transformation of Stuttgart's inner-city railroad terminal, allowing the reclamation of 109 hectares of underutilized real estate, is at the core of the very controversial planning initiative Stuttgart 21. The Stadtbibliothek, part of this urban redevelopment project, was initially envisioned in 1997 as "Bibliothek Stuttgart 21". It is placed as a translucent monolith on a small quadrilateral block and conceived as space and platform for community and the collection of knowledge. Eun Young Yi reinterprets archetypal space configurations, proportions and geometries ingrained into the collective memory of humanity. A cube or hexahedron is associated with the classical element "earth", and as the only

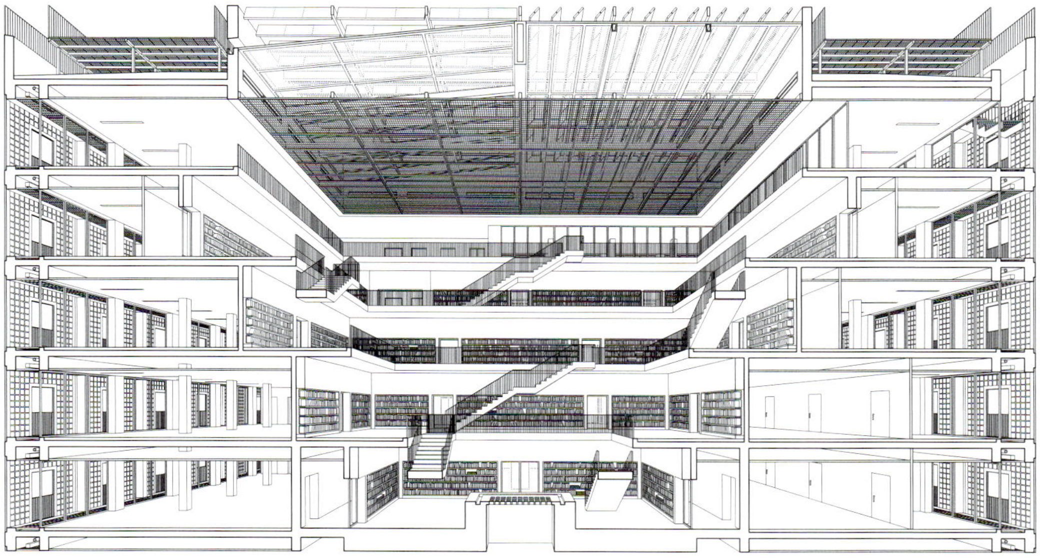

Section perspective

regular Platonic solid able to tessallate Euclidian space, generates the volume of the library. A regular grid of in-situ concrete frames, filled with frosted glass blocks around a rectangular, unprotected opening, constitutes the exterior skin of the double-envelope system, ensuring high-density light levels and even glare-free distribution. At night, blue LED lights transform the white crystalline day appearance of the building into a light sculpture.

Nestled in the plan center of the large cube is a smaller hexahedron, referred to as the "heart". This communal meditative space, the inner sanctum, void of any function, serves the purpose of deceleration; the volume, like the outer cube, bears no orientative suggestions and is accessible from the exterior square loop through openings on all four sides. Rectangular wall incisions in the form of windows or indentations and the small, square, skylight-like coffers and oculi, respectively paired with the proportional qualities of a cube, are reminiscent of the archetypal paradigm of the pantheon.

The "heart" is encapsulated by an enclosed, circumferential helical stair system providing access to the four colonnade-like library floors surrounding the central space; above the "heart", the stairs open up onto the ground level of the reading gallerias designed in the shape of an inverted stepped pyramid with linear bookshelves lining the outer perimeter of the terraces. Abundant daylight, directed by adjustable photovoltaic-clad louvers, floods into the negative, ziggurat-like form through a large skylight. The unifying monochromatic color concept of the exterior skin finds continuation on the interior; only the book spines set colorful accents. Typically, double-faced shelving units are arranged within the inner circumferential loop in a perpendicular fashion, while work spaces and meeting rooms occupy the periphery along the inner thermal glass facade. The cube displays the word "library" in different languages. ***wr***

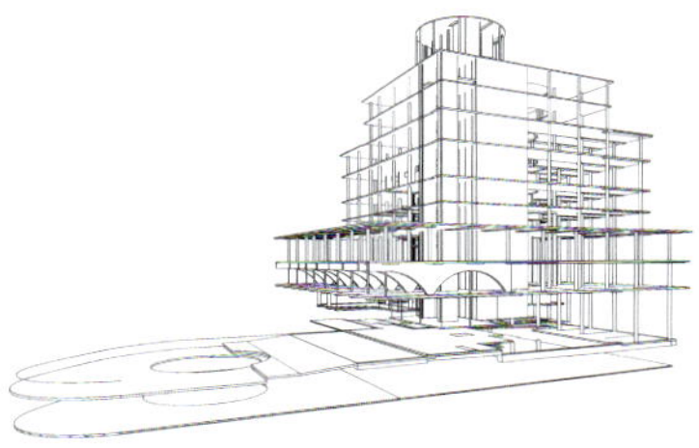

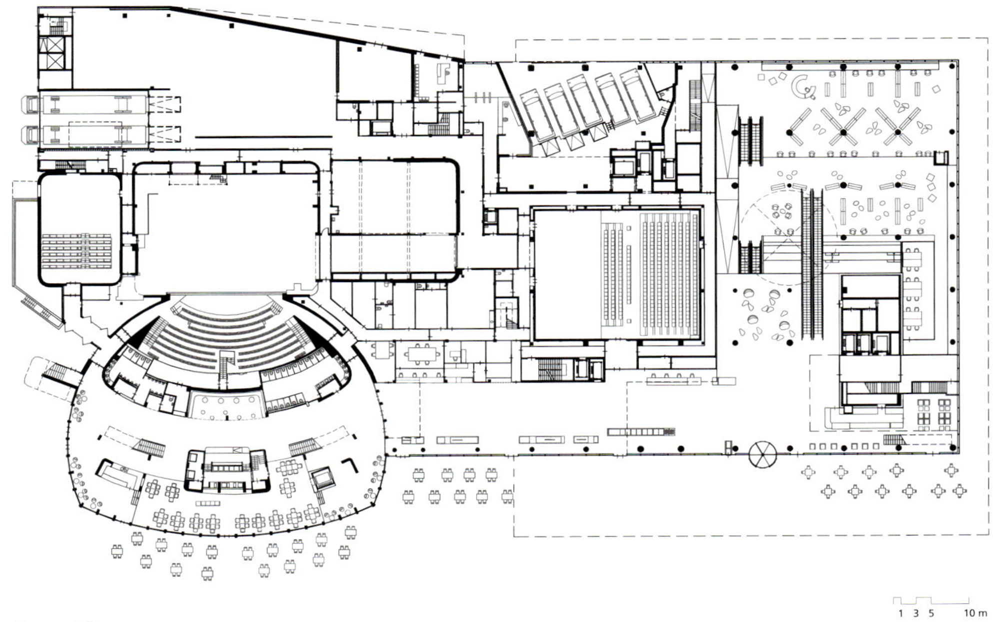

Ground floor

Library of Birmingham

Birmingham, UK

Architect	Mecanoo
Client	Birmingham City Council
Completion	2013
Floor area	31,000 m²
Number of volumes	1 million
Seating capacity	300 (auditorium)

The Library of Birmingham opened in late 2013 as a grand addition to the second largest metropolitan economy in the United Kingdom. Sited in Centenary Square, it replaces the previous library of Birmingham, a concrete icon of British Brutalism, and fulfills previously frustrated intentions for a landmark in the central city. Wrapped in a distinctive facade of aluminum filigree circles, the 31,000 m² library transforms the square, providing a new cohesion with the adjacent 1960s Repertory Theatre and the 1936 Baskerville House. Facing the busiest pedestrian route in the city, the ten-story structure is a visible statement of today's library as both civic icon and informal public place.

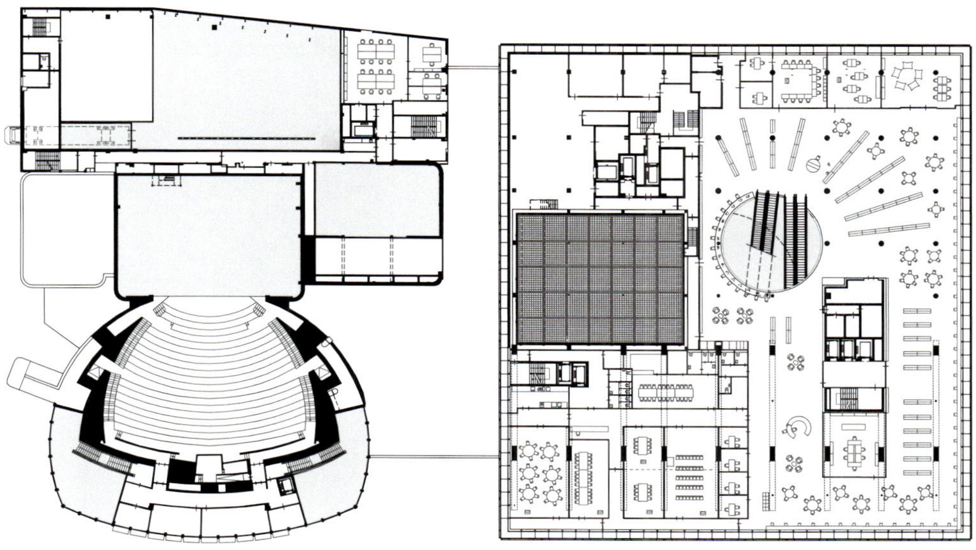

First floor

The library as part of Centenary Square | View of sunken outdoor performance space | The facade consists of two layers of circular aluminum sections

Mecanoo's creative director Francine Houben states that libraries are "the cathedrals of nowadays..." (Source: *The Observer*) and the Library Birmingham, as one of the largest institutions of its kind in Europe, withstands such a comparison in scale and scope. Designed to serve 10,000 patrons daily, the extensive program includes not only the adults' and children's library but also a music library, several study areas, health services, multi-media center, archives, exhibition halls, cafés, lounge space and a shared performance space with the newly renovated Repertory Theatre. These numerous spaces are arranged vertically with public service areas on the lower floors, and archives and the relocated Shakespeare Memorial Room on the upper levels. These designations between the quotidian and the precious are additionally differentiated in the glazed facade through the gray and gold bands; gold bands indicate the location of the treasures such as the Shakespeariana archive and renowned documents of the Industrial Revolution.

The floor plans of the above-ground levels, each a simple square, are distinguished from one another by different-sized circular openings in the floors. The resulting eight, unaligned, overlapping spaces offer unique glimpses into the areas directly above and below. Mecanoo describes these spaces as rotundas that play an important role in connecting the library physically and with light and ventilation. Some hold special significance within the library. The rooftop rotunda houses the relocated Shakespeare Memorial Room, a Victorian reading room designed in 1882 as the first Birmingham Central Library. A recessed rotunda in the plaza accommodates an outdoor performance center and connects with the Repertory Theater.

In another aspect comparable to church congregations, libraries, too, must attract and maintain their audience. Houben's goal at Birmingham is to "promote the informal" and to "seduce people into coming in" to this "cathe-

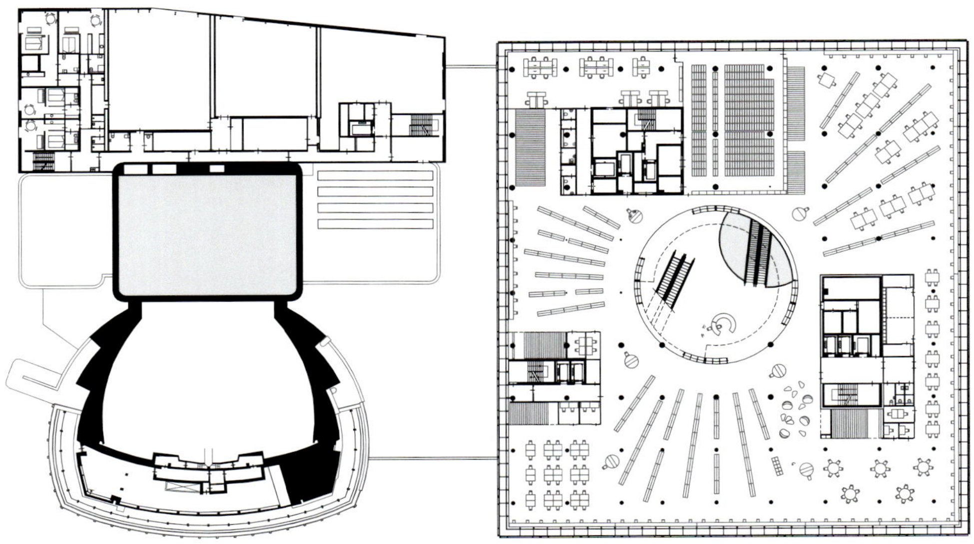

Second floor

dral" of knowledge. The rotundas, many of which are connected with escalators, recall the pedestrian movements of shopping malls. Here, though, their eccentric placement in plan resembles Deconstructivist compositions and creates dynamic movement amongst the many varying spaces, both interior and exterior. This retail-inspired strategy serves the library well in creating social spaces amongst the books for many types of interaction in what Houben calls "the most public space in the knowledge economy". (Source: *The Observer*)

The successful completion of the new library – on time, below budget and with a BREEAM Excellent rating – is in itself a civic statement. The realization of such a large-scale public project in the current global economy is the product of a design project management that foresaw the selection of an architectural firm well after the start of the process. With the City Council as client, the process also involved many sub-consultants including a design manager for the development of an integrated building design approach. Mecanoo's success in this respect is the ability to negotiate such bureaucracy with grace, wit and fiscal wisdom.

The City Council conceived of the new Library of Birmingham as a place of learning and community. Mecanoo's ambition for a "people's palace" (Source: *press kit*) as such a place is part of the search for a new paradigm in 21st century public library design. ***lw***

ESPON (European Spatial Planning Observation Network) Project 1.4.3 Study on Urban Functions, March 2007, p. 119.

Rowan Moore, "Library of Birmingham – Review", *The Observer*, August 31, 2013, p. 2.

Mecanoo Architecten, *press kit*.

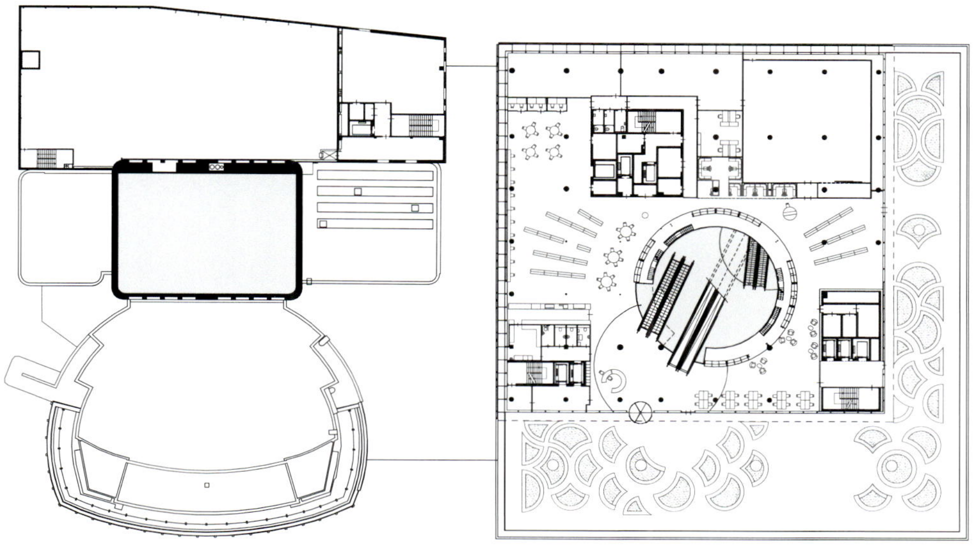

Third floor

Section through major segments | Escalators connect the many shifting rotunda spaces

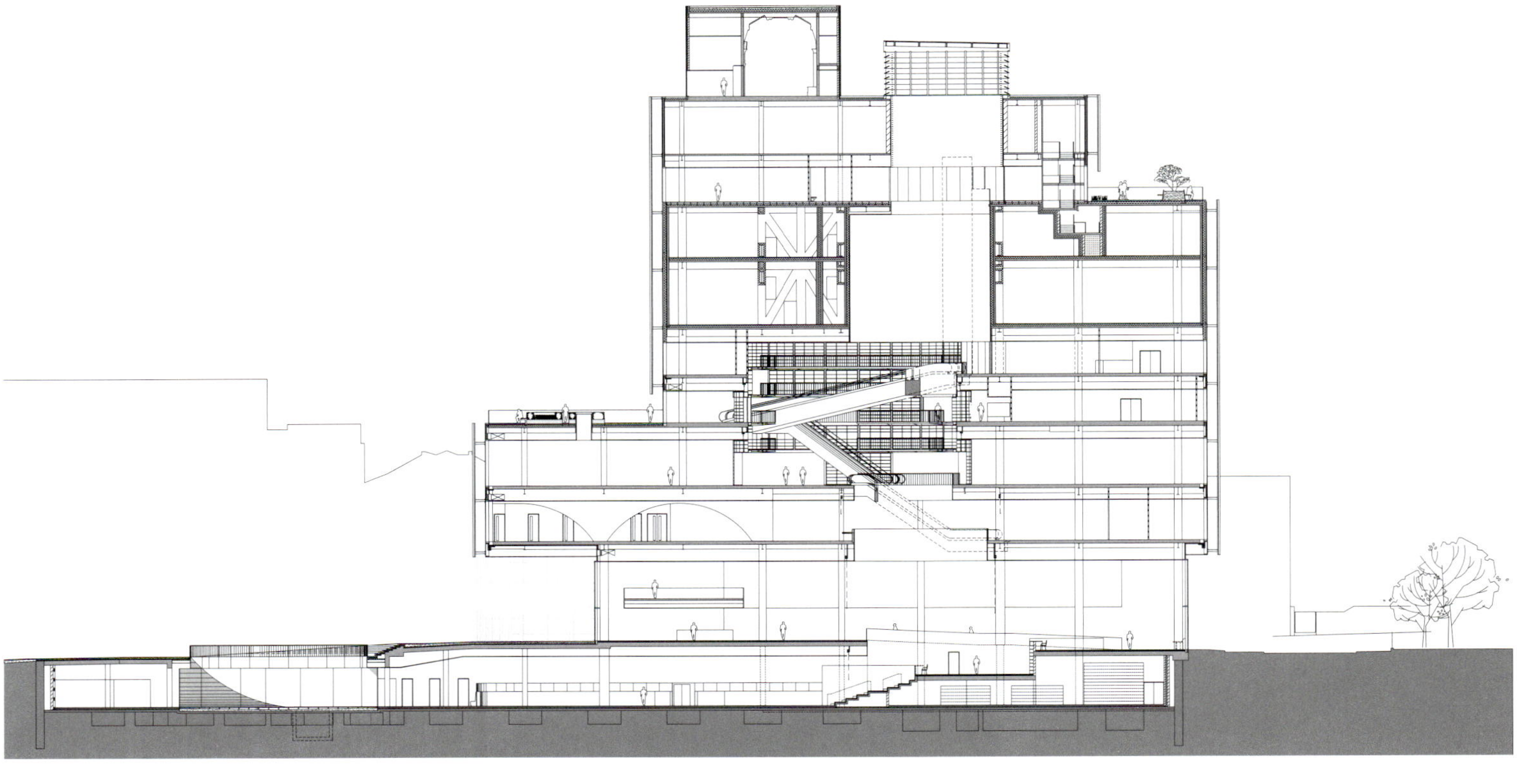

Section

View through overlapping rotundas | Stacks and reading | Informal seating in the children's room | View toward seating lounge

Small Public Libraries

Small and large public libraries are, at the same time, very similar and extremely different. Their basic structure is, in many ways, identical. They share a mission and many of the same 21st century concerns and objectives, especially for maintaining relevance in the era of digital technology. In the fulfillment of these objectives, however, the similarities diverge. Due to the dramatic differences in size between small and large public libraries – from the size of a room up to approximately 10,000 m^2 on the one hand and up to 40,000 m^2 on the other – the realization of like-minded goals are achieved through diverse paths.

By the democratic underpinnings of the public library, small public libraries serve communities with lesser population. Small public libraries fall into two categories; those that serve town communities and those that serve a small neighborhood of a larger community. In the former, the small library serves the entire population of a town. In the latter, the library serves one of many sectors of a greater metropolitan community, as a branch library of a large public library system. Metropolitan libraries often have up to 25–40 branches. The New York Public Library is an example of a mega-system with 92 branch libraries serving all of its boroughs. Small-town libraries enjoy an autonomy of structure, budget and operation. Branch libraries work within the structure predetermined by the larger system through which it exists. With this dependence, branch libraries sometimes fall victim to budget cuts and, in difficult economic times, are closed down. In serving a smaller number of citizens, small public libraries attend to a less dramatically diverse community of patrons.

Small libraries are neighborhood-centric. Centrally located, they are often found in close proximity to other civic establishments such as a post office, the town hall, a fire station and perhaps a public pool. By association, the library is assumed into an informal governance of the town structure, and its community meeting space plays a valuable role in day-to-day town life. It regularly hosts municipal gatherings such as community mentoring, town planning, school committees and, at times of local and national elections, voting. Through such involvement the small public library is tightly knit into the civic life of the small town.

Outside the immediate municipal structure, the small library is similarly connected to local and grass-roots organizations. Town functions from minor drama productions to local artists' demonstrations make use of the library as a venue. These events follow no specific agenda but can include the arts as well as technology, catering to both the young and the old. Classes such as "how to watercolor" are as popular as classes on "protecting one's online identity". The involvement of the library in these events broadens a program repertoire that by fiscal necessity would otherwise be more limited. The variety of such attractions appeals to and entices patrons of all ages.

As part of smaller communities the patrons are defined by relative similarity of per capita income and, as a group, are less diverse. Through an institution embedded within a relatively homogeneous community the programs of the small public library cater to less divergent needs than those of large metropolitan communities. The patrons of affluent neighborhoods, for example, share comparable concerns that differ completely from those of disadvantaged or crime-ridden neighborhoods: the desire for immediate access to newly published books as opposed to afterschool programs for latchkey kids. In a large public library, all of these concerns coexist and must be addressed within the confines of a finite budget. The small library faces only the needs of like-minded citizens.

Small-library service operates at its own scale. While all public libraries provide a basic level of service to its patron groups, the magnitude of the small public library's endeavors is a product of its significantly smaller patron groups. This scalar difference is, in fact, inversely related to its size; fewer patrons allow for a concentrated use of resources. This is exemplified by the needs of older patrons. Universally addressed, services for the elderly range from barrier-free accommodations to physical amenities such as large-print and audio books, low-vision readers, and magnifiers for text enhancement. In the small library, with less demand, this can also include more costly items such as lendable e-book readers with font enlargement capability and Text-to-Speech features. With fewer patrons to serve, outreach programs for the elderly in the small library can extend beyond the requisite physical needs to those of social and even emotional well-being: for example, social gatherings organized specifically to provide regular engagement for an older patronage in the form of garden clubs or reading groups for the elderly. In some libraries, a delivery program brings books and other media to elderly homebound patrons. With smaller populations and inherently fewer demands, small libraries have the ability to expand and personalize service, distinguishing its character by the scale of its gestures.

Within communities characterized by similar demographics – economics, locale, and, sometimes, race – the actions of the small public library are often fueled and supported by consensus. Without the necessity to provide outreach efforts for many diverse needs, the small library focuses its work and budget on unified objectives. The power of such solidarity can apply to many different aspects of the library. Nowhere is this more evident than with young readers. With a ubiquitous emphasis on learning and the young, today's public libraries of all sizes provide enhanced service in children's spaces. In contrast to large libraries with many groups to serve, small libraries can often offer a more individualized service. For instance, service for an autistic child might, in a large public library, consist of online resources while in a small library it might be addressed in person, if necessary. Further, the fulfillment of very specific needs in a small library can manifest itself in an exuberant and, at times lavish, manner. They range from those of underserved neighborhoods for safe afterschool environments with homework programs, relaxed activities and healthy snacks to the desire for enhanced math and science focus for precocious preschoolers in affluent communities. In many instances these efforts are quite expensive, requiring a majority vote for the approval of funds beyond operational spending. These efforts are not exclusive to the needs of the young. In an agrarian community where farming is a shared value, a small public library in Onondaga, NY, loans out plots of land for patrons interested in experimenting with new organic farming practices. With a unified vision amongst its patrons, such expenditure in a small library constitutes an investment in the community and results in extraordinary efforts.

The role of architecture in these efforts is unique. Within the small library, there are many opportunities for the creation of experience through the library interior. With the diverse range of small communities, the library interior as a representation of these characteristics is a chance for the exploration of style. There are also occasions for new expression in exterior form – expressions premised upon the individual agenda of the community rather than a development in the library typology; for example, the expression of the library form as a protective fortress within an underprivileged community or as a modern sculpture in an affluent community. Together, the architecture of the interior and the exterior form a fascinating picture of a diverse library patronage.

The small public library is a unique case of democracy in action. It remains, as its 19th century predecessor, characterized and empowered by community. As a type, it has not had to alter dramatically as it expands the concept of "access for all" beyond the commodities of books and technology. Today's small library trades in human interests as knowledge, with lendable collections from plots of land for gardening to musical instruments (as it is the case at the Lopez Island Library in Washington State), providing a relevance in daily life that is immutable in the rapidly changing digital landscape. ***lw***

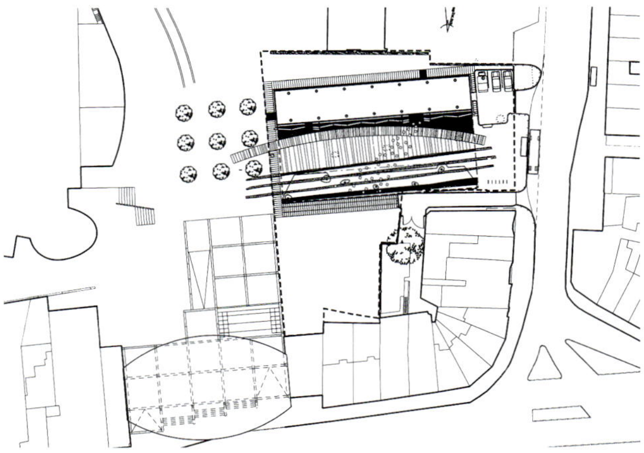

Site plan

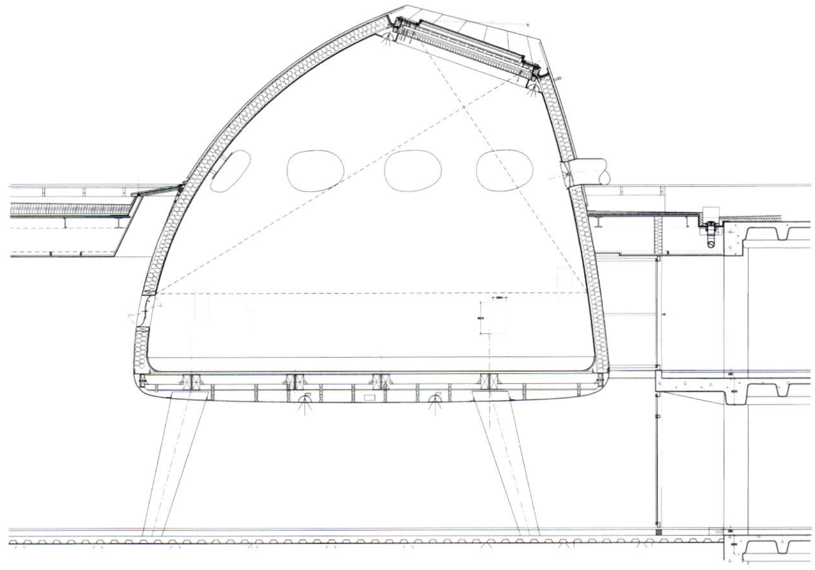

Section through one of the three "pods"

Peckham Library and Media Centre

London, UK

Architect	Alsop + Störmer Architects
Client	London Borough of Southwark
Completion	2000
Floor area	2,500 m²
Number of volumes	60,000
Seating capacity	110

Designed by Alsop + Störmer Architects, the Peckham Library and Media Centre with its 2.1 m high stainless steel letters spelling "LIBRARY" is identified by its bold form, vibrant color and a heroic orange rooftop protuberance. The library is an inverted L with a generous entry plaza created by an enormous overhanging volume resting on spindly posts. With its gravity-defying form and unique juxtaposition of color and materials, the library is a bold and quirky structure that redefines the role of the library in the local community.

Peckham, in the borough of Southwark, is a dense, urban district of South London marked by

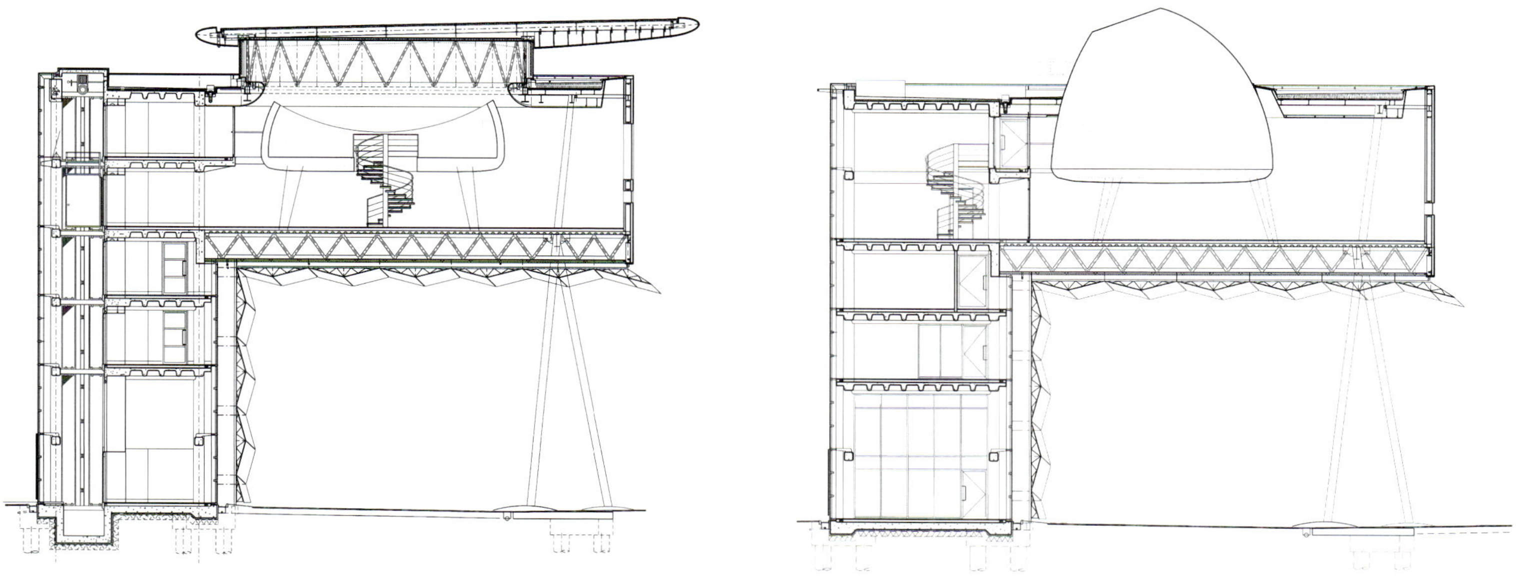

Sections

View of north facade | Billboard-type advertisement on the entrance facade | Entry plaza | View of third floor stacks with pods beyond

crime and gang violence. Located in a highly diverse area, the ethnic make-up of this working class community includes Africans (more than one third of the population), Caribbeans, Asians, Irish and Bangladeshi. The library project was completed in 2000 as part of a £290 million urban renewal and regeneration program, which also included new low-rise housing and a health center. The library and its plaza serve as an informal connector between the new programs, extending the limits of Peckham Square.

The inverted L-shaped volume is divided into the lending library and administrative services. Administrative services include information equipment, a social meeting space and a media center that are housed in the five-story linear bar, the vertical portion of the inverted "L". The lending library occupies the two-story horizontal volume that hovers 12 m above the plaza, supported on 12 slender, skewed columns. This double-height space serves both as reading room and the stacks for 60,000 volumes. While prototypical library elements of shelves, tables and chairs are present, the reading room is dominated by the presence of three enormous "pods", supported on legs, that float above the stacks. Formed from curved timber ribs and structural plywood, each pod serves a unique function: a children's room, a meeting place and a special collection of Afro-Caribbean literature.

The exterior is characterized by a panoply of shapes, textures and color. Seamed, horizontal pre-patinated copper cladding defines the east and west facades as well as the overhanging volume. The north and entry facades are glazed; the north side characterized by windows of intense colors and the entry by a sheet of undulating metal mesh suspended from the glass and soffit.

The wit and seeming irreverence of the library belies the social mission of Alsop's first major building in London. Its unconventional use of

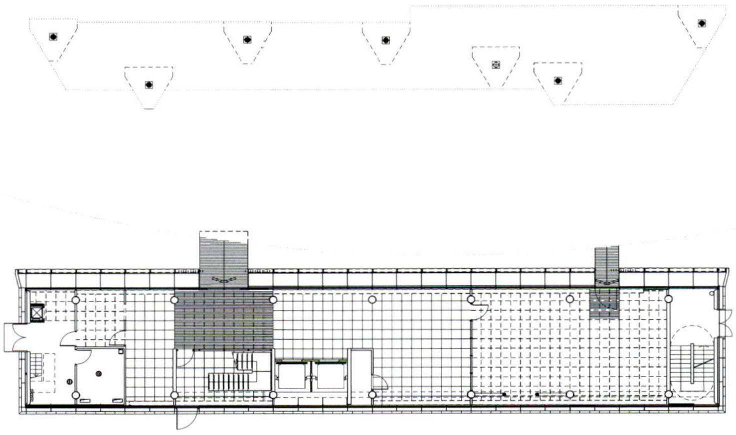

Ground floor

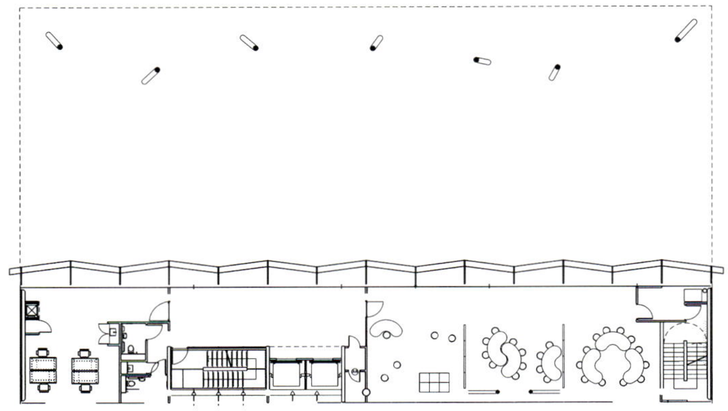

First floor

Views of the plywood-clad pods | Interior of Afro-Caribbean literature pod

form, materials and color is not only lighthearted but is, in fact, an embrace of civic responsibility. The institution of the library is reinterpreted through architectural language, transforming the traditional and the staid to the whimsical and fun. In doing so, the library is made accessible to a user population of immigrants and attractive to children and teens. This is best illustrated by the architectural language of the "pod", which gives life and prominence to the Afro-Caribbean Collection. The exuberant use of colored glass facades is not simply decorative but a part of an energy strategy to provide natural light and natural ventilation. These ethics are best exemplified by the signature orange "beret" or "tongue" protruding from the roof inviting speculation while it provides shade for the ventilation shafts located on the south side.

With almost half a million annual visitors, the Peckham Library and Media Centre is the busiest of Southwark's libraries. It is the recipient of numerous awards, from the prestigious RIBA Stirling Award (2000) for the best building in Britain to the Civic Trust Award in 2001 for excellence in public architecture. This array of prizes recognizes the breadth of this design, which simultaneously addresses issues of urban intervention, library design and community renewal.

In this project, Alsop demonstrates the far-reaching power of architecture. ***lw***

Stephen Shukor, "Guns Plague Peckham Despite Investment", BBC News, February 8, 2007.

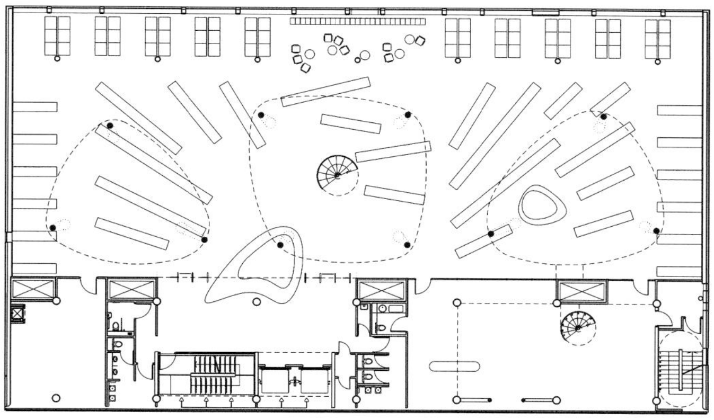

Third floor

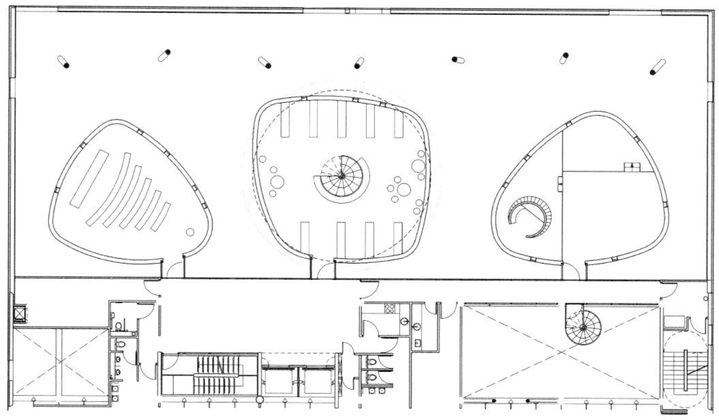

Fourth floor

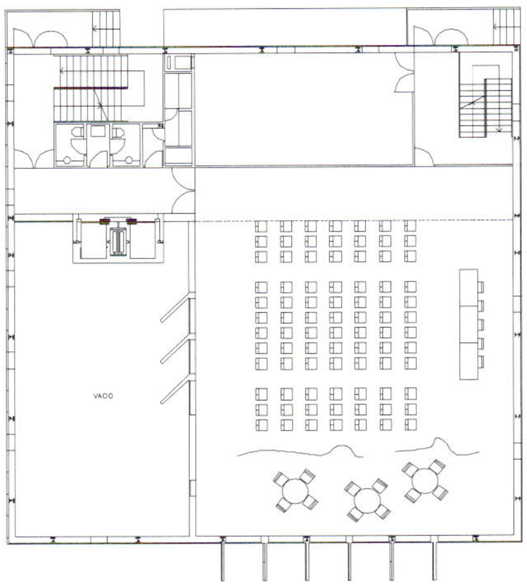

First floor

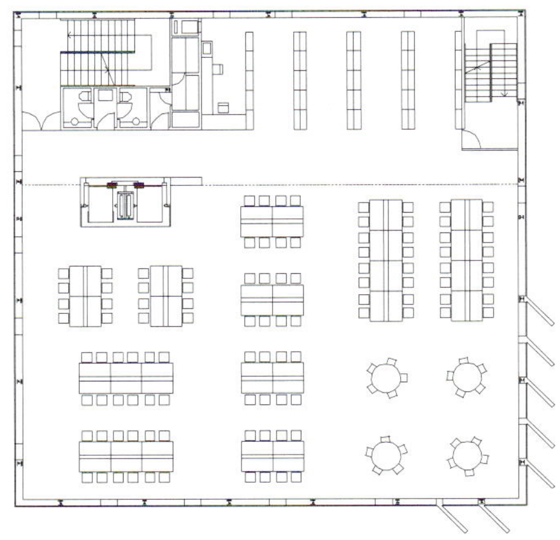

Second floor

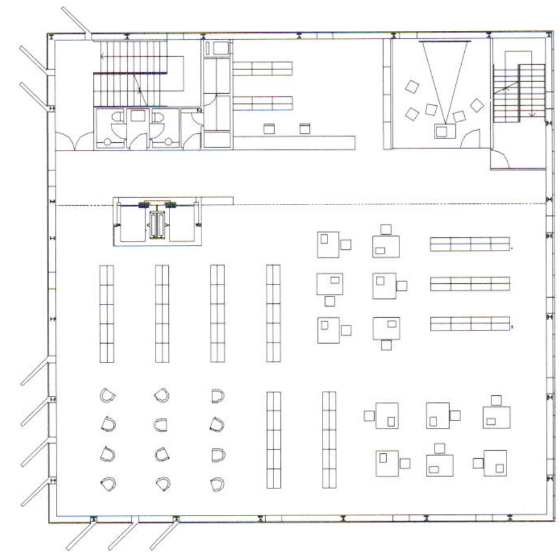

Third floor

Biblioteca Pública Usera José Hierro

Madrid, Spain

Architect	Ábalos & Herreros
Client	Comunidad de Madrid
Completion	2004
Floor area	3,500 m²
Number of volumes	60,000
Seating capacity	218

As part of the Community of Madrid's extensive library system, the Biblioteca Pública Usera José Hierro serves a southern district of Madrid of the same name. Completed in 2003, the Biblioteca Pública Usera is one in a network dedicated to reaching a metropolitan population of 7 million. The winning competition entry of architects Iñaki Ábalos and Juan Herreros, the library acknowledges through design the issues of a district troubled by poverty, high levels of unemployment and crime. Rising out of the suburban landscape of Usera, the 3,500 m² library is distinctly divided into two parts; a concrete plinth and a tower clad in prefabricated metal panels. The plinth houses a car

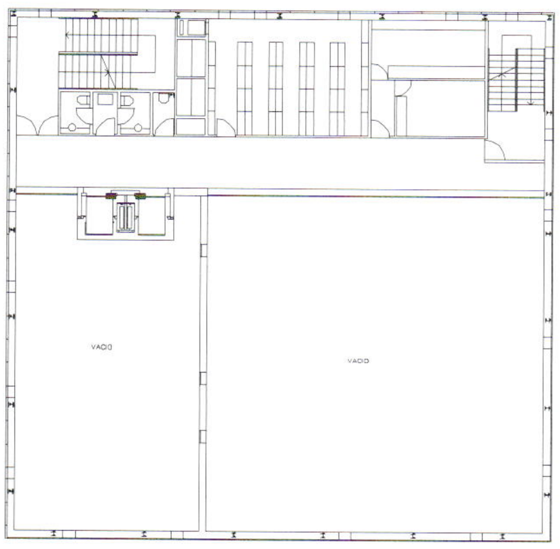

Plan of first mezzanine

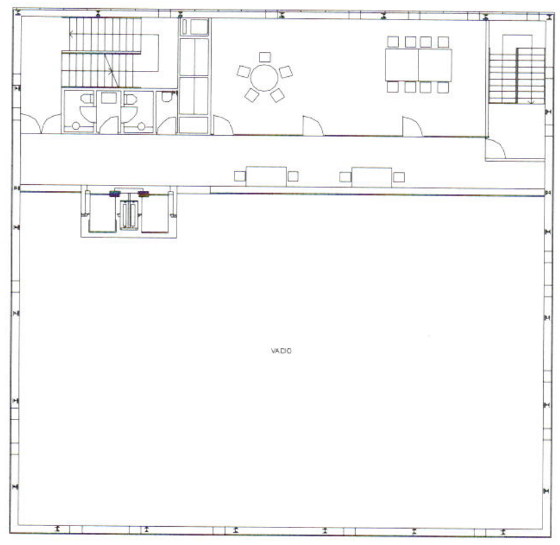

Plan of second mezzanine

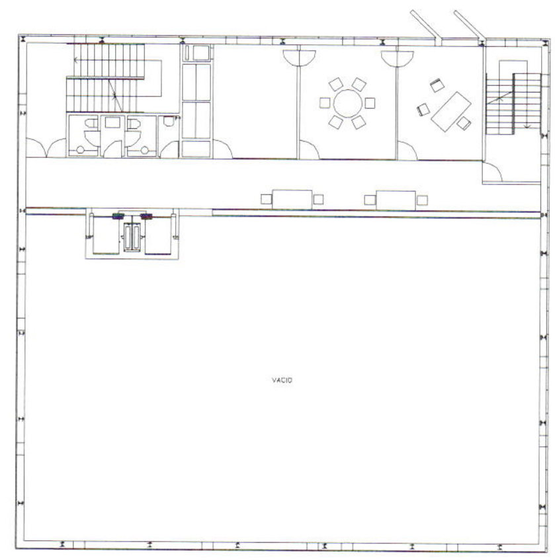

Plan of third mezzanine

View from Avenida de Rafaela Ybarra | Views of exterior facade and shutters

and bicycle park and its roof serves as the base of an urban, outdoor plaza. The tower consists of four double-height levels and seven mezzanine levels that, with the exception of a small elevator core, are entirely free of vertical structure. The incorporation of the structural elements into the facade permits the creation of open spaces and reading rooms that are both well proportioned and secure. Stairs, restrooms, stacks and program services densely placed within the mezzanine floors overlook these double-height spaces creating a relationship of dualities.

The library is sited amidst an urban open space within the dense apartment blocks and busy streets of Usera. Perched on a hill, the library looms above the street like a modern fortress with its long and narrow apertures. Ábalos and Herreros' proposal for a vertical scheme occupying only a portion of this rectangular parcel of public land allows for a substantial part of the parcel to be dedicated as public open space. These include a more formal garden on the south side and an informal urban plaza at the entry off the Avenida de Rafaela Ybarra. In doing so, the architects extend the library as a common "living room" to the outdoors. The architects describe their design as a "catalytic converter which recognizes this space of collective activity in Usera, establishing it as a centerpiece and giving it urban meaning." (Source: www.herrerosarquitectos.com)

In this intense, sunlit neighborhood of Madrid, the interior of the library is purposefully designed as an atmosphere of semi-darkness – a cool atmosphere pierced by rays of light from the narrow slits in the facade. This marked transition from the exterior is most evident in the lofty shaft-like entrance hall. The spaces are minimal and spare, punctuated only by windows that are proportioned as slots and surfaces covered in wallpaper designed by artist, Peter Halley. This wallpaper with its abstract pattern of different colors is allegedly derived from a Jorge Luis Borges story.

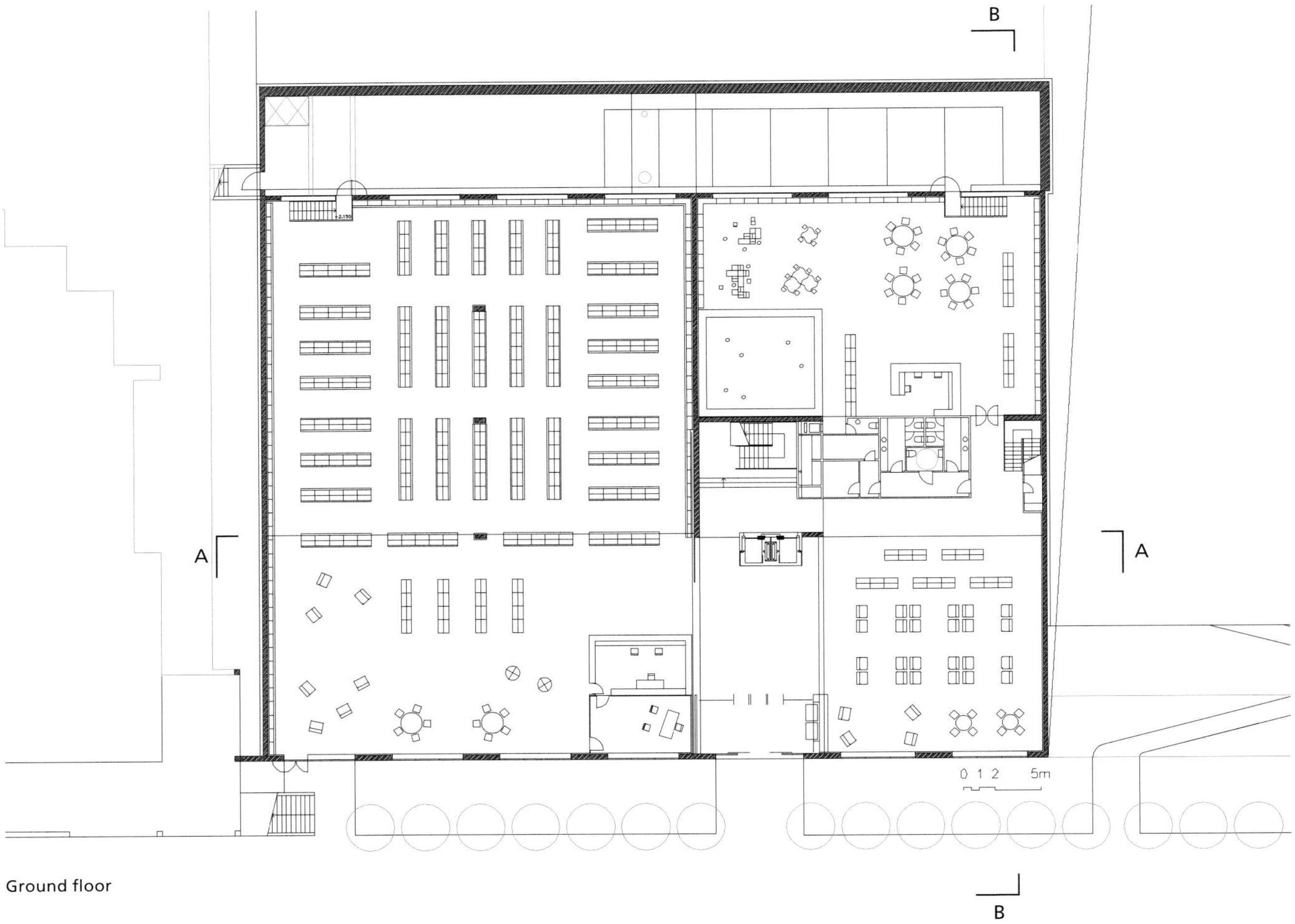

Ground floor

Exterior shutters frame the view outside | Views of reading room with Peter Halley wallpaper

Reminiscent of both graffiti art and the actual graffiti scrawled on the lower portions of the facade, the use of this wallpaper creates an internal environment that is deliberate and poetic within a language of the streets. This wallpaper also covers the interior surface of the shutters of certain fixed windows, windows that narrowly frame views of this district against the distant backdrop of Madrid. These controlled perspectives are appropriated as part of the interior of the library, providing views of a seemingly ordered world in a disordered environment.

Named after José Hierro, one of Spain's contemporary poets known for his existential style, the Biblioteca Pública Usera is a spare and moving work of architecture that captures the essence of a gritty, modern existence. With the ever changing nature of the muted but slightly reflective facade, the tower is at once a mirror of its surroundings and a refuge from it. Ábalos and Herreros were able to put into form that which was articulated by Peter Halley: "We had some provocative things to say about the underlying structure of the world we all experience that most people really didn't want to face." (Source: petter-halley.blogspot.de) In post-Franco Spain, these thoughts are expressed with simplicity in the Biblioteca Pública Usera. ***lw***

"Peter Halley talks to Dan Cameron – '80s Then – Interview", http://petter-halley.blogspot.de/

http://www.herrerosarquitectos.com/EN_Ind_proyectos.html

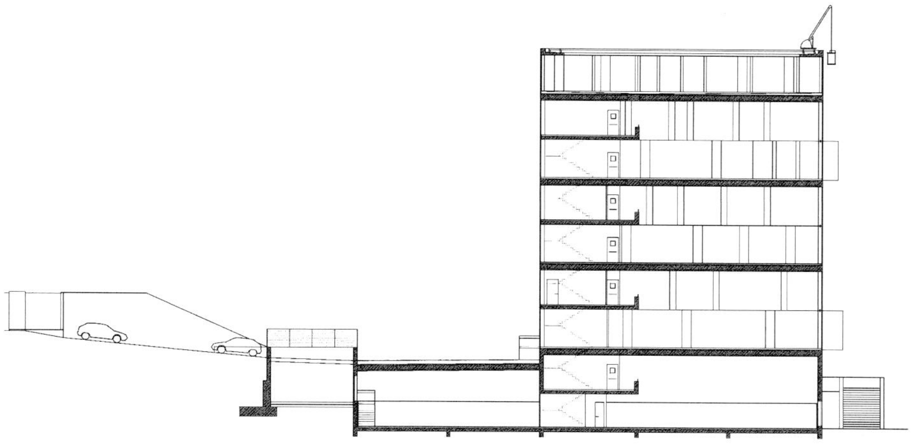

Section B–B

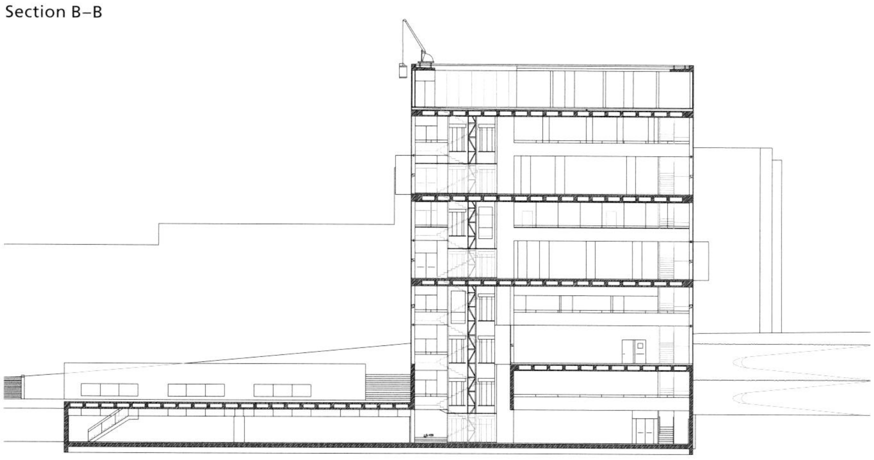

Section A–A through reading room

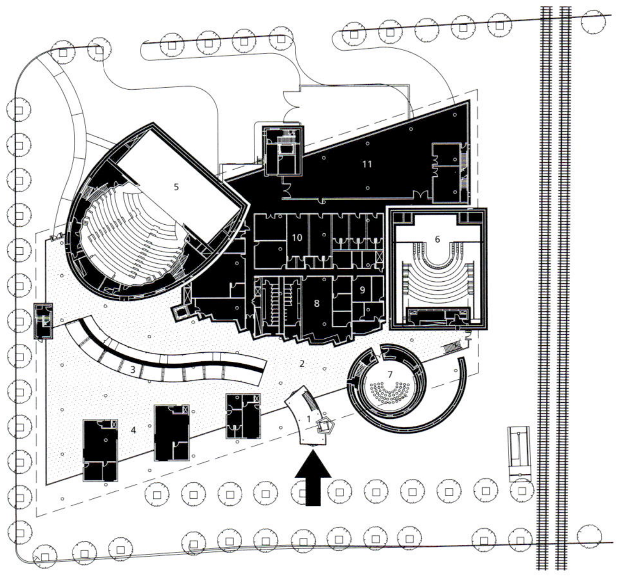

Ground floor

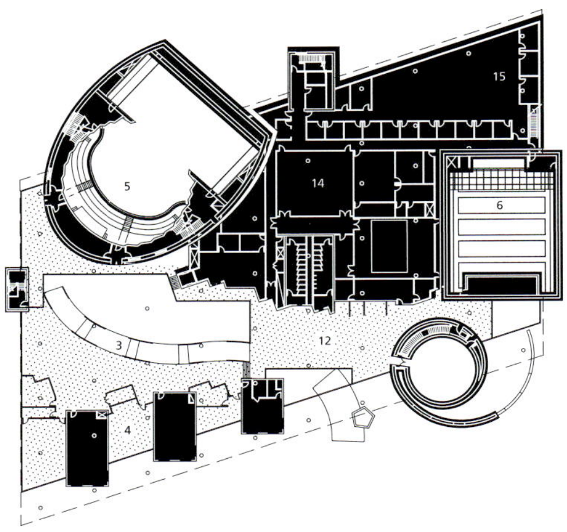

First floor

1 Entry vestibule
2 Lobby
3 Ramp
4 Children's library
5 550-seat proscenium theater
6 250-seat studio theater
7 Story room
8 Circulation desk
9 Box office
10 Performers' support
11 Scene shop
12 Teen loft
13 Art, dance and acting studios
14 Rehearsal rooms
15 Administrative offices

ImaginOn: The Joe & Joan Martin Center

Charlotte, North Carolina, USA

Architect	Holzman Moss Bottino with Gantt Huberman Architects
Client	Public Library of Charlotte; Mecklenburg County; Children's Theater of Charlotte
Completion	2005
Floor area	10,590 m²
Number of volumes	n/a
Seating capacity	250 and 550 (theaters)

An exuberant exploration of geometry, ImaginOn is a collaboration of the Charlotte-Mecklenburg Public Library and the Children's Theater. Dedicated to philanthropists Joe and Joan Martin, this 10,590 m^2 project extending over one city block of downtown Charlotte has drawn record numbers of visitors since its opening in 2005.

Part library, part theater, ImaginOn is a unique amalgamation of public and private investments with a shared mission to bring "stories to life through extraordinary experiences that challenge, inspire and excite young minds", as postulated on the library's website. It consists of a vast parallelogram-shaped open-plan struc-

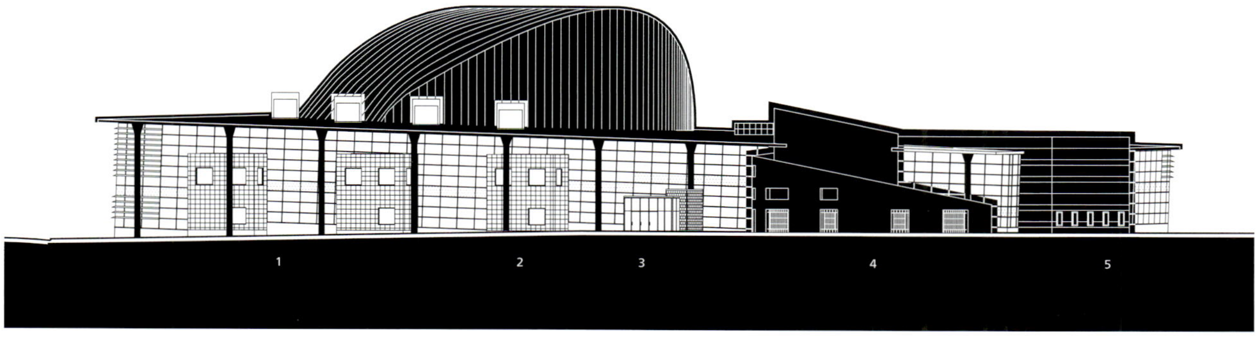

1 Children's library
2 550-seat proscenium theater
3 Entry vestibule
4 Story room
5 250-seat studio theater

South elevation

Night view | Library and theater have a commanding street presence | A ramp connects the floors

ture, intersected by volumes defined by programmatic elements that include two theaters, production studios, scene and paint shops, dressing rooms, a technology center and a library. With the aim of creating "experience", the open plan and the lack of architectural clues allow a child to move randomly from one attraction to the next, creating a new and different encounter each time. A curving ramp connecting the two floors is one discernible element of architectural order in a riotous array of shapes, colors and materials. Several environmental strategies have resulted in a LEED Silver rating for the building in the U.S. Green Building Council's certification program.

The new library program comprises the Spangler Library for young children, the Story Lab, a space called "The Loft" for teens from ages 12 to 18 and Tech Central with more than 30 computer stations, a demonstration classroom and a multi-media production studio with blue-screen technology. The relocation of the children's department from the main Charlotte Mecklenburg Library in 2005 to its new home in ImaginOn carried on a century of history that began with the library's opening in 1903 as a Carnegie Free Library. The upgrade is evident in scale and digital sophistication. And the removal of the children's library from the main public library and the resultant loss of interaction with adult services are believed to be compensated for by a different type of interaction. With a fully integrated services approach exemplified by the co-existence of the circulation desk and box office as a single space, library users co-mingle freely with the users of the theater, with the anticipated result of an enriched experience.

At a time when libraries strive to redefine themselves in the age of electronic media, ImaginOn's objective to provide the experience of the written word in its many present-day forms – spoken, electronic, visual – is one solution. In choosing a path of sensory stimulation, ImaginOn tackles this problem in a distinctly American fashion. ***lw***

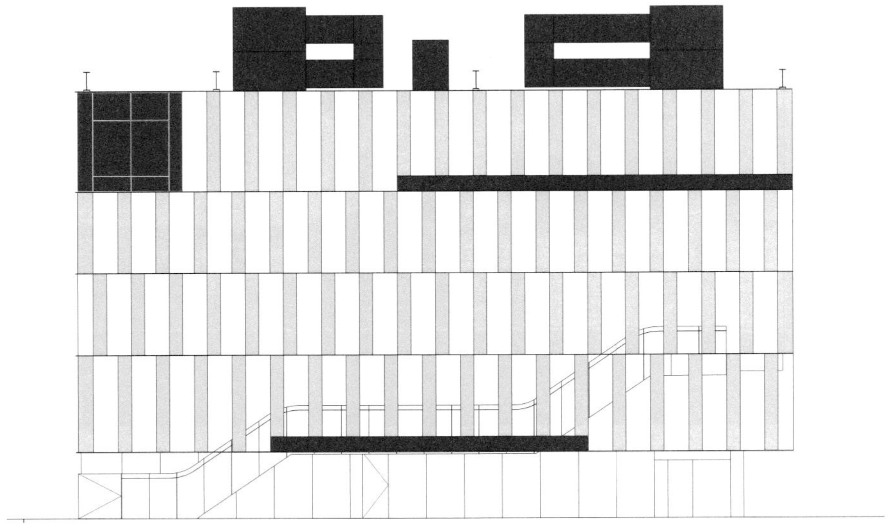

South elevation

Whitechapel Idea Store

London, UK

Architect	Adjaye Associates
Client	London Borough of Tower Hamlets
Completion	2005
Floor area	4,500 m²
Number of volumes	n/a
Seating capacity	134 seats, 55 computer terminals

The Whitechapel Idea Store is the flagship of seven "idea stores", the reincarnation of a library system in East London. The "idea store" is the result of a major campaign, begun in the 1990s, to rejuvenate the Tower Hamlets library system in addressing the contemporary needs of the district. Designed by Adjaye Associates and completed in 2005, the Whitechapel Idea Store exemplifies an unabashed use of retail design and marketing in rethinking the concept of the library and its community. Historically recognized as the impoverished sector of Victorian London of the infamous "Jack the Ripper", many parts of the present-day Borough of Tower Hamlets remain characterized

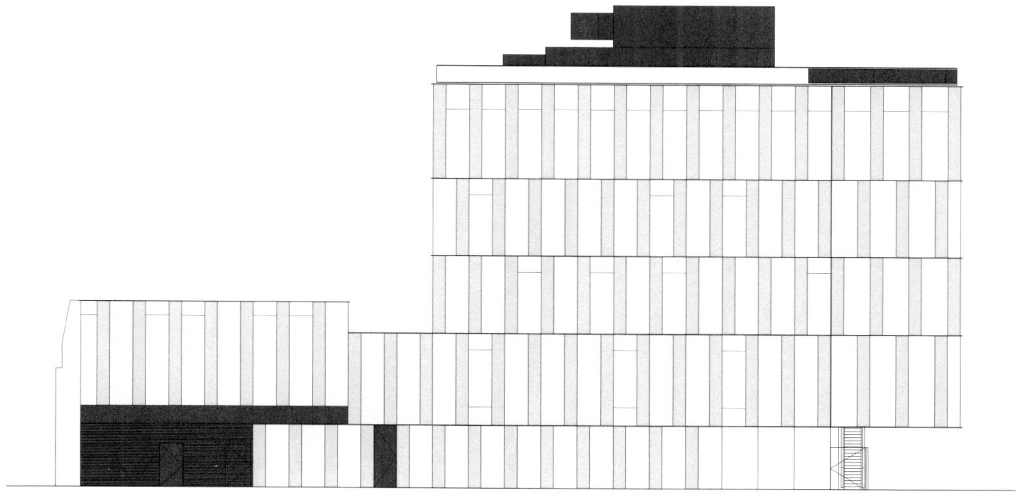

West elevation

The Idea Store in the colorful context of Tower Hamlets Borough | View of open-air entrance escalators | Book stacks

by high unemployment, low levels of education and one of the country's least-used library systems. The inadequacy of this system with its historic, aging buildings prompted one of the most extensive library surveys in the history of London. Responses were unequivocal in condemning the system as outdated and rundown. They were equally clear in expressing a prioritized need for books and technology over an upgrade of the existing structures.

The branding of the library as an "idea store" signals a deliberate departure from the antiquated library system, its institutional connotations of class and education and the resultant inaccessibility of such a system to its present-day community. With the introduction of the Idea Store, the library is envisioned anew as a learning center integrating the resources of a modernized Tower Hamlets library with those of Lifelong Learning Services, an agency of the borough that offers credit and non-credit courses serving as feeder for colleges and vocational training programs. The merger of the two institutions makes available books, media, technology and walk-in access to 900 courses. Drawing on retail concepts, the Idea Store sells learning in its tangible form as books and its intangible form as education. The Idea Stores also address the problematic issue of location, an issue that has contributed to the failure of the existing library system. The lack of patronage of the old facilities was, in part, due to their placement within a city of a different era – a placement that lacks relevance in today's borough. Rather, each of the new Idea Stores is sited amidst the circuit of everyday 21st century life – near retail establishments, malls, supermarkets and banks. Anne Cunningham, the Head of Libraries, said, "If McDonald's or the major supermarkets wouldn't site a store there, neither would we." (Source: *Library Journal*) As the flagship store, the Whitechapel Idea Store is positioned on a major thoroughfare near several markets, a gas station,

View of adult collections

a pharmacy and the Whitechapel Underground station. A five-level structure with multiple entrances, access to Whitechapel includes an escalator in an open-air atrium that spills directly onto the street. The Whitechapel Idea Store is a straightforward stack of five floor plates in which 10 % of the program is devoted to retail while the remainder is equally divided between the books/media and the classrooms. A café with panoramic views of St. Paul's Cathedral is placed at the highest level, employing a classic retail design device to draw the public through the building. These programs are unified by a facade of aluminum panels and alternating clear and colored glass that incorporates a logo as well as a high-tech informational display system. This appealing modern facade in translucent hues of blue and green has become the signature of the Idea Store. As such, its architectural palette as a branding device derives iconic aspects from the highly successful Apple store.

The vision to replace all the existing libraries in Tower Hamlets with Idea Stores has implications for cost and infrastructure. It is estimated that the cost of operating each new store is 25 % above current library expenditures, due to expanded hours and services. These costs will be subsidized, in part, by the borough and the government and, in part, through the revenue derived from retail sales and the café. The existing libraries will not be demolished but, rather, be reused, where possible, for other community events. Patronage has increased dramatically since the opening of the Idea Stores. While the word "library" is scrupulously avoided – this includes the substitution of the position of "ideas supervisor" for that of "librarian" – this new attitude towards books, media and learning is a positive step in the development of the library in the UK of the 21st century. ***lw***

Thomas Patterson, "An Experiment in the Blighted East End Redeploys and Revamps Library Service", *Library Journal*, January 5, 2001.

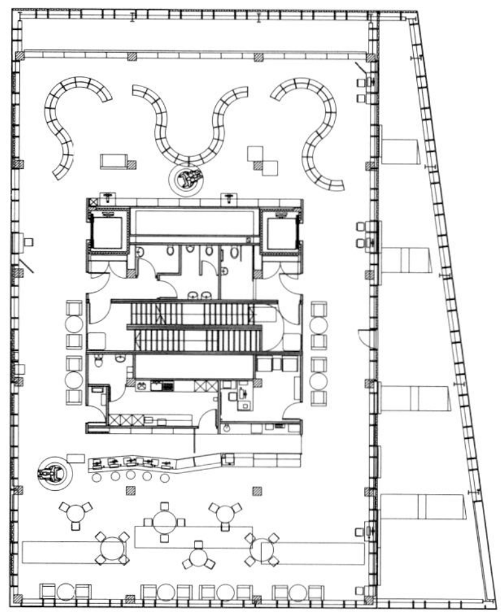

Fourth floor

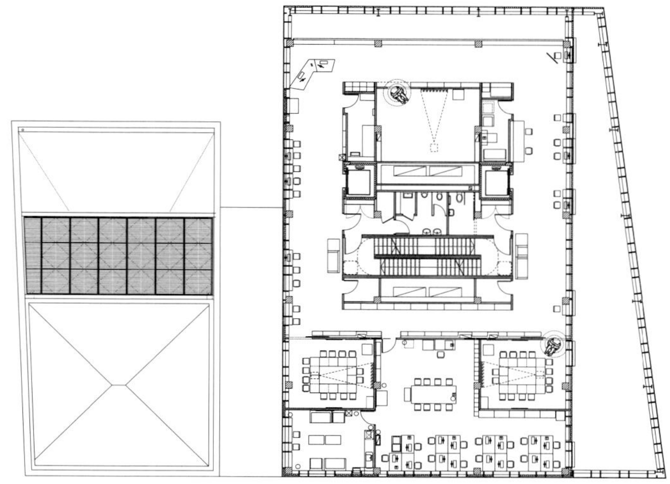

Third floor

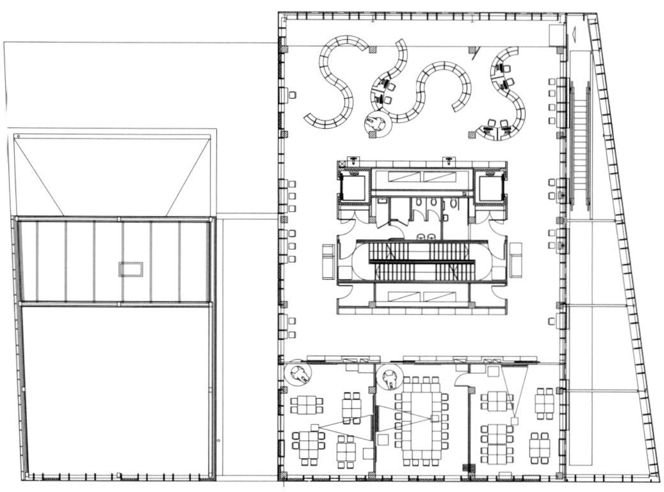

Second floor

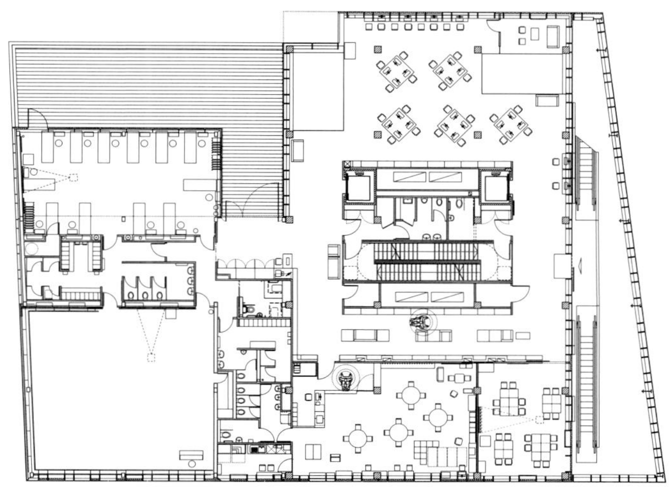

First floor

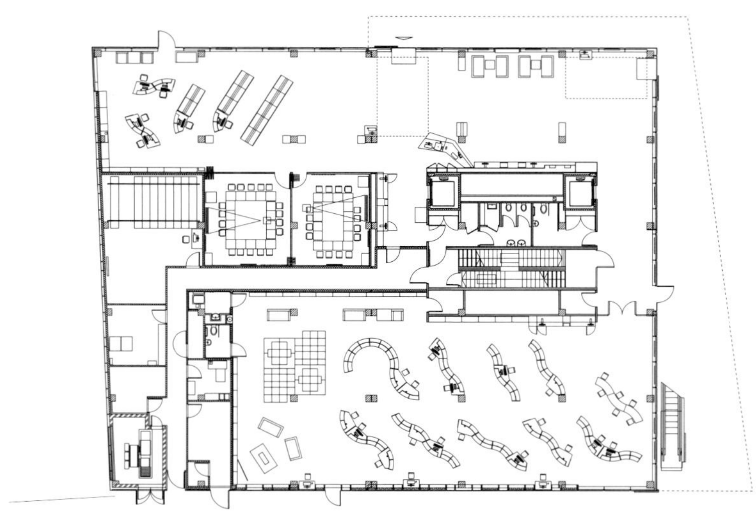

Ground floor

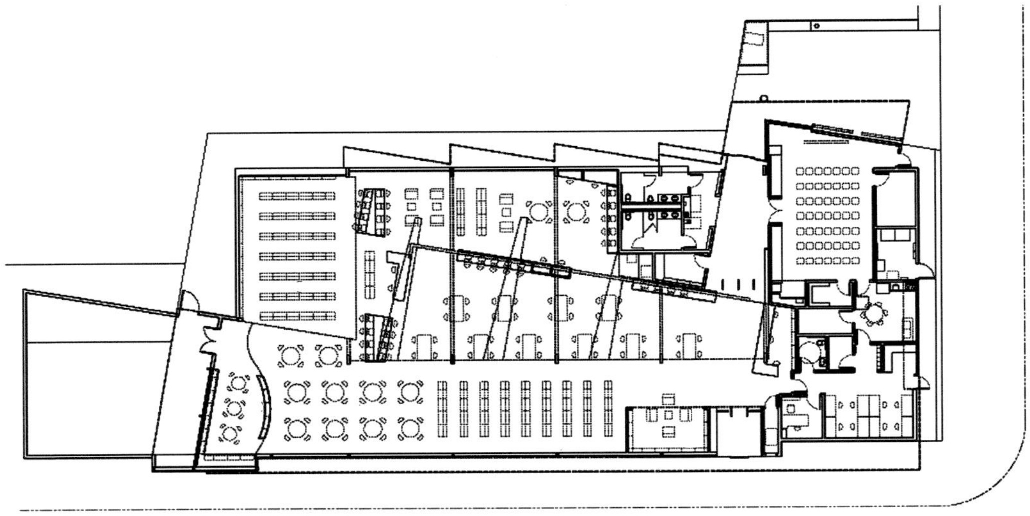

Ground floor

Miriam Matthews Hyde Park Branch Library

Los Angeles, California, USA

Architect	HplusF Architecture and Design
Client	Board of Library Commissioners, LAPL
Completion	2006
Floor area	975 m²
Number of volumes	40,000
Seating capacity	125 (general seating); 50 (multi-purpose room)

Constructed in 2006 in Hyde Park, on a burnt-out site of the 1992 Los Angeles riots, the Miriam Matthews Hyde Park Branch Library exemplifies the opportunity for architecture in the rebuilding of a community. One of 72 branch libraries in the Los Angeles network, this library is named after the first African American librarian in California whose 33-year tenure in the Los Angeles Library system from 1927–1960 was dedicated to the preservation of black history.

With the exception of staff offices and a meeting space, this small branch library consists of one open space for adults and children. Divisions of space are made through the energetic manipula-

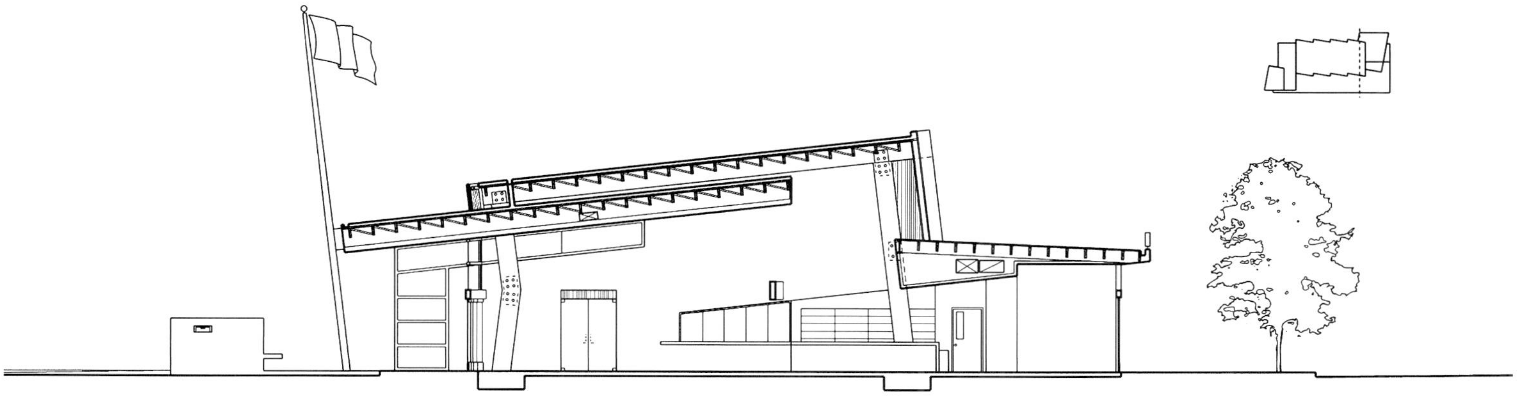

Transverse section

View of the side facade | View of the open interior | Detail at the windows: small apertures and clerestory

tion of the 6.7 m high ceiling and sectional devices rather than walls serve to delineate boundaries. These sectional changes are articulated as a medley of forms and materials that are subsequently expressed on the exterior. The composition of slanted and skewed shapes is anchored against the rhythmic expression of the structural supports and mechanical ductwork.

The library engages the intersection of Florence and Van Ness Streets with a bold, sculptural presence expressed in cement board, glass and copper-tinted metal. Natural light filters through the clerestory windows in horizontal bands high above the level of the street in acknowledgement of the need for security and problems such as drive-by shooting. The large expanses of the otherwise blank exterior facade are animated by the constant changing of materials in scale and direction as well as the vibrant mural of artist Robin Strayhorn. The ceramic mural titled "Transformation Through Education", which includes tiles made by the children of the local elementary schools, is integrated into both the front and back facades.

A simple rectangle in plan, the library with its four different facades is volumetrically a composition imbued with a sense of rhythm. An exuberant array of sawtooth roof forms, beams, ducts and awning supports alludes to a syncopated movement both on the interior and the exterior. The resulting work with its multi-layered, multi-textured forms is a hybrid of many ideas.

The building received an LEED Silver rating for sustainability and it improved upon its service most notably through increases in volumes from 25,000 to 40,000 and a tripling of computer stations. The goal was to provide a library that "is in complete response to the people who occupy it", as architect Craig Hodgetts stated. In the first year after completion, statistics showed that patronage and book circulation tripled from previous use. ***lw***

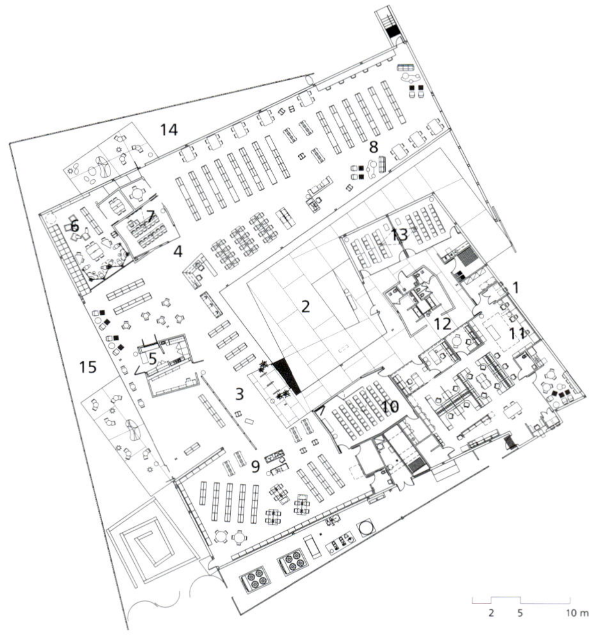

1 Entry
2 Program courtyard
3 Lobby
4 Service desk
5 Bookstore/café
6 Teen area
7 Computer training
8 Adult collection
9 Children's area
10 Program room
11 Staff
12 Restrooms
13 Meeting rooms
14 Reading court
15 Café court

Ground floor with furniture

Arabian Public Library

Scottsdale, Arizona, USA

Architect	Richärd + Bauer
Client	City of Scottsdale
Completion	2007
Floor area	1,939 m²
Number of volumes	120,000
Seating capacity	56 (meeting room)

The Arabian Public Library sits low amid the arid Arizona landscape, a sculptural volume of rusted and tilted metal planes. Four branch libraries, each named after a local horse breed, serve Scottsdale's affluent and highly educated population of 245,000. In this city the per capita income is 2.5 times the national average. Located in a sprawling suburban neighborhood, this branch library serves patrons accustomed to a culture of gated communities and shopping malls. Library service for this group with its particular demands has shaped the direction of the design.

Richärd + Bauer's design approaches the project through the lens of retail design. On the exterior,

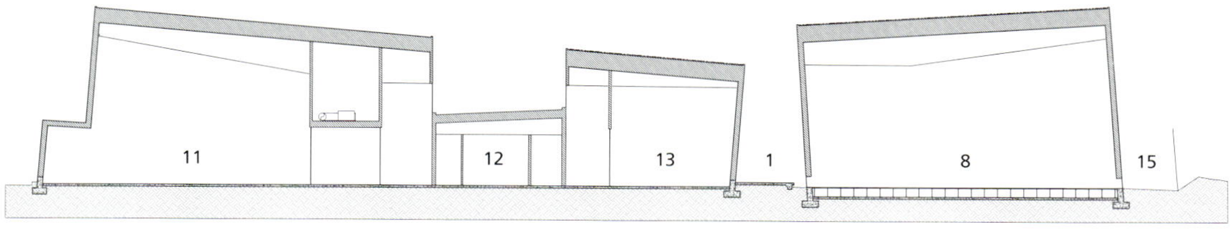

Cross section

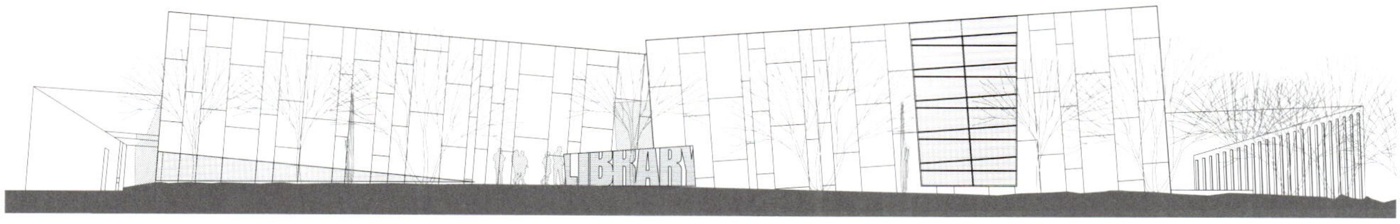

North elevation

Low volumes of the library in the desert landscape | Periodicals and collection | Metal plates of the exterior

the blank facades of monolithic, rusted, metal planes serve to focus one's attention inwards and towards the books while obscuring the surrounding suburban context. Architect Jim Richärd explained that he "struggled with the ordinariness of the surroundings, with the minimarts, the chain stores and the surface lots" (Source: *Architectural Record*) and that the resultant forms are instead inspired by the slot canyons of the Arizona deserts. The drama of these passageways in the rock walls is replicated in the library entrance with its art installation by Norie Sato as well as in the narrow, daylit corridors along the courtyard through deftly placed architectural forms. The result is a series of interesting vistas that serve to draw the user through the library. On the interior, in a one-story open plan arranged around an internal courtyard, patrons are encouraged to roam as if in a stylized bookstore café. The lack of circulation and reference desks and the use of self-check stations make this experience entirely plausible. The library's strategy is to attract occupants with beautifully displayed merchandise and showroom furnishings. The library has even established a remote online reservation system with a drive-thru pick-up. The spaces are carefully designed to maximize the use of natural light and to create an atmosphere conducive to computer use and reading. An under-floor ventilation system resides in the 46 cm raised floor – it not only reduces the visual clutter of ductwork but also serves to circulate air.

While the Arabian Public Library achieves the aim of the library to "merchandise", the deliberate exclusion of the context in the design begs consideration. In turning inwards, the project turns its back to the immediate albeit ordinary suburban setting. In doing so, the project has given up an important role of the library to be part of a civic community. ***lw***

Levinson, Nancy. "Arabian Public Library", *Architectural Record*, June 2008.

Design sketch

1 Foyer
2 Bar
3 Information desk
4 Multi-function space
5 Office
6 Meeting room
7 Stack area
8 Store
9 IT area
10 Multi-media and audio-visual
11 Children's library

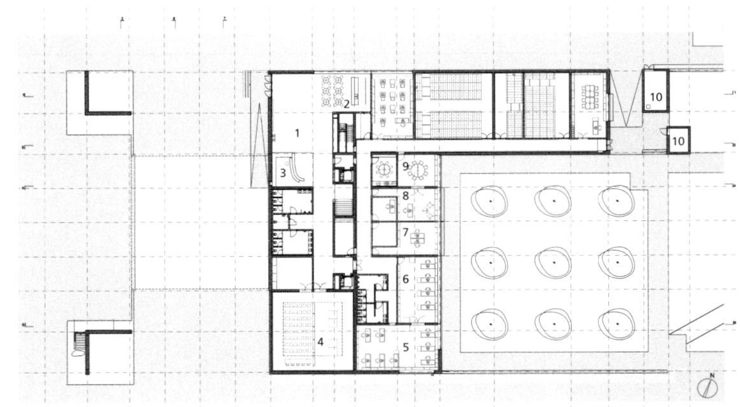

Ground floor

Biblioteca Municipal

Viana do Castelo, Portugal

Architect	Álvaro Siza
Client	Município de Viana do Castelo
Completion	2007
Floor area	3,130 m²
Number of volumes	140,000 documents
Seating capacity	408

The library, sited on the northern bank of the Lima River, acknowledges the significance of the water to the history of this town in the northern Portuguese region of the Alto Minho. Once a fishing village, Viana do Castelo reached its Golden Age in the 15th and 16th centuries as the harbor from which sailed many of Portugal's celebrated voyagers.

The library is part of a master plan for the reorganization and development of the waterfront. Constructed of white concrete with a continuous stone base, the library consists of two parts: a low L-shaped volume, raised 65 cm above the level of the land, and a 45 × 45 m volume that is raised one

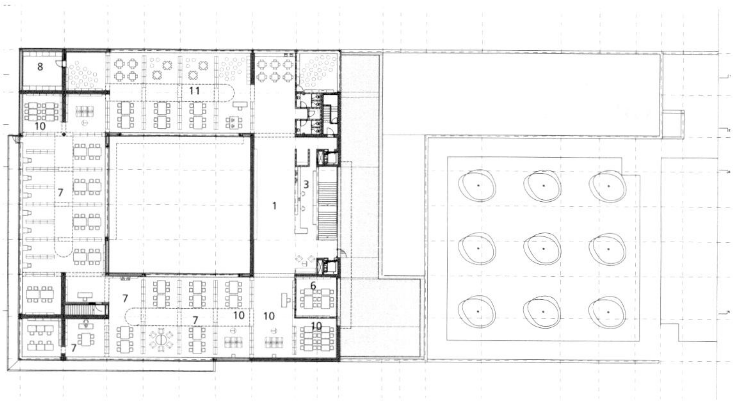

First floor

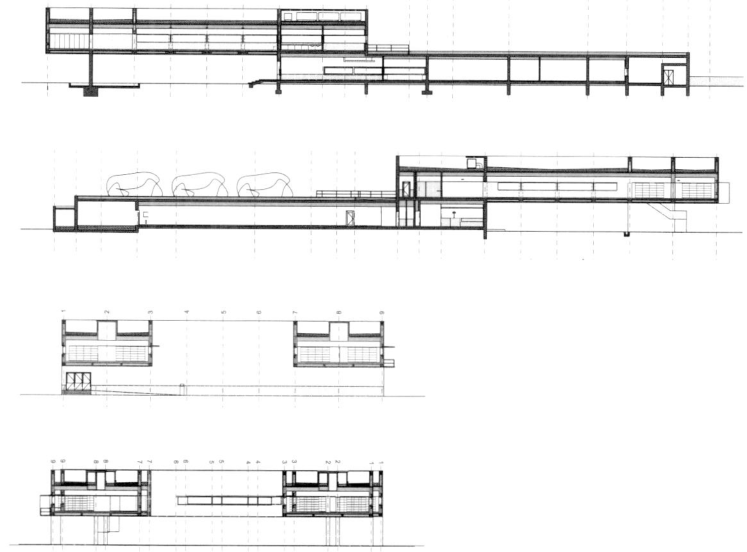

Sections

The library, raised one level above ground | View of the skylight in the reading room | Bands of windows frame views of the city

story around a 20 × 20 m central void. The raised volume is designed to permit a full view of the river both at a pedestrian level and from a considerable portion of the building interior.

The library program is divided between the raised volume that houses the reading rooms and books and the lower L-shaped building that contains administrative offices, meeting rooms, reception and archives. Public access is through a set of doors within the space of the void while staff access is placed at the eastern end of the lower block. Through the use of two minimal supports, the raised volume allows for an expansive vista of the river, expressing the horizontal line of the river bank without a self-conscious framing of the view. This vista is reinforced on the interior through bands of windows in the reading rooms.

The structure of the library is similarly differentiated between the upper and lower volumes. The lower L-shaped building is a typical construction of solid/steel concrete mixed slabs resting on reinforced concrete load-bearing walls with foundations. The raised volume with its expansive horizontal view is achieved through the use of long-span construction. The structure, prefabricated in sections in the shop, consists of a grid of latticed beams supported at one end upon the lower building and, at the other end, upon the two expressed supports. In 2009, the official citation from RIBA in honoring Siza with the Royal Gold Medal stated that "the forging of a masterful and seemingly inevitable architecture out of the possibilities of a site is one of the supreme characteristics of Álvaro Siza's architecture." The Biblioteca Municipal exemplifies this statement in its profound simplicity, its spare and minimal response to the physical context of the river and its relationship to the city. ***lw***

"RIBA Honors Álvaro Siza with 2009 Royal Gold Medal", http://www.bustler.net/index.php/article/riba_honors_alvaro_siza_with_2009_royal_gold_medal/

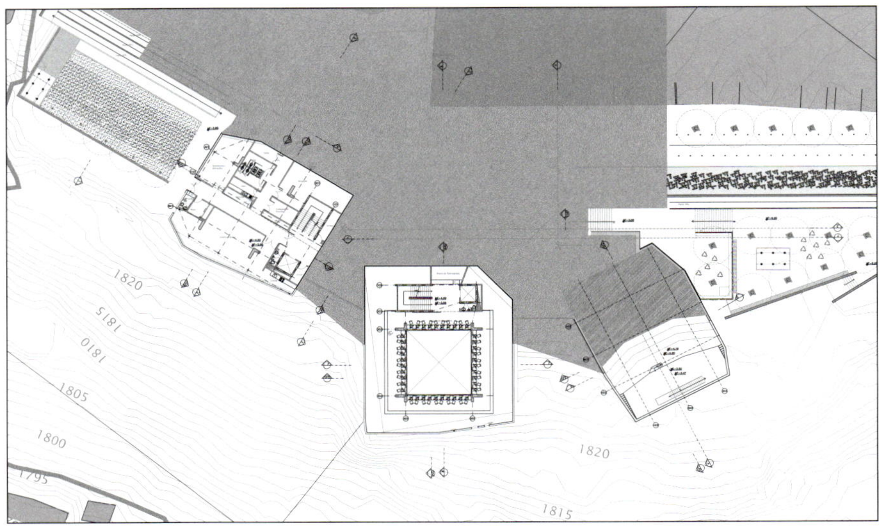

Level -1

Parque Biblioteca España

Medellín, Colombia

Architect	Giancarlo Mazzanti
Client	Alcaldia de Medellín
Completion	2007
Floor area	2,960 m² (gross)
Number of volumes	12,000
Seating capacity	175 (auditorium)

Three black, monolithic blocks jutting from the hills of Medellín, Colombia, serve as a library for the neighborhood of Santo Domingo Savio, once believed to be one of the most violent in Latin America. At one time the domain of drug cartels, Medellín, like the rest of Colombia, has in the 21st century undergone a dramatic transformation due to urban reform legislation. Law 388, enacted in 1997, required the drafting of public space renovation plans in the major cities and resulted in the Plan de Ordenamiento Territorial (POT). In the city of Medellín, Mayor Sergio Fajardo (2003–2007), a strong advocate for civic commitment, focused on rectifying social

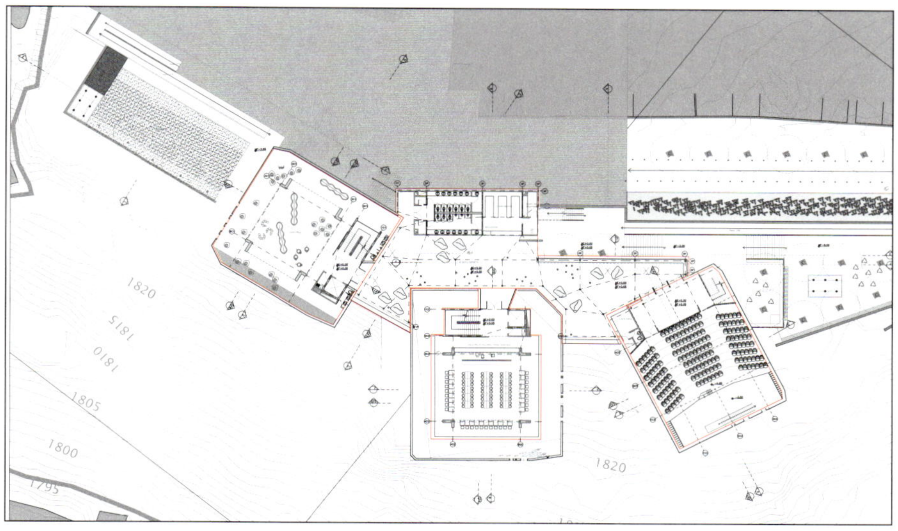

Ground floor (level 0)

The library amidst the barrio Santo Domingo Savio | The library's black volumes contrast with the brick houses of the barrio | View from the plaza

inequities in the most impoverished sectors of the city through the implementation of this plan.

The Santo Domingo Savio barrio is one such district that has benefited from Mayor Fajardo's plan of "social urbanism", which included a series of "library parks" to promote education, culture and recreation. Designed by Giancarlo Mazzanti in an open competition and completed in 2007, the 2,960 m^2 Parque Biblioteca España, named for Spain's contribution towards the project, comprises two distinct parts: the three volumes constituting the library on the one hand and a platform that both integrates the separate buildings and provides a plaza and meeting place with striking views of the valley below. The irregular and monumental forms of the buildings loom above the surrounding simple brick houses of the barrio, engaging the mountainous landscape beyond.

The three discrete volumes correspond in function to the programmatic requirements of library, community center and auditorium. The center volume houses the library functions with three vertically stacked, double-height reading rooms surrounded by overlooking mezzanines filled with computer stations. The community center houses event space, classrooms, an exhibition area and a daycare center. The auditorium inhabits the third volume with seating that corresponds to the steep incline of the hillside.

The library and community center are double structures; the external envelope of stone tile is supported by a steel structure while the internal core is a poured-in-place concrete frame. The programmatic functions take place within the spaces of the internal core, physically and philosophically removed from the exterior that can only be glimpsed through a few openings in the facade. The double structure allows for the placement of skylights along the periphery of the roof between the two systems. Natural light washes down the multi-storied void between

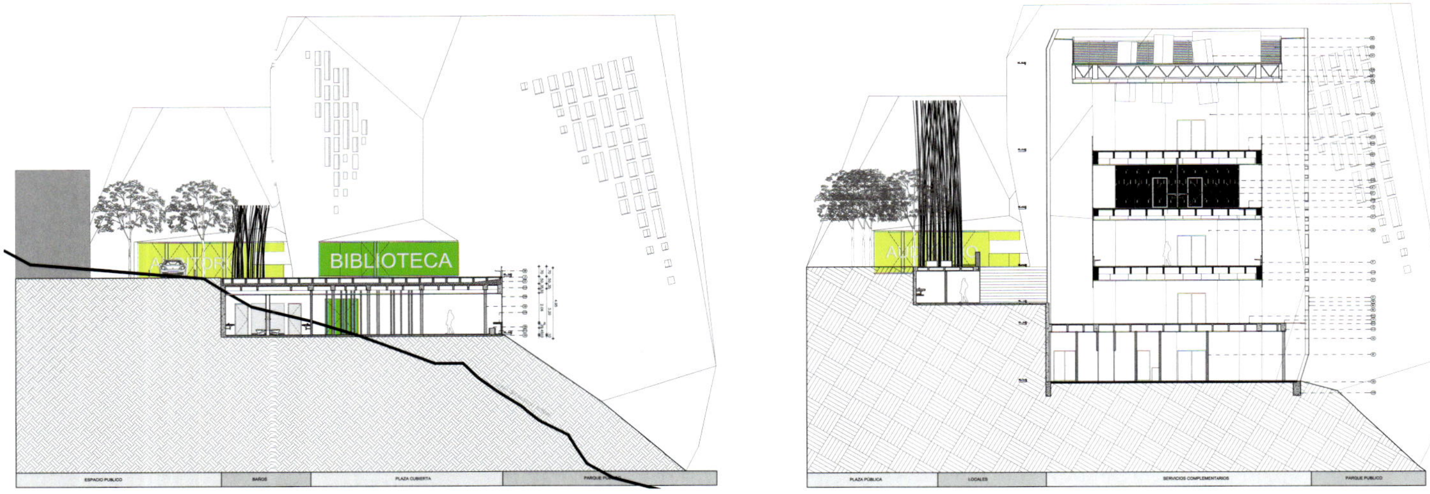

Sections

the exterior skin and interior core, augmenting the otherwise scarce daylight entering through the limited number of windows. The primarily blank facades were part of Mazzanti's intent to create an inward-turning building for this community. He states that it "disconnects the people temporarily from their context" so as "to take people from this poor community into another place and change their reality." (Source: *Architectural Record*)

The monumental, boulder-like Parque Biblioteca España has changed the reality of the Santo Domingo barrio. Its iconic forms have become a symbol of the new Medellín, attracting a record number of visitors each day to what had once been an inaccessible district of 170,000. Where the Santo Domingo residents once endured a two-hour climb home from their workplace in the city center, this neighborhood is now connected by Metrocable, a mass transport rail with a stop leading directly to the Parque Biblioteca España. While the structure has not aged well – water damage, efflorescence and loss of facade tiles – due in part to low-skilled labor and a sophisticated construction, the project has succeeded in improving life in the community. As a "library park", its function extends well beyond that of book lending to include business training, art gallery, community center, auditorium, gym space, children's play area and an outdoor space. Most importantly, due to the courageous efforts of Mayor Fajardo, the Parque Biblioteca España has catalyzed a community and created a pride of place for this impoverished neighborhood. ***lw***

Beth Broome, "Parque Biblioteca España", Architectural Record ital., November 2008. http://archrecord.construction.com/projects/portfolio/archives/0811parque-1.asp

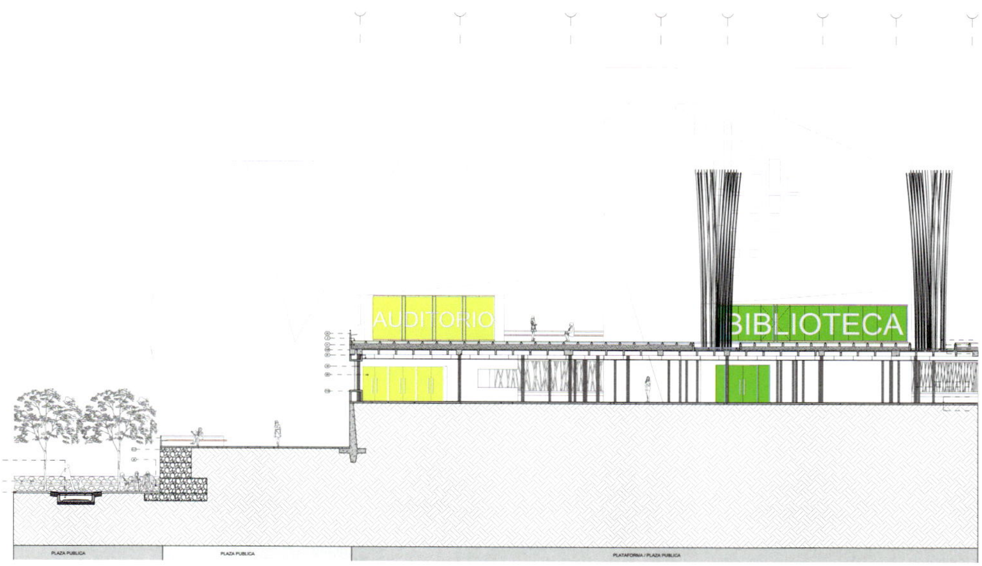

Section

Reference section | Views of the three discrete black stone-clad volumes of the complex | View from the plaza

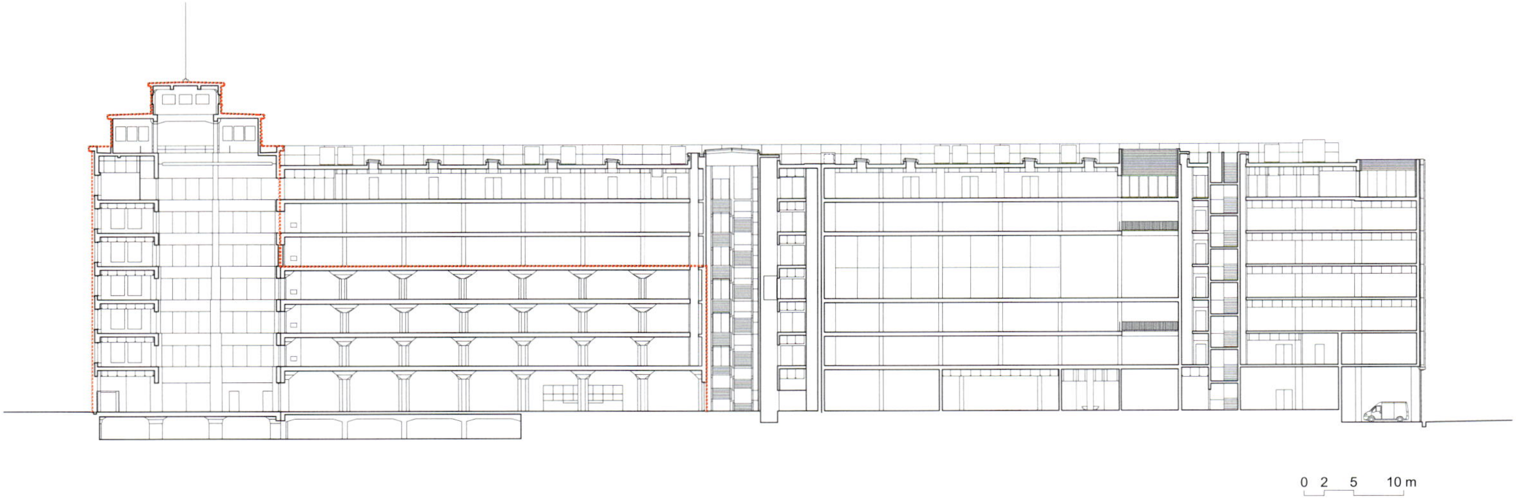

South elevation

Médiathèque André Malraux

Strasbourg, France

Architect	Jean Marc Ibos, Myrto Vitart
Client	Ville de Strasbourg
Completion	2008
Size	11,800 m²
Number of volumes	160,000 documents
Seating capacity	1,000

Located in the heart of Strasbourg, the home of Johannes Gutenberg and one of the earliest centers of printing, the Médiathèque André Malraux is the largest library in eastern France. Designed by Jean Marc Ibos and Myrto Vitart, this project is one of several planned for the conversion of the former industrial port, Bassin d'Austerlitz, to one of the city's "cultural islands". In keeping with the objectives of the Société d'Aménagement et d'Equipement de la Région de Strasbourg (S.E.R.S.) "to preserve existing buildings and develop them", the new library is exemplary in its adaptive reuse of a decommissioned grain silo and warehouse.

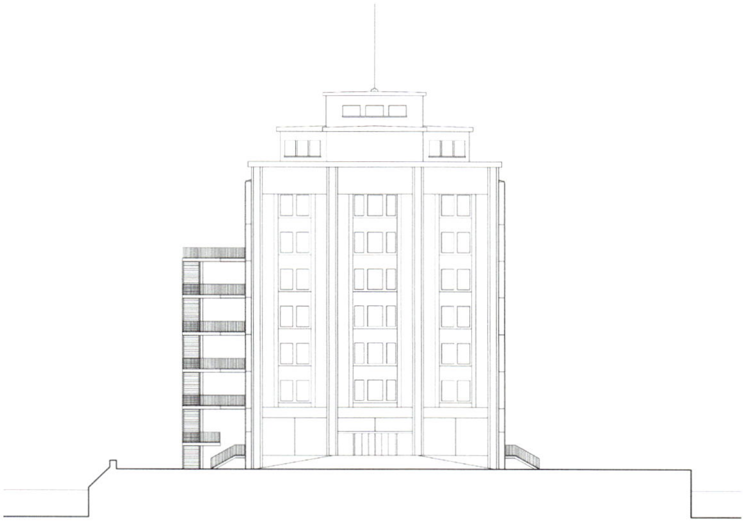

West elevation

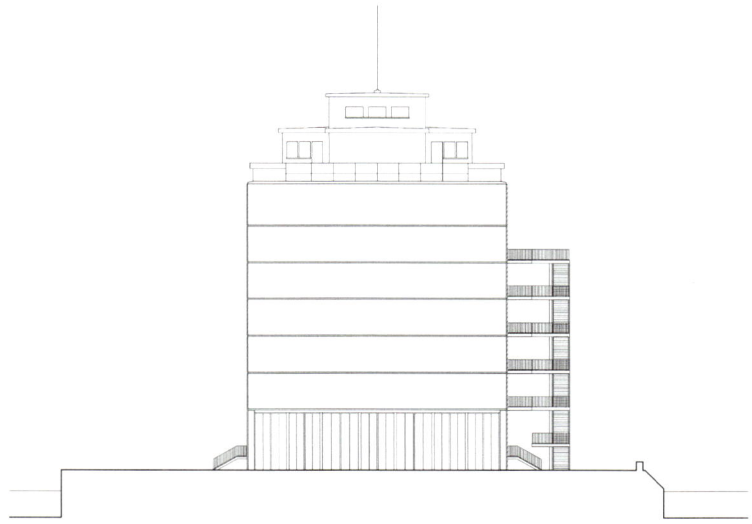

East elevation

New glazed facade on the former warehouse | Former grain silo structure used as entry to library | Reading area with low ceilings characteristic of a warehouse | Collection area prior to inauguration

The library site on the long and narrow peninsula next to the Bassin d'Austerlitz is part of the industrial docks of the Seegmuller pier. A former grain silo and warehouse built in the 1930s, its conversion to a library included both renovation and extension. The interior of the ten-story silo was stripped of its grain storage cells but its structure and full height of 47 m were retained as the entrance atrium for the library, a dramatic space that each floor overlooks. In the adjacent warehouse with its low floor-to-ceiling heights, the structural frame of massive concrete columns and floors was retained and even extended in a small addition on the east side. The long facades were removed and replaced with a metal and glass skin that allows light to penetrate the low and dark floor plates. A series of exterior metal stairs were added on the north side providing a rhythm to the glazed facade along the waterway. In explaining their work, the architects stated that "... everything obeys the logic of the waterway: linearity of embankments, extent of the pier, alignment of trees. Even the buildings, set in profile from one end the other, are in perfect continuity parallel to the embankments, with their silos, like prows, vertically punctuating the extremities." (Source: www.ibosvitart.com) The presence of the industrial past, most notably the elements of raw concrete, the structural grid, the repetitive bays and the linear form, is juxtaposed with the present through the use of color and graphics. Old and new are visibly intertwined in the interior by the application of a bold red color, painted directly on the concrete traversing the length of the building in rectilinear planes and linear shards. Moving from the floor plane to the column capitals, onto the vertical wall surfaces and along the expanse of low ceilings, the ribbon of color that begins on the surface of the entry plaza serves as a device that guides the user through this 11,800 m² library, simultaneously breaking and reinforcing its linearity. The furniture, too, complements this device of color through a palpable plasticity in the same shade of red.

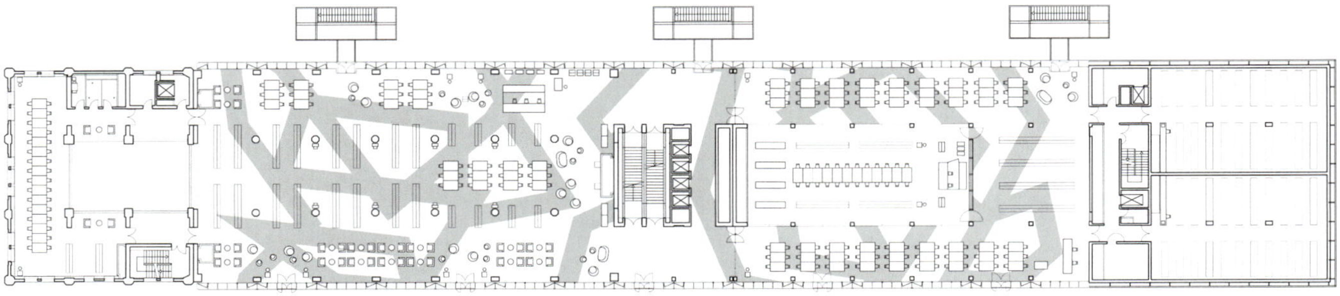

Third floor plan

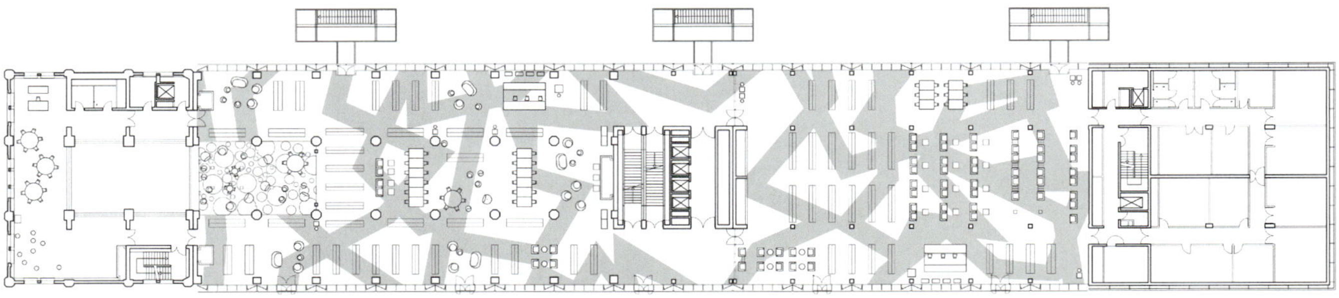

First floor plan

The signage and wayfinding for this library of "8 departments over 6 levels ... 160,000 documents, ... 20 kilometers of shelves" and 1,000 seats are the work of Intégral Ruedi Baur et Associés. Using texts "escaped" from books to "punctuate the space ... and reveal the materials", the signage is incorporated into the red ribbon; etched on the floor, moving up the columns, onto the walls and even the facade of the painted silo itself. This use of text and text fragments creates an ambiguity, blurring the line between function and art. At night, the glass facades dematerialize allowing for a view of the library and revealing it as a masterful fusing of past and present. ***lw***

"La Médiathèque André Malraux ouvrira ses portes le 20 september", September 13, 2008, http://www.bibliofrance.org

"Presqu'île André Malraux", http://www.sers.eu/Austerlitz-la-bataille-du-mole-DNA

"La Médiathèque André Malraux", http://www.ibosvitart.com/en/projects.php

"Strasbourg : la médiathèque Malraux bientôt inaugurée", http://www.libestrasbourg.fr/

http://www.integral.ruedi-baur.eu/

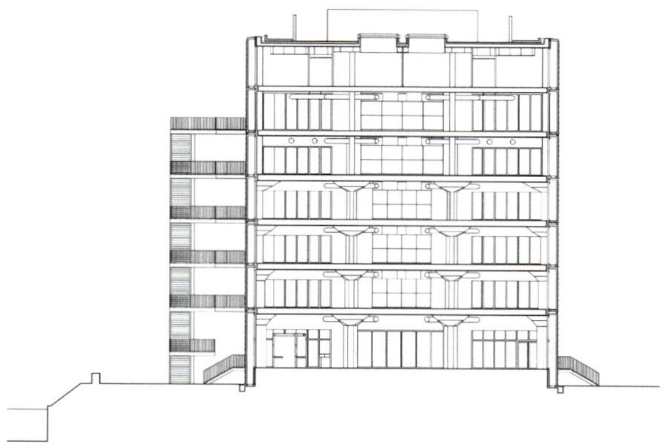

Transverse sections

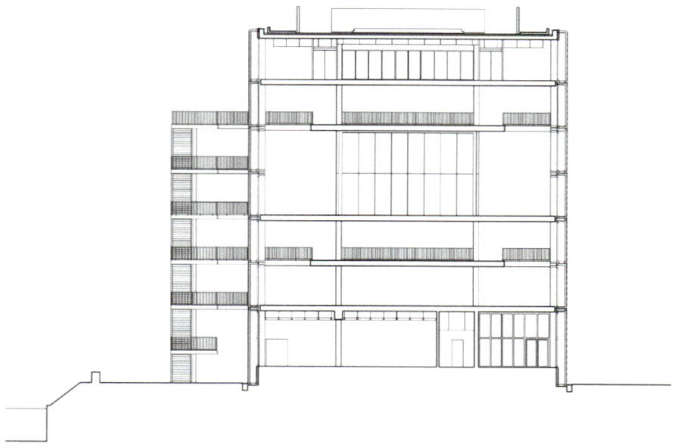

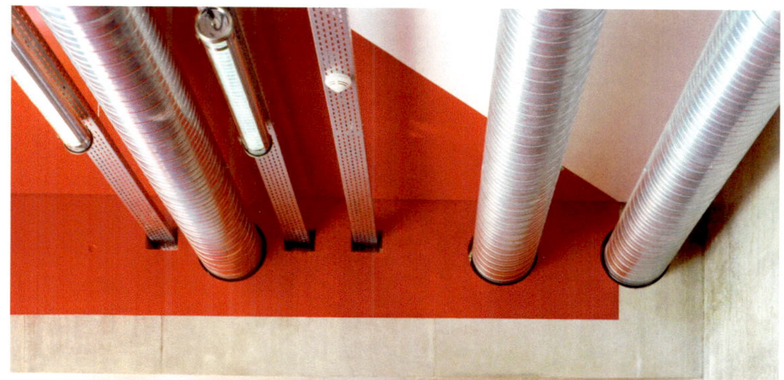

Lounge seating | Periodicals area | The use of bold color, furniture and graphic design integrates the existing concrete structure with the new library program

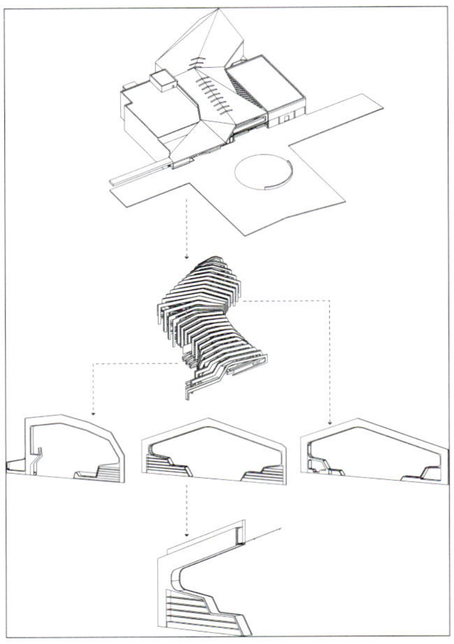

Axonometric showing sequence of integration

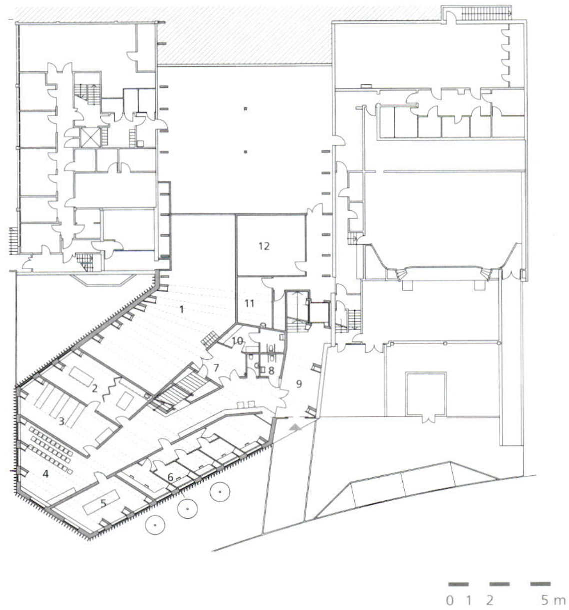

1 Technical room
2 Meeting/study room
3 Local history collection
4 Storytelling rooms
5 Classroom
6 Offices
7 Storage
8 Toilets
9 Lower foyer
10 Wardrobe
11 Cleaning room
12 Magazines
13 Existing toilets
14 Café
15 Library
16 Children and youth collection
17 Existing hall
18 Amphitheater

Lower level plan

Vennesla Bibliotek og Kulturhus

Vennesla, Norway

Architect	Helen & Hard
Client	Vennesla Kommune
Completion	2011
Size	1,990 m²
Number of volumes	30,000
Seating capacity	85 (library); 50 (study rooms)

Designed by the Stavanger architectural firm Helen & Hard, the Vennesla Bibliotek og Kulturhus, housing the library and cultural center serves a small municipality in Vest-Agder, Norway. The 1,990 m^2 facility opened in 2011 after a 2005 decision to relocate to the town center. In its reincarnation as part of the main square, this project exemplifies some of the key characteristics of the 21st century public library.

Directly facing the town square, the library occupies a prominent infill site between an existing adult learning center and a community center with cinema. In adapting to the adjacent buildings, the library footprint angles from the

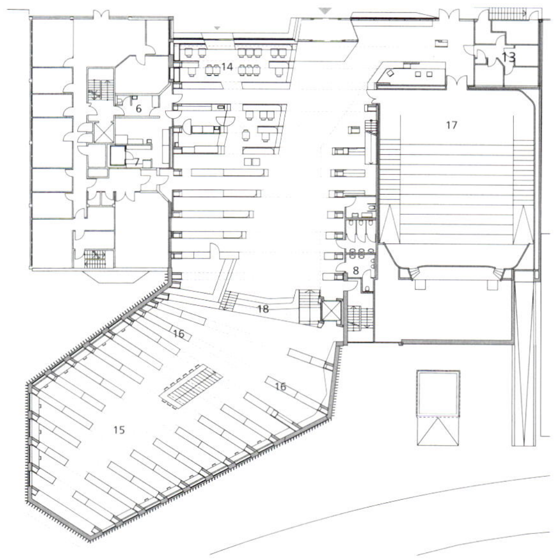

Ground floor plan

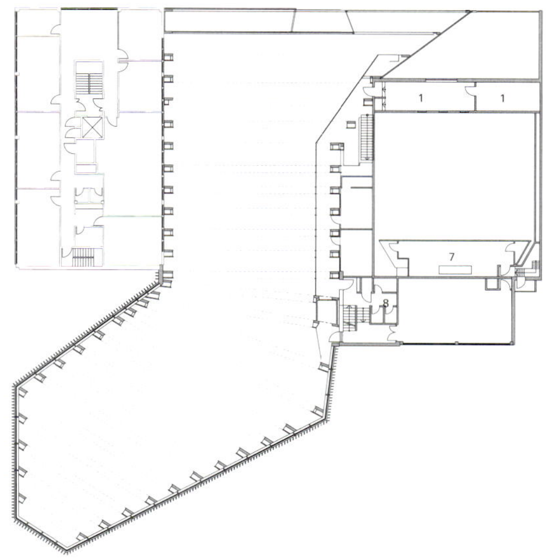

Mezzanine plan

Entry facade on the town square | Rear facade with its vertical sun shading fins | View of rear entrance

pedestrian thoroughfare through to the block behind. A new glass facade on the square extends the length of both the library and the community center. Common entrances, a covered exterior loggia, a passageway through the library connecting the front and back and a shared lobby space merge the library and community center under the auspices of a Cultural Center (Kulturhus). In the first year, the combined activities provided by both programs brought in an excess of 100,000 visitors to this community of over 12,000.

The library comprises a single open room of books and reading, a small café, administrative offices and meeting rooms. Matching and, in parts, exceeding the height of the adjacent three-story buildings, the library is divided into a main level with a mezzanine and a lower level. At an imposing height of almost 6 m at the apex, the mezzanine level lifts up from the main floor to allow for the creation of the lower level. Books and reading space occupy the main level with offices and meeting rooms directly below.

Twenty-seven timber arches span the length of the irregularly shaped main level. Made possible by CNC technology, the arches stretch and shift to adapt to the geometry of the angled space while maintaining a constant center profile. Made from prefabricated glue-laminated timber, these arches are first structural ribs that support the roof. Each rib is constructed as a box unit in varying thickness, especially at the base. Faced by bent plywood, the depth of each unit is used for many secondary functions. It holds shelves, seats, lighting, and is habitable in parts. Its functions range from shelving to furniture, light fixture, space divider, signage, display, storage and HVAC chase. The architecture is performative in this concept of usable hybrid structures, a reflection of an ingrained 21st century trait, namely multi-tasking.

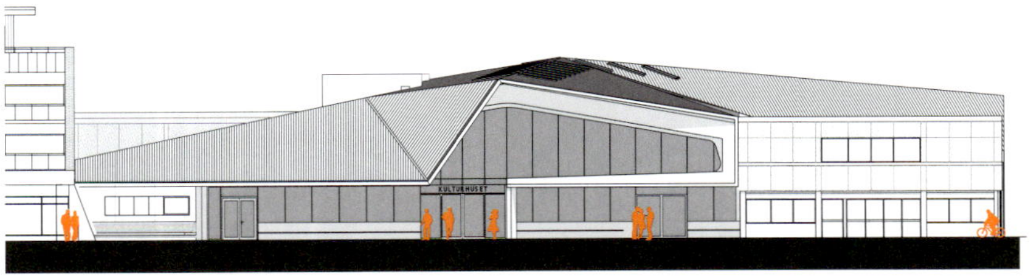

East elevation

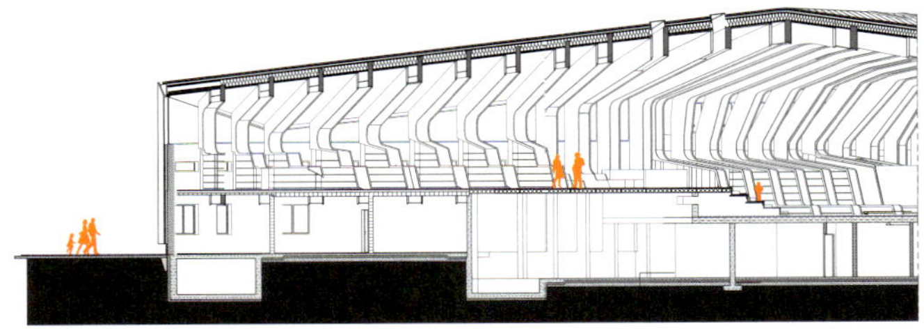

Longitudinal section

The use of wood as a material is pervasive not only in the interior, but throughout. Wood defines the exterior from the folding roof form to the vertical sun-shading wood fins that are highly visible on the side and the rear facades. Less visible elements such as the slab and the elevator shaft are also of wood, contributing to a total quantity of 450 m^3 of glue-laminated timber in the project. This use of wood – in itself a symbol of Norwegian culture – is an embrace of renewable building materials that contributes to the library's designation as a Class "A" low-energy Norwegian building.

The design of the Vennesla Library and Cultural Center is indicative of the many changes that have transformed the public library of old. Here, a move to the center of town results in a civic monumentality that is not premised on size. Engaged in its community, broadened in scope through borrowed program, constructed through digital construction technology and imbued with a material conscience, the Vennesla Library demonstrates the evolution of the 19th century one-room library model and the changing face of the 21st century public library. ***lw***

Vennesla Library, http://www.librarybuildings.info

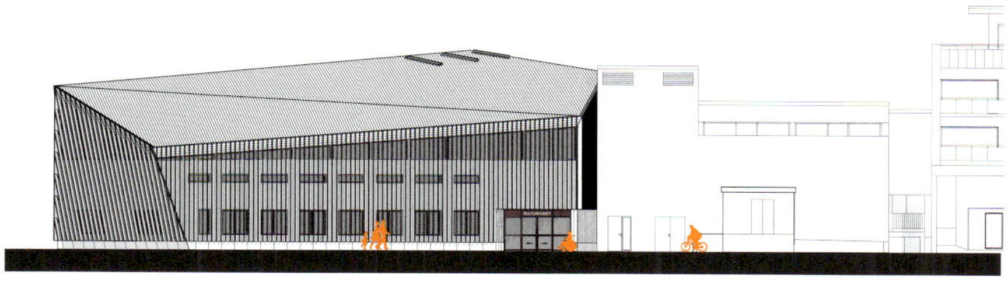

West elevation

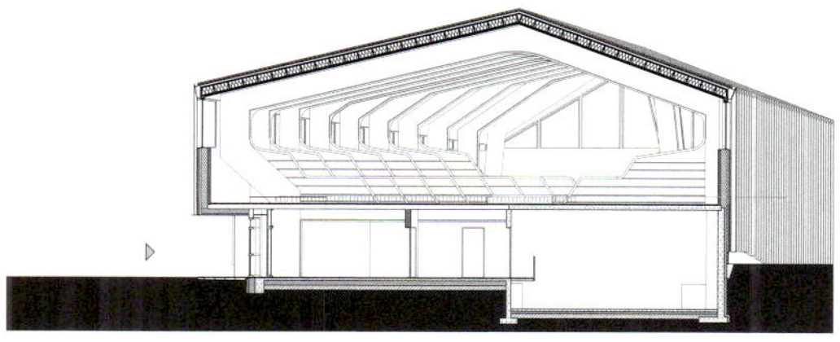

Cross section

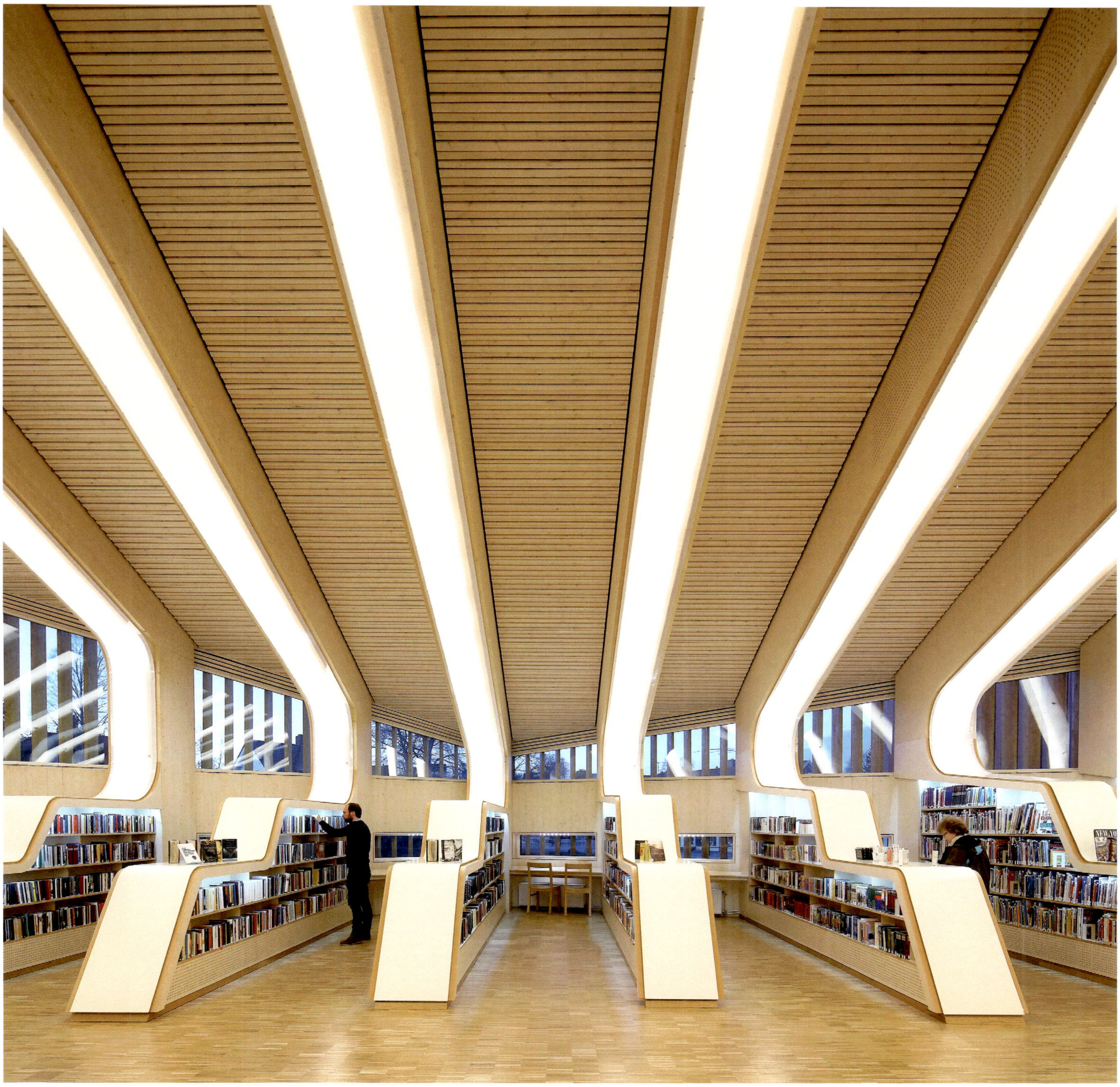

The interior of the library is formed by 27 structural ribs | The ribs are multi-functional as structure, lighting, bookcase and seat

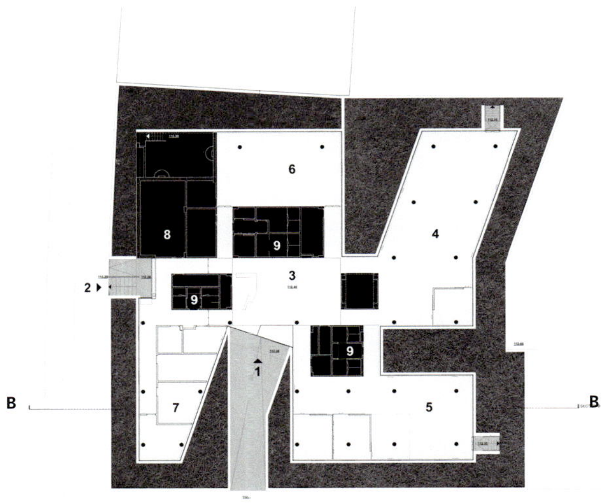

Ground floor

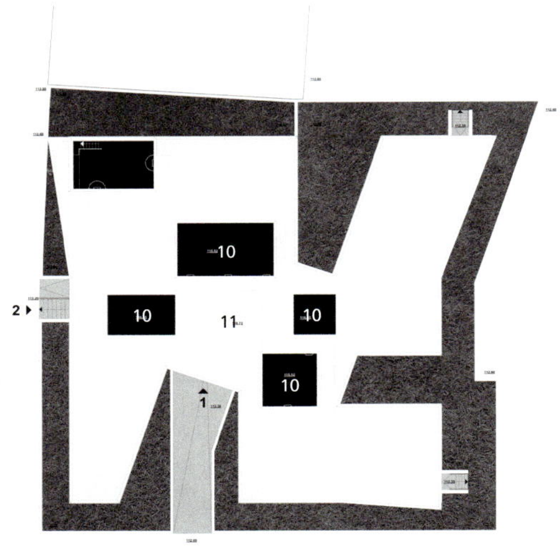

Roof plan

1 Main entrance
2 Service entrance
3 Entrance hall
4 Adults' reading room
5 Children's reading room
6 Conference and exhibition room
7 Office spaces
8 Storage
9 Toilets
10 Technical areas/colored patios
11 Stone terrace

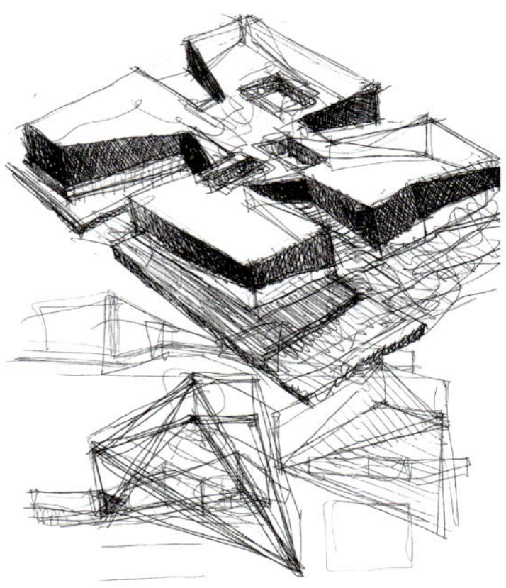

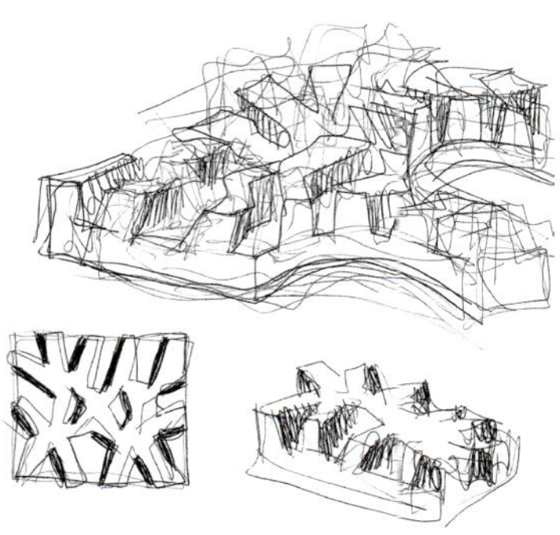

Biblioteca Municipal de Almada

Almada, Portugal

Architect	Santa-Rita Arquitectos
Client	Municipio de Almada
Completion	2012
Floor area	800 m²
Number of volumes	15,000
Seating capacity	50

Situated on the opposite bank of the Tagus River from greater metropolitan Lisbon, Almada houses a significant part of the service workforce of the capital city. In the 1960s, it was the refuge of citizens from both the nearby countryside and from the former Portuguese colonies of Cape Verde, Angola and Mozambique in search of work in the capital. Since the 1990s, development in Almada has resulted in improved infrastructure for transportation, water and sanitation.

Completed in 2012, the Biblioteca Municipal de Almada was part of a vision for renewal in this dense and underserved neighborhood. Located within the Parque do Fróis and near the high

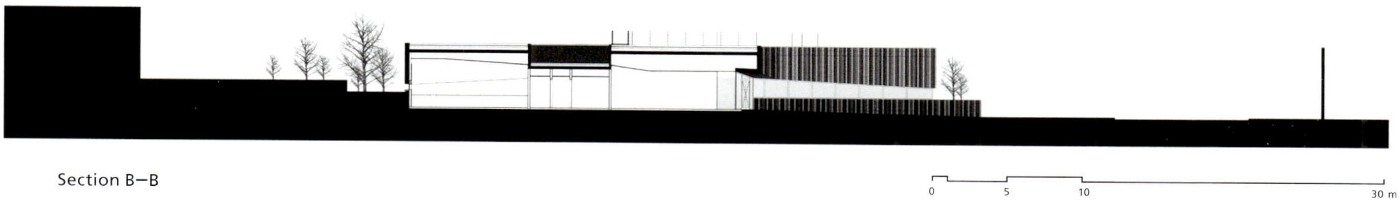

Section B—B

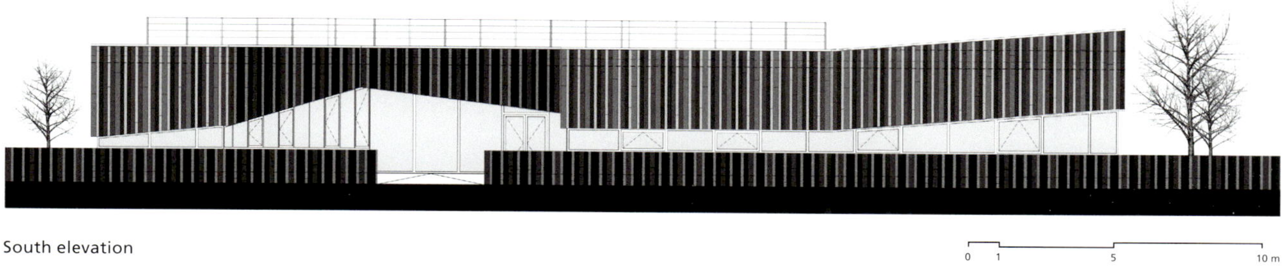

South elevation

The library against the backdrop of Almada's housing blocks | Raised outdoor rooms provide sheltered green views through the continuous ribbon of glass

school, the simple and elegant library serves a low-income population of which 30 % is under the age of 20. Sited on a barren hill amid conventional housing blocks, the concrete and glass library takes the form of a quasi pinwheel. The concrete of the building, formed with vertical striations, is a playful ribbon that floats above a horizontal continuum of glass, a welcome contrast to the perfunctory openings in the surrounding housing flats.

A square in concept, the library plan is eroded by a series of outdoor rooms set upon a low base planted with trees. These deep and narrow courtyards inhabit the negative space of the pinwheel and separate the programmatic functions of the adult section, the children's room, a multipurpose community space and the administrative wing. On the exterior they serve as outdoor meeting spaces for this community but within the interior, they provide a sheltered view for the various reading rooms. Through a sectional relationship between the low green plinth on the exterior and the seemingly sunken interior floor plane, the readers, both old and young, are offered a view into a verdant oasis in this gritty urban neighborhood. The relationship between the exterior and the interior is both subtle and gentle in its proffer of a protected place from which community building can begin to take place.

The design of the Biblioteca Municipal de Almada aims to foster autonomy and social diversification through reading, culture and learning. The work of Santa-Rita Arquitectos is exemplary of a new type of library as a place for community engagement. ***lw***

Câmara Municipal of Almada, http://www.m-almada.pt/

"Urban Policy in Portugal", European Urban Knowledge Network, August 4, 2010, http://www.eukn.org

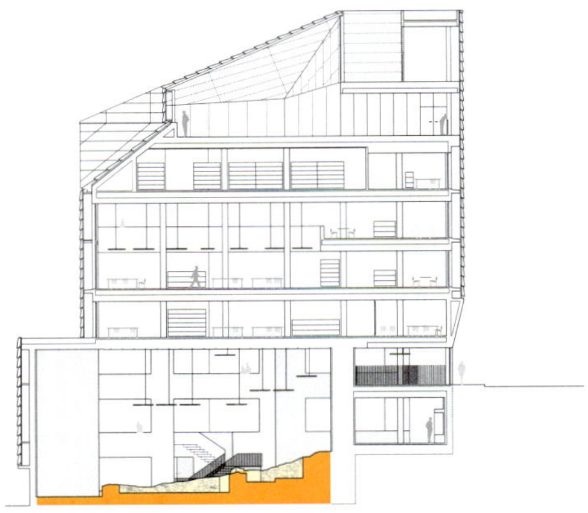

Cross section

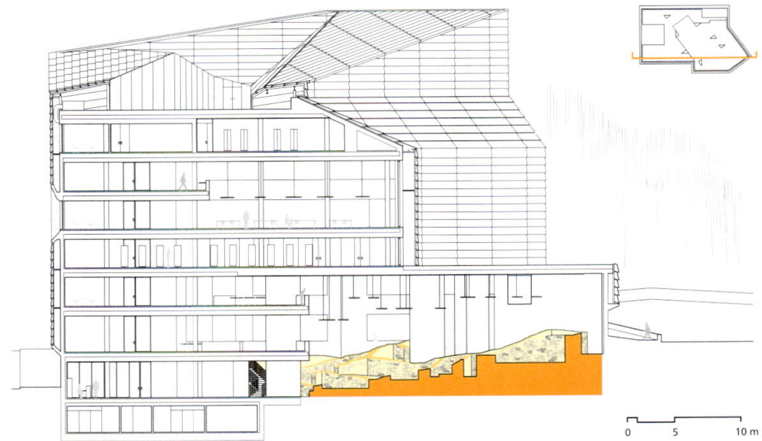

Longitudinal section

Biblioteca Pública de Ceuta

Ceuta, Spain

Architect	Paredes Pedrosa Arquitectos
Client	Ministero de Cultura, Educación y Deporte
Completion	2013
Floor area	6,200 m²
Number of volumes	130,000
Seating capacity	400

The Biblioteca Pública de Ceuta is the unique combination of a library, an archaeological site and a visitors' center. Completed in 2013, this 6,200 m² facility is the winning entry of a 2007 competition by the Madrid-based firm Paredes Pedrosa Arquitectos. Situated on a promontory of the northern Moroccan coast, the project occupies a Janus-faced site at the confluence of the Mediterranean Sea and the Atlantic Ocean. The project straddles not only bodies of water but through its architecture also the past and present history of this unique Spanish city, one of two autonomous Spanish territories on mainland Africa.

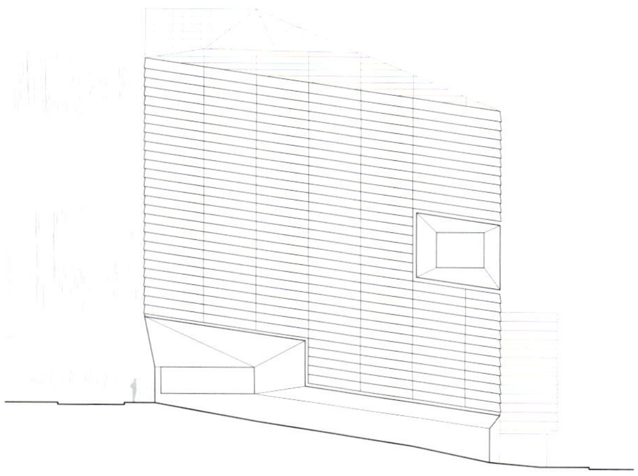

North elevation

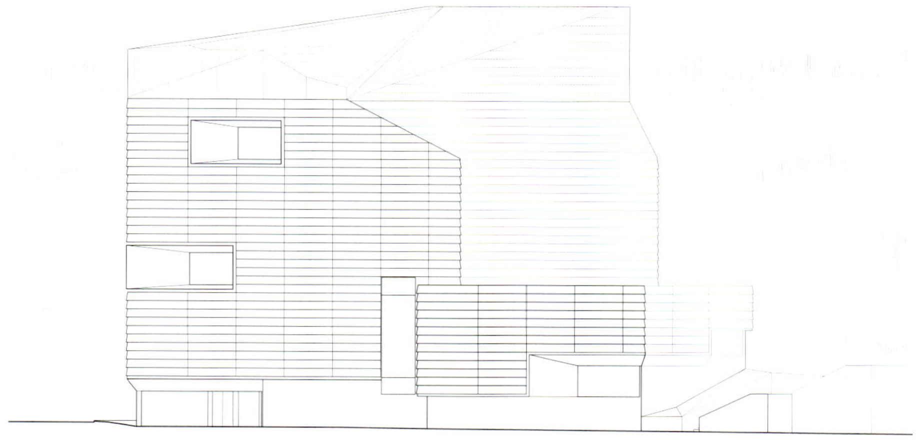

East elevation

View of the library near the top of the sloping city | Exterior materials of concrete and steel mirror the building's internal structure | The metal facade is layered to reduce heat and solar gain

The Biblioteca Pública de Ceuta is located on the compact, sloping site of an archaeological excavation near the water's edge. The facility comprises eight levels above ground, a ground level, and a below ground level. The program includes the requisite library functions of reading, collection, manuscript archive, children's and teen library, audio-visual room, research labs and the remains of a 14th century Marinid settlement. Remnants of an Arabic dynasty of Berber descent that ruled Ceuta from the 13th to the 15th century, these ruins are the focal point of the building and occupy a prominent, three-story open space on the ground level. Terraces with library functions open onto this space, providing a visual connection between the two programs. While accessed by separate entrances on different levels of the nearby streets, the library and visitors' center are integrated as a single design by the archaeological ruins on the lower level.

The library's geometry, a trapezoidal form with steps and folds, is derived from the intersection of overlapping urban grids. A rectangular form on one front aligns with the orthogonal contemporary city grid, while the triangular form on another front aligns with the medieval city of the ruins. The acknowledgement of both cities recognizes the existence of Arabic rule, a significant part of the city's history prior to Spanish allegiance. Through the library's form past and present are united within the building.

The structural concept for the building similarly focuses on the archaeological ruins as a demarcation of two systems, one concrete and one steel. The concrete structure wraps and supports the ruins and the lower levels that connect to the archaeological site. Seven triangular concrete columns – the geometry once again a product of the city grids – support the triple-height space of the archaeological finds. In counterpoint, the levels above the archaeological site are supported by a separate light-weight steel structure.

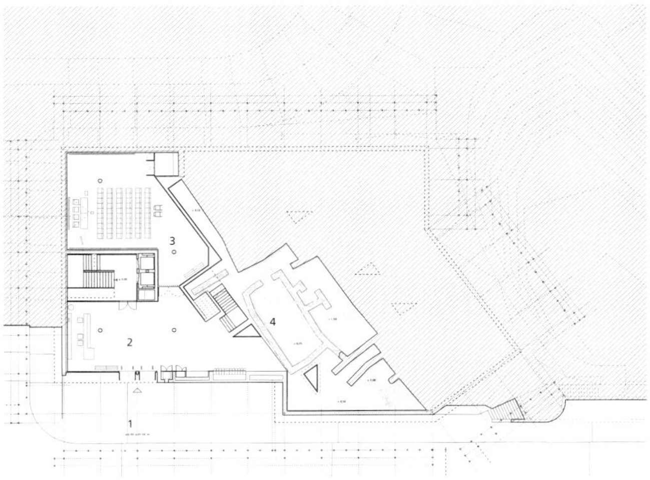

Ground floor

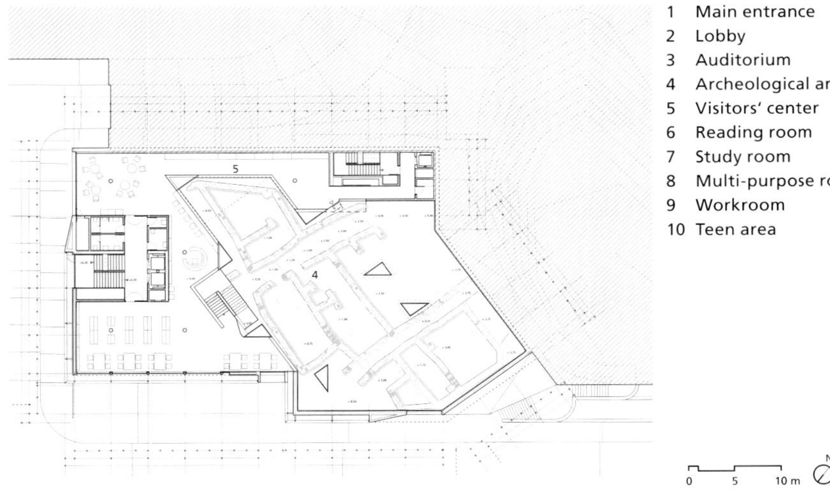

Level 1

1 Main entrance
2 Lobby
3 Auditorium
4 Archeological area
5 Visitors' center
6 Reading room
7 Study room
8 Multi-purpose room
9 Workroom
10 Teen area

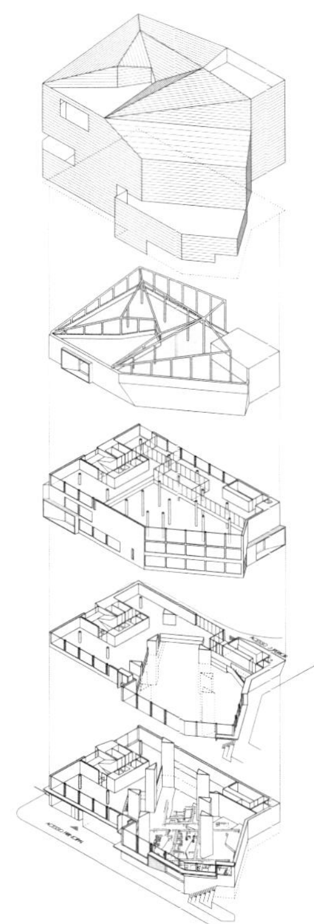

View of archaeological remains in a triple-height space | Axonometric drawing showing the building's stratification | View of reading room

The facades correspondingly divide into concrete and metal as distinctive exterior materials.

The concrete lower structure emerges, plinth-like, at the entry levels. The concrete surface reveals itself as a horizontal band, faceted and folded, around windows and entryways that are viewpoints towards the city and the water. Above the concrete base, the volume is clad in an energy-efficient aluminum skin. Differentiated by orientation through slight variations in make-up, the facade is a system of different layers; a habitable air space sandwiched between an internal glass layer and an outer perforated metal layer. They work together as "veils" in the North African climate to reduce solar gain and glare and to maximize the use of natural daylight.

The Biblioteca Pública de Ceuta is part of a new typology of public libraries in which library functions are enhanced through an expanded scope. Through the incorporation of additional and often unrelated programs, the library broadens its knowledge base, gaining new users. In this area of North Africa with a history encompassing both Arabic and Spanish rule, the integration of this past through architecture is also an act of acceptance. ***lw***

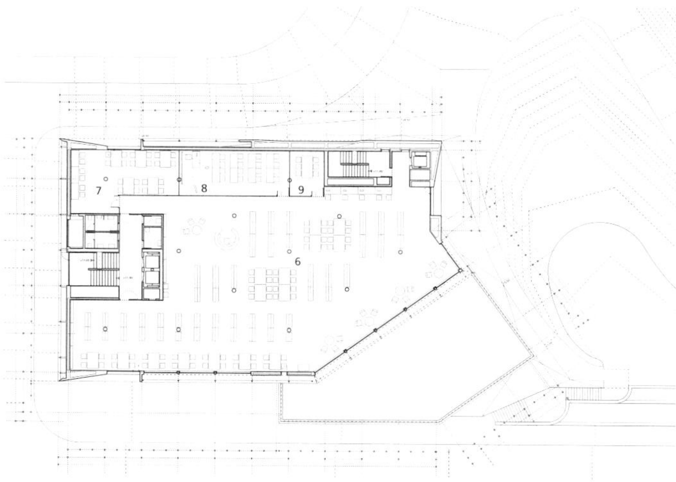

Level 3

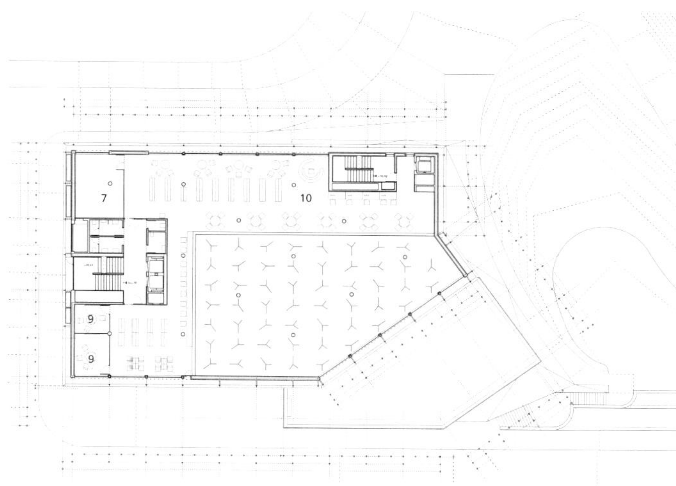

Level 5

1 School building
2 School extension
3 Teachers' housing
4 Women's association center
5 School library
6 Secondary school

0 50 100 m N

Site plan

Gando School Library

Gando, Burkina Faso

Architect	Diebedo Francis Kéré
Client	Gando Community; Schulbausteine für Gando e. V.
Completion	2014
Floor area	460 m²
Number of volumes	approx. 4,500 (140 m)
Seating capacity	75

The Gando School Library serves approximately 3,000 villagers. Architect Kéré designed the library and orchestrated its realization with little financial support and through the efforts of the community. A native of Gando at a time when no primary school existed, Kéré, the son of the village chief, was sent away to school at age 7. After having obtained a degree through a scholarship from the German government, Kéré's success abroad inspired him to provide educational opportunities for children back in his village. The Gando Primary School that opened in 2001 is the result of a dedicated journey to build a school through fund raising, both private and government, and community endeavor.

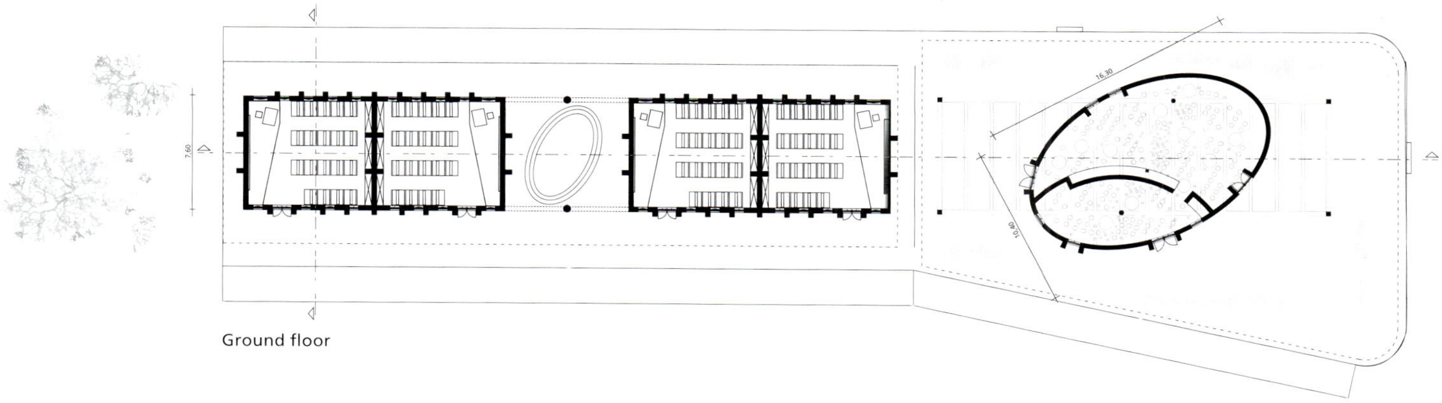

Ground floor

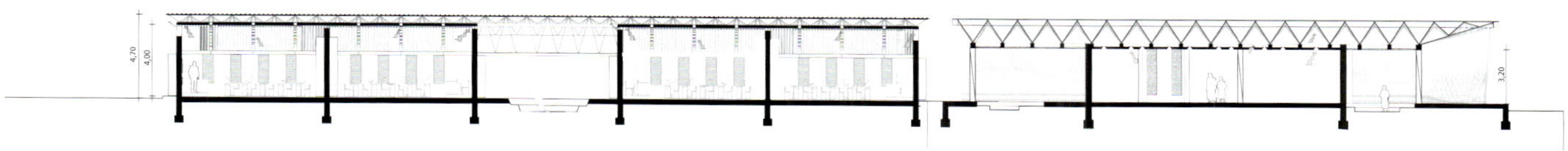

Section

Traditional clay pots were transformed into skylights | Exterior view from above | The overhang protects the walls against rain | On the interior, the clay pots provide daylight and ventilation

Built of indigenous materials by the citizens of the village, the school has been a great success, earning Kéré an Aga Khan Award and giving rise to additional projects related to the school and in surrounding areas.

The School Library is sited with the school buildings in an L-configuration. The library occupies the corner and forms a joint between the school building and the extension. All three buildings are similarly conceived as structures centrally placed between oversized rectilinear earthen plinths and overhanging tin roofs. The library structure is a 460 m^2 elliptical form with a single curved interior wall dividing the library into two; a small private reading room and a larger public one. Additional reading space is provided in the shallow curved spaces sunken into the earthen floor in the exterior space covered by the overhanging roof.

The materials for the library are local to the area: load-bearing walls of compressed earth, packed earth floor, corrugated tin roof. At the library two additional indigenous materials are used for the first time in construction: eucalyptus and clay pots. Eucalyptus, a weed typically used for firewood, serves to support the overhanging roof edge on the two long sides of the rectangular plinth. As slender columns, they form a screen façade along the front and the back, providing further spatial delineation in the buffer zone between the interior and the exterior. The clay pots are cast into the ceiling as skylights for light and ventilation. Construction methods, too, are simple to enable the participation of an unskilled community. Compressed earth bricks were produced through human efforts and hand-assembled on site. The clay pots were transformed into skylights on site with the removal of their two ends with a handsaw. In terms of environmental control, overhanging roofs protect walls against heat gain and rain while creating shaded internal spaces. The elevation of the roof surface above trusses increases air circulation. ***lw***

University Libraries

Universities founded throughout Europe during the high and late Middle Ages, such as the Universities of Bologna in Italy, Paris in France, Salamanca in Spain and Oxford in England to name a few of the oldest institutions, described a new educational model and necessitated the future conception of the academic library as type. Originally the university was not associated with a particular built environment, but rather defined as a community of scholars, and the teaching took place in non-designated spaces. However, with the increased forming of colleges in the 15th and 16th centuries a geographic locus paired with first, an unsystematic, and later intentional, form-giving building program was established, including scholarly libraries, archives and protective vaults, besides spaces for teaching, assembly, administration and residential purposes.

Higher education, the *septem artes liberalis*, imparted knowledge in the subjects of rhetoric, grammar and dialectics as well as arithmetic, geometry, astronomy and music and the higher faculties of theology, medicine and law. The degree of Baccalaureus Artium in the *artes liberalis* was the prerequisite for the study of the three superior disciplines, with theology considered the most complex and prestigious. In accordance with the philosophies of the Middle Ages with their Christian focus, the primary purpose and focus of a university system was the education of the clergy, a concept that was still carried into the New World with the founding of the first universities in the Americas in the 16th and 17th century.

Early universities, in order to be recognized as teaching institutions and eligible to bestow degrees, required a political mandate, funding through the church – in rare instances the state – and almost without exception papal approval. The attainment of monastic libraries in times of religious suppression, bequests by sovereigns, scholars and bibliophiles, and endowments commonly established the core of academic collections and provided for their conservation and growth. Books were often laid out on desks, a space-consuming storage method, limiting the number of users. Further, due to the rarity of the books, often only scholars with the academic degree of a Magister had free access to early library holdings and in early modern times, when academic libraries became more accessible to a wider community of scholars, hours of operation were often strongly curtailed. By the end of the 15th century Europe counted almost 90 established universities with affiliated libraries. Current statistics provided by the Online Computer Library Center, OCLC, lists an astounding 42,675 academic libraries worldwide.

Today, academic main libraries constitute the heart of the intellectual life of universities and often, at least in the modern Anglo-Saxon model of higher education, define the geographic center of a university campus as well. In their architectural language and iconic quality, or even in the array of amenities not tied to the core functions of the library such as cafés, restaurants, auditoria, multi-media facilities and bookstores they differ little from large contemporary urban public libraries. Instead the distinction is predominately apparent in their institutional integration, and their organizational and spatial structure is tailored to a very particular academic realm defined by the student and faculty body, the learning objectives, the teaching philosophies and the research orientations.

Exposed to a rapidly and constantly changing knowledge environment, the effectiveness of university libraries is highly dependent on the composition and calibration of the printed and digital collection, access to scientific databases and subscriptions to electronic publications. To assure relevance in proximity to the institution's mission statement, to maintain collection currency and to guarantee user service centricity, sophisticated monitoring tools assist librarians in collecting data on information seeking and studying behavior, the attraction and retention of students and faculty, the link between library use and learning success and scholarly competitiveness. Library administrators are obliged to establish user relations through library steering committees engaging stakeholders across the whole user spectrum in a dialogue, with the objective to establish strategic planning goals concerned with the future status of the collection, spatial configuration and service structure. Fostering public relations to external research facilities, academic institutions and industries creates valuable synergies between the institution and the outside world.

Exceedingly qualified and specialized librarians are instrumental in shaping academic research and teaching through the systematization of digital knowledge, the filtration of relevant and reputable information, the participation in the digitization of holdings, the integration of printed and digital materials, and the hyperlinking of databases and digital content for interdisciplinary collaborations. Extensive university systems with all-encompassing faculties and disciplines often are confronted with the logistic necessity to establish within the genre of academic libraries, smaller specialty libraries housing so-called niche collections and archives dedicated to a particular school. When in 1683, the theologian John Harvard bequeathed his private library of 400 books to Harvard University, the nucleus to a collection containing today more than 18 million volumes housed in 79 libraries and one depository within the Harvard University Library System was established. Access to printed material without major delays is critical within an academic setting, and a network of libraries and off-site depositories consequently constitutes a logistic and economic challenge since the option of browsing, an important component of literature research, becomes more difficult to ensure.

A radical approach to the organization and shelving of a collection was devised in the Joe and Rika Mansueto Library (2011, pp. 244–247), designed by Helmut Jahn for the University of Chicago library system. By depositing 3.5 million volumes of little browsing interest within an automated storage and retrieval system below the actual library, valuable shelving space was freed up for browsing attractive material while the robotic system retrieves ordered materials within minutes. The construction of the Jacob-und-Wilhelm-Grimm-Zentrum (2009, pp. 232–237) of the Humboldt Universität in Berlin, designed by Max Dudler, allowed the consolidation of all faculty internal library holdings, providing access to the information not only for the community of the university but also the greater public at one central location.

Modern academic libraries are not isolated entities within a university system but rather assume the role of communication hubs fostering interdisciplinary discourse, providing the bases for social interactions, opportunity for contemplation, "save haven" functions for incoming students and room for interactive learning experiences in laboratories, technology-infused meeting spaces and multi-media labs. The integration of library research components into course curricula, introduction to literature research strategies and library outreach programs such as writing centers, and library-associated learning commons are fundamental components of academic libraries supporting learning success, information literacy and the completion of degree programs. Intra-library loans assuring access to holdings of individual schools and faculties as well as interlibrary loan agreements between leading library systems extend the availability of institution-owned printed knowledge. Sophisticated library portals and the configuration of high-speed networks accomplish access of digital library content from locations throughout the university system at all times.

Despite the relentless voices prophesizing the demise of libraries the analysis of most commonly used resources offered by libraries of academic institutions reveals that the use of the printed book prevails by far over the use of electronic primary sources and if predictions are correct, print media will remain in this position for the foreseeable future. The appreciation of acquiring knowledge, regardless of fluctuations in learning strategies and information gathering, will always demand a supportive, human-centered spatial quality, and academic libraries today and in the future need to meet the challenge. Technology, however, is to be seen as a decisive catalyst in delineating academic library planning concepts, creating the foundation for flexible service structures, transformations in user interface and the management of a constantly morphing knowledge environment. *wr*

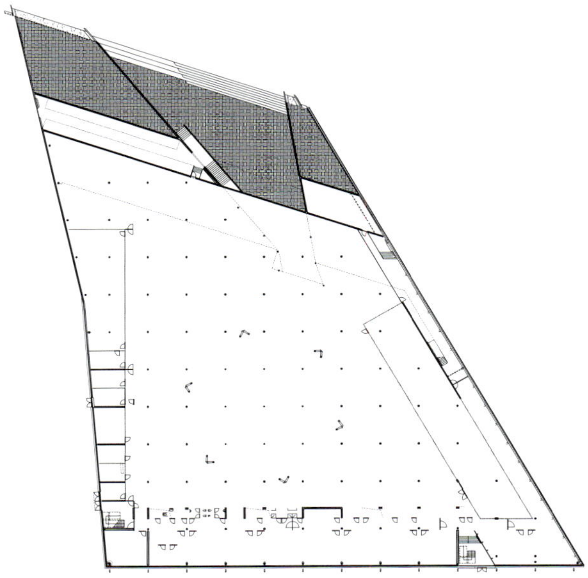

Basement plan

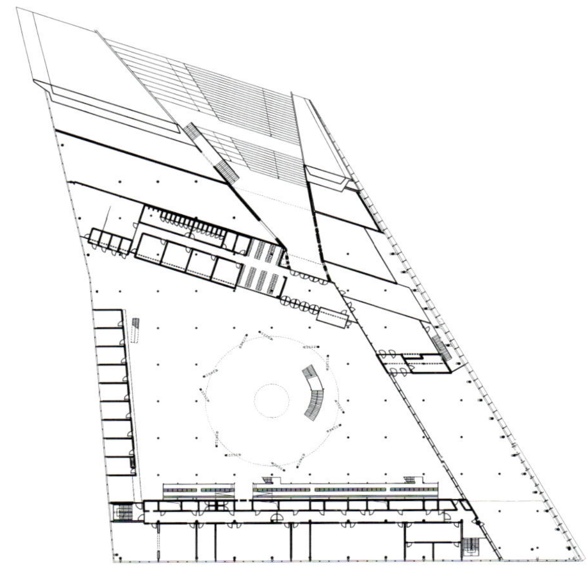

Ground floor

0 5 10 20 m

Central Library

Technische Universiteit Delft
Delft, the Netherlands

Architect	Mecanoo
Client	ING Vastgoed, Den Haag
Completion	1998
Floor area	15,000 m²
Number of volumes	980,000
Seating capacity	1,000

The Central Library at Technische Universiteit Delft (Delft Technical University) is the national library of technology and the center of technical and scientific information in the Netherlands. With its extensive physical collection and electronic information services, it serves both the university population and the commercial and industrial sectors. Designed by the Dutch firm Mecanoo, this library is noted for its iconic form – an expansive green roof pierced by a conic structure. Completed in 1998, this library represents a *tour de force* in sustainable practice that was much ahead of its time.

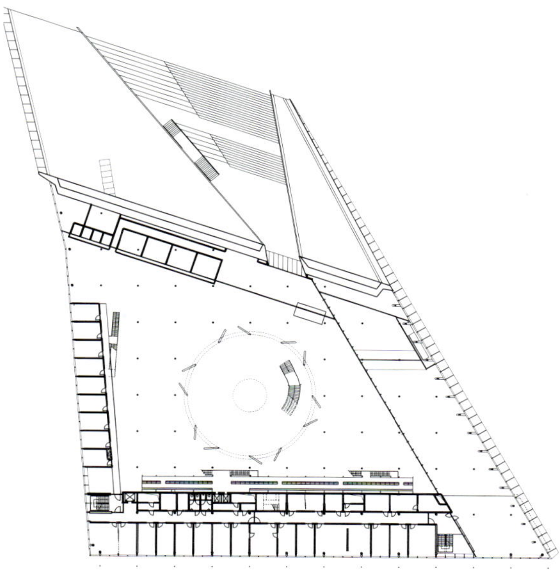

First floor

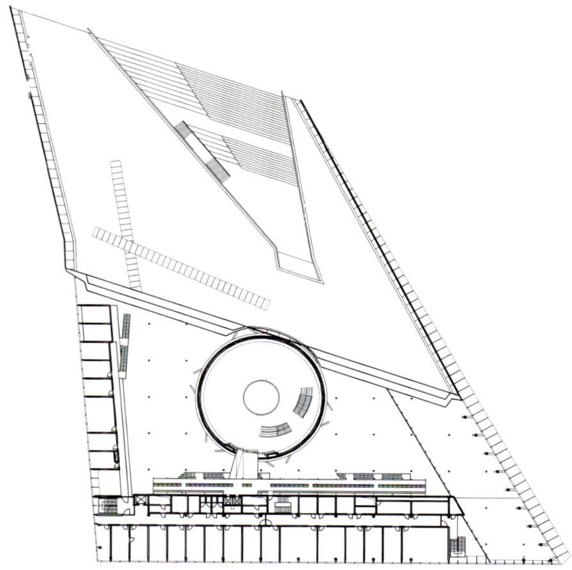

Second floor

The library is presented as a landscape and in juxtaposition with the Brutalist auditorium directly across | The conical structure is a beacon on campus | Glazing around the conical structure provides natural light on the interior

The library is sited opposite the lecture hall designed by Team X architects Van den Broek and Bakema. The Brutalist concrete auditorium wields a forceful presence, physically as a massive structure and ideologically as a benchmark in the history of architecture. This imposing context was the impetus for Mecanoo's shift from a focus on form alone. Instead the library is presented as a landscape – an extension of the campus and a place for human interaction.

On the western edge, facing the auditorium, the library begins as a continuation of the campus lawn. It is subsequently lifted into the air as a vast and sloping expanse of green. This design strategy places the library entirely beneath a grass roof that is freely accessible for walking and lounging. The roof is supported on a system of slender columns within a huge volume enclosed by canted, glazed walls on three sides. It is pierced by a massive cone structure that extends 40 m above grade. Open at the top, this iconic form is a beacon on the campus both during the day and at night.

Accessed through a broad flight of steps in the grass, the library consists of a large reading room with administrative offices and computer rooms on the eastern and southern perimeters. The cone structure rests on splayed steel columns in the center of an irregular trapezoidal floor plan and houses the circulation desk and four levels of study spaces. The majority of the collection is stored in temperature- and humidity-controlled storerooms in the basement and is retrieved upon request. 80,000 volumes of the most requested books are displayed in a four-story, suspended, steel-framed bookcase on the north perimeter, silhouetted in front of a wall painted in signature Mecanoo ultramarine. Glazing both within and encircling the cone provides light for the main library as well as the study spaces.

Concern for a clear environmental strategy is seen in the critical roles played by key components

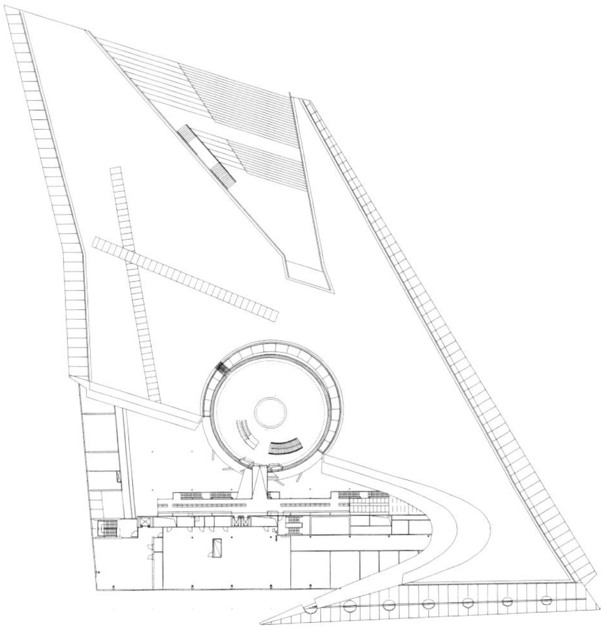

Third floor

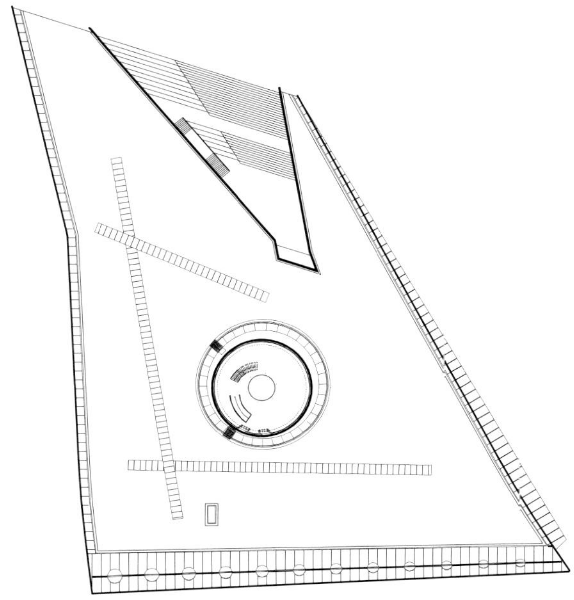

Roof plan

View of four-story suspended bookcase | View of study spaces | The most requested books are displayed on a four-story bookshelf

of this design. The vast grass surface with its density and mass provides thermal insulation as well as acoustic soundproofing for the interior. The rainwater held by the vegetation also contributes to natural cooling in the summer. The glazed facades consist of a system of outer glazing, a 140 mm wide air cavity and a sliding inner glass. Air is drawn through the cavity and removed at the top level. For the heating and cooling of the building itself, a cold storage system is used in which heat and cold are stored in groundwater. In this case, two tubes are placed 60 m apart in a layer of sand 45–70 m below grade. In the winter, warm groundwater is pumped through one tube to the building and, when cooled, exits through the other. In the summer, cool groundwater is used similarly for cooling.

The Central Library at TU Delft predates the dilemma of the 21st century library as it adapts to a world of technology and new media. At TU Delft, books and media are assumed and co-exist without fanfare. The design with its iconic grass roof posits with success the library as an environmentally conscious place for the meeting of people and ideas. ***lw***

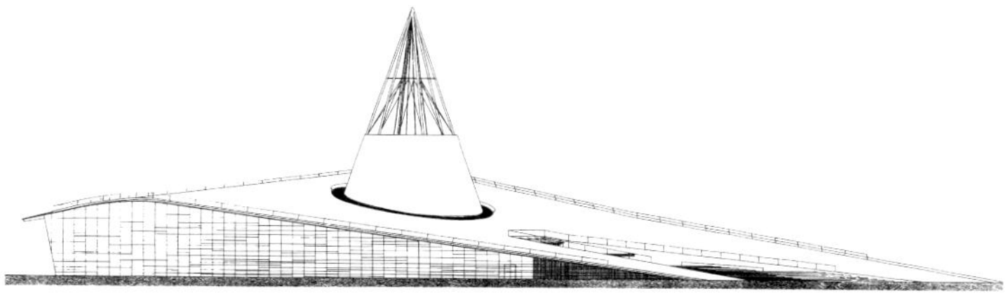

North elevation

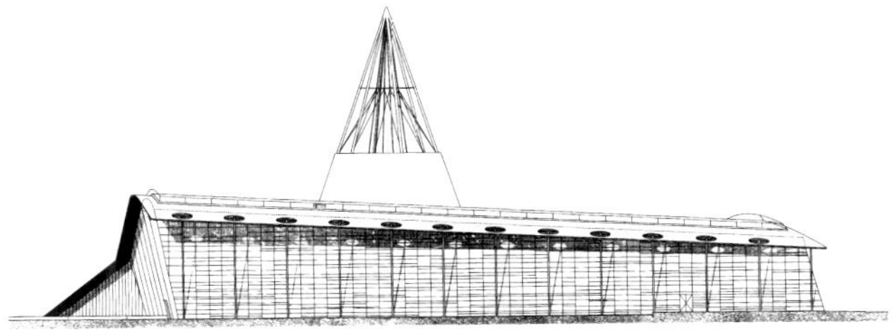

East elevation

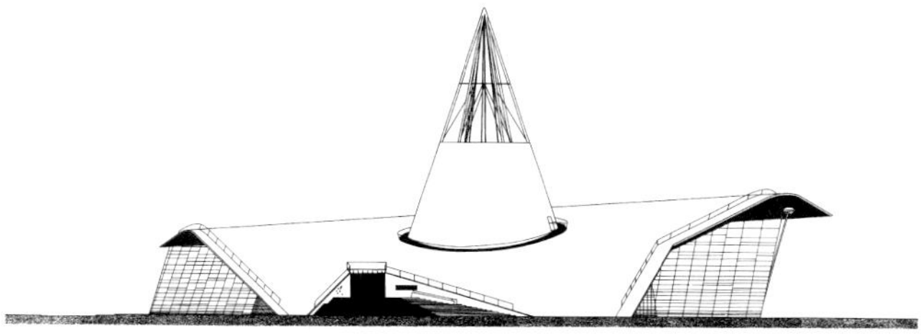

West elevation

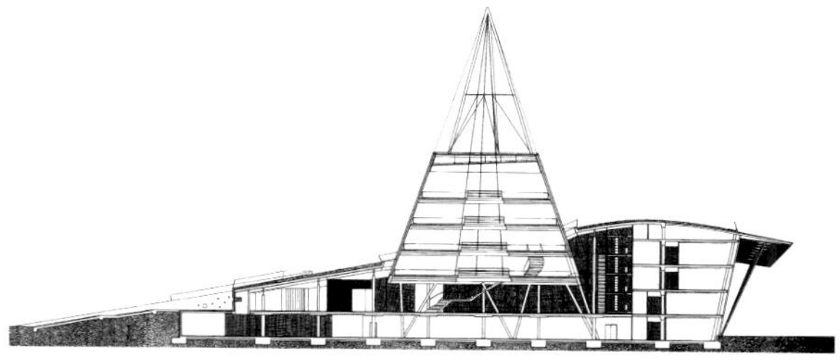

Section

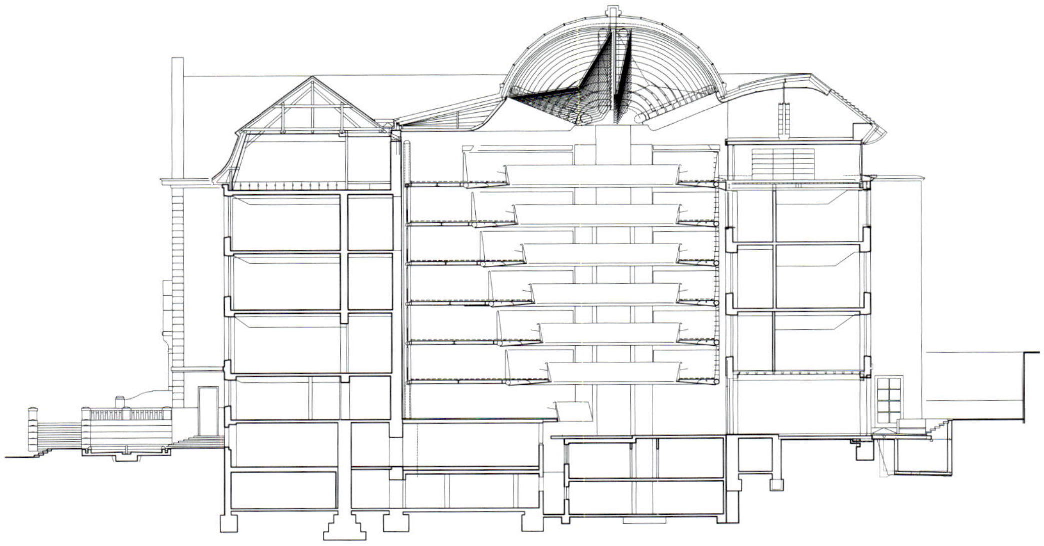

Section

Exterior view of refurbished school | Vaulted skylight arching over the atrium | Tapered steel ribs radiating from an elliptical, tubular ring support the cantilevered floor above | Space between the elliptically shaped library floors and the courtyard walls of the historic building

Law Library

Universität Zürich

Zurich, Switzerland

Architect	Santiago Calatrava
Client	Universität Zürich
Completion	2004
Floor area	4,800 m^2
Number of volumes	170,000 books, 700 journals
Seating capacity	500

The Bibliothek des Rechtswissenschaftlichen Instituts, designed by Santiago Calatrava for the Faculty of Law at the University of Zurich, is formed by a series of seemingly floating, hollow elliptical plates inscribed into the rectilinear courtyard of a historic building. Formerly accommodating the Alte Kantonsschule (secondary school), the complex, designed in 1909 by the cantonal chief architect Herman Friez, featuring Neo-Baroque and Art Nouveau style elements, was adapted for the use by the Law Faculty. When seen from the street, the intervention is restricted to the new glass dome and the appearance of the historic building was preserved.

A narrow passageway congruent with the minor axis of the elliptical plan leads from an external

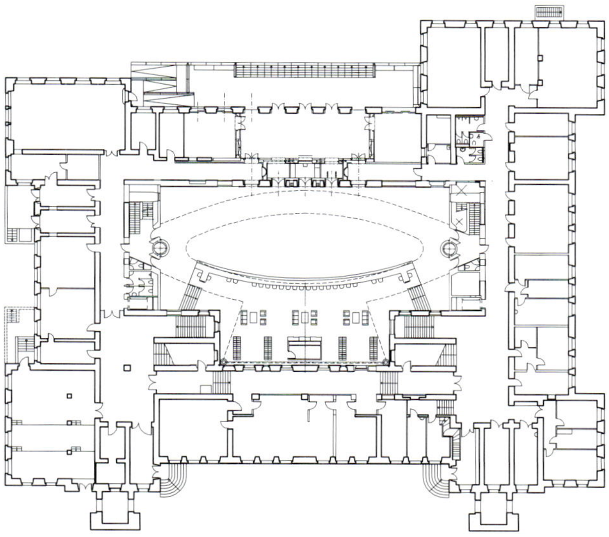

Ground floor

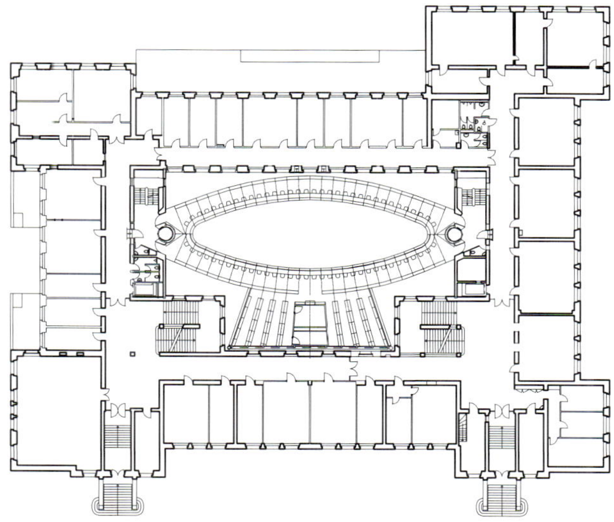

First floor

lobby onto the library's stone-paved entry plaza. Seven floors above, a steel-framed arched skylight, connecting the foci of the outer ellipse, funnels an abundance of natural light through the eye of the library. Towards the top of the lightwell the center void increases gradually in diameter, resulting in the volumetric shape of a reverse elliptical cone. The visual effect of an almost continuous surface is strengthened by surrounding, inclined, tall balustrades clad with vertically oriented maple wooden slats.

While traveling between floors, cylindrical glass-enclosed elevators at opposite ends of the major axis offer a dramatic view into the lightwell. The collection is placed on linear wooden shelves following the circumference of the outer ellipse. Conveniently accessible by the scholars, the wall of books also provides a colo-ful enclosure to the study space. Solid maple panels forming the back of the shelving system create a serene surface complementing the white plaster of the historic facade. Highly tensional/interstitial, compressed and decompressed volumes generated by the insertion of an elliptical sphere nto a rectangular cube are omnipresent within the library while framed views of the juxtaposition are offered through preserved and new window openings into the transformed space.

Both the solitaire character and the suspended nature of the inserted library body are enabled by the structural concept. The tubular steel skeleton of the inserted volume is anchored back to the existing structure in a method that eliminates not only the need for columns on the entry level, but also limits the necessity for structural bridging along the perimeter. Expressed tapered steel ribs radiating from the exterior tubular ring support the cantilevered library floor. Light coffers formed by the plates enhance the dynamic curvature of the floor plates and create a central void. Two glass-enclosed stories, housing offices on the lower level and a study zone above, were added to the back of the existing structure. Enclosure of the once open courtyard reduced the exposure to weather, resulting in energy savings. ***wr***

b-tu Brandenburg University of Technology Cottbus - Senftenberg

Logotype for Brandenburg Technical University: The iconographic waveform and color scheme of the center are carried over into the graphic layout of printed material

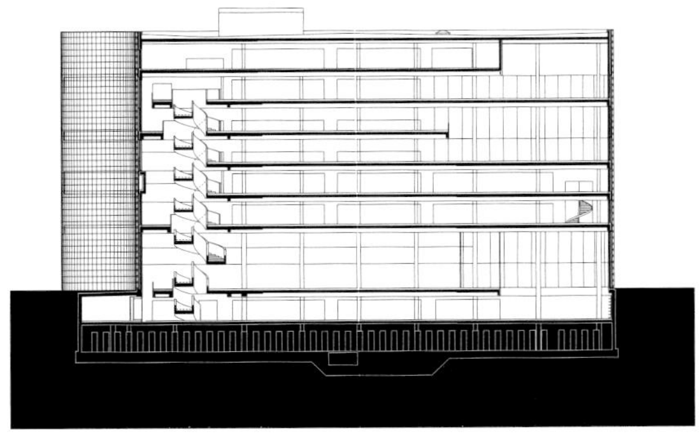

Cross section

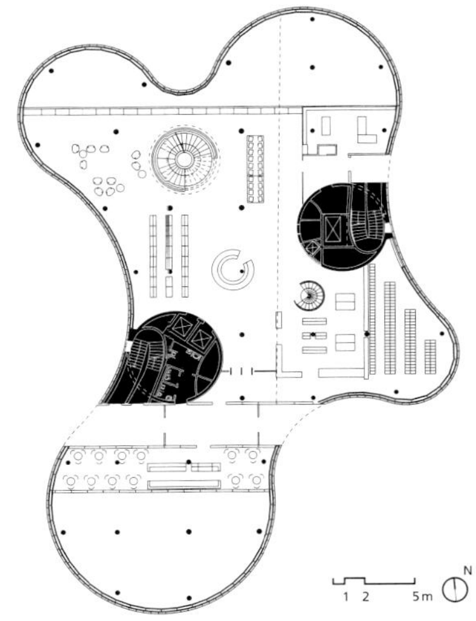

Ground floor

IKMZ – Informations-, Kommunikations- und Medien- zentrum

Brandenburgische Technische Universität Cottbus, Germany

Architect	Herzog & de Meuron
Client	Brandenburgische Technische Universität Cottbus, Landesbauamt
Completion	2004
Floor area	7,630 m²
Number of volumes	900,000
Seating capacity	597

The IKMZ (Information Communication and Media Center) of the Brandenburgische Technische Universität (Brandenburg Technical University) in Cottbus was designed by Herzog & de Meuron as a tall, abstract solitaire positioned in the center of a wide, unobstructed and sparsely landscaped site, visually mediating between the inner city of Cottbus and the campus.

Insulated by multi-lane streets, the center connects the two poles by a pedestrian passageway cut right through the building's otherwise unbroken envelope. Wrapped entirely in a shroud made of glass, superimposed with white raster images of intertwined and

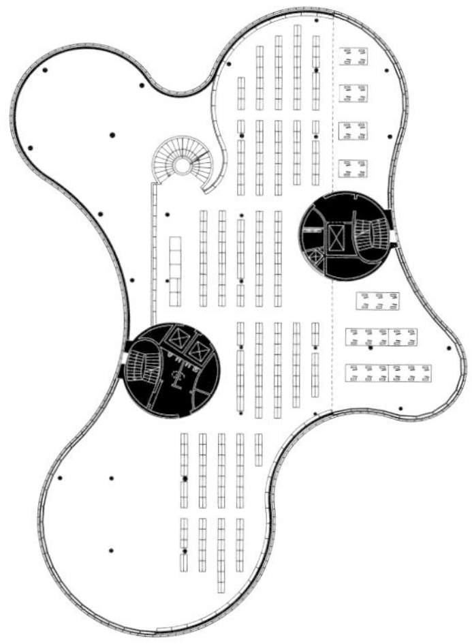

Third floor

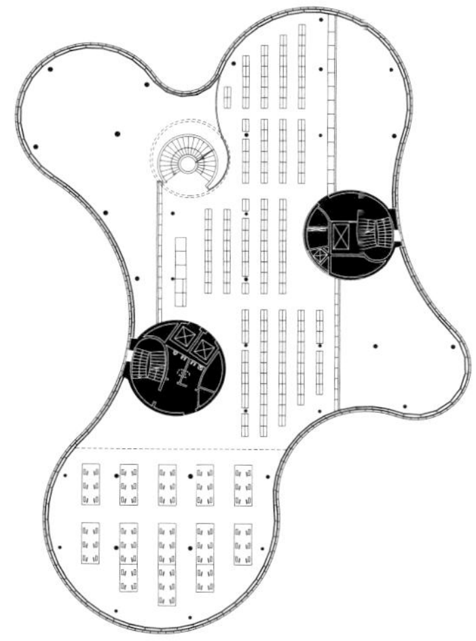

Fourth floor

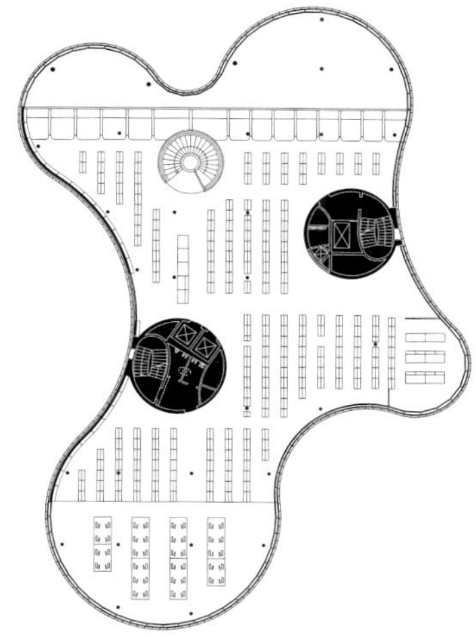

Sixth floor

Designed as an abstract solitaire, the center mediates visually between the inner city of Cottbus and the university campus | Entrance | Workspaces illuminated by custom-designed chandeliers

meandering language fragments, the building appears, in daylight, as a scale-less and nearly opaque monolith. Only at night, when the interior illumination penetrates the translucent double-skin glass facade and renders the inner skeleton consisting of cores, columns and slabs visible, does the building undergo a transformation from abstractness to comprehensible reality.

The meandering ground figure is achieved by connecting alternating convex and concave circle segments to a continuous curve. Projected up over seven floors, a non-directional object is created that permanently fluctuates in volume, and vanishes and engulfs depending on the viewing angle, point of focus and the intensity of reflections. Paired with the sun's path, the change in weather and the course of seasons provoke the glass skin to cycle through endless color modifications from a modulated frosty white to a dark green, then followed by a warm glow at night, giving the building a remarkable sculptural quality. The iconographical strength of the structure is heightened by the fact that the IKMZ is seemingly situated on top of a gently sloped mound, a cost-cutting measure to avoid expansive excavation for the two lower, subterranean floors, housing closed stacks and multi-media presentation rooms.

The main entry vestibule, as part of the passageway, offers access into a light-flooded, multi-chromatic circulation and information space dominated by three elements – a free-floating monumental spiral staircase cast of concrete, the concrete columns organized in a nearly orthogonal grid, and the custom-designed helix-shaped chandeliers. Electric green, magenta, yellow and a dark blue are reserved for all collection and reference locations, areas of service and information, as well as circulation and infrastructural elements. Clearly distinguished from the psychedelic and exuberant display of color are the tranquility-demanding reading rooms and

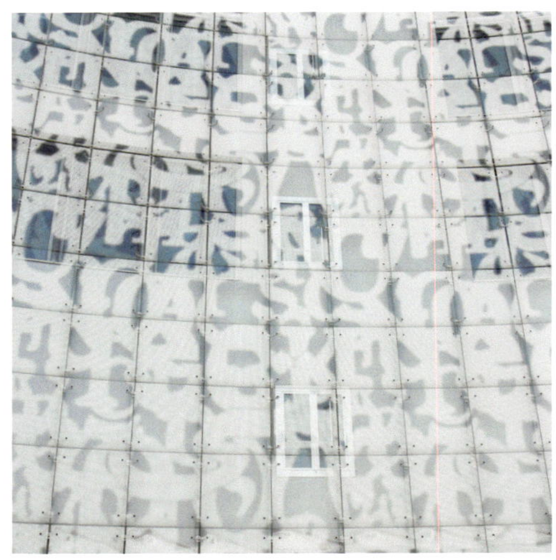

White raster images of intertwined and meandering language fragments are superimposed onto the glass panels, forming the outer layer of the double-skin facade | Modulation of raster screen creating images of language fragments

study areas, which are predominantly rendered in white and gray. It is in these locations where the white, cryptic patterns dissolved in pixels and printed on the exterior glass cloak, achieve a decoupling of the interior space by abstracting the built environment beyond.

Two circular concrete service cores, contributing to the lateral stability of the structure, generate the only visible acute angles inside the library by tangentially touching the inner glass envelope, thus interrupting the flow of motion while at the same time redirecting it. To a varying extent, following the orthogonal structural grid, slabs are cut back from the envelope in patterns alternating from floor to floor, creating intercommunicating floors, double-height spaces for assembly, collaboration or reading. Complex views are offered from galleries into glass-enclosed voids or back into the building's exposed skeleton.

The IKMZ combines library and multi-media functions to a modern e-learning center; through the integration of a high-capacity glass fibre infrastructure, connecting the university's operational data processing center with the individual network nodes, the future of information flow appears secured.

The new logotype of the institution, as well as the pictograms identifying five areas of focus – environmental studies, energy, material sciences, architecture and information & communication technology – are derived from the undulating shape of the library. Besides the iconographic waveform, the building's interior color concept, a means of orientation and a wayfinding system in itself, is replicated in the graphic design concept and layout of the university's printed material. ***wr***

Central spiral staircase connecting all library floors | Entry lobby

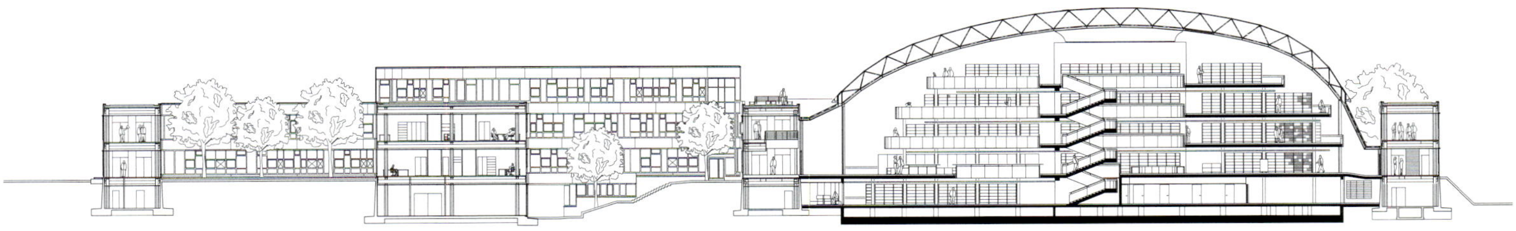

Elevation of institute building and section of library

Philological Library

Freie Universität
Berlin, Germany

Architect	Foster + Partners
Client	Senatsverwaltung für Stadtentwicklung
Completion	2005
Floor area	6,290 m²
Number of volumes	800,000
Seating capacity	650

The Freie Universität or Free University, whose name references its placement in then West Berlin, was founded in 1948 as an alternative to the Humboldt Universität in the Russian sector of the postwar city. Originally housed in various villas in the suburb of Dahlem, in 1973, the campus complex was completed as a group of buildings designed from a 1963 prize-winning competition entry by the partnership of Candilis, Josic, Woods. The design is a manifesto of Team X's ideological departure from CIAM and reflected their humanistic ideology that "in everyday usage ... the inextricable complexity of urban life is expressed." (Source: *Another Modern*) In the case of the Free University this ideology

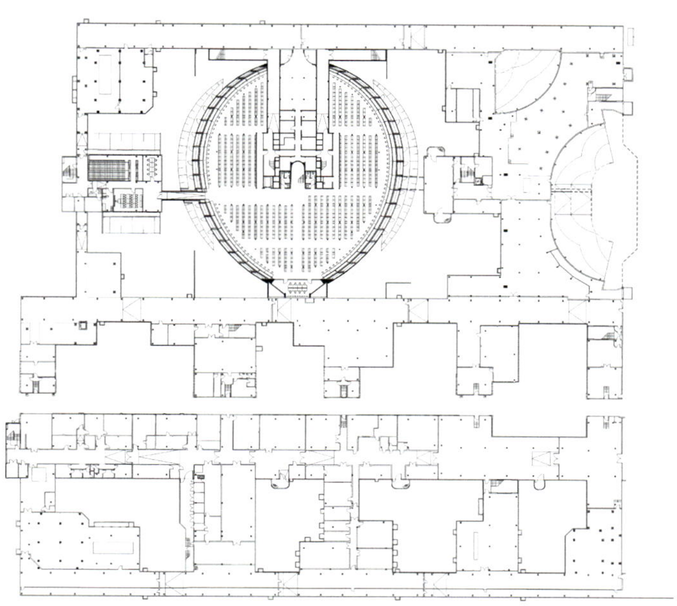

Ground floor

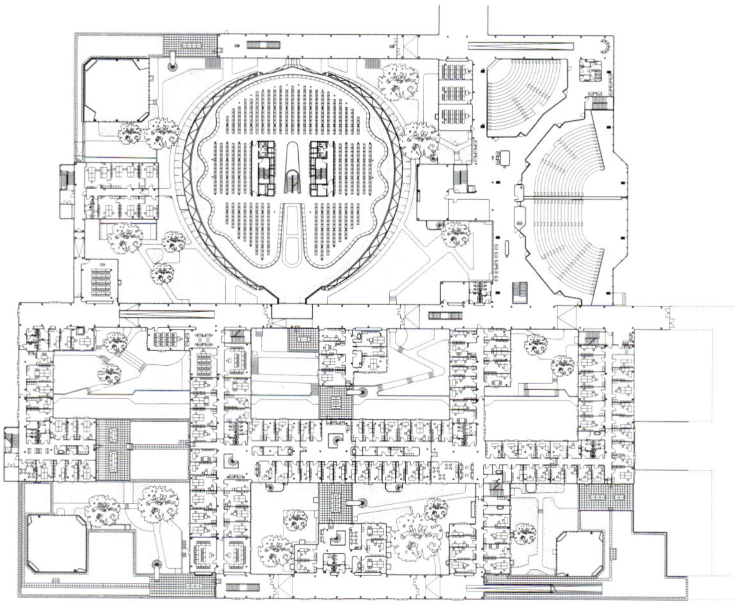

Second floor

View of the library on campus | Circulation in the atrium | The ovoid roof of glazed and aluminum panels

led to the use of communication, both physical and visual, as one of the most important factors within a university to give "access to other disciplines and to other ideas and philosophies." This idea manifested itself in a "continuous building complex organized around built and non-built zones ... along an orthogonal street system or a diagonal path system from courtyard to courtyard." (Source: *Free University Berlin*)

As part of the redevelopment of the campus 34 years later, Norman Foster received the commission to refurbish the Candilic, Josic, Woods complex and to design a new library for the Faculty of Philology and Humanities. Sited within a space previously occupied by six courtyards of the complex, Foster's new library integrates ten separate, departmental libraries. The five-story, glass and concrete ovoid structure occupies the majority of the newly created courtyard. It connects to the existing complex at the two extreme ends of the oval form on its principal axis of rotation. These connections replace the many purposefully indirect and meandering paths that were the hallmark of the original design. Four serpentine floor plates, one above the other and receding in size, are centered on this axis in an open structure. On each floor, books are located at the center while users are allocated space on the perimeter at continuous, curvilinear built-in reading desks and guardrails. Accommodating more than 600 users in adjacent, unidirectional seats, the design promotes quiet study and research.

A curved, double-layered dome of glazed and aluminum exterior panels contains the concrete internal structure. The inner layer, a membrane of glass fiber, is attached to the external glass skin through a yellow-painted, wide-span steel structure. Operable apertures in both membranes allow for the circulation of fresh air and, ultimately, provide natural ventilation for more than 50 % of the year. The inner layer also serves to filter the daylight entering through the external glazing, providing readers with a diffused,

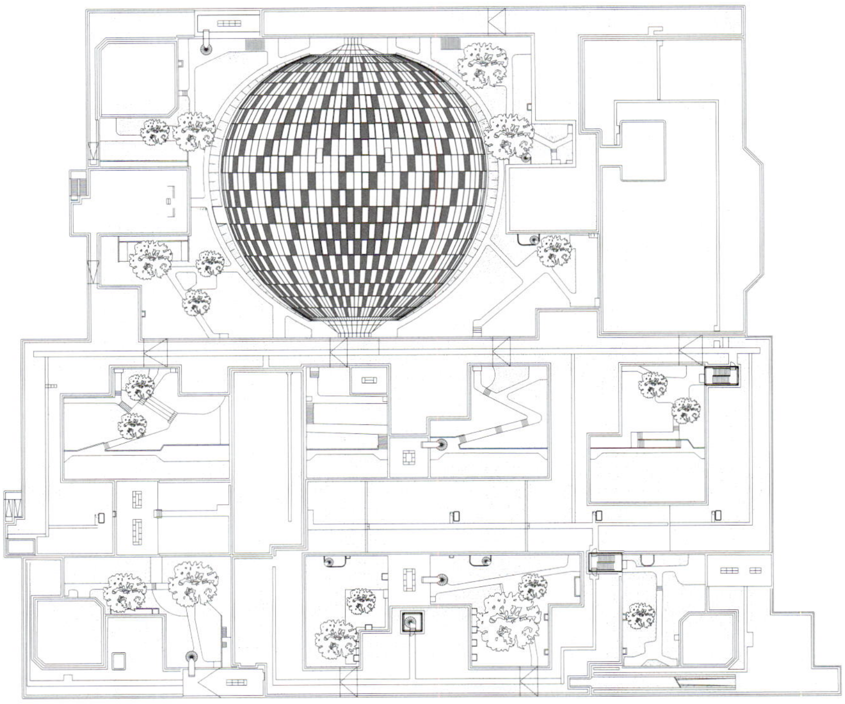

Roof plan

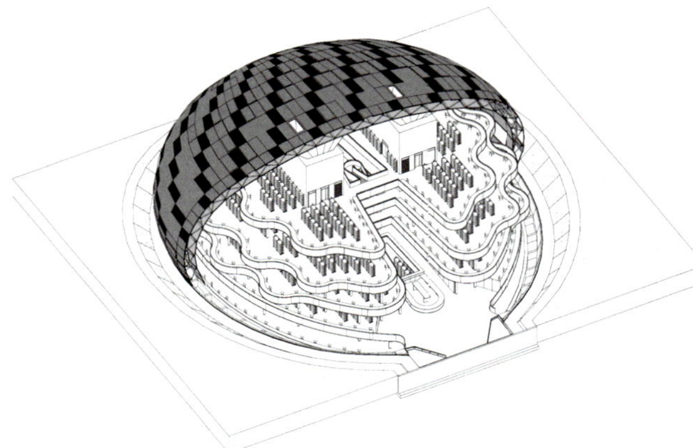

Cutaway axonometric

Entrance | View looking down the atrium

natural light. At the time of completion, the library was noted as one of Foster's greatest efforts toward sustainability and reflected the firm's commitment to research in the use of active and passive technologies.

The library's cranial-like floor plan and volume have earned it the nickname of "Berlin Brain". While valve-like entrances and other physiological analogies make this comparison plausible, the library as a variation on the curved, monumental structure is part of a Foster evolution that includes the American Air Museum, the Great Glass House, Canary Wharf Underground Station, the Reichstag and the London City Hall. Utilizing the analogy of the brain as the center of the human nervous system, the new Philological Library similarly assumes a central importance within the Candilis, Josic, Woods complex – an importance that refutes the principles of its Modernist host. The judgment to use this project as a vehicle for the exploration of form within a site imbued with such historical and theoretical significance is perhaps an indication of progress and its costs – the subject of Le Corbusier's letter to the final CIAM congress before its succession by Team X. ***lw***

Tom Avermaete, *Another Modern, The Postwar Architecture and Urbanism of Candilis-Josic-Woods*. Rotterdam: Nai Publishers, 2005.

Candilis, Josic, Woods, Schiedhelm. *Free University Berlin*. London: AA Publications, 1999.

Study counters receive optimum daylight from the dome | The glass fiber membrane on the interior of the dome

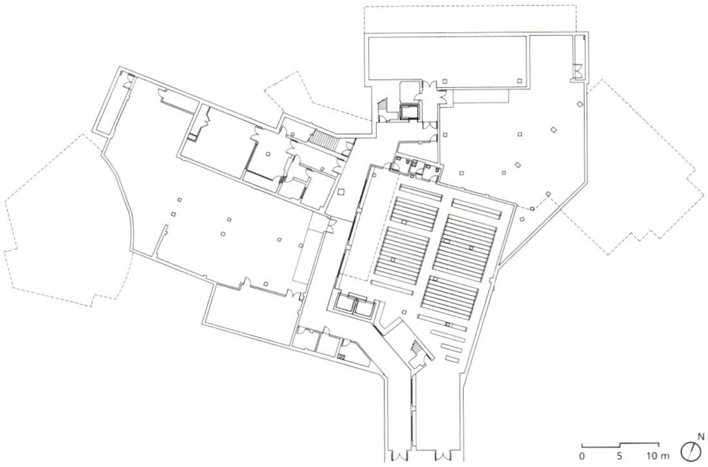

Ground floor

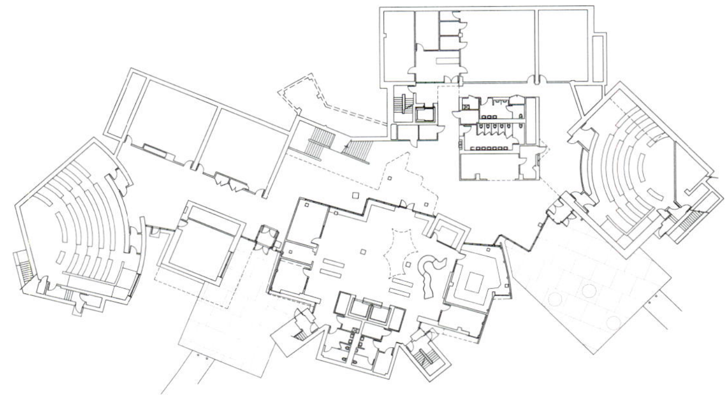

First floor

Cafe seating at "The Street", near the entrance | The distinct volumes of the library | View of atrium skylight at main entrance

Lewis Library

Princeton University

Princeton, New Jersey, USA

Architect	Gehry Partners
Client	Princeton University
Completion	2008
Floor area	8,082 m² (gross)
Number of volumes	350,000 (print collection)
Seating capacity	400 (classrooms/study rooms)

A distinct composition of steel, glass, brick and stucco on 8,082 m^2, the Lewis Library is Princeton University's library of science and research, consolidating several departmental libraries previously spread across campus. With this plan, six librarians and 14 administrative support staff relocated from their respective libraries to establish a joint presence at Lewis Library. This strategy of integration allows for greater efficiency in managing resources, information and services.

Of equal importance, the new program also includes the Office of Information Technology's Education Technologies Center and New Media

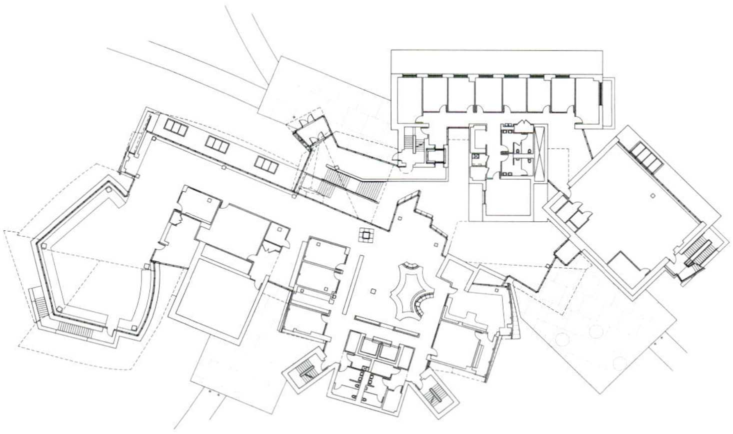

Second floor

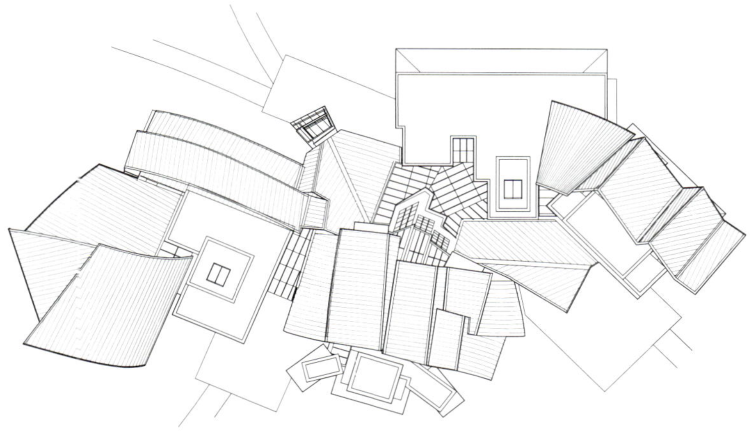

Roof

Center, a new Broadcast Center, operated by the Office of Information Technology (OIT) and the Princeton Institute for Computational Science and Engineering, and OIT's computational science and engineering support group. The New Media Center will more than double its previous floor space for workstations that support software and hardware for creating and manipulating digital objects. These spaces will be dedicated to visualization technology that will aid researchers in rendering, analyzing and displaying their data.

These planning strategies provide a raison d'être for Gehry's undefined architectural forms. At the Lewis Library, they divide into approximately three dissimilar masses; a two-story wing and a four-story tower housing the collection and a three-story wing accommodating the Education Technologies Center, New Media Center and the computational science and engineering support groups. Gehry claims that the massing (involving 40 tonnes of embossed stainless steel, 562 tonnes of clay for bricks, 2,415 m^2 glass and 1,022 m^2 of stucco) is "a sculptural body-language" that is contextual with Princeton's signature Gothic campus. In Gehry style, these exterior sculptural forms result in clashing shapes and geometry that are irregular and constructed only through the programming platform, CATIA (Computer Aided Three-dimensional Interactive Application). While students enjoy the intrigue of the jarring shapes and bold colors, they have difficulty navigating the library itself. Similarly, book stacks are located primarily below ground where an orthogonal space is possible. The geometry, however, has created some interesting interior spaces that include the skylit entry atrium formed by the intersection of different materials, a star-shaped drywall opening between two levels, and a 10.3 m high glass-enclosed reading room nicknamed "The Tree House". ***lw***

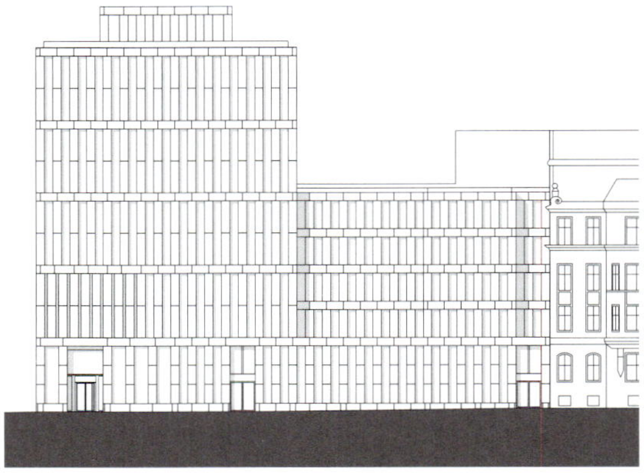

East elevation

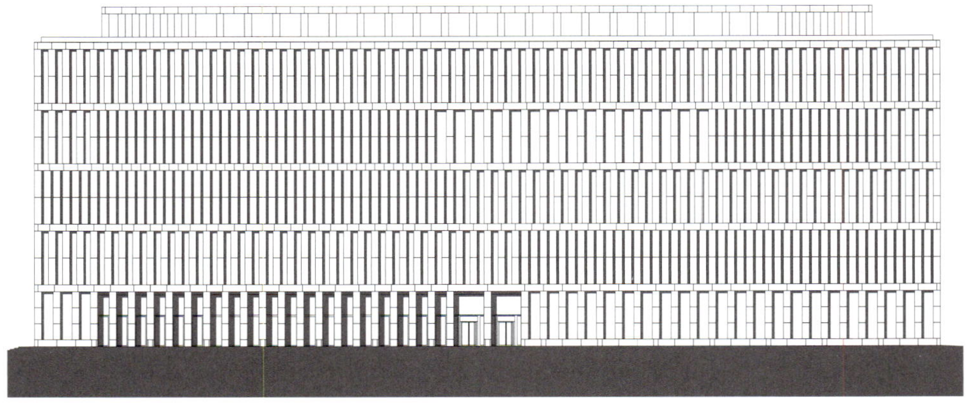

South elevation

Jacob-und-Wilhelm-Grimm-Zentrum

Humboldt Universität
Berlin, Germany

Architect	Max Dudler
Client	Humboldt Universität, Technische Abteilung
Completion	2009
Floor area	4,500 m²
Number of volumes	2.5 million (2 million accessible)
Seating capacity	1,200

The Jacob-und-Wilhelm-Grimm-Zentrum designed by Max Dudler for the Humboldt Universität in Berlin realizes for the first time in the nearly 180-year history of the institution the vision of a library open to the public. It comprises the central library and twelve distinct departmental library collections. Located along the elevated train line between Bahnhof Friedrichstraße and Hackescher Markt, the building completes the southern edge of a typical Berlin city block. Bearing the name of the Grimm Brothers, who were appointed to the Prussian Academy of Sciences in Berlin in 1840, the library innovatively combines core library functions with computer and media services. The precious private library of

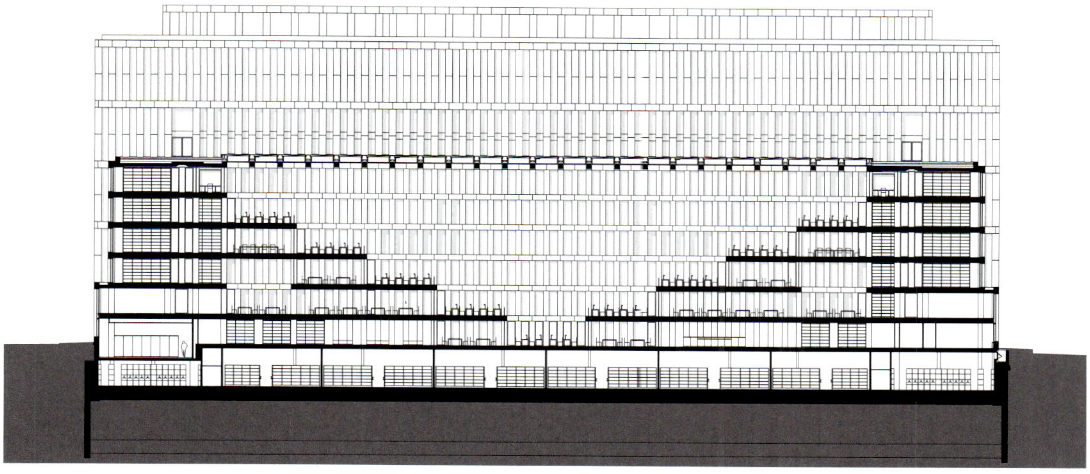

Longitudinal section

At night the illuminated long and narrow apertures emphasize the rigor of the construction module | The library completes the edge of a typical Berlin city block, with the lower volume of the central reading room continuing the cornice height of the adjacent historic buildings

Jacob and Wilhelm Grimm is preserved in a vault located on the top floor of the new facility.

Clearly delineated zones establish the spatial organization of the building and consequently induce the aesthetic rigor innate in the expression of the exterior and interior facades. Max Dudler interprets the entity of a book as the smallest Gestalt-giving module, creating a "sculpture made of stone." Light spilling out of the long and narrow apertures, varying in width and cut deep into the stone envelope, transforms the rather monolithic day-time appearance of the sculpture into a vibrant body at night, revealing both the shelving units on the interior in rhythm with the window openings and the exterior impression of books aligned on shelving.

An urban longitudinal plaza increasing the setback between train viaduct and building, the entrance hall external to the secured core, the internal circulation spine and finally the library's central terraced reading room encapsulated by the collection, all follow the underlying principle of linearity, symmetry and an orientation-enhancing order.

Inside the tiered volume of the reading room, the orthogonal structural grid was increased threefold in density by column enclosures functioning as vertical shafts for the routing of building systems. This departure from the typical bay pattern introduces a three-dimensional skeleton of a scale apart from the surrounding floors. Vertical and horizontal glass panels inserted into this wood-clad framework create a unique interplay between light and dark, transparency and opaqueness. Outside the library's nucleus, the concept of open and obscured views is continued on the surrounding stack floors. Library aisles establish view corridors connecting back to the reading room and diametrically offer a visual link to the city. The dialectic between the secluded space, traditionally associated with limited-access stack concepts, and the outside world, manifests

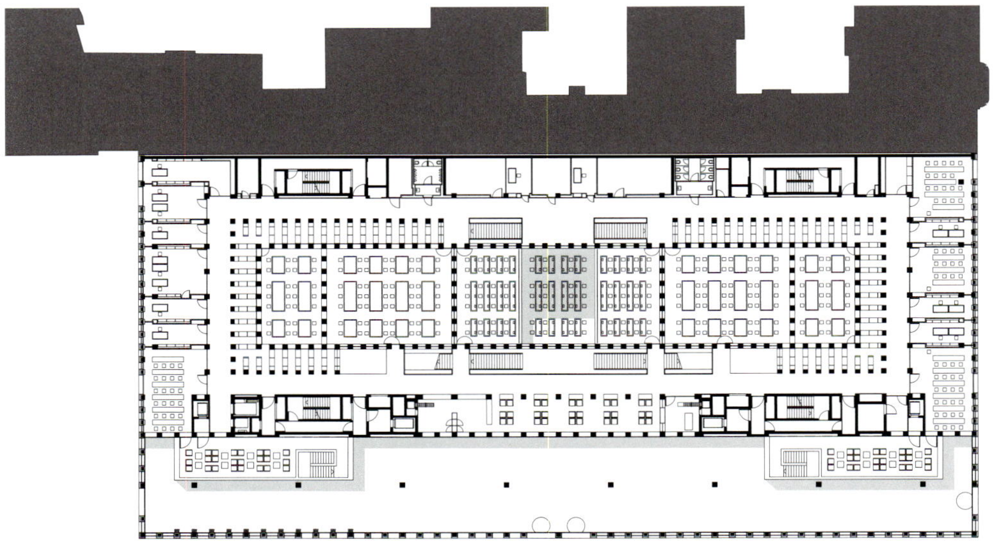

First floor

Worktables along the exterior wall respond to the rhythm of the fenestration | Entry hall serving as a meeting point, information commons and distribution hub | The central terraced reading room is encapsulated by the collection and roofed by expansive skylight panels

itself in the 2 million books, freely accessible to the scholar and the public alike. By offering the invaluable experience of browsing, distinctive intellectual pursuits are taken out of isolation and a far richer explorative fabric is woven.

The tall light-filled entry hall serves as a meeting point, an information commons, a dining hall and a distribution hub providing access to lower floor locker rooms, mezzanine seating areas, book drops and the library core. Accessible from three sides, this gathering space constitutes a lively public forum in contrast to the stillness of the inner building beyond. Multi-media teaching and learning facilities occupy the voids formed under the lower tiers of the cascading reading room. Acoustically separated from the central space by glazing, the classrooms benefit from the abundant daylight infiltrating the great reading room.

Along the first floor circulation spine, equipped with self-checkout stations, display windows reveal the technical complexity of two automated book sorting and vertical routing systems. Original card catalogue units still serving parts of the historic collection are integrated into a modern, data-based reference library playing off on the omnipresent dialogue between tradition and modernity. The concept challenges the expensive and overrated request for flexibility in anticipation of future library infrastructural changes by emphasizing aesthetic, environmental and ergonomic qualities. Along the stack floor perimeters specially dimensioned shelving units can be substituted for seating, while removable shaft enclosures provide maintenance access to building systems. A co-generation energy concept paired with daylight harvesting and air duct activated concrete slabs contribute to a sustainable library for the future. ***wr***

Max Dudler, Humboldt Universität zu Berlin; *Jacob-und-Wilhelm-Grimm-Zentrum*, Zurich: Niggli Verlag, 2010.

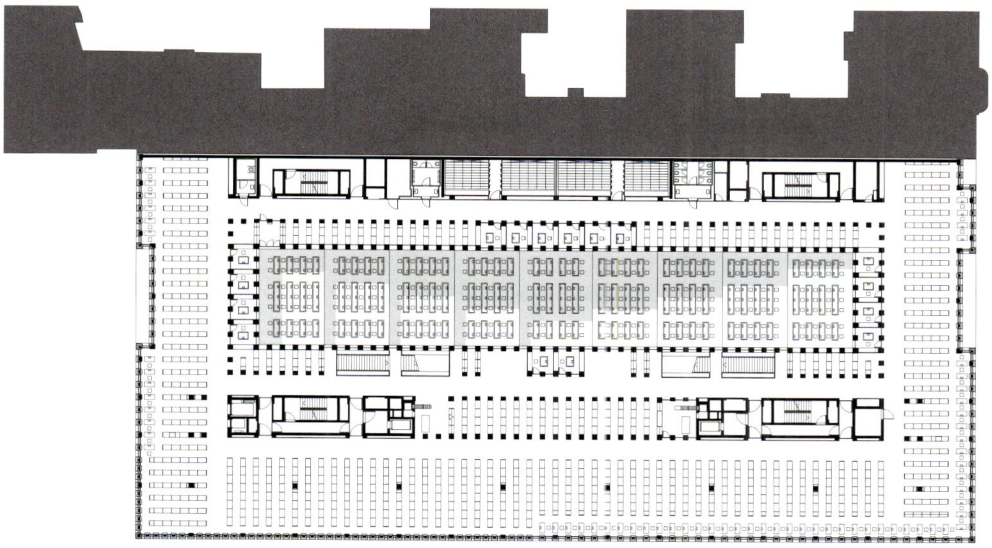

Fifth floor

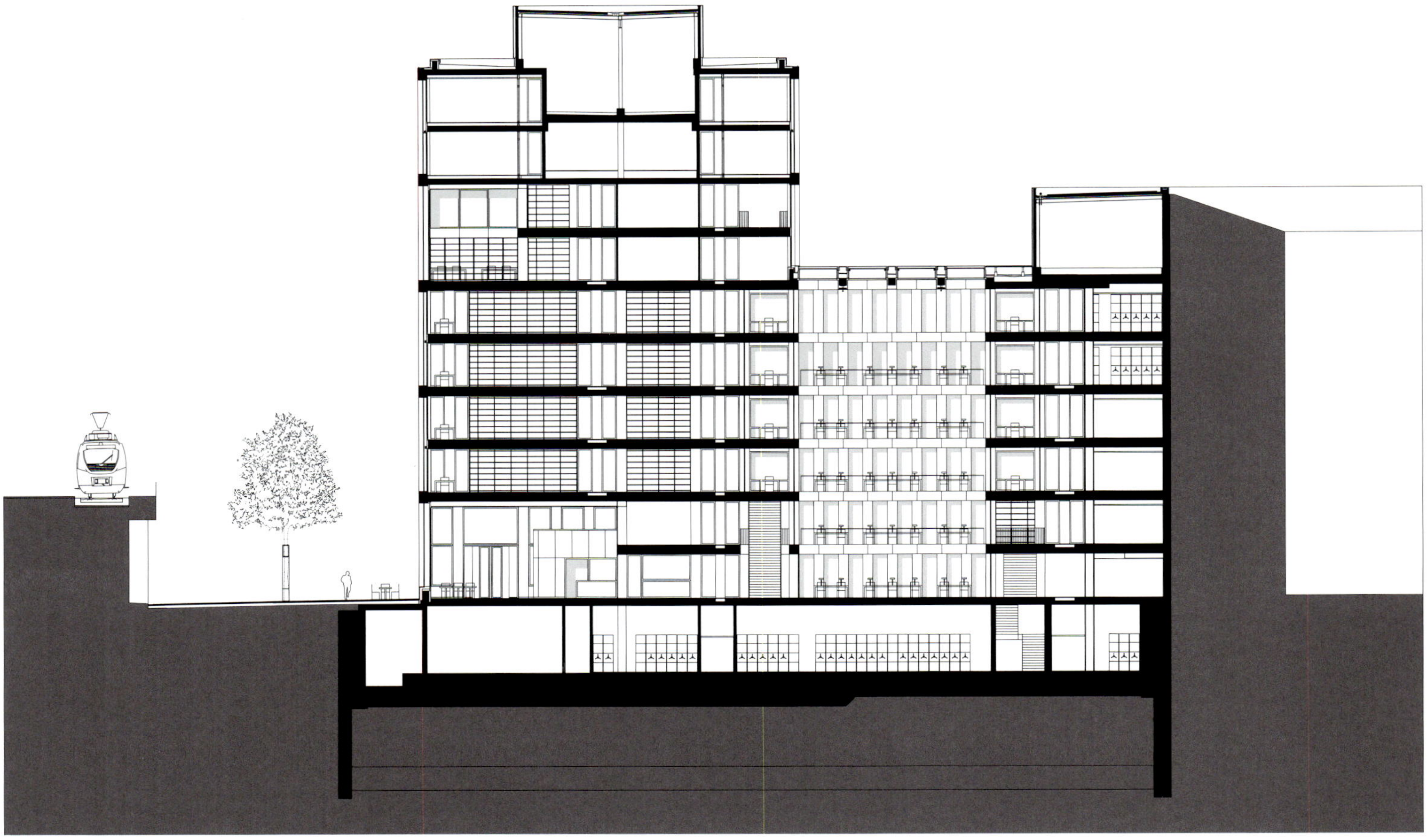

Cross section

The construction grid is derived from a 0.6 m shelving unit and an aisle width of 0.9 m | A small cafeteria supports the concept of the entry hall as communication hub and meeting point | Rows of custom-designed tables provide study space on the terraces of the wood-paneled central reading room

Floor plan under shell

Rolex Learning Center

Ecole Polytechnique Fédérale de Lausanne Lausanne, Switzerland

Architect	SANAA
Client	Ecole Polytechnique Fédérale de Lausanne (EPFL)
Completion	2010
Floor area	20,200 m² (37,000 m² including storage and basement parking)
Number of volumes	500,000
Seating capacity	600-seat auditorium/total occupant load 860

The topographic architecture of the Rolex Learning Center generates a unique environment for innovative learning concepts based on research conducted at the EPFL Institute for Pedagogical Research and Support (Centre de Recherche et d'Appui pour la Formation et ses Technologies – CRAFT), while providing a research and experimentation laboratory for the study of current learning behaviors and the implementation of future pedagogical technologies. Serving a population of 7,000 students and 4,000 researchers, the core components of the Learning Center include a large scientific library housing 500,000 volumes of scientific literature, a multi-media library offering access to 10,000 online journals

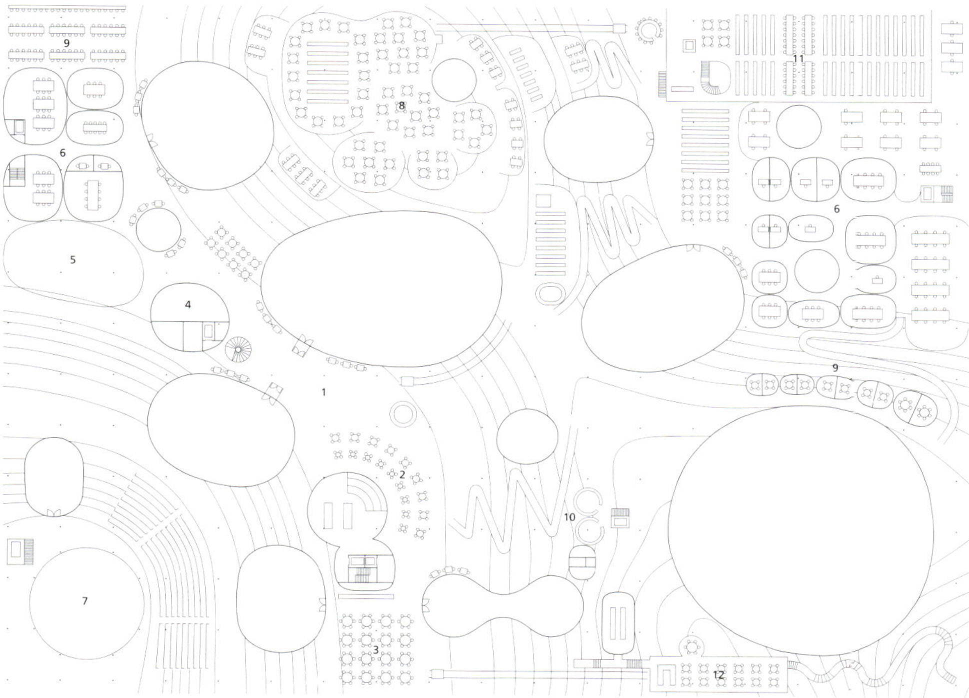

Ground floor

1 Main entrance
2 Café
3 Food court
4 Bank
5 Bookshop
6 Offices
7 Multi-purpose hall
8 Library
9 Work area
10 Ancient book collection
11 Research collection
12 Restaurant

Fourteen curvilinear patios varying in shape and ranging in diameter from 7 to 50 m punctuate the rectangular single-story volume measuring 166 × 121 m | The distant alpine mountain range inspired the undulating architectural concept

and 17,000 e-books, a language and multi-media center, study and teaching facilities, a 600-seat amphitheater and the CRAFT laboratory. A cybercafé, multi-media bookstore, cafeteria and a restaurant overlooking Lake Geneva complement the space program and enhance the experiential qualities.

Indicative of the Oblique Function Theory (La fonction oblique) devised in 1966 by the French architect Claude Parent and the French theorist, philosopher and urban planner Paul Virilio, who promoted the idea of the inclined plane in architecture enhancing the relationship between the built environment and the occupant, the undulating floor plate, in excess of 20,000 m², generates a continuous and seemingly boundary-free landscape. The user is forced to engage physically with the architecture, formed of valleys and mounds, by ascending and descending slopes, and sensing acceleration and resistance due to the oblique angle formed between the body's gravitational vector and the inclined walking surface, a phenomenon non-existent in a level environment. A multi-faceted inhabitable circulation fabric, into which the many program elements are woven, not only furthers the amalgamation of architecture and user as imagined by Parent and Virilio, but also invites interdisciplinary discourse and varying forms and levels of sociability.

Navigating the undulations of the floor, the user experiences a dynamic environment with constantly shifting spatial and experiential qualities, nuanced by the travel of sound waves, the infiltration of light, the framing of views, and the phenomenon of emerging and vanishing horizons. Space characteristics reach from introverted and silent areas for individual learning and thought to areas suitable for group studies, discussions and presentations.

Complex shell structures, innately suitable for column-free spans and slender construction, are commonly associated with roofs. The Rolex Learning Center, however, reverses the concept

By employing the principle of shell structures characterized by wide, column-free spans for the construction of the floor plate, the exceptional effect of a sinuously curving and rolling topography is achieved | **Next spread:** Night views of the complex | The courts offer space for socializing

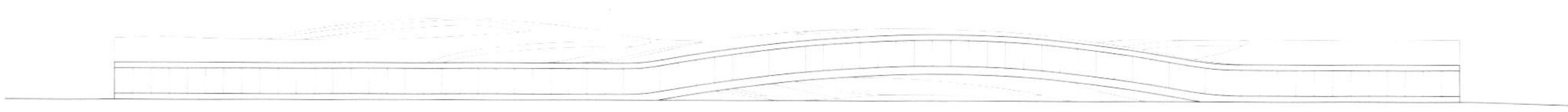

North elevation

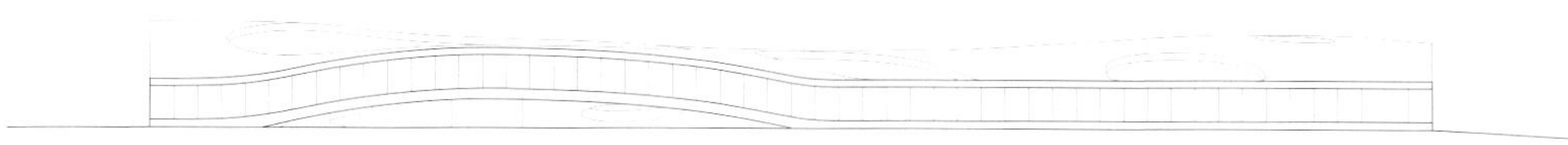

East elevation

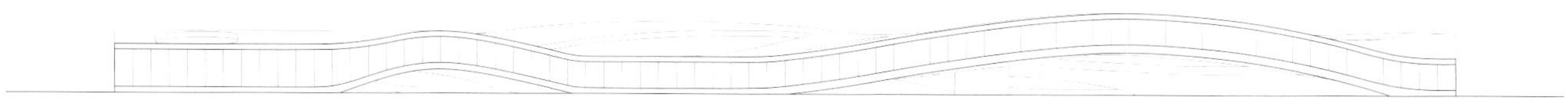

South elevation

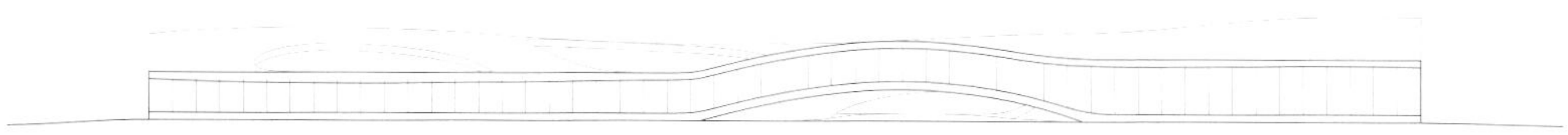

West elevation

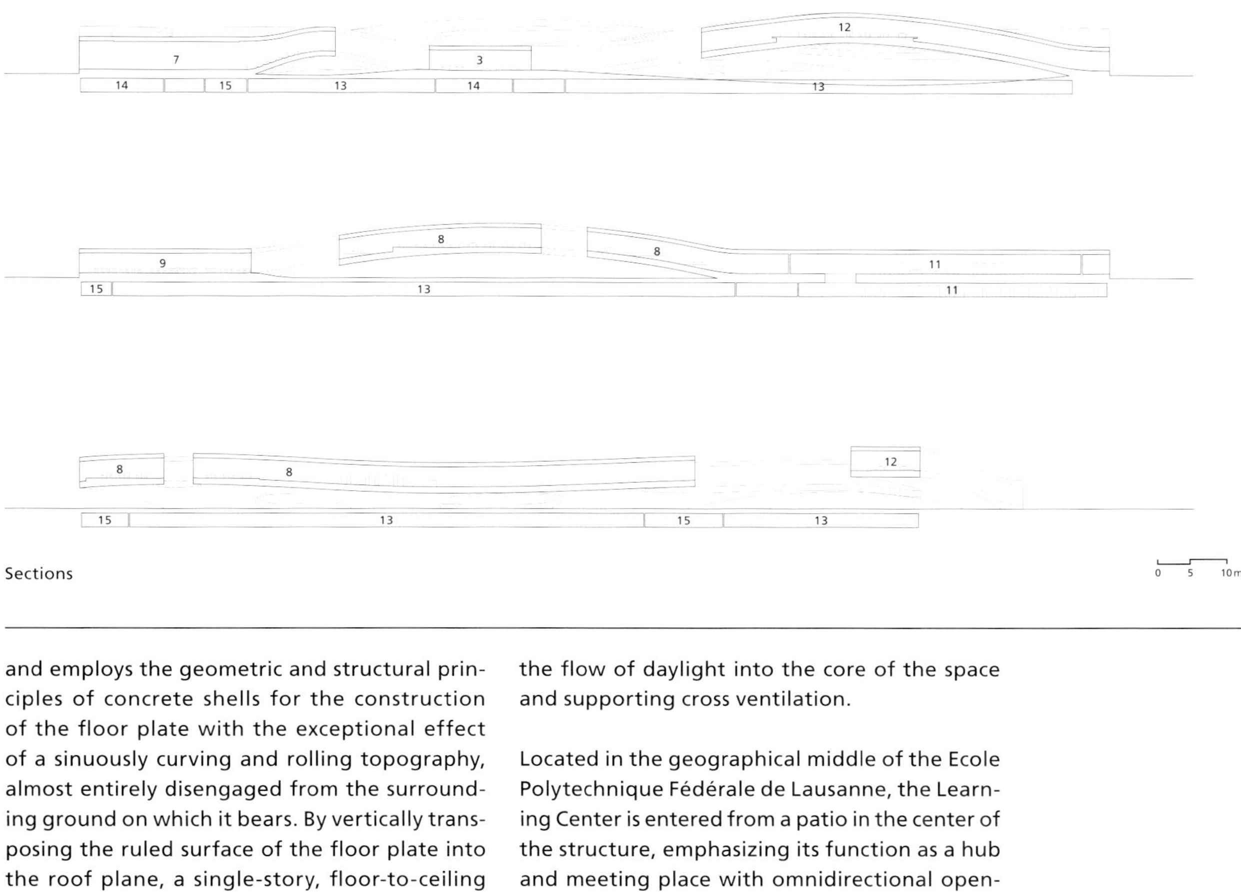

3 Food court
7 Multi-purpose hall
8 Library
9 Work area
11 Research collection
12 Restaurant
13 Parking
14 Storage
15 Mechanical

Sections

and employs the geometric and structural principles of concrete shells for the construction of the floor plate with the exceptional effect of a sinuously curving and rolling topography, almost entirely disengaged from the surrounding ground on which it bears. By vertically transposing the ruled surface of the floor plate into the roof plane, a single-story, floor-to-ceiling glazed volume takes shape, creating the envisioned space continuum on the interior while providing reference to the alpine landscape in the distance. Fourteen circularly formed patios of varying shape and diameter are punctured into the expansive rectangular floor plate, allowing the flow of daylight into the core of the space and supporting cross ventilation.

Located in the geographical middle of the Ecole Polytechnique Fédérale de Lausanne, the Learning Center is entered from a patio in the center of the structure, emphasizing its function as a hub and meeting place with omnidirectional openness to all users instilled with the vision that only interdisciplinary collaboration and dialogue can advance humanity. ***wr***

Design sketch

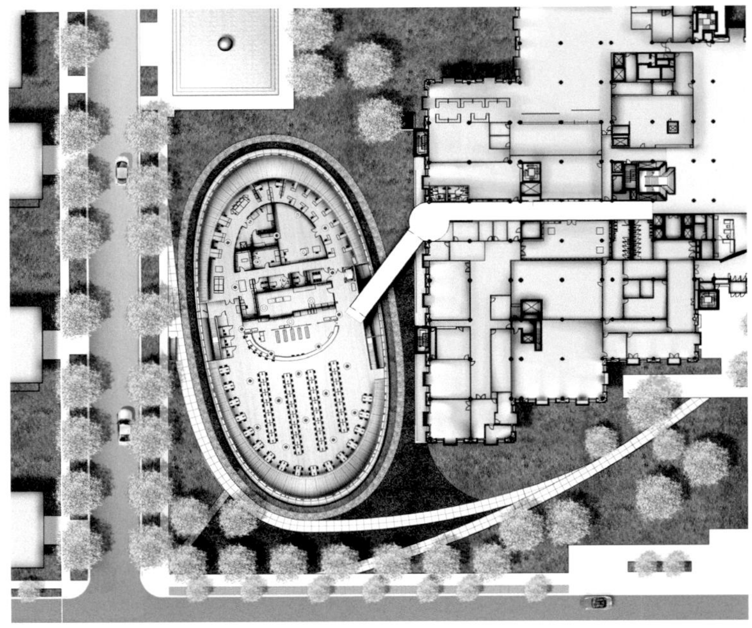

Site plan

Joe and Rika Mansueto Library

Chicago, Illinois, USA

Architect	Helmut Jahn
Client	University of Chicago
Completion	2011
Floor area	5,453 m²
Number of volumes	3.5 million
Seating capacity	180 (reading room)

On an architecturally diverse quadrangle of the University of Chicago's campus, the Joe and Rika Mansueto Library is neighbor to Henry Moore's bronze sculpture *Nuclear Energy*, a Ricardo Legorreta dormitory and SOM's limestone Brutalist Regenstein Library. The U.S. $ 25 million Mansueto Library, designed by Helmut Jahn as an addition to the Regenstein Library, opened in 2011 to great acclaim.

While it is chiefly known for its iconic glass-domed reading room and its underground robotic stacks, the significance of the Mansueto Library in an age of digital technology is its affirmation of accessible print for the research library.

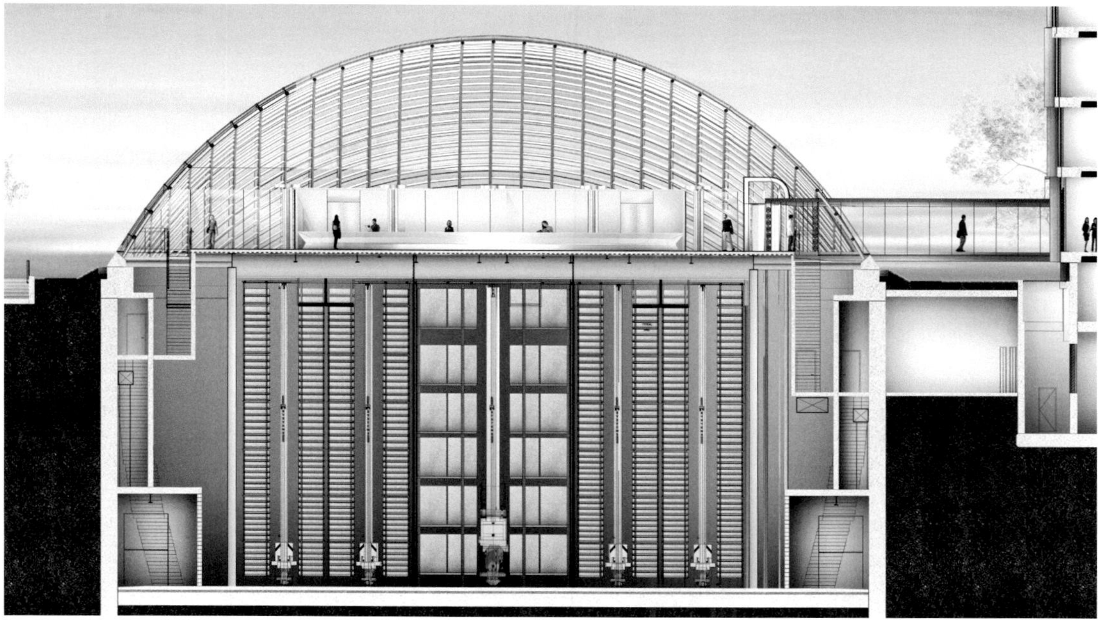

Section through the underground book storage system

Views of the glass-domed grand reading room

With a university acquisition rate of 150,000 volumes a year, the Regenstein Library, completed in 1970, was operating at full capacity. A university task force considered and rejected the prevalent solutions of "browseable" high-density shelving and off-site storage. It also declined to digitize and dispose of less-used collections, a solution embraced by similar academic institutions. With a circulation of 600,000 items in 2004 and the fact that "copyright law prevents the university from offering full digital access to about 80 % of its holdings" (Source: *The Chronicle of Higher Education*), an on-site expansion was recommended. The design brief requested an addition to the Regenstein Library of a storage facility and an underground reading room. Helmut Jahn's solution is unique in reversing these programmatic requirements while employing an automated storage and retrieval system (ASRS).

Used for years in industrial settings, the automated storage and retrieval system consists of racks, storage bins and a robotic crane for retrieval. The ASRS requires one seventh of the space required on traditional shelving and, at the time of the opening of the Mansueto Library, only 25 or fewer ASRS had been used in academic library applications. Mansueto's 15.2 m high system, the largest in North America, employs 1,200 racks to yield a capacity of 3.5 million volumes. The library has identified 1 million items for such storage, items that are deemed too fragile or not required for browsing on open stacks. The items are recorded in the library systems through scanned barcodes and stored by size rather than classification. Patrons fill online requests that trigger a retrieval sequence. One of five robotic cranes identifies the bin, retrieves it and delivers it to a loading dock in three minutes. To date, the ASRS at Mansueto has remaining storage capability for the next two decades.

In reversing the design brief and placing the book storage underground, Jahn has created a new

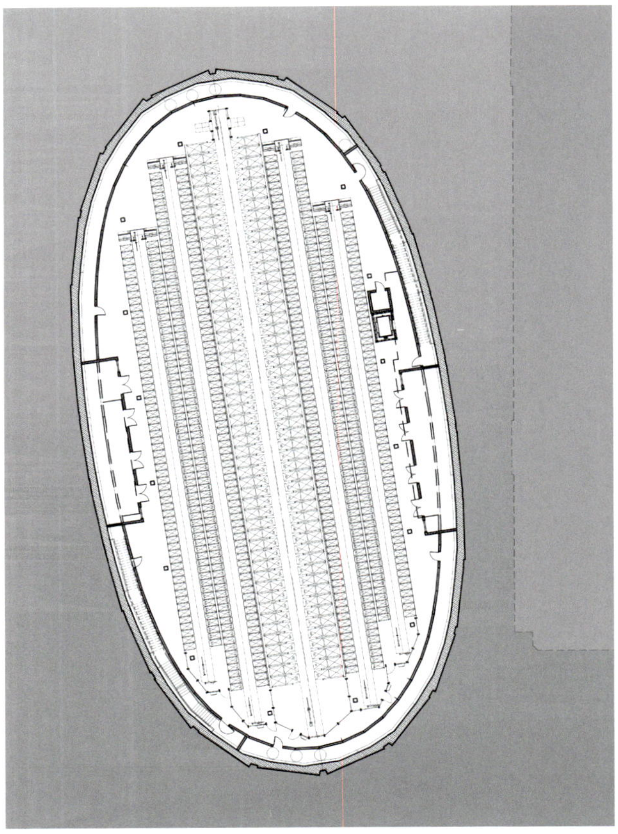

Basement plan

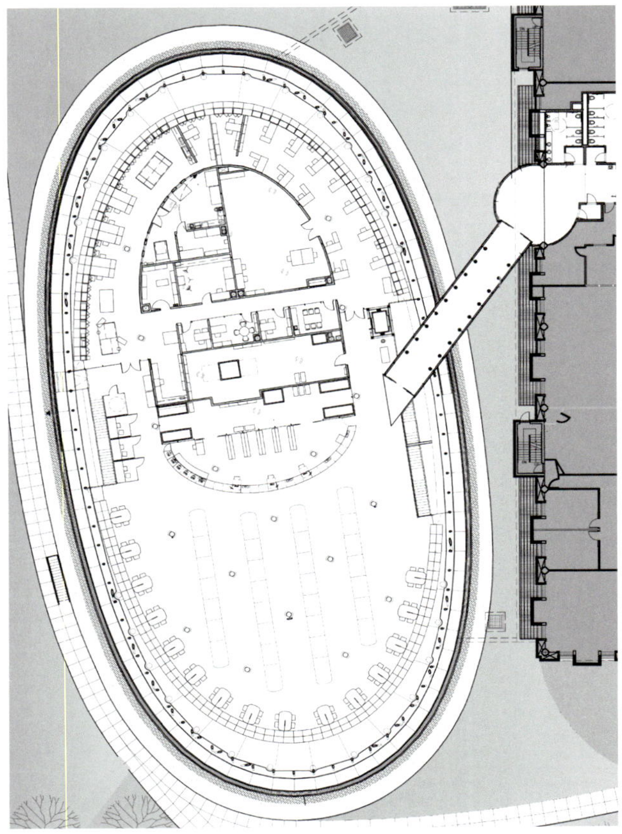

Ground floor

Automated storage and retrieval system | Seating inside the grand reading room | Reading room with workspaces | Glass entrance

Chicago icon in the 12.2 m high, glass-encased steel structure. The elliptical dome houses a 180 person, 743 m² reading room, a circulation service center and the conservation laboratory. Constructed as an insulated glass canopy of 700 segments of fritted glass, the dome's exterior layer rejects solar gain and provides shading while admitting visible light to the reading room within. The quality of natural light within the interior environment is well-suited to reading or repairing of books, corroborating the library's emphasis on printed matter. Artificial lighting is discreetly placed within the ventilation kiosks and integrated into the steel structure. White oak tables and chairs trimmed with stainless steel, designed by Yorgo Lykouria, further enhance the minimalist interior of the reading room. In her decision to privilege site storage, Library Director Judith Nadler was in no way rejecting digital collections. A contributor to the Google Books project since 2010, Nadler recognizes the potential of technology, employs it intelligently and efficiently to enhance reading and the book in "a bold statement of continued centrality of libraries for modern culture." (Source: www.uchicago.edu) *Wired* magazine's accolade, "library of the future", is apt as this dual embrace of technology and print is truly prescient for the future of libraries in the 21st century. ***lw***

Andrew Abbott, "The University Library" (recommendations of the University of Chicago Task Force about the future of the University libraries), May 2006, p. 6.

Susie Allen, "Mansueto Library Emerges as a Chicago Icon", November 2011. http:// www.uchicago.edu/features/20111010_mansueto/

Marc Parry, "A High-tech Library Keeps Books at Faculty Fingertips – With Robot Help", *The Chronicle of Higher Education*, July 24, 2011.

Benjamin Recchie, "Librodome", *The University of Chicago Magazine*, September/October 2011.

Angela Watercutter, "Robots Retrieve Books in University of Chicago's New, Futuristic Library", *Wired*, May 11, 2011.

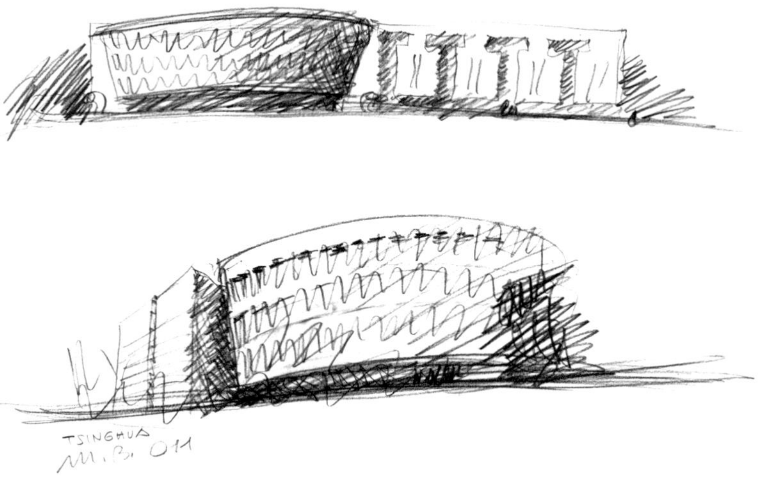

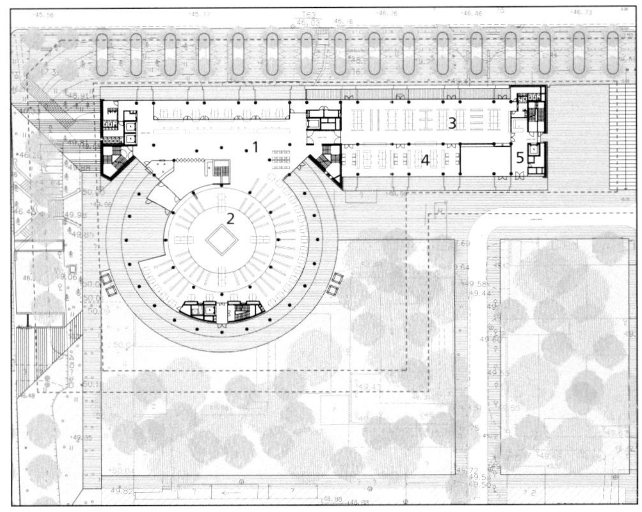

Ground floor

1 Entrance hall/ reception desk
2 Open shelves area
3 Index hall
4 Offices
5 Lobby

10 m

Kai Feng Humanities and Social Sciences Library

Tsinghua University
Beijing, China

Architect	Mario Botta (local architects: Ecadi, Shanghai)
Client	Shanghai Real Estate (Group) Co, Ltd., Shanghai Shentong Underground Railway Assets Mgmt. Co.
Completion	2011
Floor area	20,000 m²
Number of volumes	1.5 million
Seating capacity	1,000

The Kai Feng Humanities and Social Sciences Library of Tsinghua University opened in 2011 on the 100th anniversary of the founding of the institution. Sited on the former imperial gardens of the Qing Dynasty in northern Beijing, Tsinghua is one of the leading universities in China. Renowned for research in sciences and engineering, it has earned the nickname, "MIT of China". Since the last decades of the 20th century the university has further developed a multi-disciplinary structure with the incorporation of 14 schools including the School of Humanities and Social Sciences. On a campus with six other libraries, the opening of the 20,000 m² library dedicated to this subject

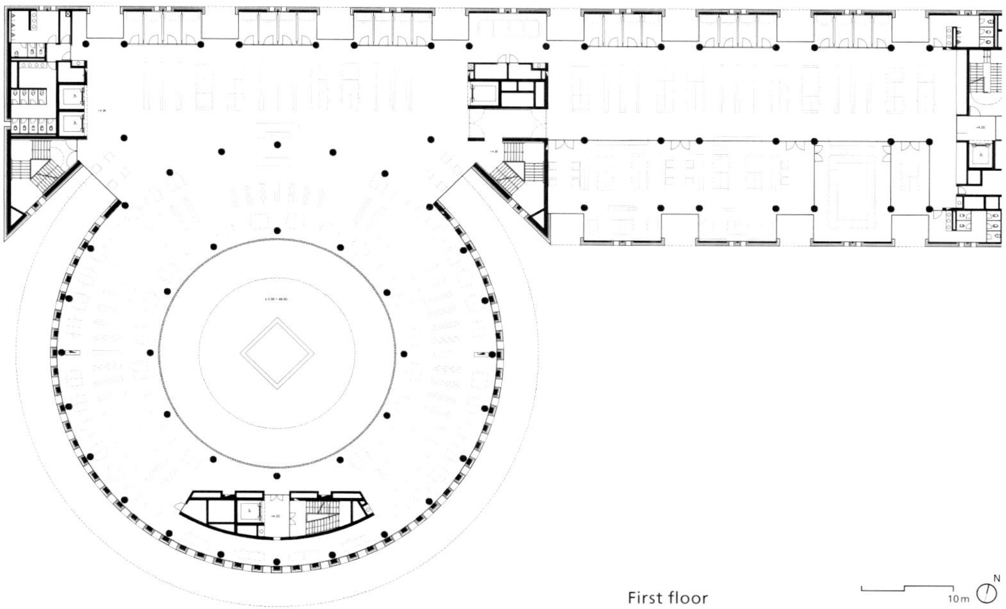

First floor

View of the brick panels at the bar building | The truncated cone structure | Grand steps towards the entry plaza

is part of what university official Hu Heping calls a "boost and a solid foundation for Tsinghua to accomplish new achievements in its humanities and social science research for the next 100 years."

Located on the east side of campus, the library is characterized by a stature distinctive to its geometry. A massive truncated cone nestles within a long bar building fronting the main campus road. The conic form increases in width from the ground level to the third level while a skylit, four-story central void within another truncated cone inversely decreases in width at the same time. The dynamic space that mediates between the expanding shell and the contracting inner void is occupied by the collection. The shelves are radially arranged with study carrels both at the deep, recessed windows on the outer edge and at the inner atrium whose edge is delineated by a delicate wood screen guardrail. The four-story bar building with its support spaces, individual study rooms, grouped carrels and a research center follows an orthogonal internal configuration validating its rectangular bar shape. The form of the bar erodes to allow the full emergence of the conic shape. This intersection is marked on each floor by "information points", small reference stations manned by a librarian. Defining the limits of each form, these points serve as the key to the building as a whole.

In an interview, Botta said that, "Architecture today often abdicates one of its primary functions; to orient us in space. Martin Heidegger said that man inhabits only when he has the possibility of orienting himself inside a space. I believe this to be a beautiful definition. Otherwise we are overwhelmed. We need reference points, to know the center and the limit of a place, two extraordinary conditions that are being forgotten these days." (Source: www.lanciatrendvisions.com) The spatial clarity of the two library volumes make evident

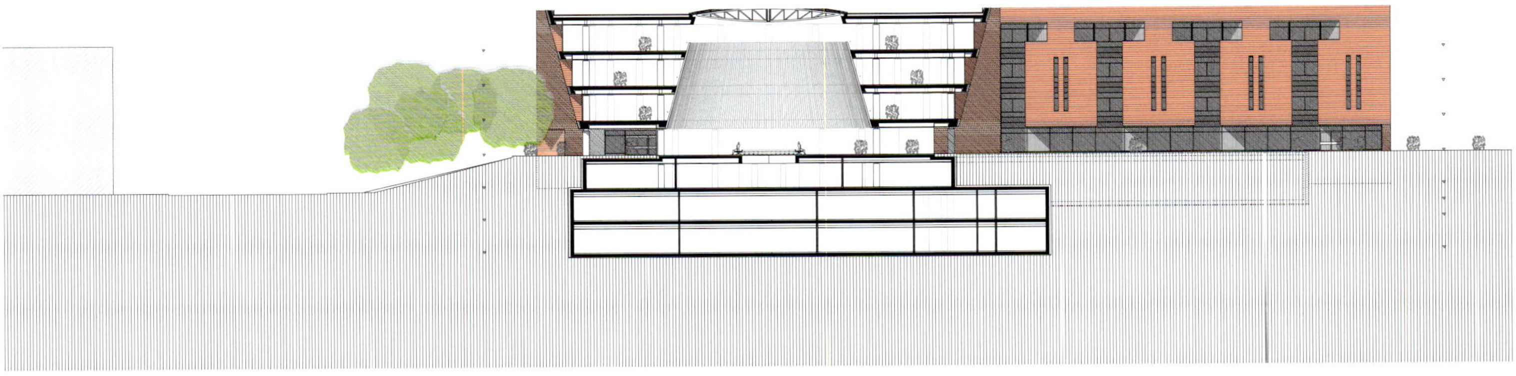

Section

View of the atrium space from within and from the stacks | The intersection of the two geometric forms

the center and the limits, a representation of Botta's belief in pure forms as a way to understanding space. While the building makes reference to primordial forms, the materials and construction details anchor it firmly in the present day. Deep openings in the brick facade of the conic volume read as massive voids from afar. They are, in fact, detailed to express the brick as thin veneer. Similarly, the T-shaped openings in the bar building resolve themselves as thin walls of brick hanging in mid-air, behind which a glazed wall is revealed. The truth told in the details corroborates Botta's belief that "Architecture is an ethical field before being an aesthetic one."

Originally the University was founded on funds from the Boxer Rebellion Indemnity Scholarship Program, suggested in 1906 by the pioneer American missionary, Arthur H. Smith, as a Chinese Student Educational Plan to President Roosevelt. The main point of the plan was to develop higher education in China, particularly by sending Chinese students to American colleges who were previously prepared for their sojourn at a school in Beijing, namely Tsinghua University. Thus the history of the University harkens back to Western ties of the early 20th century. An architectural manifestation of this connection can be seen on the old campus in the 1917 Grand Auditorium, a campus centerpiece premised upon Thomas Jefferson's Rotunda at the University of Virginia. In the 21st century rush to globalize, China, too, "has pushed its universities to be more internationalized." As Tsinghua announces intentions to build a closer relationship with the University of Oxford, it is fitting that its new library ties back to the West through the unique vision of Swiss architect Mario Botta. ***lw***

"Tsinghua University Kai Feng Humanities and Social Sciences Library is Established", *Kai Feng News*, http://www.kaifengfoundation.org

"The Antiquity of New: Interview with Architect Mario Botta", *Lancia Trendvisions*, http://www.lanciatrendvisions.com, November 23, 2012.

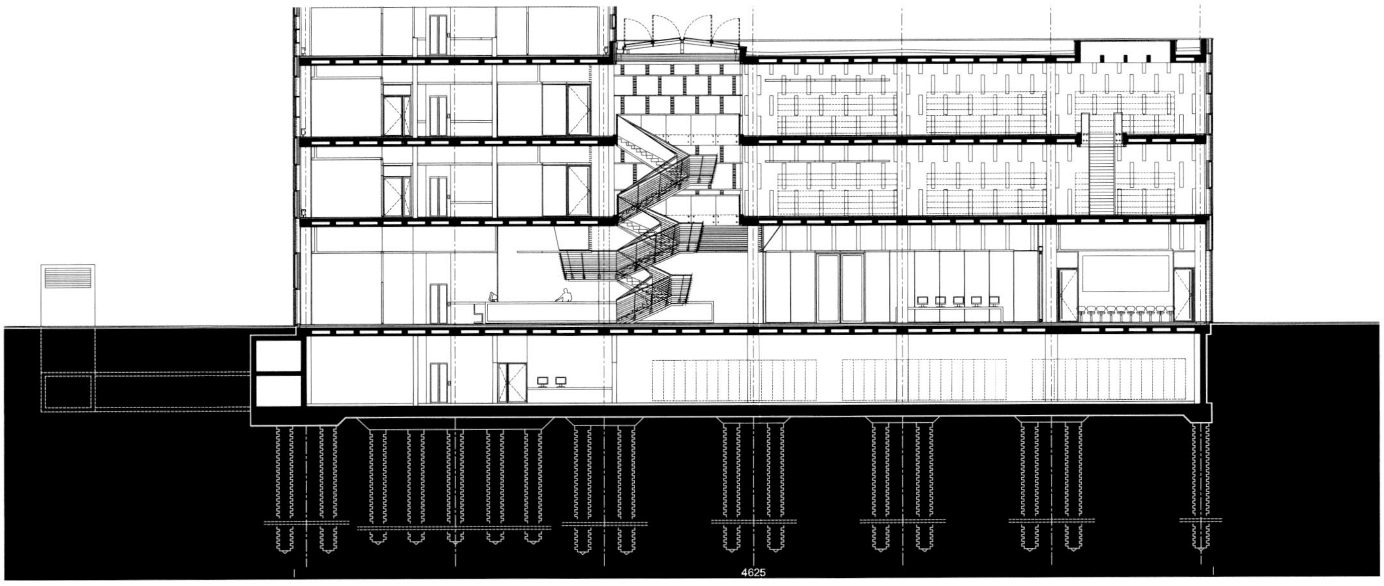

Longitudinal section

CINiBA – Centrum Informacji Naukowej i Biblioteka Akademicka

Uniwersytet Śląski

Katowice, Poland

Architect	HS99
Client	Consortium of the University of Silesia and University of Economics
Completion	2012
Floor area	13,260 m² (GFA)
Number of volumes	340,000 (open collection); 460,000 (closed collection)
Seating capacity	460 (levels 1–3)

The Scientific Information Center and Academy Library, known by its Polish acronym CINiBA, was a joint project of the University of Silesia (Uniwersytet Śląski) and the University of Economics. It opened in 2012 and is located on the University of Silesia campus in Katowice, Poland. Founded in 1928 as part of the Institute of Education the campus is housed primarily in the former Teachers' Training College.

In search of its own iconic presence, the university issued an international competition in 2002 for a new scientific research library, won by the Koszalin architectural firm HS99. The 13,260 m² facility fulfills an objective to stimulate campus

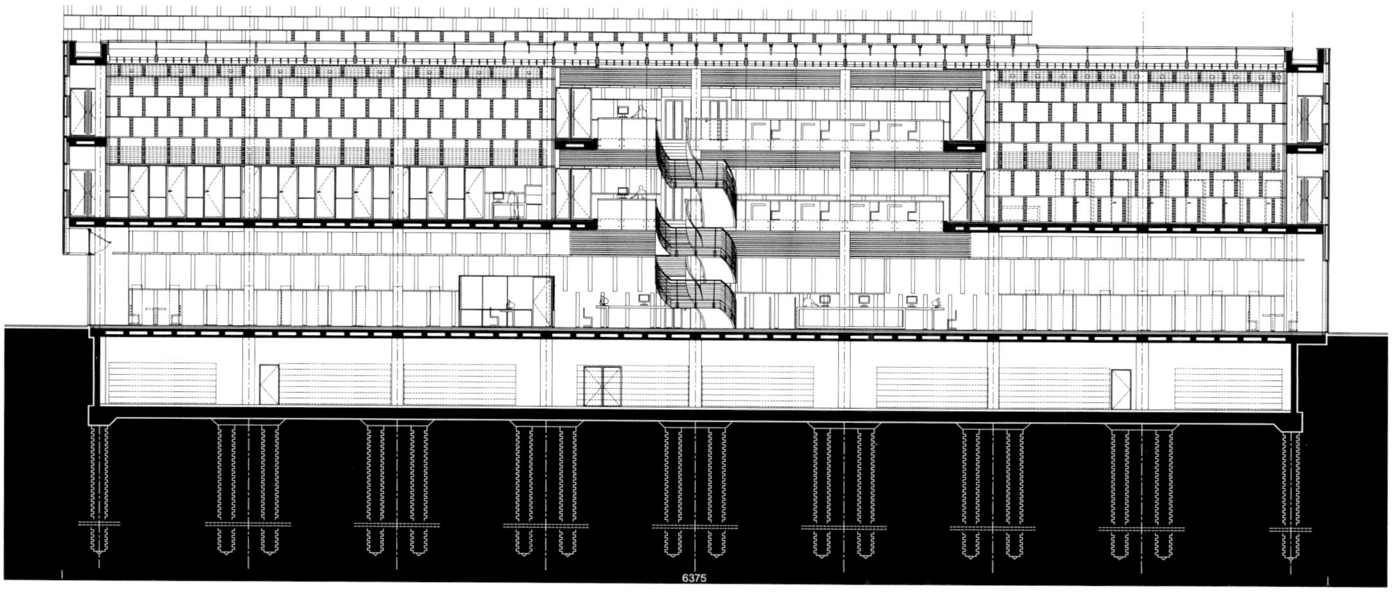

Cross section

Glazed entry opening onto the Forum, a university square | The sandstone panels in the facade reference the running bond of brickwork with gaps concealing windows. As one looks upwards, a perspective is created through the decreasing panel heights

redevelopment that reflects the prestige of the university in this city at the heart of the Upper Silesian industrial region.

Sited at the intersection of the east-west campus spine and the primary north-south axis, intended for future planning, CINiBA opens onto the Forum, a university square. The library's main entrance, a continuous glazed area in a solid facade, visually connects this civic gathering place with the main three-story atrium of the library. On a campus without the cohesion of an articulated plan the significant placement of the library expresses and reinforces an organization for the growth of the campus.

The plan is a rational one, with the clear and discernible presence of a structural grid designed for the accommodation of book shelves. The building is defined by a six by eight bay configuration, employing a classic strategy in which the dimensions of the whole relate to the capacity and efficiency of the individual bay. Two continuous bays along the eastside are devoted to enclosed spaces such as reading rooms, group study areas, conference rooms, individual workspaces and egress. The remainder of the library is open, designed to accommodate a growth to 2 million volumes. Designed for an efficient combination of stack ranges and aisles, the bay, in its most dense state, accommodates five ranges of shelving, each six units long, and an exit aisle. In areas intended for social interaction shelving ranges are exchanged for seating, resulting in bays of lower density. The flexibility of this design was instrumental to the successful completion of the project when in 2004 the project scope was expanded to include the collections of the University of Economics without a change in the overall size of the building.

For the campus and this area of Katowice, the architecture of CINiBA is both contextual and distinctive. Primarily a three-level building, the library's height corresponds to the average height of adjacent campus buildings.

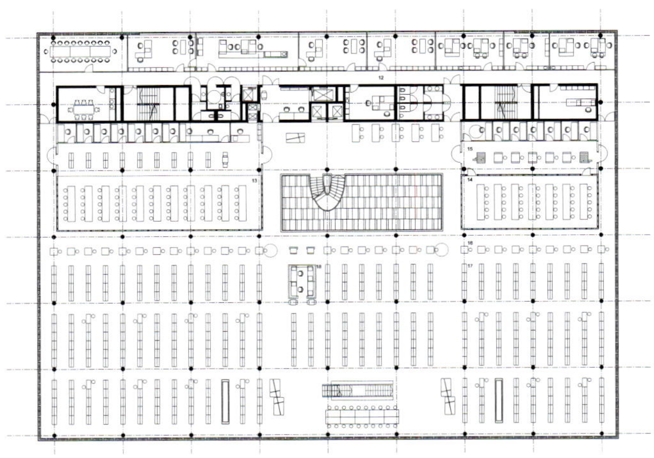

Ground floor

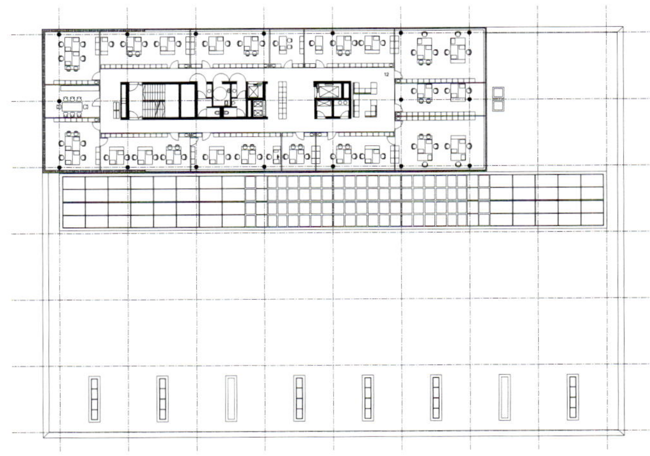

Third floor

Books occupy the tables of a reading area prior to the opening of the library, waiting to be placed on the shelving. | The grand stair provides a sculptural element in the atrium. | The glazed facade of the entry allows visual access from the Forum to the atrium.

On the northeast corner a narrow bar holding the library's closed collections extends seamlessly an additional three levels above the roof, anchoring and asserting the presence of the library and of the Forum. Clad in sandstone called Rich Kahan Red, CINiBA relates to and distinguishes itself from the surrounding clay brick buildings. The facades are composed of large, irregularly cut panels, separated by gaps and arranged in rows. Referencing brickwork, these huge rows, one on top of the next, simulate a quasi-gargantuan running bond in which the narrow gaps conceal windows and appear as abstract mortar joints. The panel heights decrease in size from bottom to top resulting in the semblance of perspective. From a monochromatic and monolithic facade emerges a subtle and complex Mannerist play in which the scale of the building disappears and reappears with different views.

On the interior, the gaps translate into a fenestration of narrow slits that together permeate the reading spaces with diffused light. These slivers of light create an introverted environment that focuses inwardly on study, shielding the readers from external diversions. At night in a complete inversion, the exterior glows with the pattern created by the multitude of lit gaps.

In CINiBA lies a catalyst for change on the Katowice campus. Through its architecture the library sets forth a new direction for future growth on campus and in the city. In looking towards a new era, it embraces yet the timeless notion of reading and solitude. ***lw***

Informatorium
Reference Desk

THE AUTHORS

Nolan Lushington (1929–2013), received an MA in history from Columbia University in 1953 and studied Library Science from 1954–1958, also at Columbia. He became a librarian at the Free Library of Philadelphia where he began to develop progressive ideas about libraries. He felt the library should be a place for citizens to learn and keep current with new concepts. From 1966–1989 he served as the Director of the Greenwich Library in Greenwich, Connecticut, where he was involved with several expansions. He was Associate Professor in the School of Library Science at Southern Connecticut State University and Chairman of the Buildings and Equipment section of the American Library Association. As a library consultant, he provided seminars and workshops on library planning and effectiveness around the USA. He wrote a number of books on library design, such as *Design and Evaluation of Public Library Buildings* (1991) and *Libraries Designed for Kids* (2008).

Wolfgang Rudorf received his diploma in Architecture and Urban Planning from the Technical University in Berlin and attended the History, Theory and Criticism of Architecture and Art program at MIT, earning a Master of Science in Architectural Studies with a research focus on the Public Works Administration's public housing initiative during the New Deal era.

He is a licensed architect in Massachusetts and a LEED accredited professional, concentrating in his practice on the interface between the architectural and engineering disciplines. Responsible for the design and construction of a number of public and university libraries, refurbishment projects, affordable housing developments, and the preservation of historic landmarks in the United States and Germany, he is a passionate supporter of an integrated project design and delivery philosophy.

Rudorf has taught for many years in the Department of Interior Architecture at the Rhode Island School of Design, where he teaches design studios and technically oriented courses on the principles of adaptive reuse of the built environment.

Liliane Wong, born in Hong Kong, is Professor and Head of the Department of Interior Architecture at the Rhode Island School of Design, where she has taught since 1998. She earned her Master of Architecture from the Harvard University Graduate School of Design and her BA in Mathematics from Vassar College. She is a registered architect in Massachusetts, and has practiced in the Boston area including in her firm, MWA, where she focuses on the design of libraries. She is a co-designer of the library furniture system, *Kore*. A long-time volunteer at soup kitchens, her teaching emphasizes the importance of public engagement in architecture and design. She is a co-founder and co-editor of the *Int|AR Journal* which promotes creative and academic explorations of sustainable environments through exemplary works of reuse.

Norma Blake received her MLS from Rutgers University in 1976 before serving over 30 years in New Jersey libraries. Blake was the state association's president and Librarian of the Year before becoming *Library Journal's* national Librarian of the Year in 2008. During her tenure as State Librarian from 2001–2012 she launched many innovative projects that made New Jersey libraries into national models for delivering services to all types of library patrons; the State Library won an innovation award for the New Jersey Knowledge Initiative, which helped libraries serve small businesses. The State Library was also awarded over U.S. $ 7 million to serve job seekers through library computer centers and received the John Cotton Dana award for library marketing. Norma Blake was a library building consultant for the state of New Jersey and privately, and 68 new or newly renovated libraries opened during her time as State Librarian.

Dr. Mohamed Boubekri is a Professor of Architecture at the University of Illinois at Urbana-Champaign. He is a William Wayne Caudill Research Fellow, and was twice a Fulbright Fellow. He received his first professional degree in architecture from the Université des Sciences et Technologie d'Oran, Algeria; a second professional master's degree from the University of Colorado-Denver and a PhD from Texas A&M University. His teaching focusses on building illumination, architectural acoustics, building economics, daylighting design, energy and building performance assessments. Author of *Daylighting Design: Planning Strategies and Best Practice Solutions* (Birkhäuser, 2014).

Rebecca Chestnutt is an architect with an office in partnership with Robert Niess, based in Berlin, Germany, and a professor at the Hochschule für Technik Stuttgart. She is currently chairman of the HFT-Stuttgart postgraduate architecture program. She has lectured at various academic institutions including Universität der Künste Berlin, Kunsthochschule Berlin-Weißensee, Kyoto Institute of Technology and Chinese University Hong Kong. She studied architecture at Virginia Tech., receiving a Bachelor of Architecture in 1980 and a Master of Architecture in 1981.

Her independent carrier as an architect began with the realization of the Luisenbad Public Library (Bibliothek am Luisenbad) in Berlin. The firm of Chestnutt Niess Architekten has successively designed a wide range of public facilities and is particularly respected for the ability to incorporate historic buildings into modern architectural schemes.

Michael Franke-Maier, born in 1972, is a scientific librarian (M.A. LIS) at the university library of the Freie Universität Berlin. After more than five years of coordinating the building of a new technical library, incorporating the libraries of 24 separate institutes of the FU library system, he became vice-director of the acquisitions department of the university library in 2013 and coordinates content cataloguing for the university library system. His interest in conventional and virtual room information systems began in 2005 and he is co-developer of v:store, a web-based software tool for managing the logistics of organizing and moving library collections.

Dr. Ursula Kleefisch-Jobst, born in 1956, studied art history, archaeology and German studies in Bonn, Munich and Rome. From 1985–1988 she undertook doctoral research at the Bibliotheca Hertziana in Rome, and worked from 1989–1990 at the State Office for the Preservation of Monuments in Berlin. Since 1990, she has been a freelance architecture critic; from 2001–2007, curator at the German Museum of Architecture in Frankfurt am Main; since 2008, executive curator at the M:AI Museum of Architecture and Engineering Art of the state of North Rhine-Westphalia. She has published widely on modern and contemporary architecture.

Karl-Heinz Schmitz, born in 1949 in Bad Godesberg, studied architecture at the University of Cape Town in South Africa (1970–1978) and at the Technical University of Karlsruhe (1985–1988). After working for several architectural practices including Haus-Rucker-Co, O. M. Ungers and Karljosef Schattner, he went on to design and realize his own buildings and has published widely on architecture and building typologies. In 1993, he joined the Bauhaus Universität Weimar as head of the Chair of Design and Theory of Building Types, where he also runs the annual international design semester iAAD, which began in 1999.

Dr. Frank Seeliger, born in 1970 in Wolfen, Saxony Anhalt, trained as an electrician and studied electrical engineering for two semesters in Leipzig. In 1999 he obtained a Master's Degree in Ethnology and Anthropology of the Americas, in 2002 his doctorate on an ethno-historical aspect of the Western Himalayas. In 2006 he became director of the library at Technische Hochschule Wildau. Since 2008, he co-organizes the annual "RFID and Beyond" libraries symposium at Wildau, and runs workshops on RFID.

Aat Vos (1964) is a Dutch architect with a substantial track record on designing library concepts and award-winning library interiors during the last 25 years. He played a leading role in the development of library design in the Netherlands, and has been planning libraries in Belgium, the UK and Norway. He is a design consultant on libraries and has developed several library furniture systems. Vos is a lecturer at the School of Architecture in Groningen, the Netherlands, and at the Masters Academy of Interior Design in Arnhem, the Netherlands.

Dr. Klaus Ulrich Werner, born in 1956, studied German studies and history in Freiburg and Vienna before undertaking a traineeship as a librarian and working in publishing. Since 1991, he has worked as a librarian at the Freie Universität Berlin. In 2000 he became founding director of the Philological Library, which moved into a new building in 2005. He is a member of the expert committee on library building at the DIN German Standards Institute and of the Board of Trustees of Architekturpreis Berlin e. V. He has been a jury member of numerous competitions and has published several anthologies on library building and library facilities, including *The Green Library* with Petra Hauke (Munich: Saur/de Gruyter, 2013). He is an author, speaker, and expert advisor and assessor in the field of library building and library management.

INDEX OF NAMES

INDEX OF PLACES

ILLUSTRATION CREDITS

The authors and the publisher thank the following photographers, architects and institutions for the kind permission to reproduce the photographs in this book. Unless noted otherwise, all drawings are courtesy of the architects. Every effort has been made to trace the copyright holders of images. We apologize in advance for any unintentional omission and would be happy to insert the appropriate acknowledgement in any subsequent edition of the manual.

Cover: Stefan Müller, courtesy of Yi Architects
8 HS99
10 Diliff/Wikimedia Commons
11 center Alex Proimos, Sydney/Wikimedia Commons
11 bottom Argonne National Laboratory/ Wikimedia Commons
12 top Courtesy of Seattle Central Library
12 bottom Jan Tik/Wikimedia Commons
13 top Gehry Partners
13 center Ceridwen/Wikimedia Commons
13 bottom left Arjen Schmitz, courtesy of Jo Coenen Architects
13 bottom right Alsop Architects
14 top Sergio Gomez, courtesy of Giancarlo Mazzanti
14 bottom Nelson Pavlovsky/Wikimedia Commons
16 left Courtesy of the City of Cerritos
16 right Chris Trader
17 top Pinnacle Exhibits
17 bottom Nova77/Wikimedia Commons
18 New Jersey State Library
20 Tom Kessler, courtesy of Holzman Moss Bottino
24 Angelika Schnell
25 top left Sailko/Wikimedia Commons
25 top right Timo Orre
25 center Elekhh/Wikimedia Commons
25 bottom Peter Márki-Zay
26 top El fosilmaníaco/Wikimedia Commons
26 bottom F. Higer/Wikimedia Commons (photo Göttweig)
27 top Reinhold Armbruster-Mayer
27 center Chapeaumelon/Wikimedia Commons
27 bottom Craig Elliott
28 center Diliff/Wikimedia Commons
29 left Vincent Desjardins/Wikimedia Commons
29 right Marie-Lan Nguyen/Wikimedia Commons
31 bottom, 32 bottom, 33 center (plan and section), 34 (plans), 37 center Drawings: Lehrstuhl Entwerfen und Gebäudelehre an der Bauhaus-Universität, Weimar
32 top Werner Szambien, *Karl F. Schinkel*, Basel: Birkhäuser, 1990, p. 24
33 top Peter Blundell Jones, *Gunnar Asplund*, London: Phaidon, 2006, courtesy of Phaidon
33 bottom Jonas Nilsson Lee/Flickr
34 top *Alvar Aalto, Complete Works*, Vol. I 1922–1962, Zurich: Artemis, 5th ed., 1990, p. 48
34 bottom Erik R. Bishoff/Flickr
35 top Matthias Wolff
35 center Badische Landesbibliothek
36 top left Toyo Ito & Associates
36 top right Max Dudler
36 bottom Sage Ross/Wikimedia Commons
37 top Horst/Flickr
37 bottom Steven Holl
38 Scott Orr/istock
39 bottom Daderot/Wikimedia Commons
40 top Marcio Silva/istock
40 bottom left and right Carol M. Highsmith/Wikimedia Commons
41 top David Iliff/Wikimedia Commons
41 bottom Sarah Stierch/Wikimedia Commons
44 Chestnutt Niess
45 Reinhard Görner, courtesy of Chestnutt Niess
46 Chestnutt Niess
47 left Werner Huthmacher
47 right Chestnutt Niess
48 top and center Chestnutt Niess
48 bottom Werner Huthmacher
49–51 Liliane Wong
52 left Stefan Müller, courtesy of Max Dudler
52 right Namijano/Flickr
53 left Walt Lockley/Wikimedia Commons
53 right Brian Kernaghan
54 Markus Berger
55 left Leonel Ponce
55 right Brian Kernaghan
56 The University of Manchester Library/ Flickr
58 top Boston Pictorial Archive, http://ark.digitalcommonwealth.org/ ark:/50959/c821h069s
58 center Markus Berger
58 bottom Lara Swimmer, courtesy of Meyer, Scherer & Rockcastle
59 top, center Michael Moran/OTTO, courtesy of Lee Skolnick, Architecture + Design Partnership
59 bottom Ken Lee/Flickr
60 top Courtesy of the City of Cerritos
60 center Ann Sofie Hildebrandt
60 bottom Emile Ashlely, courtesy of Helen & Hard
61 Michael Moran, courtesy of Rice+Lipka
62 Klaus Ulrich Werner
64 Ulrike Lickert, commissioned by Senatsverwaltung für Stadtentwicklung und Umwelt Berlin
66 Klaus Ulrich Werner
72: 1, 2; 73: 3; 74: 4, 5 Wolfgang Rudorf
75: 6 Stefan Müller, courtesy of Max Dudler
75: 7 Max Dudler
75: 8, 9; 77: 12, 13 Toyo Ito & Associates,
76: 10; 77: 11 Wolfgang Rudorf
78: 14 DVD R W/Wikimedia Commons
78: 15 Brian Kernaghan
78: 16, 17 Bollinger + Grohmann Ingenieure
82 top and bottom Kiefer Luft- und Klimatechnik
83 top Toyo Ito & Associates
83 bottom Foster + Partners
84 top AFC Air Flow Consulting AG
84 bottom Wolfgang Rudorf
85 top left and right Lamilux, Heinrich Strunz GmbH
85 bottom Wolfgang Rudorf
86 top Pemba Mpimaji/Wikimedia Commons
86 bottom Ragesoss/Wikimedia Commons
87 Wolfgang Rudorf
88 Toyo Ito & Associates
89 top Stefan Müller, courtesy of Max Dudler
89 center left Nigel Young, Foster + Partners
89 center left Wolfgang Rudorf
90: 1 Mohamed Boubekri
91: 1–5 Mohamed Boubekri
92: 6, 8 Mohamed Boubekri
92: 7 HMC Architects
93: 9, 10, 11, 13 Mohamed Boubekri
94: 14, 15 Mohamed Boubekri
95: 16, 17, 18, 19 Christian Richters
96–98 Sketches: aatvos
99 top Jan Bartelsman
99 bottom Stijn Poelstra
100 Sketches: aatvos
102 top Holger Ellgaard/Wikimedia Commons
102 bottom From: Snead & Company Iron Works, *Library Planning, Bookstacks and Shelving*, Jersey City, NJ: The Snead & Company Iron Works, 1911.
103 top Nolan Lushington
103 center Stefan Müller, courtesy of Max Dudler
103 bottom Drawing: Liliane Wong
104 Toyo Ito & Associates
105 Courtesy of Seattle Central Library
106 Klaus Ulrich Werner
107 top Michael Franke-Maier
107 bottom Nolan Lushington
108 left Michael Franke-Maier
108 right arTec – visual solutions
109 top Georges Fessy, courtesy of Jean-Marc Ibos, Myrto Vitart

109 center Rolf Duden
109 bottom Wolfgang Rudorf
110 Michael Franke-Maier
111 top Christian Hallmann
111 bottom Melanie Kleist
112 left Klaus Ulrich Werner
112 right Michael Franke-Maier
113 NTK, Czech National Library of Technology
115 Andreas Schröder
117, 118 May-Britt Grobleben, Verbund der Öffentlichen Bibliotheken Berlins
122, 125 Ralph Richter Photography, courtesy of Schmidt Hammer Lassen
123, 124 Adam Mørk, courtesy of Schmidt Hammer Lassen
126–129 T. R. Hamzah & Yeang International
130–133 Alberto Moreno Guzmán, courtesy of Pei Partnership Architects
134–139 Hans Schlupp Photography, courtesy of KSP Jürgen Engel Architekten
140 Luftbildpilot Harald Anders, courtesy of Gabriele Glöckler Architektur
141, 142, 143 Maix Mayer, courtesy of Gabriele Glöckler Architektur
146 left Tim Hursley
146 right Bill Timmerman, courtesy of Will Bruder
147, 148–149 top Courtesy of Will Bruder
148 bottom Matt Winquist, courtesy of Will Bruder
149 bottom Bill Timmerman, courtesy of Will Bruder
150, 151, 152 left, 153 Peter Mackinven/ VIEW
152 right Courtesy of Michael Hopkins Architects
154 left DVD R W/Wikimedia Commons
154 right Lembi Buchanan/istock
155, 156 left and top right, 157 Brian Kernaghan
156 bottom right Nolan Lushington
158–163 Arjen Schmitz, courtesy of Jo Coenen Architects
164 bottom left, 165 bottom left and right Stefan Müller, courtesy of Eun Young Yi
164 bottom right Min-Gi Hong
166–171 Christian Richters
174–177 Alsop Architects
178, 179 left, 180 Paolo Roselli, courtesy of Ábalos & Herreros
179 right, 181 bottom Roland Halbe
181 top Bleda & Rosa, courtesy of Ábalos & Herreros
182–183 Tom Kessler, courtesy of Holzman Moss Bottino
184–187 Adjaye Associates
188–189 Benny Chan Photography, courtesy of HplusF Architecture and Design
190–191 Bill Timmerman, Mark Boisclair, courtesy of Richärd + Bauer
192–193 Duccio Malagamba
194 Carlos Tobón, courtesy of Giancarlo Mazzanti
195 left and right, 196, 197 top, bottom left and right Sergio Gómez, courtesy of Giancarlo Mazzanti
198, 199 right, 201 top, Georges Fessy, courtesy of Jean-Marc Ibos, Myrto Vitart
199 left, 200, 201 bottom, Philippe Ruault, courtesy of Jean-Marc Ibos, Myrto Vitart
202–205 Helen & Hard
206–207 Fernando Guerra | FG+SG, courtesy of Santa-Rita Arquitectos
208–211 Fernando Alda, courtesy of Paredes Pedrosa Arquitectos
212–213 Diebedo Francis Kéré, courtesy of Kéré Architecture
216–219 Christian Richters
220 left Hochbauamt des Kantons Zürich
220 right Heinrich Helfenstein, courtesy of Santiago Calatrava
221 left and right Wolfgang Rudorf
222–225 Wolfgang Rudorf (photos)
226–229 Nigel Young, courtesy of Foster + Partners
230–231 Gehry Partners
232–237 Stefan Müller, courtesy of Max Dudler
238–243 SANAA
244, 245 left, 246 left, 247 top Rainer Viertlboeck, courtesy of Helmut Jahn
245 right, 246 right, 247 bottom Tom Rossiter, courtesy of Helmut Jahn
248, 249, 250 left, 251 Fu Xing, courtesy of Mario Botta
250 right Julia Ruane
252–255 HS99